THE
unofficial GUIDE®
ᵀᴼ Disneyland®

2012

THE *unofficial* GUIDE®
ᴛᴏ Disneyland*

2012

BOB SEHLINGER, SETH KUBERSKY, AND LEN TESTA

*Disneyland® is officially known as the Disneyland Resort®.

WILEY

This book makes reference to various Disney copyrighted characters, trademarks, marks, and registered marks owned by The Walt Disney Company and Disney Enterprises, Inc.

Please note that prices fluctuate in the course of time and that travel information changes under the impact of many factors that influence the travel industry. We therefore suggest that you write or call ahead for confirmation when making your travel plans. Every effort has been made to ensure the accuracy of information throughout this book, and the contents of this publication are believed to be correct at the time of printing. Nevertheless, the publishers cannot accept responsibility for errors or omissions, for changes in details given in this guide, or for the consequences of any reliance on the information provided by the same. Assessments of attractions and so forth are based upon the author's own experience; therefore, descriptions given in this guide necessarily contain an element of subjective opinion, which may not reflect the publisher's opinion or dictate a reader's own experience on another occasion. Readers are invited to write the publisher with ideas, comments, and suggestions for future editions.

Published by:
John Wiley & Sons, Inc.
111 River Street
Hoboken, NJ 07030-5774

Produced by Menasha Ridge Press

Cover design by Paul Dinovo

Interior design by Vertigo Design

For information on our other products and services or to obtain technical support, please contact our Customer Care Department within the United States at 800-762-2974, outside the United States at 317-572-3993, or by fax at 317-572-4002.

John Wiley & Sons, Inc., also publishes its books in a variety of electronic formats. Some content that appears in print may not be available in electronic formats.

ISBN 978-1-118-01228-4

Manufactured in the United States of America

5 4 3 2

CONTENTS

LIST *of* MAPS

ACKNOWLEDGMENTS

A BIG SALUTE TO OUR WHOLE *UNOFFICIAL* TEAM, who rendered a Herculean effort in what must have seemed like a fantasy version of Jean-Paul Sartre's *No Exit* to the tune of "It's a Small World." We hope you all recover to tour another day.

Special thanks to dining critic Pete Johnson; Disney historian Jim Hill; cartoonist Tami Knight; *Unofficial Guide* research director Len Testa; child psychologist Karen Turnbow, PhD; *Unofficial Guide* statistician Fred Hazleton; "Unheralded Treasures" writer Lani Teshima; and *Unofficial* friends Genevieve Bernard, Mike Scopa, David Swanson, Ken Warhola, and Henry Work.

Amber Kaye Henderson, Darcie Vance, Annie Long, Ritchey Halphen, and Holly Cross all contributed energetically to shaping this latest edition. Much appreciation also goes to editorial-production manager Molly Merkle, cartographer Steve Jones, and indexer Ann Cassar.

—*Bob Sehlinger*

INTRODUCTION

WHY "UNOFFICIAL"?

DECLARATION OF INDEPENDENCE

THE AUTHOR AND RESEARCHERS OF THIS GUIDE specifically and categorically declare that they are and always have been totally independent of the Walt Disney Company, Inc., of Disneyland, Inc., of Walt Disney World, Inc., and of any and all other members of the Disney corporate family.

The material in this guide originated with the authors and researchers and has not been reviewed, edited, or in any way approved by Walt Disney Company, Inc., Disneyland, Inc., or Walt Disney World, Inc.

This guidebook represents the first comprehensive *critical* appraisal of Disneyland. Its purpose is to provide the reader with the information necessary to tour the theme parks with the greatest efficiency and economy and with the least amount of hassle and standing in line. The researchers of this guide believe in the wondrous variety, joy, and excitement of the Disney attractions. At the same time, we realistically recognize that Disneyland is a business, with the same profit motivations as businesses all over the world.

With no obligation to toe the Disney line, we represent and serve you, the reader. The contents were researched and compiled by a team of evaluators who are completely independent of the Walt Disney Company, Inc. If a restaurant serves bad food, if a gift item is overpriced, or if a ride isn't worth the wait, we say so. And in the process, we hope to make your visit more fun, efficient, and economical.

DANCE TO THE MUSIC

A DANCE HAS A BEGINNING AND AN END. But when you're dancing, you're not concerned about getting to the end or where on the dance floor you might wind up. In other words, you're totally in the moment. That's the way you should be on your Disneyland vacation.

You may feel a bit of pressure concerning your vacation. Vacations, after all, are very special events, and expensive ones to boot. So you work hard to make your vacation the best that it can be. Planning and organizing are essential to a successful Disneyland vacation, but if they become your focus, you won't be able to hear the music and enjoy the dance.

So think of us as your dancing coach. We'll teach you the steps to the dance in advance so that when you're on vacation and the music plays, you will dance with effortless grace and ease.

THE IMPORTANCE OF BEING GOOFY

DISNEY'S DIRECTOR OF CHARACTER AFFAIRS was reviewing budget estimates for bringing the Seven Dwarves' diamond mine into OSHA compliance when his assistant burst into the room.

"Wally, watch the wood paneling! What's the matter this time?" the director sighed.

"Big trouble brewing, boss. It's . . . the union!"

"Oh, no, not again!" cried the director, beating his head against against a miniature desktop Zen garden. "We can't afford another PR disaster like that last strike, with all those Mary Poppins penguins waddling on the picket line."

"I wish it were that simple. Those penguin pushovers negotiated away their health care for halibut. The Arctic Avian Artisans' Guild were birdbrains compared to what we're facing this time."

"Well, who's making the noise this time? The Brotherhood of Professional Pirates? International Association of Snakes, Tigers, and Elephants? Quacker's Equity?"

"Worse, boss. It's the biggest union of them all—the AFL-CIO!"

"You mean the Animated Film Likenesses and Cartoon Interpreters Organization?" the director sputtered. "But how is that possible? We've had their leadership in our back pocket for decades!"

"We used to, but not any more. There's been a shake-up at the top. Our man is out, and the new president is out for our blood."

"I don't understand! Everyone knows that seniority is the only thing that counts in union politics. We've been depositing Cheddar in Mickey's off-shore accounts since before you were born, Wally. Where did they find a member more senior than the Big Cheese himself?"

"Funny story, sir. Remember how you thought it would be a good business move to buy back Oswald the Lucky Rabbit?"

"Huh? Oh, right. Walt lost the rights to that ancient relic way before Mickey was even around. Sure, we got him for a song in a swap with Universal Studios. Figured that the kids just love that retro junk these days. Plus, I heard he's big in Japan. It's a win-win, right?"

"Brilliant as always, boss. But then, remember how you said we should bring old characters out of retirement to help with the refurbishment of our California Adventure park?"

"Of course, there's nothing better for classing up someplace tacky than a few well-placed antiques. I learned that watching HGTV. Besides, they were just sitting around collecting pensions. I figured that we could put them to work dirt cheap!"

"And it worked great, boss. Surveys say that most of our guests think these vintage characters show we now respect our history, with only one in three still calling us 'cynical artistic strip miners.' "

"Wow, that's quite an improvement! So what's the problem then?"

"It seems that we forgot to read the fine print in the union charter. By bringing Oswald back into the fold and reactivating all these old performers, we've given them the right to reclaim their seniority status, with all related privileges."

"My goodness, think of the back pay and accrued vacation time! We'll be ruined!"

"That's the least of our worries, boss. With their newfound clout, the old characters have rallied around Oswald, who is still pretty sore about being on the shelf for so many years. He called for a no-confidence vote against Mickey Mouse, and our man was unseated. The rabbit's in charge of the union now, and he's just issued a list of the members' demands."

"All right, Wally, give it to me straight. What's the lagomorph looking for? Is this a bunny we can bargain with?"

"For starters, on behalf of Horace Horsecollar, he's insisting that the horses that draw the carriages down Main Street USA be allowed to go anywhere in the park that they like, instead of being 'forced to perform repetitive motions in an ergonomically injurious fashion.' "

"We'll have a few more trampled-child liability lawsuits, but we can work with that. What's next?"

"Peg Leg Pete wants a lifetime special assistance pass, and the Three Little Pigs say that they refuse to serve any pork products in their new cafe. Turns out that they're kosher."

"Guess I'll have to go elsewhere for bacon cheeseburgers. Done!"

"About those cheeseburgers . . . Clarabelle Cow is calling for us to stop selling meat throughout the resort. She's bringing out the big guns: PETAAA."

"People for the Ethical Treatment of Anthropomorphic Animated Animals? Oy vey!"

"Clarabelle also wants a full FBI investigation into whatever happened to Minnie Moo. She claims that there was some sort of 'cookout conspiracy' and says that an informant called Deep Snout has the smoking grill."

"Give her whatever she wants; we don't want the feds poking around in that mess!" whispered the director, looking around furtively. "Is that the end?"

"One last thing, but it's a doozy. Oswald himself is demanding equal billing with Mickey in all media, past and present. Parades, fireworks, meet and greets: wherever the Mouse goes, the rabbit wants to be right by his side. Even old films—Oswald is insisting on being inserted into *Fantasia* as the leader of the enchanted brooms!"

"Yikes, the CGI bills alone will bust us! And Mickey will never allow it—you know what his ego is like." The director mused. "Maybe we can buy the bunny off. I've got a great script for a film noir featuring a rabbit, but Roger is still drying out in rehab for dip addiction. Tell Oswald the part is his—all he has to do is say 'p-p-p-please.' "

"I'll give it a shot, boss," said Wally. "But we may need to sweeten the pot. How do you like the sound of *Oswalds of the Caribbean*?"

And so it goes . . .

The Death of Spontaneity

One of our all-time favorite letters is from a man in Chapel Hill, North Carolina. He writes:

> *Your book reads like the operations plan for an amphibious landing: Go here, do this, proceed to Step 15. You must think that everyone is a hyperactive, type-A theme-park commando. What happened to the satisfaction of self-discovery or the joy of spontaneity? Next you will be telling us when to empty our bladders.*

As it happens, we at the *Unofficial Guide* are a pretty existential crew. We are big on self-discovery when walking in the woods or watching birds. Some of us are able to improvise jazz without reading music, while others can whip up a mean pot of chili without a recipe. When it comes to Disneyland, however, we all agree that you either need a good plan or a frontal lobotomy. The operational definition of self-discovery and spontaneity at Disneyland is the "pleasure" of heat prostration and the "joy" of standing in line.

It's easy to spot the free spirits at Disneyland Park and Disney California Adventure, particularly at opening time. While everybody else is stampeding to Splash Mountain or Toy Story Midway Mania!, they're the ones standing in a cloud of dust puzzling over the park map. Later, they're the folks running around like chickens in a thunderstorm trying to find an attraction with less than a 40-minute wait. Face it: Disneyland Resort is not a very existential place. In many ways it's the ultimate in mass-produced entertainment, the most planned and programmed environment imaginable. Self-discovery and spontaneity work about as well at Disneyland as they do on your tax return.

We're not saying that you can't have a great time at Disneyland. Bowling isn't very spontaneous either, but lots of people love it. What we *are* saying is that you need a plan. You don't have to be inflexible about it. Just think about what you want to do—before you go. Don't delude yourself by rationalizing that the information in this modest tome is only for the pathological and super-organized.

HOW *This* GUIDE WAS RESEARCHED *and* WRITTEN

WHILE MUCH HAS BEEN WRITTEN CONCERNING Disneyland Resort, very little has been comparative or evaluative. In preparing this guide, nothing was taken for granted. The theme parks were visited at different times throughout the year by a team of trained observers who conducted detailed evaluations, rating the theme parks along with all of their component rides, shows, exhibits, services, and concessions according to formal, pretested rating criteria. Interviews with attraction patrons were conducted to determine what tourists of all age groups enjoyed most and least during their Disneyland visit.

Although our observers are independent and impartial, we do not claim special expertise or scientific background relative to the types of exhibits, performances, or attractions viewed. Like you, we visit the Disneyland parks as tourists, noting our satisfaction or dissatisfaction. Disneyland offerings are marketed to the touring public, and it is as the public that we have experienced them.

The primary difference between the average tourist and the trained evaluator is that the latter approaches attractions equipped with professional skills in organization, preparation, and observation. The trained evaluator is responsible for much more than simply observing and cataloging. While the tourist is being entertained and delighted by the *Enchanted Tiki Room,* the professional evaluator seated nearby is rating the performance in terms of theme, pace, continuity, and originality. The evaluator also checks out the physical arrangements: Is the sound system clear and audible without being overpowering; is the audience shielded from the sun or rain; is seating adequate; can everyone in the audience clearly see the stage? Similarly, detailed and relevant checklists are prepared by observer teams and applied to rides, exhibits, and concessions, as well as to the theme park in general. Finally, observations and evaluator ratings are integrated with audience reactions and the opinions of patrons to compile a comprehensive profile of each feature and service.

In compiling this guide, we recognize the fact that a tourist's age, gender, background, and interests will strongly influence his or her taste in Disneyland offerings and will account for his or her preference of one ride or feature over another. Given this fact, we make no attempt at comparing apples with oranges. How, indeed, could a meaningful comparison be made between the serenity and beauty of the Storybook Land Canal Boats and the wild roller-coaster ride of California Screamin'? Instead, our objective is to provide the reader with a critical evaluation and enough pertinent data to make knowledgeable decisions according to individual tastes.

The essence of this guide, then, consists of individual critiques and descriptions of each feature of the Disneyland parks, supplemented with some maps to help you get around and several detailed touring plans to help you avoid bottlenecks and crowds. Because so many Disneyland guests also visit Universal Studios Hollywood, we have included comprehensive coverage and a touring plan for that park as well.

A WORD TO OUR READERS ABOUT ANNUAL REVISIONS

SOME OF YOU WHO PURCHASE EACH NEW EDITION of the *Unofficial Guide* have chastised us for retaining examples, comments, and descriptions from previous years' editions. This letter from a Grand Rapids, Michigan, reader is typical:

> *Your guidebook still has the same little example stories. When I got my [new] book, I expected a true update and new stuff, not the same-old, same-old!*

First, the *Unofficial Guide* is a reference work. Though we are flattered that some readers read the guide from cover to cover, and that some of you find it entertaining, our objective is fairly straightforward: to provide information that enables you to have the best possible Disneyland vacation.

Each year during our revision research, we check every attraction, restaurant, hotel, shop, and entertainment offering. Although there are many changes, much remains the same from year to year. When we profile and critique an attraction, we try to provide the reader with the most insightful, relevant, and useful information, written in the clearest possible language. It is our opinion that if an attraction does not change, then it makes little sense to risk clarity and content for the sake of freshening up the prose. Disneyland guests who try the Mad Tea Party, Peter Pan's Flight, or the *Enchanted Tiki Room* today, for example, experience the same presentation as guests who visited Disneyland in 2007, 1990, or 1986. Moreover, according to our extensive patron surveys (about 1,000 each year), today's guests still respond to these attractions in the same way as prior-year patrons.

The bottom line: We believe that our readers are better served if we devote our time to that which is changing and new as opposed to that which remains the same. The success or failure of this *Unofficial Guide* is determined not by the style of the writing but by the accuracy of the information and, ultimately, whether you have a positive experience at Disneyland. Every change to the guide we make (or don't make) is evaluated in this context.

WE'VE GOT ATTITUDE

SOME READERS DISAGREE with our attitude toward Disney. One, a 30-something woman from Golden, Colorado, lambasted us, writing:

> *I read your book cover to cover and felt you were way too hard on*

Disney. It's disappointing, when you're all enthused about going, to be slammed with all these criticisms and possible pitfalls.

A reader from Little Rock, Arkansas, also took us to task:

Your book was quite complimentary of Disney, perhaps too complimentary. Maybe the free trips you travel writers get at Disneyland are chipping away at your objectivity.

And from a Williamsport, Pennsylvania, mother of three:

Reading your book irritated me before we went because of all the warnings and cautions. I guess I'm used to having guidebooks pump me up about where I'm going. But once I arrived, I found I was fully prepared and we had a great time. In retrospect, I have to admit you were right on the money. What I regarded as you being negative was just a good dose of reality.

A Vienna, Virginia, family chimed in with this:

After being at Disney for 3 days at the height of tourist season, I laughed out loud at your "Death of Spontaneity" section. We are definitely free-spirit types who don't like to plan our days when we are on vacation. A friend warned us, and we got your guidebook. After skimming through it before we left, I was terrified that we had made a terrible mistake booking this vacation. Thanks to your book, we had a wonderful time. If it had not been for the book, we definitely would have been trampled by all the people stampeding to Space Mountain while we were standing there with our maps.

Finally, a reader from Phoenixville, Pennsylvania, prefers no opinions at all, writing:

Although each person has the right to his or her own opinion, I did not purchase the book for an opinion.

For the record, we've always paid our own way at Disneyland Resort: hotels, admissions, meals, the works. We don't dislike Disney, and we most definitely don't have an ax to grind. We're positive by nature and much prefer to praise than to criticize. Personally, we have enjoyed the Disney parks immensely over the years, both experiencing them and writing about them. Disney, however, as with all corporations (and all people, for that matter), is better at some things than others. Because our readers shell out big bucks to go to Disneyland, we believe they have the right to know in advance what's good and what's not. For those who think we're overly positive, please understand that *The Unofficial Guide to Disneyland* is a guidebook, not an exposé. Our overriding objective is for you to enjoy your visit. To that end we try to report fairly and objectively. When readers disagree with our opinions, we, in the interest of fairness and balance, publish their point of view right alongside ours. To the best of our knowledge, the *Unofficial Guides* are the only travel guides in print that do this.

THE SUM OF ALL FEARS

EVERY WRITER WHO EXPRESSES AN OPINION is quite accustomed to readers who strongly agree or disagree. It comes with the territory. Troubling in the extreme, however, is the possibility that our efforts to be objective have frightened some readers away from Disneyland, or stimulated in others a state of apprehension. For the record, if you enjoy theme parks, Disneyland and Walt Disney World are as good as they get: absolute nirvana. They're upbeat, safe, fun, eye-popping, happy, and exciting. Even if you arrive knowing nothing about the place and make every possible touring mistake, chances are about 90% that you'll have a wonderful time anyway. In the end, guidebooks don't make or break great destinations. They are simply tools to help you enhance your experience and get the most vacation for your money.

As wonderful as Disneyland is, however, it is nevertheless a complex destination. Even so, it's certainly not nearly as challenging or difficult as visiting New York, San Francisco, Paris, Acapulco, or any other large city or destination. And, happily, there are numerous ways, if forewarned, to save money, minimize hassle, and make the most of your time. In large measure, that's what this guide is about: giving you a heads-up regarding potential problems and opportunities. Unfortunately, some folks reading the *Unofficial Guide* subconsciously add up the various warnings and critical advice and conclude that Disneyland is altogether too intimidating or, alternatively, too expensive or too much work. They lose track of the wonder of Disneyland and become focused instead on what might go wrong.

Our philosophy is that knowledge is power (and time and money too). You're free to follow our advice or not at your sole discretion. But you'd be denied the opportunity to exercise that discretion if we failed to fairly present the issues.

With or without a guidebook, you'll have a great time at Disneyland. If you let us, we'll help you smooth the potential bumps. We are certain that we can help you turn a great vacation into an absolutely superb one. Either way, once there, you will get the feel of the place and quickly reach a comfort level that will allay your apprehensions and allow you to have a great experience.

THE *UNOFFICIAL GUIDE* PUBLISHING YEAR

WE RECEIVE MANY QUERIES each year asking when the next edition of the *Unofficial Guide* will be available. Usually our new editions are published and available in the stores by late August or early September. Thus the 2013 edition will be on the shelves in the autumn of 2012.

WHERE'S THE INDEX?

TO ELIMINATE YOUR HAVING TO CARRY THIS TOME around the theme parks, we've created quite a few tear-out pages with maps, touring plans, survey forms, and more at the end of the book.

Consequently, we've moved the index from its usual position as the last thing in the book to immediately precede the tear-out pages.

LETTERS, COMMENTS, AND QUESTIONS FROM READERS

MANY OF THOSE WHO USE *The Unofficial Guide to Disneyland* write to us, asking questions, making comments, or sharing their own strategies for visiting Disneyland. We appreciate all such input, both positive and critical, and encourage our readers to continue writing. Readers' comments and observations are frequently used in revised editions of this *Unofficial Guide* and have contributed immeasurably to its improvement.

Reader Questionnaire

At the back of this guide is a short questionnaire that you can use to express opinions about your Disneyland Resort visit. The questionnaire is designed to allow every member of your party, regardless of age, to tell us what he or she thinks. Clip the questionnaire on the dotted lines and mail it to:

Reader Survey
The Unofficial Guide to Disneyland
P.O. Box 43673
Birmingham, AL 35243

If you prefer, you can also fill out our reader survey online by visiting **touringplans.com/disneyland-resort/survey.** If you write us or return our reader-survey form, you can rest assured that we won't release your name and address to any mailing-list companies, direct-mail advertisers, or other third party. Unless you instruct us otherwise, we will assume that you do not object to being quoted in a future edition.

How to Contact the Author

Write to Bob Sehlinger, care of *The Unofficial Guide to Disneyland* at the address above, or e-mail him at **unofficialguides@menasharidge. com.** When you write, put your address on both your letter and envelope; sometimes the two get separated. It is also a good idea to include your phone number and e-mail address. If you e-mail us, please tell us where you're from. Remember, as travel writers, we're often out of the office for long periods of time, so forgive us if our response is slow. *Unofficial Guide* e-mail is not forwarded to us when we're traveling, but we will respond as soon as possible when we return.

Questions from Readers

Questions frequently asked by readers are answered in an appendix at the back of this *Unofficial Guide.*

DISNEYLAND RESORT:
an OVERVIEW

IF YOU'VE NOT BEEN TO DISNEYLAND for a while, you'll hardly know the place.

First, of course, there is **Disneyland Park,** the original Disney theme park and the only one that Walt Disney saw completed in his lifetime. Much more than the Magic Kingdom at Walt Disney World, Disneyland Park embodies the quiet, charming spirit of nostalgia that so characterized Walt himself. The park is vast yet intimate, steeped in the tradition of its creator yet continually changing.

Disneyland was opened in 1955 on a 107-acre tract surrounded almost exclusively by orange groves, just west of the sleepy and little-known Southern California community of Anaheim. Constrained by finances and ultimately enveloped by the city it helped create, Disneyland operated on that same modest parcel of land until 2001.

Disneyland Park is a collection of adventures, rides, and shows symbolized by the Disney characters and Sleeping Beauty Castle. It's divided into eight subareas, or "lands," arranged around a central hub. First encountered is **Main Street, U.S.A.,** which connects the Disneyland entrance with the central hub. Moving clockwise around the hub, the other lands are **Adventureland, Frontierland, Fantasyland,** and **Tomorrowland.** Two major lands, **Critter Country** and **New Orleans Square,** are accessible via Adventureland and Frontierland but do not connect directly with the central hub. Another land, **Mickey's Toontown,** connects to Fantasyland. All eight lands will be described in detail later.

Growth and change at Disneyland (until 1996) had been internal, in marked contrast to the ever-enlarging development of Walt Disney World near Orlando, Florida. Until recently, when something new was added at Disneyland, something old had to go. The Disney engineers, to their credit, however, have never been shy about disturbing the status quo. Patrons of the park's earlier, modest years are amazed by the transformation. Gone are the days of the "magical little park" with the Monsanto House of the Future, flying saucer–style bumper cars, donkey riders, and Captain Hook's Pirate Ship. Substituted in a process of continuous evolution and modernization are state-of-the-art fourth-, fifth-, and sixth-generation attractions and entertainment. To paraphrase Walt Disney, Disneyland will never stop changing as long as there are new ideas to explore.

Disneyland Park was arguably Walt Disney's riskiest venture. It was developed on a shoestring budget and made possible only through Disney's relationship with ABC Television and a handful of brave corporate sponsors. The capital available was barely sufficient to acquire the property and build the park; nothing was leftover for the development of hotels or the acquisition and improvement of property adjoining the park. Even the Disneyland Hotel, connected to the theme park by monorail, was owned and operated by a third party until 1989.

Disneyland's success spawned a wave of development that rapidly surrounded the theme park with whimsically themed mom-and-pop motels, souvenir stands, and fast-food restaurants. Disney, still deep in debt, looked on in abject shock, powerless to intervene. In fact, the Disneyland experience was etched so deeply into the Disney corporate consciousness that Walt purchased 27,500 acres and established an autonomous development district in Florida (unaccountable to any local or county authority) when he was ready to launch Disney World.

Though the Florida project gave Disney the opportunity to develop a destination resort in a totally controlled environment, the steady decline of the area encircling Disneyland continued to rankle Walt. After tolerating the blight for 30 years, the Walt Disney Company (finally flush with funds and ready for a good fight) set about putting Disneyland Park right. Quietly at first, then aggressively, Disney began buying up the mom-and-pop motels, as well as the few remaining orange and vegetable groves near the park.

In June 1993 the City of Anaheim adopted a Disney plan that called for the development of a new Disney destination resort, including a second theme park situated in what was once the Disneyland parking lot; a Disney-owned hotel district with 4,600 hotel rooms; two new parking facilities; and improvements, including extensive landscaping of the streets that provide access to the complex. City of Anaheim, Orange County, and State of California infrastructure changes required to support the expanded Disney presence included widening I-5, building new interchanges, moving a major power line, adding new sewer systems, and expanding utilities capacity.

By the end of 2000, all of the changes, modifications, and additions were finished, and Disneyland began the new century as a complete multitheme park resort destination. The second and newest park, **Disney California Adventure** (or DCA to the initiated), celebrated its grand opening on February 8, 2001.

DCA is an oddly shaped park built around a lagoon on one side and the Grand Californian Hotel on the other, with one of Disney's trademark mountains, **Grizzly Peak,** plopped down in the middle. **Buena Vista Street,** an entranceway evoking 1920s Los Angeles, leads to five "lands." Inside the front gate and to the left is **Hollywood Studios Backlot** (which may be renamed Hollywood Land by the time you visit), a diminutive version of the Disney's Hollywood Studios theme park at Walt Disney World. Then there's **Golden State,** a catch-all district that combines California's industry, cuisine, natural resources, people, and history. Next is **a bug's land,** with characters and attractions based on the Disney/Pixar film *a bug's life.* Opening in 2012, **Cars Land** is dedicated to the desert town of Radiator Springs from Disney/Pixar's *Cars.* Finally, **Paradise Pier** recalls the grand old seaside amusement parks of the early 20th century. DCA is described in detail later in the guide.

Critical Comparison of Attractions Found at Both Parks*

ADVENTURELAND

Enchanted Tiki Room About the same at both parks.

Jungle Cruise More-realistic audio-animatronic (robotic) animals and longer ride at Disney World.

CRITTER COUNTRY

Splash Mountain Better scenery and a bigger drop at the Magic Kingdom.

The Many Adventures of Winnie the Pooh Longer and with more motion at the Magic Kingdom.

FANTASYLAND

Carrousels About the same at both parks.

Castles Far larger and more beautiful at the Magic Kingdom.

Dumbo the Flying Elephant About the same at both parks. However, the WDW version is about to get a new theme and will double in size.

It's a Small World Disneyland version renovated in 2008.

Mad Tea Party The same at both parks.

Peter Pan's Flight Shorter but with better lighting effects at Disneyland.

Snow White's Scary Adventures Magic Kingdom version is better (but it's set to close in Florida soon).

FRONTIERLAND

Big Thunder Mountain Railroad About the same; sights and special effects are better at the Magic Kingdom.

Pirate's Lair on Tom Sawyer Island Comparable, but a little more elaborate and with a pirate theme at Disneyland.

Various river cruises (canoes, boats, and such) More interesting sights at Disneyland, and only Disneyland offers canoes.

MAIN STREET, U.S.A.

WDW/Disneyland Railroad The Disneyland Railroad is far more entertaining by virtue of the Grand Canyon Diorama and the Primeval World components not found at the Magic Kingdom.

NEW ORLEANS SQUARE

The Haunted Mansion Slight edge to the Magic Kingdom version.

Pirates of the Caribbean Far superior at Disneyland.

TOMORROWLAND

Astro Orbitor About the same at both parks, but much higher in the air at the Magic Kingdom.

Autopia/Tomorrowland Speedway Disneyland version is superior.

Buzz Lightyear More mobile guns and better game-play at Disneyland.

Space Mountain Much better at Disneyland.

*It should be noted that several of the attractions at Disney California Adventure, such as The Twilight Zone Tower of Terror, *Disney Junior, It's Tough to Be a Bug!*, Toy Story Midway Mania!, *Turtle Talk with Crush*, and *Muppet-Vision 3-D*, appeared first at one of the Walt Disney World theme parks. A version of Soarin' Over California is the first DCA attraction exported to Walt Disney World. None of the remaining DCA attractions are found at Walt Disney World, though Ariel's Undersea Adventure is scheduled to open there in 2012.

The entrances to Disneyland Park and DCA face each other across a palm-studded pedestrian plaza called the **Esplanade,** which begins at Harbor Boulevard and runs west, between the parks, passing into **Downtown Disney,** a dining, shopping, entertainment, and nightlife venue. From Downtown Disney, the Esplanade continues via an overpass across Downtown Drive and past the monorail station to the **Disneyland** and **Paradise Pier hotels.**

Sandwiched between the Esplanade and Downtown Disney on the north and DCA on the south is the 945-room **Grand Californian Hotel** and the 50-unit **Grand Californian Villas.** Designed in the image of rustic national-park lodges, the Grand Californian supplants the Disneyland Hotel as Disneyland's prestigious lodging property.

North of the hotels and across West Street from Disneyland Park is a huge multistory parking garage that can be accessed directly from I-5. This is where most Disneyland guests park. Tram transport is provided from the garage, the adjacent oversize-vehicle lot, and from outlying lots to the Esplanade. Kennels are located by the parking garage. Ticket booths are situated along the Esplanade.

SHOULD I GO TO DISNEYLAND PARK IF I'VE SEEN WALT DISNEY WORLD?

DISNEYLAND PARK IS ROUGHLY COMPARABLE to the Magic Kingdom theme park at Walt Disney World near Orlando, Florida. Both are arranged by "lands" accessible from a central hub and connected to the entrance by a main street. Both parks feature many rides and attractions of the same name: Space Mountain, Jungle Cruise, Pirates of the Caribbean, It's a Small World, and Dumbo the Flying Elephant, to name a few. Interestingly, however, the same name does not necessarily connote the same experience. Pirates of the Caribbean at Disneyland Park is much longer and more elaborate than its Walt Disney World counterpart. Big Thunder Mountain is more elaborate in Florida, and Dumbo is about the same in both places.

Disneyland Park is more intimate than the Magic Kingdom, not having the room for expansion enjoyed by the Florida park. Pedestrian thoroughfares are narrower, and everything from Big Thunder Mountain to the castle is scaled down somewhat. Large crowds are more taxing at Disneyland Park because there is less room for them to disperse. At Disneyland Park, however, there are dozens of little surprises, small unheralded attractions tucked away in crooks and corners of the park, which give Disneyland Park a special charm and variety that the Magic Kingdom lacks. And, of course, Disneyland Park has the stamp of Walt Disney's personal touch.

A Minnesota couple who have sampled Disney both east and west offered this observation:

We have been to WDW in Florida several times. This was our first visit to Disneyland. For parents with children 10 years of age and younger, I highly recommend Disneyland instead of WDW. Its size is much more manageable. You can stay within walking distance of the front gate. That makes it practical and easy to get to the gates early in the morning (an absolute imperative) and get away in the afternoon for a break (always helpful). The size and scale of WDW make this impractical.

A Salem, Massachusetts, family who had visited WDW 3 years prior to their Disneyland trip, agreed:

We heard from many that Disneyland was small, that the castle was underwhelming, and that DCA was a disappointment. But the Disney magic was there and we had a great time exploring what was unique about each park. We spent three days at the parks and wished we had planned to be there longer. The parks may be smaller but there is still plenty to see and do.

Disneyland first-timers are rewarded with a special pin, as this Oregon mom relates:

When I went to pick up something at Town Hall on Main Street, I realized that they had pins to proudly announce it was a first visit to DL. I don't recall reading anything about this in your book and would have taken advantage of it with my older son's first visit. Fortunately, there is no date on it, so I got one for each son and told them that no one would know it was the older one's second time.

To allow for a meaningful comparison, we have provided a summary of those features found at Disneyland Park and not WDW's Magic Kingdom (listed alphabetically below), accompanied by a critical look at the attractions found at both parks on page 12.

ATTRACTIONS FOUND ONLY AT DISNEYLAND PARK

ADVENTURELAND
Indiana Jones Adventure
Tarzan's Treehouse

FANTASYLAND
Alice in Wonderland
Casey Jr. Circus Train
Matterhorn Bobsleds
Mr. Toad's Wild Ride
Pinocchio's Daring Journey
Sleeping Beauty Castle
Snow White's Scary Adventures*
Storybook Land Canal Boats

FRONTIERLAND
Fantasmic! (also at Disney's Hollywood Studios; seasonal)
Sailing Ship *Columbia*

MAIN STREET, U.S.A.
The Disneyland Story presenting *Great Moments with Mr. Lincoln*

MICKEY'S TOONTOWN
Chip 'n Dale Treehouse
Gadget's Go Coaster
Goofy's Playhouse
Mickey's House
Minnie's House
Miss Daisy, Donald's Boat
Roger Rabbit's Car Toon Spin

TOMORROWLAND
Finding Nemo Submarine Voyage
Star Tours (also at Disney's Hollywood Studios)
Captain EO (also at Epcot)

*WDW's version will close sometime in 2012.

PART ONE

PLANNING *before* YOU LEAVE HOME

GATHERING INFORMATION

IN ADDITION TO THIS GUIDE, we recommend that you first visit our website, **touringplans.com,** which offers essential tools for planning your trip and saving you time and money. One of the most popular parts of **touringplans.com** is our Crowd Calendar, which shows crowd projections for Disneyland and Disney California Adventure for every day of the year. Look up the dates of your visit, and the calendar will not only show you the crowd level predicted for each park but will also give you projected wait times for each day.

We've also created many Disneyland and Disney California Adventure touring plans in addition to those in this book, featuring variations for holidays, seniors, Morning Magic Hours, and those who like to sleep in. If our plans aren't quite what you're looking for, **touring plans.com** lets you create your own, either from scratch or by using one of ours as a template, and share it with family and friends.

Our most popular feature for subscribers is Lines, a mobile application that provides continuous real-time updates on wait times at the Disneyland Resort. Using a combination of our in-park research and updates sent in by readers, this tool allows you to see all current wait and Fastpass-distribution times at every attraction in each park, as well as our estimated wait times for these attractions for the rest of today and tomorrow. If you have an Internet-enabled phone, you'll be able to see instantly where the shortest lines are at any time of day. You can also use Lines to view touring plans and look up crowd calendars. The app is available for **touringplans.com** subscribers on the Apple iPhone and iPad on the iTunes Store (search for "TouringPlans"; requires iPhone OS 3.0 or later) and Android Market; owners of other phones can use the Web-based version at **m.touringplans.com.**

As long as you have that smartphone handy while visiting the Land, we and your fellow *Unofficial Guide* readers would love it if you could report on the wait times you see while you're there. Open up Lines, log in to your user account, and click "+Time" in the upper right corner to help everyone out (and earn nifty virtual "badges" for your efforts).

Much of our Web content—including the online trip planner, resort photos and video, and errata for this book—is completely free for anyone to use. Access to part of the site, most notably the Crowd Calendar, additional touring plans, and in-park wait times, requires a small subscription fee (current-book owners get a substantial discount). This nominal charge helps keep us online and costs less than lunch at the French Market restaurant in Disneyland. Plus **touring plans.com** offers a 45-day money-back guarantee.

In addition we recommend that you obtain copies of the following publications:

1. DISNEY RESORT TRAVEL SALES CENTER CALIFORNIA BROCHURE This full-color booklet describes Disneyland in its entirety and lists rates for the Disneyland hotels. Also described are Disneyland package vacations with lodging options at more than 25 nearby hotels. The brochure is available from most full-service travel agents, or it can be obtained by calling the Walt Disney Resort Travel Sales Center at ☎ 714-520-7070 or get the e-brochure at **kingdommagictravel.com/disneyland.**

2. DISNEYLAND GUIDEBOOK FOR GUESTS WITH DISABILITIES If members of your party are sight- or hearing-impaired or partially or wholly nonambulatory, you will find this small guide very helpful. Disney does not mail them, but copies are readily available at the park. You can also download the guide at **disneyland.com** by clicking on "Guest Services" at the bottom of the page.

3. ROOMSAVER CALIFORNIA/NEVADA GUIDE Another good source of lodging discounts throughout the state of California, the *RoomSaver California/Nevada Guide* can be obtained by calling ☎ 800-222-3948, Monday–Friday, 8:30 a.m.–5:30 p.m. EST, or visiting **roomsaver.com.** The guide is free, but you will be charged $3 for postage and handling. Similar guides to other states are available at the same number.

Disneyland Main Information Phone and Website

The following phone numbers and website provide general information. Inquiries may be expedited by using phone numbers specific to the nature of the inquiry (other phone numbers are listed elsewhere in this chapter, under their relevant topics).

Disneyland Guest Relations
☎ 714-781-4565 for recorded information; ☎ 714-781-7290 for live operator
disneyland.com

The Phone from Hell

Sometimes it is virtually impossible to get through on the Disneyland information numbers listed above. When you get through, you will get a recording that offers various information options. If none of the

IMPORTANT DISNEYLAND RESORT PHONE NUMBERS	
Anaheim Travel Information	☎ 714-765-8888
Disney Cruise Line	☎ 888-325-2500
Disney Guided Tours	☎ 714-781-4400
Disneyland Hotel	☎ 714-778-6600
Disneyland Resort Room Reservations	☎ 714-956-6425
Disneyland Vacation Packages	☎ 714-520-7070
Foreign Language Assistance	☎ 714-781-7290
Grand Californian Hotel	☎ 714-635-2300
Fantasmic! Balcony Reservations	☎ 714-781-4400
Information: Live	☎ 714-781-7290
Information: Recorded	☎ 714-781-4565
Lost & Found	☎ 714-781-4765
Paradise Pier Hotel	☎ 714-999-0990
Priority Seating for Restaurants	☎ 714-781-3463, Option 4

recorded options answer your question, you will have to hold for a live person. Eat before you call—you may have a long wait. If, after repeated attempts, you get tired of a busy signal in your ear or, worse, 20 minutes' worth of singing mice warbling "Cinderellie" in alto falsettos while you are on hold, call the Disneyland Hotel at ☎ 714-778-6600.

RECOMMENDED WEBSITES

A NUMBER OF GOOD Disneyland information sources are on the Web. The following are brief profiles of our favorites:

BEST OFFICIAL THEME PARK SITES The official Disneyland website, **disneyland.com,** is so loaded with videos, photos, and gimmicks that it's slow to load and cumbersome to search unless you have a fast computer and high-speed Internet. For those who do, there's a ton of information to be had, but even so it usually takes a lot of clicks to find what you're looking for. While **disneyland.com** has been upgraded recently, it still lags behind its sister site, **disneyworld.com,** especially in the area of online dining reservations. The Universal Studios website is **universalstudioshollywood.com.** Like the Disneyland site, it has a lot of bells and whistles. As far as your computer's concerned, be new, be fast, or be gone.

BEST OFFICIAL AREA WEBSITE **Anaheimoc.org** is the official website of the Anaheim–Orange County Visitors and Convention Authority. You'll find everything from hotels and restaurants to weather and driving instructions on this site.

BEST GENERAL UNOFFICIAL WEBSITES We recommend the following websites for general information related to the Disneyland Resort.

Mouseplanet.com is a comprehensive resource for Disneyland data, offering features and reviews by guest writers, information on the Disney theme parks, discussion groups, and news. The site includes an interactive Disney restaurant and hotel review page, where users can voice opinions on their Disney dining and lodging experiences. We particularly enjoy the weekly Disneyland update column.

Intercotwest.com (Internet Community of Tomorrow–West) is a website filled with detailed information on every corner of Disneyland Resort. Featured are frequent news updates and descriptions, reviews, and ratings of every attraction, restaurant, and shop at the resort.

Deb Wills's **allears.net,** which maintains a fantastic site for Walt Disney World, also has a growing Disneyland sister site. It includes extensive information about the Disney resorts and attractions, including reader reviews. The site is updated several times a week and includes Disney restaurant menus, ticketing information, maps, and more.

Wdwinfo.com has a vibrant Disneyland section that can be found at **wdwinfo.com/disneyland.** It includes up-to-date dining menus, attraction reviews, touring tips, and more.

BEST DISNEYLAND HISTORY WEBSITE At **yesterland.com** you can visit the Disneyland of the past, where retired Disneyland attractions are brought back to life through vivid descriptions and historical photographs. Yesterland attraction descriptions relate what it was once like to experience the Flying Saucers, the Mine Train through Nature's Wonderland, the Tahitian Terrace, and dozens of other rides, shows, parades, and restaurants.

BEST WEBSITE FOR RUMORS AND THE INSIDE SCOOP **Jimhillmedia.com** is perfectly attuned to what's going on behind the scenes—Jim Hill always has good gossip. He works with the *Unofficial Guides* as our resident historian and contributes sidebars and anecdotes to our Disney titles.

BEST DISNEYLAND NEWS SITES **Micechat.com,** with a dedicated group of local editors, is the definitive on-the-ground coverage of the Disneyland Resort. Be sure to check out "Dateline Disneyland" and "In The Parks," two weekly columns that stay on the pulse of the parks, complete with photos. For official news, the Disney Parks Blog (**disney parks.com/blog**) covers news from all Disney resorts, including teasers about the continued construction at Disney California Adventure.

BEST MONEY-SAVING SITE **Mousesavers.com** specializes in finding you the deepest discounts on hotels, park admissions, and rental cars. MouseSavers does not actually sell travel but rather unearths and publishes special discount codes that you can use to obtain the discounts. It's the first place we look for deals when we go to Disneyland Resort.

BEST DISNEY DISCUSSION BOARDS The best online discussion of all things Disney can be found at **micechat.com/forums, mousepad.mouse**

planet.com, and **disboards.com.** With tens of thousands of members and millions of posts, they are the most active and popular discussion boards on the Web. There is also a rousing chat room inside our own mobile application, Lines (learn more at **touringplans.com/lines.**)

BEST DISNEY PODCASTS Our favorite Disneyland-centric podcast is Mousetalgia, found at **mousetalgia.com,** which covers Disneyland, Disney California Adventure, and everything else Disney. The hosts appreciate the history of the resort while maintaining balanced coverage of new Disneyland developments.

BEST DISNEY TWITTER FEEDS If you want your Disney news and rumors in 140 character bites, follow these prolific park Tweeters: @disneyparks, @disneyland, @touringplans, @micechat, @disneylandlive, @latimesfunland, @thedisneyblog, and @skubersky.

ADMISSION OPTIONS

THEME PARK ADMISSION OPTIONS ARE pretty straightforward at Disneyland Resort. You have only two things to decide:

1. How many days admission you'll need.
2. Whether you want to go to both Disneyland Park and Disney California Adventure on the same day. This is known as park hopping.

Tickets expire 14 days after the first use, so you don't want to buy more days than you'll need. Needless to say, tickets expire after you've used the number of days purchased even if 14 days haven't passed yet.

All admissions can be purchased at the park entrance, at the Disneyland Resort hotels, from the Walt Disney Travel Sales Center, on the Disneyland website, and at most Disney stores in the western United States. One- and 2-year-olds are exempt from admission fees.

Admission Costs and Available Discounts

It's possible to obtain discounts on all multiday tickets, but only in the 1%–7% range. One place to purchase admissions at a discount is **disneyland. com,** where Disney sells "bonus" tickets. These tickets, in addition to the dollar discount, allow you to enter the theme park 1 hour earlier than the general public one time during your visit. The bonus feature is offered only on 3-, 4-, 5-, and 6-day Park Hopper tickets.

unofficial **TIP**
The money you can save makes researching Disney's dizzying array of ticket options worthwhile.

If you purchase tickets on the Disneyland website, you can choose between "hard" tickets, which will be shipped to you, or e-tickets, which can be downloaded as PDF files and printed at home. An e-ticket printed from your home computer will show two bar codes. A cast member will scan these at the turnstiles. Once the bar codes are read, the cast member can issue your actual ticket.

The deepest discounts we've found are from **ARES Travel** (**arestravel. com**). ARES usually beats the Disney advance purchase price by $4–$6 per ticket and also includes the early-entry bonus feature. ARES will send you the tickets by FedEx for a flat fee of $10 per order, plus a $1-per-ticket convenience fee. You can order online or call ☎ 800-434-7894.

Military discounts are available for all Disney theme parks, usually in the 7%–25% range. Check with your base Morale, Welfare, & Recreation office for info. Military ID may be required at the gate. Many readers report buying military tickets for friends and relatives who used them without problems.

Admission prices increase from time to time. For planning your budget, however, the chart below provides a fair estimate.

1-day, One-park Ticket

This pass is good for 1 day's admission at your choice of Disneyland Park or Disney California Adventure. As the name implies, you cannot "hop" from park to park.

Park Hopper Tickets

These are good for 1, 2, 3, 4, 5, or 6 days, respectively, and allow you to visit both parks on the same day. These multiday tickets do not have to be used on consecutive days, but they do expire 14 days after their first use.

ADMISSION OPTIONS		
	AT THE GATE *ADULT | *CHILD	ADVANCE PURCHASE *ADULT | *CHILD
1-day, One-park Ticket	$80 | $74	$80 | $74
1-day Park Hopper	$105 | $99	$105 | $99
2-day, One-park Per Day Ticket	$158 | $146	$158 | $146
2-day Park Hopper	$173 | $161	$173 | $161
3-day, One-park Per Day Ticket	$209 | $193	$199 | $183
3-day Park Hopper	$224 | $208	$214 | $198
4-day, One-park Per Day Ticket	$234 | $216	$219 | $201
4-day Park Hopper	$249 | $231	$234 | $216
5-day, One-park Per Day Ticket	$251 | $231	$231 | $211
5-day Park Hopper	$266 | $246	$246 | $226
6-day, One-park Per Day Ticket	$256 | $236	$236 | $216
6-day Park Hopper	$271 | $251	$251 | $231
Deluxe Annual Passport *(some blackout dates)*	$379	$379
Premium Annual Passport *(no blackout dates)*	$499	$499
Disney Premier Passport *(no blackout dates; valid at all California and Florida parks)*	$749	$749

*Adult (age 10 and up) | *Child (ages 3–9)

The 14-day expiration is in marked contrast to similar passes sold at Walt Disney World for which you can purchase a No Expiration option. If you mistakenly bought multiday tickets because you were not aware of the 14-day expiration, call ☎ 714-781-7290 or ☎ 714-781-4565 and ask to be connected to Guest Communications, which has the authority to issue you a voucher for the unused days on your ticket.

Anytime before a pass expires, you can apply the value of unused days toward the cost of a higher priced ticket. If you buy a 4-day Park Hopper ticket, for example, and then decide you'd rather have an Annual Passport, you can apply the value of unused days on the former toward the purchase of the latter.

Annual Passports

*uno*fficial **TIP**
If you visit Disneyland 3 or more days each summer, an Annual Passport is a potential money saver.

The Disneyland Resort offers several Annual Passports. The Premium Annual Passport is good for an entire year with no blackout dates. The pass costs $499 and is good for admission to both parks (excluding arcades). Southern California Annual Passports, priced at $276, provide admission to both parks for a year, excluding preselected blackout dates. These are available to residents in zip codes 90000 to 93599 and to Baja California residents in Mexico postal codes 21000 to 22999. Prices for children are the same as those for adults on all Annual Passports. All of these passes are a good idea if you plan to visit Disneyland parks 5 or more days in a year. If you purchase your Annual Passport in July of this year and schedule your visit next year for June, you'll cover 2 years' vacations with a single pass.

Admission passes can be ordered by calling ☎ 714-781-4400 or visiting the Disneyland website. They can also be purchased in advance from Disneyland Resort hotels, Disney Stores in the Western United States, and the Walt Disney Travel Sales Center at ☎ 800-854-3104.

Rides and Shows Closed for Repairs or Maintenance

Rides and shows at Disneyland parks are sometimes closed for maintenance or repairs. If there is a certain attraction that is important to you, call ☎ 714-781-7290 before your visit to make sure that it will be operating. We also maintain an unofficial schedule of current and upcoming closures at **touringplans.com/disneyland-resort/closures.** A mother from Dover, Massachusetts, wrote us, lamenting:

> We were disappointed to find Space Mountain and the Riverboat closed for repairs. We felt that a large chunk [of the park] was not working, yet the tickets were still full price and expensive!

HOW MUCH DOES IT COST TO GO TO DISNEYLAND FOR A DAY?

LET'S SAY WE HAVE A FAMILY OF FOUR—Mom and Dad, Tim (age 12) and Tami (age 8)—driving their own car. Since they plan to be in the area for a few days, they intend to buy the 3-day Park Hopper Tickets. A typical day would cost $484.99, excluding lodging and transportation. See the chart below for a breakdown of expenses.

HOW MUCH DOES A DAY COST?	
Breakfast for four at Denny's with tax and tip	$40.00
Disneyland parking fee	$15.00
1 day's admission on a 3-Day Park Hopper Pass	
Dad: **Adult, 3-day = $214 divided by 3 (days)**	$71.33
Mom: **Adult, 3-day = $214 divided by 3 (days)**	$71.33
Tim: **Adult, 3-day = $214 divided by 3 (days)**	$71.33
Tami: **Child, 3-day = $198 divided by 3 (days)**	$66.00
Morning break **(soda or coffee)**	$14.00
Fast-food lunch **(burger, fries, and soda; no tip)**	$36.00
Afternoon break **(soda and popcorn)**	$20.50
Dinner in park at counter-service restaurant with tax	$41.50
Souvenirs **(Mickey T-shirts for Tim and Tami) with tax***	$38.00
1-day total **(not including lodging and travel)**	**$484.99**

Cheer up—you won't have to buy souvenirs every day.

TIMING *Your* VISIT

SELECTING THE TIME OF YEAR FOR YOUR VISIT

CROWDS ARE LARGEST at Disneyland during the summer (Memorial Day–Labor Day) and during specific holiday periods throughout the rest of the year. The busiest time of all is Christmas Day–New Year's Day. Thanksgiving weekend, the week of Washington's birthday, spring break for schools and colleges, and the 2 weeks around Easter are also extremely busy. To give you some idea of what *busy* means at Disneyland, more than 77,000 people have toured Disneyland Park in 1 day! While this level of attendance is far from typical, the possibility of its occurrence should prevent all but the ignorant and the foolish from challenging this mega-attraction at its busiest periods. Historically, attendance at Disney California Adventure has been about one-third that of Disneyland Park, but thanks to new attractions such as The Little Mermaid and *World of Color*, that gap is tightening.

unofficial **TIP**
You can't pick a less crowded time to visit Disneyland than the period following Thanksgiving weekend and leading up to Christmas.

The least-busy time of all is from after Thanksgiving weekend until the week before Christmas. The next slowest times are September

TOP 10 AMERICAN THEME PARKS

THEME PARK	ANNUAL ATTENDANCE	AVERAGE DAILY ATTENDANCE
Walt Disney World's Magic Kingdom	17.0 million	46,499
Disneyland	16.0 million	43,781
Epcot	10.8 million	29,658
Animal Kingdom	9.7 million	26,537
Disney's Hollywood Studios	9.6 million	26,310
Disney California Adventure	6.3 million	17,200
Islands of Adventure	5.9 million	16,299
Universal Studios Orlando	5.9 million	16,233
SeaWorld Orlando	5.1 million	13,973
Universal Studios Hollywood	5.0 million	13,808

Source: Themed Entertainment Association

through the weekend preceding Thanksgiving, January 4 through the first week of March, and the week following Easter up to Memorial Day weekend. At the risk of being blasphemous, our research team was so impressed with the relative ease of touring in the fall and other "off" periods that we would rather take our children out of school for a few days than do battle with the summer crowds. Though we strongly recommend going to Disneyland in the fall or in the spring, it should be noted that there are certain trade-offs. The parks often close earlier on fall, winter, and spring days, sometimes early enough to eliminate evening parades, fireworks, and other live-entertainment offerings such as *Fantasmic!* Also, because these are slow times of the year at Disneyland, you can anticipate that some rides and attractions may be closed for maintenance or renovation. Finally, if the parks open late and close early, it's tough to see everything, even if the crowds are light.

Most readers who have tried Disney parks at varying times of the year concur. A wintertime visitor from Sacramento, California, agrees:

Although there was a torrential storm on 2 days of our 4-day visit, I can safely say that I will never visit in high season again. Yes, we were wet. Yes, there were attractions and rides closed for refurb. BUT, the longest line we waited in was 25 minutes to see the princesses. There were characters EVERYWHERE, and access to them was easy as pie. There were no issues with heat or sunburn. It felt like an adventure. And we saved a boatload of money and were able to splurge on a view room at the Grand Californian.

unofficial **TIP**
In our opinion, the risk of encountering colder weather and closed attractions during an off-season visit to Disneyland is worth it.

Not to overstate the case: We want to emphasize that you can have a great time at the Disneyland parks regardless of the time of year or

Anaheim Convention and Special-event Calendar

DATES	CONVENTION/ EVENT	NUMBER OF ATTENDEES
2011		
Sept. 28–Oct. 7	Microsoft SharePoint Conference	6,000
Oct. 9–16	Confidential Group	8,000
Oct. 26–29	Confidential Group	6,000
Nov. 8–14	National Assn. of Realtors Convention & Trade Expo	20,000
Nov. 30–Dec. 3	Apostolic Assembly of Faith in Christ Jesus Conference	7,500
2012		
Jan. 19–22	NAMM/International Music Products Assn. Show	89,000
Jan. 29–Feb. 1	Craft & Hobby Assn. Convention & Trade Show	18,000
Feb. 14–16	UBM Canon Technology Expo	25,000
Mar. 8–11	Natural Products Expo West Trade Show	50,000
Mar. 14–19	United Spirit Assn./All Stars & College	13,500
Mar. 22–25	Religious Education Congress	41,000
Mar. 30–Apr. 4	United Spirit Assn./Spirit and Dance Nationals	33,000
Apr. 11–14	Pri-Med West Conference and Exhibition	14,000
Apr. 11–15	Varsity Spirit Corporation/American Championships	20,000

crowd level. In fact, a primary objective of this guide is to make the parks fun and manageable for those readers who visit during the busier times of year.

Of course, crowds are not the only consideration when deciding what time of year to visit Disneyland. Holidays are celebrated at Disneyland like nowhere else, and the festive decor is almost worth the price of admission. The parks are decked out for Halloween from late September until the end of October. Be aware that after-hours extra-cost Halloween parties (tickets are about $60) cause Disneyland to close early to day guests on several evenings in the fall, as a Tucson, Arizona, family found:

unofficial **TIP**
If it's not your first trip to Disneyland and you must join the holiday-weekend crowds, you may have just as much fun enjoying Disney's fantastic array of shows, parades, and fireworks as you would riding the rides.

The Halloween event from mid-September to end of October changes the low season to a zoo. Every local with an annual pass showed up in the afternoon. The park closed early for this event [and] DCA backed up because of the early closure of Disneyland [Park].

Christmas trappings transform Disneyland Park from mid-November until after New Year's Day. There's also a Christmas parade, and several attractions such as The Haunted Mansion and It's a Small World offer a special holiday version.

DATES	CONVENTION/ EVENT	NUMBER OF ATTENDEES
2012 *(continued)*		
Apr. 20–22	US Finals West Coast Cheer & Dance	8,100
May 4–6	California Dental Association Spring Scientific Sessions	30,000
June 5–14	Million Dollar Round Table Summer Convention	7,300
June 21–27	American Library Assn. Conference	25,000
Aug. 12–14	Western Foodservice & Hospitality Expo	12,500
Aug. 21–30	American Public Works Assn. Congress & Expo	6,000
Aug. 31–Sept. 2	SCRC Annual Convention	7,000
Oct.. 2–4	California Assn. of Realtors Meetings & Expo	8,000
Oct. 16–20	Natl. Recreation and Park Assn. Conference & Expo	7,200
Oct. 21–31	Produce Marketing Assn. Fresh Summit	19,000
Nov. 30–Dec. 5	Confidential Group	5,000
2013		
Jan. 12–15	Craft & Hobby Assn. Convention & Trade Show	18,000
Jan. 17–20	NAMM/International Music Products Assn. Show	89,000
Feb. 12–14	UBM Canon Technology Expo	25,000

THE SPOILER

SO YOU CHOOSE YOUR OFF-SEASON DATES and then find it almost impossible to find a hotel room. What gives? In all probability you've been foiled by a mammoth convention or trade show at the Anaheim Convention Center. One of the largest and busiest convention venues in the country, the convention center hosts meetings with as many as 75,000 attendees. The sheer numbers alone guarantee that hotel rooms will be hard to find. Compounding the problem is the fact that most business travelers don't have roommates. Thus a trade show with 8,000 people registered might suck up 13,000 rooms (including people who registered late)! The final straw as you might expect is that room rates climb into the stratosphere based on the high demand and scarcity of supply. In regard to increased crowds at the theme parks, it's estimated that less than 10% of convention attendees will find time to enjoy the parks. It's also true, however, that business travelers are more likely to bring their spouse and even kids to a convention held in Anaheim. The bottom line is that you don't want to schedule your vacation while a major event is going on at the convention center. To help you avoid major trade shows and conventions, we've created a calendar of meetings scheduled through February 2013, showing the number of expected attendees of each (see above).

SELECTING THE DAY OF THE WEEK FOR YOUR VISIT

THE CROWDS AT WALT DISNEY WORLD in Florida comprise mostly out-of-state visitors. Not necessarily so at Disneyland Resort, which, along with Six Flags Magic Mountain, serves as an often-frequented recreational resource for the greater Los Angeles and San Diego communities. To many Southern Californians, Disneyland Park and Disney California Adventure are their private theme parks. Yearly passes are available at less cost than a year's membership to the YMCA.

What all this means is that weekends are usually packed. Saturday is the busiest day of the week. Sunday, particularly Sunday morning, is the best bet if you have to go on a weekend, but it is also extremely busy.

During the summer, Monday and Friday are very busy, Tuesday and Wednesday are usually less so, and Thursday is normally the slowest day of all. During the off-season (September–May, holiday periods excepted), Thursday is usually the least crowded day, followed by Tuesday.

In Florida, there are four Disney theme parks with a substantial daily variance in attendance from park to park. At Disneyland Resort, Disneyland Park usually hosts crowds three times larger than those at Disney California Adventure, but because DCA is smaller, crowd conditions are comparable. Expressed differently, the most crowded and least crowded days are essentially the same for both Disneyland parks.

EARLY ENTRY

ANYONE WHO BUYS a 3-or-more-day Park Hopper admission in advance (that is, not at the theme park) may enter Disneyland Park 1 hour before the park is opened to the general public only on 1 day. You can exercise your early-entry privilege on Tuesday, Thursday, Saturday, or Sunday. During this Morning Magic Hour, most of the Fantasyland attractions—along with Space Mountain, Finding Nemo Submarine Voyage, Astro Orbitor, Buzz Lightyear, and Star Tours in Tomorrowland—will usually be open. The rest of the park's attractions (and all Fastpass machines) will remain off-limits until the official opening time.

Guests at the Paradise Pier, Grand Californian, and Disneyland hotels and those who purchase a package vacation from the Walt Disney Travel Company can participate in Mickey's Toontown Morning Madness. In this program, package purchasers can enjoy the attractions in Mickey's Toontown 1 hour before the general public on Monday, Wednesday, Friday, and Saturday. Note that Mickey's Toontown opens 1 hour later than the rest of Disneyland Park. Thus, if the park opens at 8 a.m. and Toontown opens at 9 a.m., you'll be eligible to enjoy Morning Madness 8–9 a.m. Though you can enter Toontown early, you actually enter the park with the general public at official opening time. In practice, unless you're among the first to enter the park, it will take you so long to clear the turnstiles and walk back to Mickey's Toontown that you'll be fortunate if you arrive in time to enjoy more than 20 minutes or so of the event. For more information, call ☎ 714-520-7070.

An Aurora, Ohio, multigenerational family echoed our comments:

Our package included a Toontown Morning Madness early entry (which was a joke because we couldn't get there in time).

OPERATING HOURS

DISNEYLAND RESORT RUNS a dozen or more different operating schedules during the year, making it advisable to visit **disneyland.disney. go.com/calendar** or call ☎ 714-781-4565 the day before you arrive for exact hours of operation.

PACKED-PARK COMPENSATION PLAN

THE THOUGHT OF TEEMING, jostling throngs jockeying for position in endless lines under the baking Fourth of July sun is enough to wilt the will and ears of the most ardent Mouseketeer. Why would anyone go to Disneyland Park or DCA on a summer Saturday or during a major holiday period? Indeed, if you have never been to the parks, and you thought you would just drop in for a few rides and a little look-see on such a day, you might be better off shooting yourself in the foot. The Disney folks, however, being Disney folks, feel kind of bad about those interminably long lines and the basically impossible touring conditions on packed days and compensate patrons with a no-less-than-incredible array of first-rate live entertainment and happenings throughout the park.

Throughout the day, the party goes on with shows, parades, concerts, and pageantry. In the evening, there is so much going on that you have to make some tough choices. Big-name musical groups perform on the River Stage in Frontierland and at the Fantasyland Theatre. Other concerts are produced concurrently at the Hyperion Theater at Disney California Adventure. There are always parades and fireworks, and the Disney characters make frequent appearances. No question about it—you can go to the Disneyland parks on the Fourth of July (or any other crowded extended-hours day), never get on a ride, and still get your money's worth. And even on the busiest days, there are attractions at each park that rarely require more than a 15-minute wait: *Great Moments with Mr. Lincoln, The Enchanted Tiki Room,* the railroad and monorail, and Innoventions at Disneyland Park; Disney Animation, Blue Sky Cellar, and the sourdough and chocolate factories at Disney California Adventure.

If you decide to go on one of the parks' "big" days, we suggest that you arrive 1 hour and 20 minutes before the stated opening time. Use the touring plan of your choice until about 1 p.m., and then take the monorail to Downtown Disney for lunch and relaxation. Southern Californian visitors often chip in and rent a room for the group (make reservations well in advance) at the Disneyland or Grand Californian hotels, thus affording a place to meet, relax, have a drink, or change clothes before enjoying the pools at the hotel. A comparable arrangement can be made at other nearby hotels as long as they furnish a shuttle service to and from the park. After an early dinner, return to the park for the evening's festivities, which really get cranked up at about 8 p.m.

GETTING THERE

DISNEY PATRONS CAN drive directly into and out of parking facilities without becoming enmeshed in surface street traffic. To avoid traffic problems, we recommend the following:

1. Stay as close to Disneyland as possible. If you are within walking distance, leave your car at the hotel and walk to the park. If your hotel provides efficient shuttle service (that is, will get you to the parks at least 30 minutes before opening), use the shuttle.

2. If your hotel is more than 5 miles from Disneyland and you intend to drive your car, leave for the park extra early, say 1 hour or more.

3. If you must use the Santa Ana Freeway (I-5), give yourself lots of extra time.

4. Any time you leave the park just before, at, or just after closing time, you can expect considerable congestion in the parking lots and in the loading area for hotel shuttles. The easiest way to return to your hotel (if you do not have a car in the Disneyland Resort parking lot) is to take the monorail to the Disneyland Hotel or walk to the Grand Californian Hotel, and then take a cab to your own hotel. While cabs in Anaheim are a little pricey, they are usually available in ample numbers at the Disneyland hotels and at the pedestrian entrance on Harbor Boulevard. When you consider the alternatives of fighting your way onto a hotel shuttle or trudging back to your hotel on worn-out feet, spending a couple of bucks for a cab often sounds pretty reasonable.

unofficial **TIP**
Warning: Most shuttles don't add vehicles at park-opening or -closing times. In the mornings, you may not get a seat.

5. If you walk or use a hotel shuttle to get to the parks and are then caught in a monsoon, the best way to return to your hotel without getting soaked is to take the monorail to the Disneyland Hotel and catch a taxi from there.

6. The Orange County Transit District provides very efficient bus service to Disneyland with three different long-distance lines. Running about every 30 minutes during the day and evening, service runs 10 a.m.–midnight, depending on the season and your location. Buses drop off and pick up passengers at the Disneyland Hotel. From there, guests can take a Disney tram to the park entrance. Trams run approximately every 6 minutes. Bus fare is about $1.50 and children age 6 and under ride free; the tram is free for everyone. A bus day pass is available for $4; 7-day passes are $20 and 15-day passes are $35. For additional information, call ☎ 714-636-7433 or 888-364-2787 or visit **octa.net.** For public transportation in the immediate area surrounding Disneyland, see our discussion of the Anaheim Resort Transit (ART) system starting on page 33.

DISNEYLAND PARKING

DISNEYLAND HAS FOUR PARKING AREAS. The main parking facility, the Mickey & Friends parking garage, can be accessed directly from I-5, Disneyland Drive, or Ball Road. One of the largest parking structures in the world, the garage is connected to Downtown Disney and the theme parks by Disney tram. If you have a noncollapsible stroller that's not permitted on the tram, the walking distance is just less than 1 mile.

The secondary parking areas are the Simba lot behind the Paradise Pier Hotel, the Pumbaa lot off Disney Way, and the Toy Story lot on the corner of Katella Avenue and Harbor Boulevard. From Simba you can walk through Downtown Disney to the parks or alternatively walk to the Downtown Disney Monorail stop and take the monorail into Disneyland Park (not Disney California Adventure). Both Pumbaa and Toy Story offer shuttles to the parks, or you can walk (about 0.5 mile for each). Parking fees for all lots are $15 for cars, $20 for RVs and oversize vehicles, and $25 for buses and tractors with extended trailers. After parking your car, save yourself a frantic search at the end of your day by taking a digital photo of the lot name and section number.

TAKING A TRAM OR SHUTTLE BUS FROM YOUR HOTEL

TRAMS AND SHUTTLE BUSES are provided by many hotels and motels in the vicinity of Disneyland. Usually without charge, they represent a fairly carefree means of getting to and from the theme parks, letting you off near the entrances and saving you the cost of parking. The rub is that they might not get you there as early as you desire (a critical point if you take our touring advice) or be available at the time you wish to return to your lodging. Also, some shuttles are direct to Disneyland, while others make stops at other motels and hotels in the vicinity. Each shuttle service is a little bit different, so check out the particulars before you book your hotel. If the shuttle provided by your hotel runs regularly throughout the day to and from Disneyland and if you have the flexibility to tour the parks over 2 or 3 days, the shuttle provides a wonderful opportunity to tour in the morning and return to your lodging for lunch, a swim, or perhaps a nap; then you can head back to Disneyland refreshed in the early evening for a little more fun.

Be forewarned that most hotel shuttle services do not add more vehicles at the parks' opening or closing times. In the mornings, your biggest problem is that you might not get a seat on the first shuttle. This occurs most frequently if your hotel is the last stop for a shuttle that serves several hotels. Because hotels that share a shuttle service are usually located close together, you can improve your chances of getting a seat by simply walking to the hotel preceding yours on the pickup route. At closing time, and sometimes following a hard rain, you can expect a mass exodus from the parks. The worst-case

continued on page 33

Southern California at a Glance

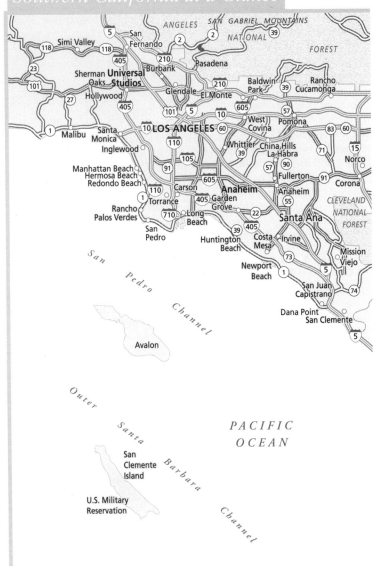

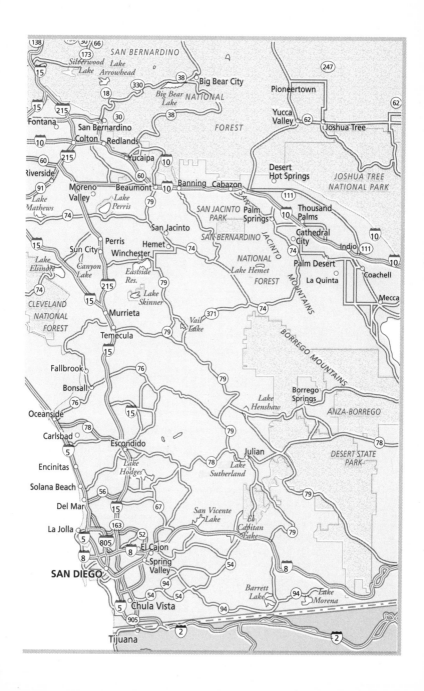

Around Disneyland

0 ——— 1,000 ft
0 ——— 200 m

N

W. Ball Rd.

Santa Ana Fwy.
5

S. Disneyland Dr.

S. Walnut Rd.

Main Parking Garage

DISNEYLAND PARK

Pinocchio Parking

tram loading

Magic Way

Disneyland Hotel Self-Parking

Downtown Disney Self-Parking and Valet

DOWNTOWN DISNEY

tram stop

hotel shuttle loading

tram stop

main pedestrian entrance

Harbor Blvd.

Fantasy Tower

Adventure Tower

DISNEYLAND HOTEL

Grand Californian Hotel Self-parking

GRAND CALIFORNIAN HOTEL

Frontier Tower

Disney California Adventure

DISNEY'S PARADISE PIER HOTEL

S. Disneyland Dr.

Downtown Disney Parking

Katella Ave.

ANAHEIM CONVENTION CENTER

continued from page 29

scenario in this event is that more people will be waiting for the shuttle to your hotel than the bus will hold and that some will be left. While most (but not all) hotel shuttles return for stranded guests, you may suffer a wait of 15 minutes to 1 hour. Our suggestion, if you are depending on hotel shuttles, is to exit the park at least 45 minutes before closing. If you stay in a park until closing and lack the energy to deal with the shuttle or hike back to your hotel, go to the Disneyland Hotel and catch a cab from there. A cab stand is also adjacent to the Harbor Boulevard pedestrian entrance and another is at the Grand Californian Hotel.

The shuttle-loading area is located on the Harbor Boulevard side of the Disneyland Park's main entrances. The loading area connects to a pedestrian corridor that leads to the park entrances. Each hotel's shuttle bus is color-coded yellow, blue, red, silver, or white. Signs of like color designate where the shuttles load and unload.

Anaheim Resort Transit

Anaheim Resort Transit (ART) provides shuttle service to Disneyland Park, Downtown Disney, and the convention center. The service operates 14 routes designated 1–16 (excluding 8 and 13). There are just three to nine well-marked stops on each route, so a complete circuit on any given route usually takes about 20 minutes, but some take up to 1 hour. All of the routes originate and terminate at Disneyland. To continue on to the convention center, you must transfer at Disneyland to Route 1–5, 9, 12, 14, or 16.

The shuttle vehicles are colorful little trolleys similar to the trolleys in San Francisco (except on wheels) and are wheelchair accessible. They ideally run every 10 minutes on peak days during morning and evening periods but can take up to 30 minutes when it's really busy, every 20 minutes during the less busy middle part of the day, and every 20 minutes all day long on nonpeak days. Service begins 1 hour before park opening and ends 30 minutes after park closing. If you commute to Disneyland on ART and then head to Downtown Disney after the parks close, you'll have to find your own way home if you stay at Downtown Disney more than 30 minutes. All shuttle vehicles and respective stops are clearly marked with the route designation.

Hotels served by ART vending kiosks, along with Denny's, sell 1-day, 3-day, and 5-day passes for $4, $10, and $16, respectively. Children age 2 years and under ride free with a paying adult. Day passes for children can be purchased for $1, a 3-day pass for $2, and a 5-day pass for $4. Children must be taken out of strollers in order to ride. Passes cannot be purchased from the driver. For more information, call ☎ 888-364-ARTS or check **rideart.org.** Passes are also available in advance or at ART's website.

A **WORD** *about* **LODGING**

TRAFFIC AROUND DISNEYLAND, and in the Anaheim–Los Angeles area in general, is so terrible that we advocate staying in accommodations within 2–3 miles of the park. Included in this radius are many expensive hotels as well as a considerable number of moderately priced establishments and a small number of bargain motels.

READERS' DISNEYLAND RESORT REPORT CARD

RELATIVELY NEW TO *THE UNOFFICIAL GUIDE TO DISNEYLAND* is the Readers' Disneyland Resort Report Card. Room quality indicates cleanliness, bed comfort, and room size. Check-in efficiency rates how quickly and accurately the hotel staff get you into your room. Quietness of room considers soundproofing from neighbors and exterior noise. Shuttle service (if available) evaluates transportation the hotel offers to Disneyland. The pool rating includes the size of the pool, how crowded it gets, and how clean the pool and pool area are. Hotel staff assesses how friendly and effective the staff are at handling problems and special requests. Our food court rating applies to any on-site counter-service dining, and the overall rating is the summary for every category.

This year, readers rated Disney's hotels better, on average, than off-site hotels. This is interesting because readers generally rate Disney's Florida resorts lower than their off-site counterparts. This indicates that Disneyland may do a better job at running their Disneyland hotels, probably because of the wide variety of alternative hotels literally next door. While Disneyland, unlike Disney World, may be surrounded by non-Disney hotels and restaurants, the net effect to consumers is a better overall experience.

Readers' Disneyland Resort Report Card

BEST WESTERN ANAHEIM INN	DISNEYLAND HOTEL	DISNEY PARADISE PIER	DISNEY'S GRAND CALIFORNIAN
ROOM QUALITY B	ROOM QUALITY B–	ROOM QUALITY B	ROOM QUALITY B
CHECK-IN EFFICIENCY B	CHECK-IN EFFICIENCY A	CHECK-IN EFFICIENCY A	CHECK-IN EFFICIENCY B
QUIETNESS OF ROOM B	QUIETNESS OF ROOM C	QUIETNESS OF ROOM A	QUIETNESS OF ROOM C
SHUTTLE SERVICE C+	SHUTTLE SERVICE N/A	SHUTTLE SERVICE N/A	SHUTTLE SERVICE N/A
HOTEL POOL C	HOTEL POOL A	HOTEL POOL B	HOTEL POOL B
STAFF B	STAFF A	STAFF A	STAFF A
FOOD COURT C	FOOD COURT –	FOOD COURT A	FOOD COURT C
OVERALL RATING C+	**OVERALL RATING B+**	**OVERALL RATING A**	**OVERALL RATING B**
EMBASSY SUITES ANAHEIM-SOUTH	HOWARD JOHNSON HOTEL ANAHEIM	MARRIOTT ANAHEIM SUITES	ALL OTHER OFF-SITE HOTELS
ROOM QUALITY B	ROOM QUALITY A	ROOM QUALITY B	ROOM QUALITY B
CHECK-IN EFFICIENCY B	CHECK-IN EFFICIENCY C	CHECK-IN EFFICIENCY B	CHECK-IN EFFICIENCY B
QUIETNESS OF ROOM B	QUIETNESS OF ROOM B	QUIETNESS OF ROOM C	QUIETNESS OF ROOM B
SHUTTLE SERVICE C	SHUTTLE SERVICE C	SHUTTLE SERVICE C	SHUTTLE SERVICE B
HOTEL POOL C+	HOTEL POOL C	HOTEL POOL B	HOTEL POOL B
STAFF B	STAFF B	STAFF C+	STAFF B
FOOD COURT C	FOOD COURT F	FOOD COURT C+	FOOD COURT C+
OVERALL RATING C+	**OVERALL RATING C+**	**OVERALL RATING C+**	**OVERALL RATING B**

– indicates not enough data.

Another reason why these results are surprising is that readers generally take into consideration their hotel's cost when answering our survey questions, even when instructed to ignore cost. And Disney's hotels are generally far more expensive than off-site alternatives. Given the state of the U.S. economy over the past few years, it's moderately surprising to see readers rate Disney's hotels this highly.

As far as off-site hotels go, the Howard Johnson Anaheim gets the highest rating from readers. The only low rating for the hotel comes from its food court. However, with a wide variety of breakfast, lunch, and dinner options available within a 5-minute walk, this should not prevent you from staying at this hotel.

WALKING TO DISNEYLAND FROM NEARBY HOTELS

WHILE IT IS TRUE THAT MOST DISNEYLAND area hotels provide shuttle service, or are on the ART routes, it is equally true that an ever-increasing number of guests walk to the parks from their hotels. Shuttles are not always available when needed, and parking in the Disneyland lot has become pretty expensive. There is a pedestrian walkway from Harbor Boulevard that provides safe access to Disneyland for guests on foot. This pedestrian corridor extends from Harbor Boulevard all the way west to the Disneyland Hotel, connecting Disneyland Park, Disney California Adventure, and Downtown Disney.

Close proximity to the theme parks figures prominently in the choice of a hotel. Harbor Boulevard borders Disneyland Resort on the east, and Katella Avenue runs along the resort's southern boundary. The closest non-Disney hotels, and the only ones really within walking distance, are on Harbor Boulevard from just south of I-5 to the north to just south of the intersection of Katella Avenue, and along Katella Avenue near Harbor. Farther south on Harbor are some of the best hotels in the area, but they are a little far removed for commuting to the parks on foot. Additionally, these hotels are close to the Anaheim Convention Center and tend to cater, though certainly not exclusively, to business travelers.

For families, a second important consideration is the quality of the hotel swimming pool. We mention this because, unfortunately, many of the non-Disney hotels closest to the theme parks have really crummy pools, sometimes just a tiny rectangle on a stark slab of concrete surrounded on four sides by a parking lot. To bring pool quality and proximity to the theme parks together, we've developed a chart (see page 36) that lists the hotels, both Disney and non-Disney, within walking distance of the theme parks.

The chart shows the walking time from each hotel to the theme-park entrances. The times provided are averages—a couple of fit adults might cover the distance in less time, and a family with small children will likely take longer. Also on the chart we rate the swimming areas of the hotels listed on a scale of 1–10, with 10 being best. As a rule of thumb, any pool with a rating less than 5 is not a place where most folks would

Walking Times to the Theme-park Entrances   Swimming-pool Ratings

HOTEL	LOCATION	WALKING TIME	POOL RATING
Alpine Inn	Katella Avenue	13:00	2
America's Best Value Fantasy Inn	Katella Avenue	15:15	2
The Anabella	Katella Avenue	14:30	6
Anaheim Camelot Inn & Suites	Harbor Boulevard	7:15	2
Anaheim del Sol Inn	Harbor Boulevard	7:00	3
Anaheim Fairfield Inn	Harbor Boulevard	9:30	4
Anaheim Plaza Hotel & Suites	Harbor Boulevard	11:00	6
Best Western Anaheim Inn	Harbor Boulevard	7:15	2
Best Western Park Place Inn	Harbor Boulevard	5:45	2
Candy Cane Inn	Harbor Boulevard	10:30	4
Carousel Inn & Suites	Harbor Boulevard	6:45	2
Castle Inn & Suites	Harbor Boulevard	12:30	1
Desert Inn & Suites	Harbor Boulevard	6:40	1
Desert Palms Hotel & Suites	Katella Avenue	13:00	2
Disneyland Hotel, Adventure Tower	Disneyland Resort	11:00	10
Disneyland Hotel, Fantasy Tower	Disneyland Resort	10:00	10
Disneyland Hotel, Frontier Tower	Disneyland Resort	12:00	10
Disney Paradise Pier Hotel	Disneyland Resort	14:00	7
Disney's Grand Californian Hotel	Disneyland Resort	4:00*	10
Holiday Inn Express	Katella Avenue	15:00	2
Howard Johnson Hotel	Harbor Boulevard	10:15	7
Jolly Roger Hotel Anaheim	Katella Avenue	16:30	4
Park Vue Inn	Harbor Boulevard	6:40	6
Portofino Inn & Suites	Harbor Boulevard	16:30	7
Ramada Maingate	Harbor Boulevard	8:20	8
Ramada Plaza Hotel	Katella Avenue	14:30	2
Sheraton Park Hotel	Harbor Boulevard	17:00	7
Super 8 Motel Near Disneyland	Katella Avenue	15:30	2
Tropicana Inn & Suites	Harbor Boulevard	6:15	3

*To Disneyland Park. The Grand Californian has an on-site entrance to DCA.

want to spend much time. Any hotel not listed is, in our opinion, too far away for walking. Note that several non-Disney hotels are closer than the Disneyland Resort hotels, except for the Grand Californian.

The chart and the above discussion might lead you to wonder whether there's any real advantage to staying in a Disney-owned hotel. The Disney hotels, of course, are very expensive, but if you can handle the tariff, here are the primary benefits of staying in one:

1. You are eligible for early entry at Disneyland Park 4 days each week.
2. You have dozens of full- and counter-service restaurants within easy walking distance.
3. The Disney hotels offer the nicest rooms of any of the hotels within walking distance.
4. The Disney hotels offer the nicest swimming pools of any of the hotels within walking distance.
5. Numerous entertainment and shopping options are in Downtown Disney.
6. It's easy to retreat to your hotel for a meal, a nap, or a swim.
7. You don't need a car.

DISNEYLAND RESORT HOTELS

DISNEY OFFERS THREE ON-SITE HOTELS: the **Grand Californian,** the **Disneyland Hotel,** and the **Paradise Pier Hotel.** The Grand Californian, built in the rustic stone-and-timber style of the grand national park lodges, is the flagship property. Newer, more elaborately themed, and closer to the theme parks and Downtown Disney than the other two on-property hotels, the Grand Californian is without a doubt the best place to stay . . . *if* you can afford it. Rooms at the Grand Californian start at about $213 (with discounts) and go up to $550 per night.

Next most convenient is the sprawling Disneyland Hotel, the oldest, but most recently renovated, of the three. Comprising three guest-room towers, the hotel is lushly landscaped with a new vintage Disney-ana theme and offers large, luxurious guest rooms. Walking time to the monorail station, with transportation to Disneyland Park, is about 3–6 minutes. Rates at the Disneyland Hotel run $210–$350 per night, depending on the season.

The east side of the third Disney hotel overlooks the Paradise Pier section of Disney California Adventure theme park, hence the name Paradise Pier Hotel. Although the guest rooms and public areas have a beach-and-boardwalk flavor, the hotel is not themed. The guest rooms here are large. Walking to to the monorail station and Downtown Disney takes about 5–10 minutes. Depending on season, room rates range $225–$255 per night. Guests at all three Disney-owned hotels can use their keys to charge dining and shopping within the resort to their room. Third-party vendors (including most Downtown Disney restaurants) are excluded, and you'll need to show photo ID along with your room key.

Disney's Grand Californian Hotel & Spa

The Grand Californian Hotel is the crown jewel of Disneyland Resort's three hotels. With its shingle siding, rock foundations, cavernous hewn-beam lobby, polished hardwood floors, and cozy hearths, the hotel is a stately combination of elements from western national park lodges. Designed by architect Peter Dominick (who also designed the Wilderness Lodge at Walt Disney World), the Grand Californian is rendered in the Arts and Crafts style of the early 20th century, with such classic features as "flying" roofs, projecting beams, massive buttresses, and an earth- and wood-tone color palette. We strongly encourage visitors with an interest in architecture to take the fascinating (and free) hour-long Art of the Craft walking tour of the resort, offered several times each week through the Guest Services desk. Most reminiscent of the Ahwahnee Hotel at Yosemite National Park, the Grand Californian combines rugged craftsmanship and grand scale with functional design and intimate spaces. Pull up a vintage rocker in front of a blazing fire, and the bustling lobby instantly becomes a snug cabin.

The hotel's main entrance off Downtown Drive is primarily for vehicular traffic. Two pedestrian-only entrances open into Downtown Disney and DCA; this last makes it a cinch to return to the hotel from DCA for a nap, a swim, or lunch.

The 945 guest rooms are livable; however, they struggle to reconcile modern luxury with the hotel's signature rustic look. Pastel bedspreads and drapes seem much too feminine and delicate to live easily with the masculine polished-wood furniture. Room features we like include excellent light for reading in bed, more-than-adequate storage space, a two-sink vanity outside the toilet and bath, and, in some rooms, a balcony. Views from the guest rooms overlook the swimming-pool area, Downtown Disney, or Disney California Adventure theme park.

Ranging $280–$550 per night, guest rooms are the most expensive at Disneyland Resort. The Grand Californian also charges $15 a day for guest parking. Valet service is available for $22, ☎ 714-635-2300.

Disney's time-share condo enterprise, the Disney Vacation Club, premiered its first West Coast property as part of the 2009 expansion of the Grand Californian. The Villas at Disney's Grand Californian consist of 50 two-bedroom equivalent villas. *Equivalent* is the term used to describe single units that can be sold (or rented) as studio suites or combined to make two- and three-bedroom villas. All villas except studio suites include kitchens, living rooms, and dining areas, as well as washers and dryers. Master bedrooms offer a king bed, while other bedrooms provide two queen beds. Studio suites come with a single queen bed. All bedrooms have a flat-panel TV, private bath, and private balcony. Though studio suites don't have full kitchens, they do include a small fridge, a microwave, and a coffeemaker. Two-bedroom villas consist of a one-bedroom villa joined to a studio suite. Three-bedroom Grand Villas are two-story affairs with the living area, kitchen, and master bedroom on the lower level and two bedrooms on the upper level. Rates for various villas range from $575 for a studio suite to $3,680 for a three-bedroom Grand Villa.

Other elements of the Grand Californian expansion include a new swimming pool for the villas and an underground parking garage. The expansion duplicates the same California Arts and Crafts architecture of the original hotel.

Inspired by Napa Valley cuisine, the Napa Rose Restaurant is the Disneyland Resort's premier fine-dining venue. Situated in a stunning room overlooking DCA, Napa Rose is very expensive but still a very good value (see a full profile on page 190). Just a notch down in price and formality, but likewise located in an exceptionally lovely (albeit more rustic) room, is the Storytellers Café, which serves breakfast, lunch, and dinner (see a full profile on page 197). The restaurant's name is drawn from period murals depicting tall tales set in early California. The fare consists of house-specialty wood-fired pizza and hearty home-style comfort food.

The resort's pool complex, beautifully landscaped with rocks and conifers in a High Sierra theme, includes a lap pool, a Mickey-shaped pool, and a kids' pool with a 100-foot-long twisting slide. The on-site Mandara Spa is one of Disney's best, offering a wide selection of treatments and a state-of-the-art fitness facility. Rounding out the Grand Californian's amenity mix are two clubby lounges and a child-care center for children ages 5–12.

The Disneyland Hotel

Walt Disney barely managed to finance the construction of the Disneyland theme park. He certainly didn't have the funds to purchase adjacent property or build hotels, though on-site hotels were central to his overall concept. So he cut a deal with petroleum engineer and TV producer Jack Wrather to build and operate the Disneyland Hotel. The deal not only gave Wrather the rights to the Disneyland Hotel but also allowed him to build other Disneyland Hotels within the state of California until 2054. It always irked Walt that he didn't own the hotel that bore his name, but Wrather steadfastly refused to renegotiate the rights. After Jack Wrather died in 1984, the Walt Disney Company bought the entire Wrather Corporation, which among other things held the rights to the *Lone Ranger* and *Lassie* TV series and, improbably, the RMS *Queen Mary*, docked at Long Beach. By acquiring the whole corporation, the Walt Disney Company brought the Disneyland Hotel under Disney ownership in 1988.

The Disneyland Hotel consists of three towers facing each other across a verdant landscaped plaza containing decorative pools, a swimming complex, restaurants, shops, and gardens. The hotel was originally connected to Disneyland Park by monorail, but a portion of the hotel was demolished during the construction of DCA and Downtown Disney, and the station was rebuilt on its original location. Guest registration for all three towers is situated in the Fantasy Tower (previously called the Magic Tower, and the Marina Tower before that), which is connected to the Disneyland Convention Center and Disneyland Hotel's self-parking garage. Though all three towers share restaurants, shopping, and recreational amenities, the Fantasy Tower is most conveniently located. It and the Adventure Tower (formerly Dreams, née Sierra) are closest to Downtown Disney and the theme parks.

Rack rates for the Disneyland Hotel range from around $210 for a city view in the off-season to more than $350 for a view of the inner pool and garden complex during holiday periods. The best views can be had from the east/west-facing Adventure Tower, which overlooks the hotel's inner plaza and pool area on the west and Downtown Disney and the theme parks to the east. The most lackluster views are the north-facing vistas of the Fantasy Tower.

In August 2009 the Disneyland Hotel embarked on an ambitious and long-overdue renovation that included major improvements to the guest rooms, as well as a modernization of the hotel's exterior. While the hotel was formerly essentially themeless, the renovation has embraced the retro-nostalgia of baby boomer Disneyland devotees and added decorative elements evoking the park's early years; look for 1950s-style signage atop each tower and a tribute to Frontierland's long-gone Old Unfaithful geysers. Conducted in phases, with the hotel remaining open, the Adventure Tower was completed first in 2010, followed by the Frontier Tower (formerly Wonder, formerly Bonita) in 2011. Renovation is scheduled to be complete on the Fantasy Tower in 2012.

The refurbished rooms abandon the heavy blond traditional guest-room furnishings and decor in favor of a sleek monochromatic contemporary look. Each room has one king- or two queen-size beds, along with a pullout couch; one-bedroom suites with a wet bar and living room are also available. Features include a headboard with a carving of Sleeping Beauty Castle; fiber optics in the headboard create a skyline with fireworks (accompanied by a tinny rendition of "When You Wish Upon a Star") at the flick of a switch. Other decorative touches include black-and-white photography depicting the history of Disneyland and hidden Mickey designs in the carpet, though the overall feel is more business modern than Disney whimsy. Each room has a flat-panel HDTV, perfect for connecting a laptop or video game console. Other room amenities include mini-refrigerators, coffeemakers, safes large enough for laptops, and high-tech phone, cable, and wireless Internet connections. Plumbing, electrical, heating, and air-conditioning systems upgrades also were included in the project.

As part of the exterior modernization, large windows were added, giving the facade a glistening sky-blue tint. The windows, which are specially designed to filter outside noise, replaced the original 8-foot sliding doors and small balconies on all rooms (except for a handful of corner suites and penthouses in the Frontier Tower). On the upside, you get a few extra square feet of living space; on the downside, you can't enjoy outside fresh air (or smog) anymore.

The bathrooms (with newly upgraded tubs) are still small for an upscale hotel, but there is a sink and vanity outside the bathrooms. As in most family hotels built in the 1950s and '60s, a connecting door, situated by the closet and the aforementioned single sink, leads to an adjoining room. Soundproofing around the connecting doors is non-existent, so be prepared to revel in the sounds of your neighbors brushing their teeth, coping with indigestion, and arguing over what to wear. Fortunately, these sounds don't carry into the sleeping area.

The original Peter Pan–themed Never Land pool has been greatly expanded into an "immersive water play area." The new complex's centerpiece is a pair of waterslides (187 feet and 112 feet long, respectively) themed to resemble vintage monorail trains, topped by the classic Disneyland block-letter logo. There's also a 19-foot kiddie slide and bubble jets for the little ones. While the 4,800-square-foot Never Land pool's footprint remained unchanged, a new 4-foot-deep pool has been added between it and the new waterslides, with a footbridge allowing easy passage from one side of the water to the other. Unfortunately, the adult-friendly quieter Cove pools were lost in the construction, reclaimed as a grassy space for special events. Though the rebuilt amenities are attractive, they still appear inadequate in light of the hotel's volume of visitors. On sunny days expect long inefficient lines for the slides, as well as a severe shortage of lounge chairs and elbow room.

Also destroyed were the fan-favorite tropical gardens with walking paths, waterfalls, and koi ponds. In their place is Tangaroa Terrace and Trader Sam's, a casual restaurant and bar that banks on fond memories of Adventureland's 1960s-era Tahitian Terrace dinner show. Disneyland Hotel's other restaurants include Steakhouse 55 and Goofy's Kitchen, the hotel's character-meal headquarters. (All Disneyland Hotel restaurants are profiled in full in Part Four.)

As concerns practical matters, parking is a royal pain at the Disneyland Hotel. The self-parking garage is convenient only to the Fantasy Tower, and even there you'll probably have a long walk. To reach the other two towers, you must pass through the Fantasy Tower and navigate across the hotel's inner plaza and pool area. The Frontier Tower on the southern end of the property has a small parking lot to the rear accessible via Downtown Drive and Paradise Way. Unfortunately, many of the already limited spaces are reserved for the adjacent Disney Vacation Club time-share sales office. Even so, if you're staying at the Frontier Tower, it's your best bet. If there's no room in the Frontier lot, you're better off parking in the Paradise Pier Hotel's lot than in the Disneyland Hotel parking garage. The only valet parking is at the Fantasy Tower, so even if you valet park, you'll still have to hoof it to the other towers.

A California family who didn't have a car to park thought the Disneyland Hotel especially convenient:

I initially thought that staying at the Disneyland Hotel was a nice treat that we might do just this once. I now see it as an absolute necessity as it allows early entry and an easy midday retreat. That plus the great service there seals the deal. One final tip: Although the rooms don't have a kitchenette, you can request a refrigerator and a coffeemaker. We used the coffeemaker to heat water for instant oatmeal and kept juice and milk in the fridge for quick breakfasts in the room.

But a Parker, Colorado, mother of two preschoolers wished she had a net:

The beds in our room were very high off the ground, and our youngest fell out of bed a few times during our stay. Weird that they would be so high at a kid-friendly hotel!

Like the Grand Californian Hotel & Spa, the Disneyland Hotel charges a $15 daily self-parking fee.

Paradise Pier Hotel

Disney acquired the independent Pan Pacific Hotel just south of the Disneyland Hotel in 1997 and changed its name to the Disneyland Pacific Hotel. Just before Disney California Adventure opened in 2001, the hotel was rechristened as the Paradise Pier Hotel in recognition of the Paradise Pier district of DCA that the hotel overlooks.

The 481-room property makes a mostly successful attempt to merge the hotel's original South Seas flavor with a vintage seaside amusement theme inspired by the attractions across the street. Concept artwork of the park (featuring now-removed Disney California Adventure rides such as the Orange Stinger) is prominently displayed in both public spaces and guest rooms. Guest rooms are furnished with blond wood furniture and the usual Disney-pastel soft goods, including bedspreads with a hidden Mickey head pattern. Somewhat more whimsical than rooms at the Disneyland Hotel or the Grand Californian, Paradise Pier rooms include accents such as Mickey Mouse table lamps and confetti-patterned carpets. Guest-room picture windows on the hotel's east side offer the best vistas of any of the Disneyland Resort hotels with a perfect view of the lights and attractions of Paradise Pier inside DCA. From rooms on the other side of the hotel you can see, well, parking lots. Rates range $225–$255, depending on season and view.

For dining, the informal Disney's PCH Grill serves a character breakfast and dinner (without characters) daily. Amenities include a fitness center and an often breezy rooftop pool complete with a waterslide (the view from the top of the slide is killer). Self-parking in Paradise Pier's on-site garage is fast and convenient. Somewhat isolated on the Disneyland Resort property, the hotel is a 14-minute hike to the theme-park entrances, farther away than most non-Disney hotels lining Harbor Boulevard on the east side of the resort.

HOW TO GET DISCOUNTS ON LODGING AT DISNEYLAND RESORT HOTELS

SO MANY GUEST ROOMS ARE in and around Disneyland Resort that competition is brisk, and everyone, including Disney, wheels and deals to keep them filled. The recession has only compounded this. It has led to a more flexible discount policy for Disneyland Resort hotels. Here are tips for getting price breaks:

1. DISNEYLAND RESORT WEBSITE Disney has become more aggressive about offering deals on its website. Go to **disneyland.com** and check the page for "Special Offers." When booking rooms on Disney's or any other site, be sure to click on "Terms and Conditions" and read the fine print *before* making reservations.

2. SEASONAL SAVINGS You can save $15–$60 per night on a Disneyland Resort hotel room by visiting during the slower times of the year. Disney uses so many adjectives (*regular, holiday, peak, value,* and such) to describe its seasonal calendar, however, that it's hard to keep up without a scorecard. To confuse matters more, the dates for each season vary from hotel to hotel. Our advice: If you're set on staying at a Disney hotel, obtain a copy of the Disney Resort Travel Sales Center California Brochure, which is described on page 16.

If you have a hard time getting a copy of the brochure, forget trying to find the various seasonal dates on the Disneyland Resort website. Easier by far is to check them out on the independent-of-Disney **mouse savers.com** site described in tip four below.

Understand that Disney seasonal dates are not sequential like spring, summer, fall, and winter. For any specific resort, there are sometimes several seasonal changes in a month. This is important because your room rate per night is determined by the season prevailing when you check in. Let's say that you checked in to the Disneyland Hotel on April 19 for a 5-night stay. April 19 is in the more expensive peak season that ends April 20, followed by the less pricey regular season beginning April 21. Because you arrived during peak season, the peak season rate will be applied for your entire stay, even though more than half of your stay will be in regular season. Your strategy, therefore, is to shift your dates (if possible) to arrive during a less expensive season.

3. ASK ABOUT SPECIALS When you talk to Disney reservationists, inquire specifically about special deals. Ask, for example, "What special rates or discounts are available at Disney hotels during the time of our visit?" Being specific and assertive paid off for an Illinois reader:

> I called Disney's reservations number and asked for availability and rates. . . . [Because] of the Unofficial Guide *warning about Disney reservationists answering only the questions posed, I specifically asked, "Are there any special rates or discounts for that room during the month of October?" She replied, "Yes, we have that room available at a special price. . . ." [For] the price of one phone call, I saved $440.*

Along similar lines, a Warren Township, New Jersey, dad chimed in with this:

Your tip about asking Disney employees about discounts was invaluable. They will not volunteer this information, but by asking we saved almost $500 on our hotel room using a AAA discount.

4. LEARN ABOUT DEALS OFFERED TO SPECIFIC MARKETS The folks at **mousesavers.com** keep an updated list of discounts and reservation codes for use at Disney resorts. The codes are separated into categories such as "for anyone," "for residents of certain states," "for Annual Passport holders," and so on. For example, the site once listed a deal targeted to residents of the San Diego area published in an ad in a San Diego newspaper. Dozens of discounts are usually listed on the site, covering almost all Disneyland Resort hotels. Usually anyone calling the Disneyland Resort Reservations Office (call ☎ 714-956-6425 and press 1 on the menu) can cite the referenced ad and get the discounted rate.

You should be aware that Disney is trending away from room-discount codes that anyone can use. Instead, Disney is targeting people with pin codes in e-mails and direct mailings. Pin-code discounts are offered to specific individuals and are correlated with that person's name and address. Pin-code offers are nontransferable. When you try to make a reservation using the code, Disney will verify that the street or e-mail address to which the pin code was sent is yours.

To enhance your chances of receiving a pin-code offer, you need to get your name and street or e-mail address into the Disney system. One way is to call the Disney Resort Travel Sales Center at ☎ 714-520-7070 and request that written info be sent to you. If you've been to Disneyland previously, your name and address will already be on record, but you won't be as likely to receive a pin-code offer as you would by calling and requesting to be sent information. The latter is regarded as new business. Or, expressed differently, if Disney smells blood, they're more likely to come after you. On the Web, go to **disneyland.com,** click on "My Disneyland," and sign up to have offers and news sent automatically to your e-mail address.

Mousesavers.com also features a great links page with short descriptions and URLs of the best Disney-related websites and a current-year seasonal rates calendar.

5. KAYAK.COM This search engine compares discounts offered by hotel chains and Internet travel sellers. With Kayak's help you can see photos and descriptions of Disneyland-area hotels and determine which seller is offering the best discounts.

6. ANNUAL PASSPORT–HOLDER DISCOUNTS Annual Passport holders are eligible for a broad range of discounts on dining, shopping, and lodging. If you visit Disneyland Resort once a year or more, or if you plan on a visit of 5 or more days, you might save money overall by purchasing Annual Passes. We've seen resort discounts as deep as 30% offered to Annual Passport holders. It doesn't take long to recoup the extra bucks you spent on an Annual Passport when you're saving that kind of money on lodging. Discounts in the 10%–15% range are more the norm.

7. TRAVEL AGENTS Travel agents are active players in the market and are particularly good sources of information on time-limited special programs and discounts. In our opinion, a good travel agent is the best friend a traveler can have. And though we at the *Unofficial Guide* know a thing or two about the travel industry, we always give our agent a chance to beat any deal we find. If our agent can't beat the deal, we let her book it if she can receive commission from it. In other words, we create a relationship that gives her plenty of incentive to really roll up her sleeves and work on our behalf.

unofficial **TIP**
For the best rates and least crowded conditions, try to avoid visiting Disneyland Resort when a major convention or trade show is in progress.

As you might expect, some travel agents and agencies specialize, sometimes exclusively, in selling Disneyland and Walt Disney World. These agents have spent an incredible amount of time at both resorts and have completed extensive Disney education programs. They are usually the most Disney-knowledgeable agents in the travel industry. Most of these specialists and their agencies display the "Earmarked" logo indicating that they are Authorized Disney Vacation Planners. These Disney specialists are so good that we use them ourselves. They save us time and money, sometimes lots of both. The best of the best include **Sue Pisaturo,** whom we've used many times and who is a contributor to this guide **(sue@wdwvacations.com)** and **Tracy Desjardin (tdwdwtravel@comcast.net).**

8. ORGANIZATIONS AND AUTO CLUBS Disney has developed time-limited programs with some auto clubs and other organizations. Recently, for example, AAA members were offered 10%–20% savings on Disney hotels and discounts on Disney package vacations. Such deals come and go, but the market suggests there will be more in the future. If you're a member of AARP, AAA, or any travel or auto club, ask whether the group has a program before shopping elsewhere.

9. ROOM UPGRADES Sometimes a room upgrade is as good as a discount. If you're visiting Disneyland Resort during a slower time, book the least expensive room your discounts will allow. Checking in, ask very politely about being upgraded to a "theme park" or "pool view" room. A fair percentage of the time, you will get one at no additional charge.

NON-DISNEY HOTELS

WHEN WALT DISNEY BUILT DISNEYLAND, he did not have the funding to include hotels or to purchase the property surrounding his theme park. Consequently, the area around the park developed in an essentially uncontrolled manner. Many of the hotels and motels near Disneyland were built in the early 1960s, and they are small and sometimes unattractive by today's standards. Quite a few motels adopted

Disneyland-area Hotels

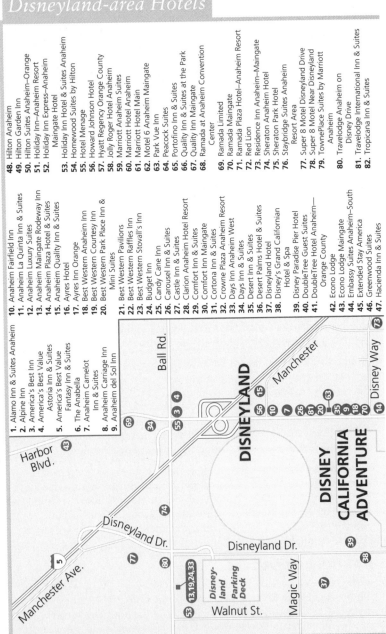

1. Alamo Inn & Suites Anaheim
2. Alpine Inn
3. America's Best Inn
4. America's Best Value Astoria Inn & Suites
5. America's Best Value Fantasy Inn & Suites
6. The Anabella
7. Anaheim Camelot Inn & Suites
8. Anaheim Carriage Inn
9. Anaheim del Sol Inn
10. Anaheim Fairfield Inn
11. Anaheim La Quinta Inn & Suites
12. Anaheim Luxury Suites
13. Anaheim Maingate Rodeway Inn
14. Anaheim Plaza Hotel & Suites
15. Anaheim Quality Inn & Suites
16. Ayres Hotel
17. Ayres Inn Orange
18. Best Western Anaheim Inn
19. Best Western Courtesy Inn
20. Best Western Park Place Inn & Mini Suites
21. Best Western Pavilions
22. Best Western Raffles Inn
23. Best Western Stovall's Inn
24. Budget Inn
25. Candy Cane Inn
26. Carousel Inn & Suites
27. Castle Inn & Suites
28. Clarion Anaheim Hotel Resort
29. Comfort Inn & Suites
30. Comfort Inn Maingate
31. Cortona Inn & Suites
32. Crowne Plaza Anaheim Resort
33. Days Inn Anaheim West
34. Days Inn & Suites
35. Desert Inn & Suites
36. Desert Palms Hotel & Suites
37. Disneyland Hotel
38. Disney's Grand Californian Hotel & Spa
39. Disney Paradise Pier Hotel
40. DoubleTree Guest Suites
41. DoubleTree Hotel Anaheim–Orange County
42. Econo Lodge
43. Econo Lodge Maingate
44. Embassy Suites Anaheim–South
45. Extended Stay America
46. Greenwood Suites
47. Hacienda Inn & Suites
48. Hilton Anaheim
49. Hilton Garden Inn
50. Hilton Suites Anaheim–Orange
51. Holiday Inn–Anaheim Resort
52. Holiday Inn Express–Anaheim Maingate Hotel
53. Holiday Inn Hotel & Suites Anaheim
54. Homewood Suites by Hilton
55. Hotel Menage
56. Howard Johnson Hotel
57. Hyatt Regency Orange County
58. Jolly Roger Hotel Anaheim
59. Marriott Anaheim Suites
60. Marriott Hotel Anaheim
61. Marriott Hotel Main
62. Motel 6 Anaheim Maingate
63. Park Vue Inn
64. Peacock Suites
65. Portofino Inn & Suites
66. Quality Inn & Suites at the Park
67. Quality Inn Maingate
68. Ramada at Anaheim Convention Center
69. Ramada Limited
70. Ramada Maingate
71. Ramada Plaza Hotel–Anaheim Resort
72. Red Lion
73. Residence Inn Anaheim–Maingate
74. Sheraton Anaheim Hotel
75. Sheraton Park Hotel
76. Staybridge Suites Anaheim
77. Super 8 Motel Disneyland Drive
78. Super 8 Motel Near Disneyland
79. TownePlace Suites by Marriott Anaheim
80. Travelodge Anaheim on Disney Drive
81. Travelodge International Inn & Suites
82. Tropicana Inn & Suites

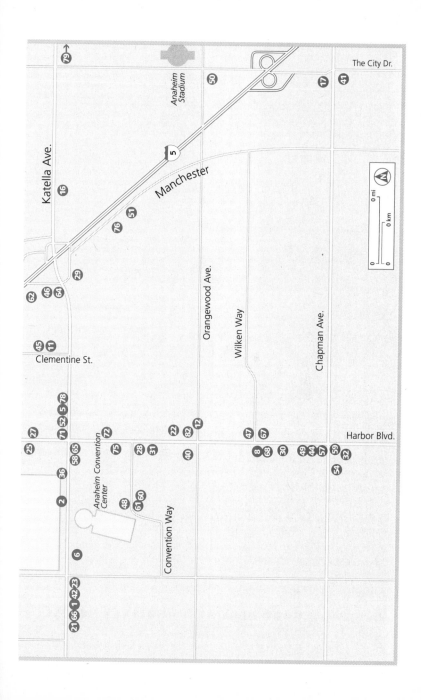

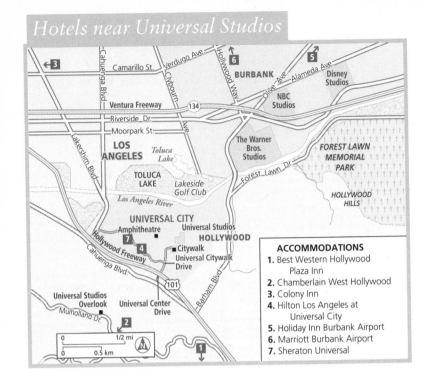

Hotels near Universal Studios

ACCOMMODATIONS
1. Best Western Hollywood Plaza Inn
2. Chamberlain West Hollywood
3. Colony Inn
4. Hilton Los Angeles at Universal City
5. Holiday Inn Burbank Airport
6. Marriott Burbank Airport
7. Sheraton Universal

adventure or fantasy themes in emulation of Disneyland. As you might imagine, these themes from five decades ago seem hokey and irrelevant today. There is a disquieting (though rapidly diminishing) number of seedy hotels near Disneyland, and even some of the chain properties fail to live up to their national standards.

If you consider a non-Disney-owned hotel in Anaheim, check its quality as reported by a reliable independent rating system such as those offered by the *Unofficial Guides,* AAA Directories, Mobil Guides, or *Frommer's* guides. Also, before you book, ask how old the hotel is and when the guest rooms were last refurbished. Be aware that almost any hotel can be made to look good on a website, so don't depend on websites alone. Locate the hotel on our street map (see pages 46–47) to verify its proximity to Disneyland. If you will not have a car, make sure the hotel has a shuttle service that will satisfy your needs.

GETTING A GOOD DEAL AT NON-DISNEY HOTELS

FOLLOWING ARE SOME TIPS AND STRATEGIES for getting a good deal on a hotel room near Disneyland. Though the following list may seem a bit intimidating and may refer to players in the travel market that are unfamiliar to you, acquainting yourself with the strategies will serve you well in the long run. Simply put, the tips we provide for getting a good deal near Disneyland will work equally well at just about any other place where you need a hotel. Once you have invested a little time and have experimented with these strategies, you will be able to routinely obtain rooms at the best hotels and at the lowest possible rates.

Remember that Disneyland Resort is right across the street from the Anaheim Convention Center, one of the largest and busiest convention centers in the country. Room availability, as well as rates, are affected significantly by trade shows and other events at the convention center. To determine whether such an event will be ongoing during your projected dates, check out the convention calendar on pages 24–25.

1. MOUSESAVERS.COM is a site dedicated to finding great deals on hotels, admissions, and more at Disneyland Resort and Walt Disney World. The site covers discounts on both Disney and non-Disney hotels and is especially effective at keeping track of time-limited deals and discounts offered in a select market—San Diego, for example. However, the site does not sell travel products.

2. KAYAK.COM is a travel search engine that searches the better hotel-discount sites, as well as chain and individual hotel websites. Websites searched vary from destination to destination but do not include Expedia and Travelocity.

3. EXPEDIA.COM AND TRAVELOCITY.COM These two websites sometimes offer good discounts on area hotels. We find that Expedia offers the best deals if you're booking within 2 weeks of your visit. In fact, some of Expedia's last-minute deals are amazing, really rock-bottom rates. Travelocity frequently beats Expedia, however, if you reserve 2 weeks to 3 months out. Neither site offers anything to get excited about if you book more than 3 months from the time of your visit. If you use either site, be sure to take into consideration the demand for rooms during the season of your visit, and check to see if any big conventions or trade shows are scheduled for the convention center.

4. PRICELINE.COM At Priceline you can tender a bid for a room. You can't bid on a specific hotel, but you can specify location ("Disneyland Vicinity") and the quality rating expressed in stars. If your bid is accepted, you will be assigned to a hotel consistent with your location and quality requirements, and your credit card will be charged in a nonrefundable transaction for your entire stay. Notification of acceptance usually takes less than an hour. We recommend bidding $35–$55 per night for a three-star hotel and $55–$80 per night for a four-star property. To gauge your chances of success, check to see if any major conventions or trade shows are scheduled for the convention center during your preferred dates.

5. OTHER WEB TRAVEL SELLERS Ever wonder which sites offer the best deals or whether you're missing some tiny boutique site offering amazing discounts? So do we. *Unofficial Guide* statistician Fred Hazleton has analyzed more than 380,000 rate quotes from dozens of Internet sellers for Disneyland Resort and Anaheim-area hotels. Fred discovered that the pricing competition for Disneyland-area hotels is a lot greater than we see in the Walt Disney World area or at our other *Unofficial Guide* destinations. Fewer than 5% of the Disneyland searches produced a single quote, while another 5% produced more than 10 quotes! The quoted rates are more varied in Anaheim than we usually see at other destinations, with a broader range between the highest and lowest rates for a given hotel. For a number of hotels, as many as six or more different rates are quoted. Fred's research has also shown that about 66% of the time the hotel website or hotel front desk will match or beat the best Internet rate available. We've also observed that Expedia and Travelocity are often the best websites for last-minute bookings.

Following are the websites that most often produce the best rate quotes for Disneyland Resort–area hotels. The percentage in parentheses tells how often the site has the winning (read: best) quote. Having the lowest rate 42% of the time, as **arestravel.com** does, may not sound like much, but consider that probably 50 other Internet travel sites are selling the same hotels.

arestravel.com (42%)   travelworm.com (40%)

hotelkingdom.com (34%)   hotels.com (32%)

lodging.com (23%)

6. ENTERTAINMENT BOOKS These area-specific guides contain discount coupons for hotels, restaurants, entertainment, shopping, and even car washes. The Anaheim version sells for about $40 at the beginning of the year but is discounted (up to $25 off) if you buy with only part of the year remaining. Sometimes the books sell out before summer. Unless you live in Orange County, you won't be able to use a lot of the coupons, but sometimes the savings on your hotel and dining will more than justify the purchase. To buy, or for additional information, visit **entertainment.com.**

If you plan to visit other Southern California attractions in addition to Disneyland, you might want to consider a **CityPass** discount booklet. Much more limited in scope than the entertainment books described above, CityPass includes a 3-day Park Hopper for Disneyland Park and DCA, including early entry to Disneyland Park for 1 day. Also included are 1 day's admission each to Universal Studios Hollywood, SeaWorld San Diego, and the San Diego Zoo or the San Diego Zoo's Safari Park. Costing $276 for adults and $229 for children ages 3–9, the booklet is valid for 14 days from first use. If you plan to visit all these parks, it will save you about 29% on admissions. If you don't use all of the admissions, however, you will save little or nothing by purchasing the CityPass booklet. The booklet does not include dining or shopping discounts. Details concerning the Southern Californian booklet as well as other CityPass destinations are available at **citypass.com.**

7. ROOMSAVER CALIFORNIA/NEVADA GUIDE This book of discount coupons for hotels throughout California is available free of charge at many restaurants and motels along the main interstates in and leading to California. However, because most folks make reservations before leaving home, picking up the coupon book en route does not help much. But for $3 ($5 Canadian) the company will mail you a copy, allowing you to examine the discounts offered before you make your reservations. The guide is free; the charge is for the postage. To order call ☎ 800-222-3948, Monday–Friday, 8:30 a.m.–5:30 p.m. EST. Or browse the guide for free at **roomsaver.com**.

8. SPECIAL WEEKEND RATES If you are not averse to about an hour's drive to Disneyland, you can get a great weekend rate on rooms in downtown Los Angeles. Most hotels that cater to business, government, and convention travelers offer special weekend discounts that range 15%–40% below normal weekday rates. You can find out about weekend specials by calling the hotel or by consulting your travel agent.

9. WHOLESALERS, CONSOLIDATORS, AND RESERVATION SERVICES Wholesalers and consolidators buy rooms, or options on rooms (room blocks), from hotels at a low negotiated rate. They then resell the rooms at a profit through travel agents, tour packagers, or directly to the public. Most wholesalers and consolidators have a provision for returning unsold rooms to participating hotels, but they are disinclined to do so. The wholesaler's or consolidator's relationship with any hotel is predicated on volume. If they return rooms unsold, the hotel might not make as many rooms available to them the next time around. Thus, wholesalers and consolidators often offer rooms at bargain rates, anywhere from 15%–50% off rack, occasionally sacrificing their profit margin to avoid returning the rooms to the hotel unsold.

When wholesalers and consolidators deal directly with the public, they frequently represent themselves as "reservation services." When you call, you can ask for a rate quote for a particular hotel or, alternatively, ask for their best available deal in the area where you prefer to stay. If there is a maximum amount you are willing to pay, say so. Chances are that the service will find something that will work for you, even if they have to shave a dollar or two off their own profit. Sometimes you will have to prepay for your room with your credit card when you make your reservation. Most often, you will pay when you check out. Listed below are two services that frequently offer substantial discounts in the Anaheim area.

ANAHEIM AREA WHOLESALERS AND CONSOLIDATORS

California reservations	☎ 800-780-5733	**hotel-locator.com**
hotels.com	☎ 800-246-8357	**hotels.com**

10. CLUBS AND ORGANIZATIONS If you belong to AAA, AARP, or a number of other organizations, you can obtain lodging discounts. Usually the discounts are modest, 5%–15%, but occasionally higher.

11. IF YOU MAKE YOUR OWN RESERVATION As you poke around trying to find a good deal, there are several things you should know. First, always call the hotel in question as opposed to the hotel chain's national toll-free number. Quite often, the reservationists at the national numbers are unaware of local specials. Always ask about specials before you inquire about corporate rates. Do not be reluctant to bargain. If you are buying a hotel's weekend package, for example, and want to extend your stay into the following week, you can often obtain at least the corporate rate for the extra days. Do your bargaining before you check in, however, preferably when you make your reservations. Work far enough in advance to receive a confirmation.

HOW TO GET THE ROOM YOU WANT

MOST HOTELS, INCLUDING DISNEY'S, won't guarantee a specific room when you book but will post your request on your reservations record and try to accommodate you. Our experience indicates that if you give them your first, second, and third choices, you'll probably get one of the three.

When speaking to the reservationist or your travel agent, it's important to be specific. If you want a room overlooking the pool, say so. Similarly, be sure to clearly state such preferences as a particular floor, a corner room, a room close to restaurants, a room away from elevators and ice machines, a nonsmoking room, a room with a balcony, or any other preference. If you have a list of preferences, type it up in order of importance, and e-mail or fax it to the hotel or to your travel agent. Be sure to include your own contact information and, if you've already booked, your reservation confirmation number. If it makes you feel better, call back in a few days to make sure your preferences were posted to your reservations record.

unofficial **TIP**
Request a renovated room at your hotel—these can be much nicer than the older rooms.

About Hotel Renovations

We have inspected almost 100 hotels in the Disneyland Resort area to compile the lodging choices presented here. Each year we phone each hotel to verify contact information and to inquire about renovations or refurbishments. If a hotel has been renovated or has refurbished its guest rooms, we reinspect that hotel along with any new hotels for the next edition of this book. Hotels that report no improvements are checked out every 2 years.

Most hotels more than 5 years old refurbish 10%–20% of their guest rooms each year. This incremental approach minimizes disruption of business but makes your room assignment a crap shoot. You might luck into a newly renovated room or be assigned a threadbare room. Disney resorts will not guarantee a recently renovated room but will note your request and try to accommodate you. Non-Disney hotels will often guarantee an updated room when you book.

Our hotel ratings are provided starting on page 62.

TRAVEL PACKAGES

PACKAGE TOURS THAT INCLUDE lodging, park admission, and other features are routinely available. Some packages are very good deals if you make use of the features you are paying for.

Finally, here's a helpful source of regional travel information:

Anaheim–Orange County Visitor and Convention Bureau
☎ 714-765-8888; anaheimoc.org

How to Evaluate a Disneyland Travel Package

Hundreds of Disneyland package vacations are offered to the public each year. Some are created by the Disney Resort Travel Sales Center, others by airline touring companies, and some by independent travel agents and wholesalers. Almost all Disneyland packages include lodging at or near Disneyland and theme-park admission. Packages offered by the airlines include air transportation.

Package prices vary seasonally, with mid-June to mid-August and holiday periods being most expensive. Off-season, forget packages; there are plenty of empty rooms, and you can negotiate great discounts (at non-Disney properties) yourself. Similarly, airfares and rental cars are cheaper at off-peak times.

Almost all package ads feature a headline stating "Disneyland for 3 Days from $298" or some such wording. The key word in the ads is *from*. The rock-bottom package price connotes the least desirable hotel accommodations. If you want better or more conveniently located digs, you'll have to pay more, often much more.

At Disneyland, packages offer a wide selection of hotels. Some, like the Disney-owned hotels, are very good. Others, unfortunately, run the quality gamut. Packages with lodging in non-Disney hotels are much less expensive.

When considering a package, choose one that includes features you are sure to use. Whether you use all the features or not, you will most certainly pay for them. Second, if cost is of greater concern than convenience, make a few phone calls and see what the package would cost if you booked its individual components (such as airfare, rental car, and lodging) on your own. If the package price is less than the à la carte cost, the package is a good deal. If the costs are about the same, the package is probably worth it for the convenience.

If you buy a package from Disney, do not expect Disney reservationists to offer suggestions or help you sort out your options. As a rule they will not volunteer information but will only respond to specific questions you pose, adroitly ducking any query that calls for an opinion. A reader from North Riverside, Illinois, wrote to the *Unofficial Guide,* complaining:

> I have received various pieces of literature from [Disney], and it is very confusing to try and figure everything out. My wife made two telephone calls and the [Disney] representatives were very courteous. However, they answered only the questions posed and were not very eager to give

advice on what might be most cost-effective. The [Disney] reps would not say if we would be better off doing one thing over the other. I feel a person could spend 8 hours on the telephone with [Disney] reps and not have any more input than you get from reading the literature.

If you cannot get the information you need from the Disney people, try a good travel agent. Chances are that the agent will be more forthcoming in helping you sort out your options.

Information Needed for Evaluation

For quick reference and to save on phone expenses, call the Disney Resort Travel Sales Center at ☎ 714-520-7070 and ask that they mail you a current Disney Resort Travel Sales Center California Brochure containing descriptions and room rates for all Disneyland lodging properties. In addition, ask for a rate sheet listing admission options and prices for the theme parks. With this in hand, you are ready to evaluate any package that appeals to you. Remember that all packages are quoted on a per-person basis, two to a room (double occupancy). Good luck.

VACATION HOMES

SOME OF THE BEST LODGING DEALS in the Disneyland Resort area are vacation homes. Prices range from about $65 a night for two-bedroom condos and town homes to $200–$450 a night for three- to five-bedroom vacation homes.

Forgetting about taxes to keep things simple, let's compare renting a vacation home with staying at a three-star hotel near Disneyland. A family of two parents, two teens, and two grandparents would need three hotel rooms at the Anaheim Fairfield Inn. At the lowest rate obtainable, they'd be spending $129 per night per room, or $387 total. Rooms are 340 square feet each, so they'd have a total of 1,020 square feet. Each room has a private bath and a TV.

Renting at the same time of year, they can rent a 2,053-square-foot, three-bedroom, two-bath vacation home with a private pool within easy walking distance of Disneyland for $375—a saving of $12 per night over the Anaheim Fairfield Inn rate. But that's not all: The home comes with a washer and dryer; an outdoor hot tub; a large, grassy play area; a barbecue grill; lounge chairs; a game room with pool table; a family room with a 52-inch high-definition TV, DVD player, and surround sound; a stereo system; a dining room with seating for eight, plus a covered patio dining area; and off-street parking. The only trade-off for our hypothetical family would be having two bathrooms instead of three.

You can see the specific home described above at **vrbo.com/175261.** VRBO stands for **Vacation Rental by Owner,** a listing service for owners of vacation properties nationwide. One thing we like about the VRBO website is that it offers detailed information, including a good number of photos of each specific home. When you book, the home you've been looking at is the actual one you're reserving. On the other hand, some vacation-home rental companies, like rental-car agencies, don't assign you a specific home until the day you arrive—these companies provide photos of a "typical home" instead of making information available on each of the individual homes in their inventory. In this case, you have to take the company's word that the typical home pictured is representative and that the property you'll be assigned will be just as nice.

Location is everything, especially in Southern California with its legendary traffic. Before renting a home, contact the owner and get the address. Then, using **mapquest.com,** obtain exact directions from the home to Disneyland. This will tell you how long and how complicated your commute will be. Avoid homes for which it's necessary to drive on a freeway for more than a couple of miles. Don't worry if the home isn't in Anaheim per se; it's the distance to Disneyland that counts.

The only practical way to shop for a rental home is on the Web. Going online makes it relatively easy to compare different properties and rental companies. The best sites are easy to navigate, let you see what you're interested in without having to log in or divulge any personal information, and list memberships in such organizations as the Better Business Bureau. Before you book, ask about minimum stays, damage deposits, cleaning charges, pets, and how any problems will be addressed once you're in the home.

HOTELS *and* MOTELS:
Rated and Ranked

WHAT'S IN A ROOM?

EXCEPT FOR CLEANLINESS, STATE OF REPAIR, and decor, most travelers do not pay much attention to hotel rooms. There is, of course, a discernible standard of quality and luxury that differentiates Motel 6 from Holiday Inn, Holiday Inn from Marriott, and so on. In general, however, hotel guests fail to appreciate that some rooms are better engineered than others.

Contrary to what you might suppose, designing a hotel room is (or should be) a lot more complex than picking a bedspread to match the carpet and drapes. Making the room usable to its

Disney Lodging for Less

Mary Waring, *Webmaster at* **mousesavers.com** *(see page 49), knows more about Disney hotel packages than anyone on the planet. Here are her money-saving suggestions.*

BOOK "ROOM-ONLY." It's frequently a better deal to book a room-only reservation instead of buying a vacation package. Disney likes to sell vacation packages because they're easy and profitable. When you buy a package, you're typically paying a premium for convenience. You can often save money by putting together your own package—just book room-only at a resort and buy passes, meals, and extras separately.

Disney now prices its standard packages at the same rates as if you had purchased individual components separately at full price. However, what Disney doesn't tell you is that components can usually be purchased separately at a discount—and those discounts are not reflected in the brochure prices of Disney's packages. (Sometimes you can get special-offer packages that do include discounts; see below.)

Keep in mind that Disney's packages often include extras you are unlikely to use. Also, packages require a $200 deposit and full payment 45 days in advance; plus, they have stringent change and cancellation policies. Generally, booking room-only requires a deposit of 1 night's room rate with the remainder due at check-in. Your reservation can be changed or canceled for any reason until 5 days before check-in.

Whether you decide to book a Disney vacation package or create your own, there are a number of ways to save:

- *Use discount codes to reduce your room-only rate.* Disney uses these codes to push unsold rooms at certain times of year. (In the past few years, however, these codes have become scarcer.) Check a website such as **mousesavers.com** to learn about codes that may be available for your vacation dates. Some codes are available to anyone, while others are just for California residents, Annual Passport holders, and so on.

  Discount codes aren't always available for every hotel or every date, and they typically don't appear until 2–6 months in advance. The good news is that you can usually apply a code to an existing

occupants is an art, a planning discipline that combines both form and function.

Decor and taste are important, certainly. No one wants to spend several days in a room where the decor is dated, garish, or even ugly. But beyond the decor, there are variables that determine how "livable" a hotel room is. In Anaheim, for example, we have seen some beautifully appointed rooms that are simply not well designed for human habitation. The next time you stay in a hotel, pay attention to the details and room-only reservation. Simply call the Disneyland Reservations Center at ☎ 714-956-6425 (or contact a Disney-savvy travel agent) and ask whether any rooms are available at your preferred hotel for your preferred dates using the code.

- **Use discount codes to reduce your vacation package rate.** Disney occasionally offers packages that include resort discounts or value-added features such as a free dining plan. For those who like the convenience of packages, these offers are well worth seeking out.

    You'll need to present a discount code to get the special package rates. Check a site such as **mousesavers.com** for more information.

    As with room-discount codes, package-discount codes aren't available for every hotel or every date, and they typically don't appear until 2–6 months in advance. You can usually apply a code to an existing package reservation. Again, call the Disneyland Reservations Center at ☎ 714-956-6425 (or contact a Disney-savvy travel agent) and ask whether any rooms are available at your preferred hotel for your preferred dates using the package code.

- **Be flexible.** Buying a room or package with a discount code is a little like shopping for clothes at a discount store: If you wear size XX-small or XXXX-large, or you like green when everyone else is wearing pink, you're a lot more likely to score a bargain. Likewise, resort discounts are available only when Disney has excess rooms. You're more likely to get a discount during less-popular times (such as value season) and at larger or less-popular resorts.

- **Be persistent.** This is the most important tip. Disney allots a certain number of rooms to each discount; reportedly this averages 100 rooms per night per code. Once the discounted rooms are gone, you won't get that rate unless someone cancels. Fortunately, people change and cancel reservations all the time. If you can't get your preferred dates or hotel with one discount code, try another one (if available) or keep calling back first thing in the morning to check for cancellations—the system resets overnight, and any reservations with unpaid deposits are automatically released for resale.

design elements of your room. Even more than decor, these are the things that will make you feel comfortable and at home.

ROOM RATINGS

TO SEPARATE PROPERTIES ACCORDING to the relative quality, tastefulness, state of repair, cleanliness, and size of their standard rooms, we have grouped the hotels and motels into classifications denoted by stars. Star ratings in this guide apply to Anaheim properties only and do not necessarily correspond to ratings awarded by Mobil, AAA, or other travel critics. Because stars have little relevance when awarded in the absence of commonly recognized standards of comparison, we have tied our ratings to expected levels of quality established by specific American hotel corporations.

Star ratings apply to *room quality only* and describe the property's standard accommodations. For most hotels and motels, a "standard accommodation" is a hotel room with either one king bed or two queen beds. In an all-suite property, the standard accommodation is either a studio or one-bedroom suite. In addition to standard accommodations, many hotels offer luxury rooms and special suites that are not rated in this guide. Star ratings for rooms are assigned without regard to whether a property has a restaurant, recreational facilities, entertainment, or other extras.

In addition to stars (which delineate broad categories), we also employ a numerical rating system. Our rating scale is 0–100, with 100 as the best possible rating. Numerical ratings are presented to show the difference we perceive between one property and another. Rooms at the Desert Palms Hotel & Suites and Howard Johnson Hotel are both rated as three and a half stars (★★★½). In the supplemental numerical ratings, the Desert Palms is rated an 82 and the Howard Johnson a 75. This means that within the three-and-a-half-star category, the Desert Palms has slightly nicer rooms than the Howard Johnson.

HOW THE HOTELS COMPARE

COST ESTIMATES ARE BASED ON THE HOTEL'S published rack rates for standard rooms. Each "$" represents $50. Thus, a cost symbol of "$$$" means a room (or suite) at that hotel will be about $150 a night (it may be less for weekdays or more on weekends).

On pages 68–71, we list a hit parade of the nicest rooms in town. We've focused strictly on room quality and have excluded any consideration of location, services, recreation, or amenities. In some instances, a one- or two-room suite can be had for the same price or less than that of a hotel room.

If you used an earlier edition of this guide, you will notice that many of the ratings and rankings have changed. In addition to the

OVERALL STAR RATINGS		
★★★★★	Superior rooms	Tasteful and luxurious by any standard
★★★★	Extremely nice rooms	What you would expect at a Hyatt Regency or Marriott
★★★	Nice rooms	Holiday Inn or comparable quality
★★	Adequate rooms	Clean, comfortable, and functional without frills—like a Motel 6
★	Budget rooms	Spartan, not aesthetically pleasing

inclusion of new properties, these changes are occasioned by such positive developments as guest-room renovation or improved maintenance and housekeeping. A failure to properly maintain guest rooms or a lapse in housekeeping standards can negatively affect the ratings.

Finally, before you begin to shop for a hotel, take a hard look at this letter we received from a couple in Hot Springs, Arkansas:

> *We canceled our room reservations to follow the advice in your book [and reserved a hotel highly ranked by the* Unofficial Guide*]. We wanted inexpensive but clean and cheerful. We got inexpensive but dirty, grim, and depressing. I really felt disappointed in your advice and the room. It was the pits. That was the one real piece of information I needed from your book! The room spoiled the holiday for me aside from our touring.*

Needless to say, this letter was as unsettling to us as the bad room was to our reader. Our integrity as travel journalists, after all, is based on the quality of the information we provide to our readers. Even with the best of intentions and the most conscientious research, however, we cannot inspect every room in every hotel. What we do, in statistical terms, is take a sample: We check out several rooms selected at random in each hotel and base our ratings and rankings on those rooms. The inspections are conducted anonymously and without the knowledge of the property's management. Although it would be unusual, it is certainly possible that the rooms we randomly inspect are not representative of the majority of rooms at a particular hotel. Another possibility is that the rooms we inspect in a given hotel are representative but that by bad luck a reader is assigned to an inferior room. When we rechecked the hotel our reader disliked so intensely, we discovered that our rating was correctly representative but that he and his wife had unfortunately been assigned to one of a small number of threadbare rooms scheduled for renovation.

The key to avoiding disappointment is to do some snooping around in advance. We recommend that you ask to get a photo of a hotel's standard guest room before you book, or at least a copy of the hotel's promotional brochure. Be forewarned, however, that some hotel chains use the same guest-room photo in their promotional literature for all hotels in the chain, and that the guest room in a specific property may not resemble the photo in the brochure. When you or your travel agent call, ask how old the property is and when the guest room you are being assigned was last renovated. If you arrive and are assigned a room inferior to that which you had been led to expect, demand to be moved to another room.

THE TOP 30 BEST DEALS

IN ADDITION TO LISTING THE BETTER ROOMS IN TOWN, we also take a look at the best combinations of quality and value in a room. The rankings are made without consideration of location or the availability of restaurants, recreational facilities, entertainment, or amenities.

The Top 30 Best Deals

RANK	HOTEL	OVERALL QUALITY RATING	ROOM QUALITY RATING	COST ($ = $50)	PHONE
1.	Ramada Limited	★★★½	75	$$–	☎ 714-999-0684
2.	Travelodge Anaheim on Disney Drive	★★★	65	$+	☎ 714-774-7600
3.	Ayres Hotel	★★★★	85	$$	☎ 714-634-2106
4.	Ramada at Anaheim Convention Center	★★★	72	$+	☎ 714-971-3553
5.	Best Western Stovall's Inn	★★★½	82	$$–	☎ 714-778-1880
6.	Extended Stay America	★★★	69	$+	☎ 714-502-9988
7.	Greenwood Suites	★★★½	82	$$	☎ 714-808-9000
8.	Homewood Suites by Hilton	★★★★	85	$$+	☎ 714-740-1800
9.	Portofino Inn & Suites	★★★½	82	$$+	☎ 714-782-7600
10.	DoubleTree Hotel Anaheim–Orange County	★★★★	84	$$$–	☎ 714-634-4500
11.	Desert Inn & Suites	★★★½	81	$$+	☎ 714-772-5050
12.	Anaheim Fairfield Inn	★★★½	75	$$+	☎ 714-772-6777
13.	Holiday Inn–Anaheim Resort	★★★½	80	$$+	☎ 714-748-7777
14.	Marriott Anaheim Suites	★★★★	83	$$$–	☎ 714-750-1000
15.	America's Best Value Astoria Inn & Suites	★★½	61	$+	☎ 714-774-3882
16.	Peacock Suites	★★★½	81	$$+	☎ 714-535-8255
17.	Anaheim Maingate Rodeway Inn	★★½	57	$+	☎ 714-533-2500
18.	Sheraton Anaheim Hotel	★★★★	87	$$$	☎ 714-778-1700
19.	DoubleTree Guest Suites	★★★★	86	$$$	☎ 714-750-3000
20.	Holiday Inn Hotel & Suites Anaheim	★★★½	82	$$+	☎ 714-535-0300
21.	Hyatt Regency Orange County	★★★★	85	$$$	☎ 714-750-1234
22.	Anaheim Plaza Hotel & Suites	★★★	65	$$–	☎ 714-772-5900
23.	Anaheim Carriage Inn	★★½	60	$+	☎ 714-740-1440
24.	Crowne Plaza Anaheim Resort	★★★★	86	$$$+	☎ 714-867-5555
25.	Motel 6 Anaheim Maingate	★★½	61	$+	☎ 714-520-9696
26.	The Anabella	★★★★	84	$$$+	☎ 714-905-1050
27.	Alpine Inn	★★½	64	$$–	☎ 714-535-2186
28.	Comfort Inn Maingate	★★½	64	$$–	☎ 714-703-1220
29.	Comfort Inn & Suites	★★★	69	$$	☎ 714-772-8713
30.	TownePlace Suites by Marriott Anaheim	★★★★	88	$$$+	☎ 714-939-9700

The Disneyland Hotel, you may notice, is not one of the best deals. This is because you can get more for your money at other properties. The Disneyland and Grand Californian hotels, however, are two of the most popular hotels in the area, and many guests are willing to pay a higher rate for their convenience, service, and amenities.

We recently had a reader complain to us that he had booked one of our top-ranked rooms for value and had been very disappointed in the room. On checking we noticed that the room the reader occupied had a quality rating of ★★½. We would remind you that the value ratings are intended to give you some sense of value received for your lodging dollar spent. A ★★½ room at $35 may have the same value rating as a ★★★★ room at $85, but that does not mean the rooms will be of comparable quality. Regardless of whether it's a good deal or not, a ★★½ room is still a ★★½ room.

Listed above are the top 30 room buys for the money, regardless of location or star classification, based on rack rates. Note that sometimes a suite can cost less than a hotel room.

MAKING *the* MOST *of* YOUR TIME

ALLOCATING TIME

THE DISNEY PEOPLE RECOMMEND SPENDING 2–4 full days at Disneyland Resort. While this may seem a little self-serving, it is not without basis. Disneyland Resort is *huge,* with something to see or do crammed into every conceivable space. In addition, there are two parks, and touring requires a lot of walking, and often a lot of waiting in line. Moving in and among large crowds all day is exhausting, and often the unrelenting Southern California sun zaps even the most hardy, making tempers short.

During our many visits to Disneyland, we observed, particularly on hot summer days, a dramatic transition from happy, enthusiastic touring on arrival to almost zombielike plodding along later in the day. Visitors who began their day enjoying the wonders of Disney imagination ultimately lapsed into an exhausted production mentality ("We have two more rides in Fantasyland; then we can go back to the hotel").

OPTIMUM TOURING SITUATION

WE DON'T BELIEVE THERE IS ONE IDEAL ITINERARY. Tastes, energy levels, and perspectives on what constitutes entertainment and relaxation vary. This understood, here are some considerations for developing your own ideal itinerary.

Optimum touring at Disneyland requires a good game plan, a minimum of 3–5 days on-site (excluding travel time), and a fair amount of money. It also requires a fairly prodigious appetite for Disney

continued on page 71

Hotel Information Chart

Alamo Inn & Suites Anaheim ★★
1140 W. Katella Ave.
Anaheim 92802
☎ 714-635-8070
thealamoinn.com

ROOM RATING	52
COST ($=$50)	$$–
POOL	•
ON-SITE DINING	–

Alpine Inn ★★½
715 W. Katella Ave.
Anaheim 92802
☎ 714-535-2186
alpineinnanaheim.com

ROOM RATING	64
COST ($=$50)	$$–
POOL	•
ON-SITE DINING	–

America's Best Inn ★★½
414 W. Ball Rd.
Anaheim 92805
☎ 714-533-2570
americasbestinnanaheim.com

ROOM RATING	58
COST ($=$50)	$$–
POOL	•
ON-SITE DINING	–

Anaheim Camelot Inn & Suites ★★★½
1520 S. Harbor Blvd.
Anaheim 92802
☎ 714-635-7275
camelotinn-anaheim.com

ROOM RATING	80
COST ($=$50)	$$$–
POOL	•
ON-SITE DINING	–

Anaheim Carriage Inn ★★½
2125 S. Harbor Blvd.
Anaheim 92802
☎ 714-740-1440
anaheimcarriageinn.com

ROOM RATING	60
COST ($=$50)	$+
POOL	•
ON-SITE DINING	–

Anaheim del Sol Inn ★★½
1604 S. Harbor Blvd.
Anaheim 92802
☎ 714-234-3411
delsolinn.com

ROOM RATING	60
COST ($=$50)	$$
POOL	•
ON-SITE DINING	•

Anaheim Maingate Rodeway Inn ★★½
1211 West Pl.
Anaheim 92802
☎ 714-533-2500
rodewayinn.com

ROOM RATING	57
COST ($=$50)	$+
POOL	–
ON-SITE DINING	–

Anaheim Plaza Hotel & Suites ★★★
1700 S. Harbor Blvd.
Anaheim 92802
☎ 714-772-5900
anaheimplazahotel.com

ROOM RATING	65
COST ($=$50)	$$–
POOL	•
ON-SITE DINING	•

Anaheim Quality Inn & Suites ★★½
1441 S. Manchester Ave.
Anaheim 92802
☎ 714-991-8100
anaheimqualityinn.com

ROOM RATING	57
COST ($=$50)	$$–
POOL	•
ON-SITE DINING	–

Best Western Courtesy Inn ★★½
1070 W. Ball Rd.
Anaheim 92802
☎ 714-772-2470
bestwestern.com

ROOM RATING	60
COST ($=$50)	$$$–
POOL	•
ON-SITE DINING	–

Best Western Hollywood Plaza Inn ★★½
2011 N. Highland Ave.
Hollywood 90068
☎ 323-851-1800
bestwestern.com

ROOM RATING	62
COST ($=$50)	$$$$+
POOL	•
ON-SITE DINING	–

Best Western Park Place Inn & Mini Suites ★★★
1544 S. Harbor Blvd.
Anaheim 92802
☎ 714-776-4800
bestwestern.com

ROOM RATING	65
COST ($=$50)	$$$–
POOL	•
ON-SITE DINING	–

Budget Inn ★★
1042 W. Ball Rd.
Anaheim 92802
☎ 714-535-5524
anaheim-budgetinn.com

ROOM RATING	50
COST ($=$50)	$$–
POOL	•
ON-SITE DINING	–

Candy Cane Inn ★★★½
1747 S. Harbor Blvd.
Anaheim 92802
☎ 714-774-5284
candycaneinn.net

ROOM RATING	78
COST ($=$50)	$$$–
POOL	•
ON-SITE DINING	–

Carousel Inn & Suites ★★★
1530 S. Harbor Blvd.
Anaheim 92802
☎ 714-758-0444
carouselinnandsuites.com

ROOM RATING	72
COST ($=$50)	$$$–
POOL	•
ON-SITE DINING	–

America's Best Value Astoria Inn & Suites ★★½
426 W. Ball Rd.
Anaheim 92805
☎ 714-774-3882
anaheimastoriainn.com

ROOM RATING	61
COST ($=$50)	$+
POOL	•
ON-SITE DINING	—

America's Best Value Fantasy Inn & Suites ★½
425 W. Katella Ave.
Anaheim 92802
☎ 714-776-2815
valueinnanaheim.com

ROOM RATING	38
COST ($=$50)	$$−
POOL	•
ON-SITE DINING	—

The Anabella ★★★★
1030 W. Katella Ave.
Anaheim 92802
☎ 714-905-1050
anabellahotel.com

ROOM RATING	84
COST ($=$50)	$$$+
POOL	•
ON-SITE DINING	•

Anaheim Fairfield Inn ★★★½
1460 S. Harbor Blvd.
Anaheim 92802
☎ 714-772-6777
marriott.com

ROOM RATING	75
COST ($=$50)	$$+
POOL	•
ON-SITE DINING	•

Anaheim La Quinta Inn & Suites ★★★½
1752 S. Clementine St.
Anaheim 92802
☎ 714-635-5000
laquinta.com

ROOM RATING	76
COST ($=$50)	$$$−
POOL	—
ON-SITE DINING	—

Anaheim Luxury Suites ★★½
620 W. Orangewood Ave.
Anaheim 92802
☎ 714-971-9000
anaheimluxurysuites.com

ROOM RATING	60
COST ($=$50)	$$−
POOL	•
ON-SITE DINING	—

Ayres Hotel ★★★★
2550 E. Katella Ave.
Anaheim 92806
☎ 714-634-2106
ayresanaheim.com

ROOM RATING	85
COST ($=$50)	$$
POOL	•
ON-SITE DINING	—

Ayres Inn Orange ★★★
3737 W. Chapman Ave.
Orange 92868
☎ 714-978-9168
ayresorange.com

ROOM RATING	66
COST ($=$50)	$$
POOL	•
ON-SITE DINING	—

Best Western Anaheim Inn ★★½
1630 S. Harbor Blvd.
Anaheim 92802
☎ 714-774-1050
anaheiminn.com

ROOM RATING	61
COST ($=$50)	$$+
POOL	•
ON-SITE DINING	—

Best Western Pavilions ★★½
1176 W. Katella Ave.
Anaheim 92802
☎ 714-776-0140
pavilionshotel.com

ROOM RATING	63
COST ($=$50)	$$−
POOL	•
ON-SITE DINING	—

Best Western Raffles Inn ★★★
2040 S. Harbor Blvd.
Anaheim 92802
☎ 714-750-6100
bestwestern.com

ROOM RATING	67
COST ($=$50)	$$+
POOL	•
ON-SITE DINING	—

Best Western Stovall's Inn ★★★½
1110 W. Katella Ave.
Anaheim 92802
☎ 714-778-1880
stovallsinn.com

ROOM RATING	82
COST ($=$50)	$$−
POOL	•
ON-SITE DINING	•

Castle Inn & Suites ★★½
1734 S. Harbor Blvd.
Anaheim 92802
☎ 714-774-8111
castleinn.com

ROOM RATING	62
COST ($=$50)	$$+
POOL	•
ON-SITE DINING	—

Chamberlain West Hollywood ★★★½
1000 Westmount Dr.
West Hollywood 90069
☎ 310-657-7400
chamberlainwesthollywood.com

ROOM RATING	81
COST ($=$50)	$$$$$
POOL	•
ON-SITE DINING	•

Clarion Anaheim Hotel Resort ★★★
616 Convention Way
Anaheim 92802
☎ 714-750-3131
clarionanaheim.com

ROOM RATING	70
COST ($=$50)	$$+
POOL	•
ON-SITE DINING	•

Hotel Information Chart (continued)

Colony Inn ★★½
4917 Vineland Ave.
North Hollywood 91601
☎ 818-763-2787
colonyinn.com

ROOM RATING	60
COST ($=$50)	$$−
POOL	−
ON-SITE DINING	−

Comfort Inn & Suites ★★★
300 E. Katella Way
Anaheim 92802
☎ 714-772-8713
comfortinnsuitesanaheim.com

ROOM RATING	69
COST ($=$50)	$$
POOL	•
ON-SITE DINING	−

Comfort Inn Maingate ★★½
2171 S. Harbor Blvd.
Anaheim 92802
☎ 714-703-1220
choicehotels.com

ROOM RATING	64
COST ($=$50)	$$−
POOL	•
ON-SITE DINING	−

Days Inn & Suites ★★½
1111 S. Harbor Blvd.
Anaheim 92805
☎ 714-533-8830
daysinn.com

ROOM RATING	56
COST ($=$50)	$$−
POOL	•
ON-SITE DINING	−

Desert Inn & Suites ★★★½
1600 S. Harbor Blvd.
Anaheim 92802
☎ 714-772-5050
anaheimdesertinn.com

ROOM RATING	81
COST ($=$50)	$$+
POOL	•
ON-SITE DINING	−

**Desert Palms Hotel
& Suites** ★★★½
631 W. Katella Ave.
Anaheim 92802
☎ 714-535-1133
desertpalmshotel.com

ROOM RATING	82
COST ($=$50)	$$$
POOL	•
ON-SITE DINING	•

DoubleTree Guest Suites
★★★★
2985 S. Harbor Blvd.
Anaheim 92802
☎ 714-750-3000
anaheimconvention
centersuites.doubletree.com

ROOM RATING	86
COST ($=$50)	$$$
POOL	•
ON-SITE DINING	•

**DoubleTree Hotel Anaheim–
Orange County** ★★★★
100 The City Dr.
Orange 92868
☎ 714-634-4500
doubletree.com

ROOM RATING	84
COST ($=$50)	$$$−
POOL	•
ON-SITE DINING	•

Econo Lodge ★
1126 W. Katella Ave.
Anaheim 92802
☎ 714-533-4505
choicehotels.com

ROOM RATING	34
COST ($=$50)	$$−
POOL	•
ON-SITE DINING	−

Greenwood Suites ★★★½
1733 S. Anaheim Blvd.
Anaheim 92805
☎ 714-808-9000
greenwoodsuites
anaheimresort.com

ROOM RATING	82
COST ($=$50)	$$
POOL	−
ON-SITE DINING	−

Hacienda Inn & Suites ★½
2176 S. Harbor Blvd.
Anaheim 92802
☎ 714-750-2101
hacienda-inn-anaheim.h-rez.com

ROOM RATING	46
COST ($=$50)	$+
POOL	−
ON-SITE DINING	−

Hilton Anaheim ★★★½
777 Convention Way
Anaheim 92802
☎ 714-750-4321
hilton.com

ROOM RATING	81
COST ($=$50)	$$$+
POOL	•
ON-SITE DINING	•

Holiday Inn–Anaheim Resort
★★★½
1915 S. Manchester Ave.
Anaheim 92802
☎ 714-748-7777
holiday-inn.com

ROOM RATING	80
COST ($=$50)	$$+
POOL	•
ON-SITE DINING	•

Holiday Inn Burbank Airport
★★★
150 E. Angeleno
Burbank 91502
☎ 818-841-4770
ichotelsgroup.com

ROOM RATING	68
COST ($=$50)	$$$+
POOL	•
ON-SITE DINING	•

**Holiday Inn Express–Anaheim
Maingate Hotel** ★★★
435 W. Katella Ave.
Anaheim 92802
☎ 714-772-7755
holiday-anaheim.com

ROOM RATING	72
COST ($=$50)	$$$
POOL	•
ON-SITE DINING	−

Cortona Inn & Suites ★★★
2029 S. Harbor Blvd.
Anaheim 92802
☎ 714-971-5000
cortonainn.com

ROOM RATING	72
COST ($=$50)	$$
POOL	•
ON-SITE DINING	—

Crowne Plaza Anaheim Resort
★★★★
12021 Harbor Blvd.
Garden Grove 92840
☎ 714-867-5555
anaheim.crowneplaza.com

ROOM RATING	86
COST ($=$50)	$$$+
POOL	•
ON-SITE DINING	•

Days Inn Anaheim West ★★½
1030 W. Ball Rd.
Anaheim 92802
☎ 714-520-0101
daysinn.com

ROOM RATING	64
COST ($=$50)	$$−
POOL	•
ON-SITE DINING	—

Disneyland Hotel ★★★★
1150 W. Magic Way
Anaheim 92802
☎ 714-778-6600
disneyland.com

ROOM RATING	89
COST ($=$50)	$$$$$+
POOL	•
ON-SITE DINING	•

Disney Paradise Pier Hotel
★★★★
1717 S. Disneyland Dr.
Anaheim 92802
☎ 714-999-0990
disneyland.com

ROOM RATING	86
COST ($=$50)	$$$$$+
POOL	•
ON-SITE DINING	•

**Disney's Grand Californian Hotel
& Spa** ★★★★½
1600 S. Disneyland Dr.
Anaheim 92802
☎ 714-635-2300
disneyland.com

ROOM RATING	90
COST ($=$50)	$$$$$$$$+
POOL	•
ON-SITE DINING	•

Econo Lodge Maingate ★★½
871 S. Harbor Blvd.
Anaheim 92805
☎ 714-535-7878
choicehotels.com

ROOM RATING	57
COST ($=$50)	$$−
POOL	•
ON-SITE DINING	—

**Embassy Suites Anaheim–
South** ★★★½
11767 Harbor Blvd.
Garden Grove 92840
☎ 714-539-3300
anaheimsouth.
  embassysuites.com

ROOM RATING	81
COST ($=$50)	$$$$−
POOL	•
ON-SITE DINING	•

Extended Stay America ★★★
1742 S. Clementine St.
Anaheim 92802
☎ 714-502-9988
extendedstayamerica.com

ROOM RATING	69
COST ($=$50)	$+
POOL	•
ON-SITE DINING	—

Hilton Garden Inn ★★★½
11777 Harbor Blvd.
Garden Grove 92840
☎ 714-703-9100
hilton.com

ROOM RATING	79
COST ($=$50)	$$+
POOL	•
ON-SITE DINING	—

**Hilton Los Angeles at
Universal City** ★★★★
555 Universal Hollywood Dr.
Universal City 91608
☎ 818-506-2500
hilton.com

ROOM RATING	87
COST ($=$50)	$$$$−
POOL	•
ON-SITE DINING	•

**Hilton Suites
Anaheim–Orange** ★★★★
400 N. State College Blvd.
Orange 92868
☎ 714-938-1111
hilton.com

ROOM RATING	86
COST ($=$50)	$$$−
POOL	•
ON-SITE DINING	•

**Holiday Inn Hotel & Suites
Anaheim** ★★★½
1240 S. Walnut Ave.
Anaheim 92802
☎ 714-535-0300
holiday-inn.com

ROOM RATING	82
COST ($=$50)	$$+
POOL	•
ON-SITE DINING	•

Homewood Suites by Hilton
★★★★
12005 Harbor Blvd.
Garden Grove 92840
☎ 714-740-1800
homewoodsuites1.hilton.com

ROOM RATING	85
COST ($=$50)	$$+
POOL	•
ON-SITE DINING	—

Hotel Menage ★★½
1221 S. Harbor Blvd.
Anaheim 92805
☎ 714-758-0900
hotelmenage.com

ROOM RATING	63
COST ($=$50)	$$+
POOL	•
ON-SITE DINING	•

Hotel Information Chart (continued)

Howard Johnson Hotel ★★★½ 1380 S. Harbor Blvd. Anaheim 92802 ☎ 714-776-6120 hojoanaheim.com	**Hyatt Regency** **Orange County** ★★★★ 11999 Harbor Blvd. Garden Grove 92840 ☎ 714-750-1234 orangecounty.hyatt.com	**Jolly Roger Hotel Anaheim** ★★★ 640 W. Katella Ave. Anaheim 92802 ☎ 714-782-7500 jollyrogerhotel.com

ROOM RATING 75 · COST ($=$50) $$– · POOL • · ON-SITE DINING —

ROOM RATING 85 · COST $$+ · POOL • · ON-SITE DINING •

ROOM RATING 68 · COST $$ · POOL • · ON-SITE DINING •

Marriott Hotel Main ★★★★ 700 W. Convention Way, Anaheim 92802 ☎ 714-750-8000 marriott.com — ROOM RATING 85 · COST $$$$– · POOL • · ON-SITE DINING •

Motel 6 Anaheim Maingate ★★½ 100 W. Disney Way, Anaheim 92802 ☎ 714-520-9696 motel6-anaheim.com — ROOM RATING 61 · COST $+ · POOL • · ON-SITE DINING —

Park Vue Inn ★★½ 1570 S. Harbor Blvd., Anaheim 92802 ☎ 714-772-3691 parkvueinn.com — ROOM RATING 59 · COST $$+ · POOL • · ON-SITE DINING —

Quality Inn Maingate ★★½ 2200 S. Harbor Blvd., Anaheim 92802 ☎ 714-750-5211 qualityinnmaingateanaheim.com — ROOM RATING 58 · COST $+ · POOL • · ON-SITE DINING —

Ramada at Anaheim Convention Center ★★★ 2141 S. Harbor Blvd., Anaheim 92802 ☎ 714-971-3553 ramada.com — ROOM RATING 72 · COST $+ · POOL • · ON-SITE DINING —

Ramada Limited ★★★½ 921 S. Harbor Blvd., Anaheim 92802 ☎ 714-999-0684 ramada.com — ROOM RATING 75 · COST $$– · POOL • · ON-SITE DINING •

Residence Inn Anaheim–Maingate ★★★½ 1700 S. Clementine St., Anaheim 92802 ☎ 714-533-3555 marriott.com — ROOM RATING 81 · COST $$$– · POOL • · ON-SITE DINING •

Sheraton Anaheim Hotel ★★★★ 900 S. Disneyland Dr., Anaheim 92802 ☎ 714-778-1700 starwoodhotels.com — ROOM RATING 87 · COST $$$ · POOL • · ON-SITE DINING •

Sheraton Park Hotel ★★★★ 1855 S. Harbor Blvd., Anaheim 92802 ☎ 714-750-1811 starwoodhotels.com — ROOM RATING 85 · COST $$$+ · POOL • · ON-SITE DINING •

Super 8 Motel Near Disneyland ★★ 415 W. Katella Ave., Anaheim 92802 ☎ 714-778-6900 super8.com — ROOM RATING 55 · COST $+ · POOL • · ON-SITE DINING —

TownePlace Suites by Marriott Anaheim ★★★★ 1730 S. State College Blvd., Anaheim 92806 ☎ 714-939-9700 tpsanaheimhotel.com — ROOM RATING 88 · COST $+ · POOL • · ON-SITE DINING —

Travelodge Anaheim on Disney Drive ★★★ 1057 W. Ball Rd., Anaheim 92802 ☎ 714-774-7600 travelodge.com — ROOM RATING 65 · COST $+ · POOL • · ON-SITE DINING —

Marriott Anaheim Suites
★★★★
12015 Harbor Blvd.
Anaheim 92802
☎ 714-750-1000
marriott.com

ROOM RATING	83
COST ($=$50)	$$$–
POOL	•
ON-SITE DINING	•

Marriott Burbank Airport
★★★½
2500 Hollywood Way
Burbank 91505
☎ 818-843-6000
marriottburbankairport.com

ROOM RATING	80
COST ($=$50)	$$$+
POOL	•
ON-SITE DINING	•

Marriott Hotel Anaheim
★★★½
700 W. Convention Way
Anaheim 92802
☎ 714-750-8000
marriott.com

ROOM RATING	82
COST ($=$50)	$$$$–
POOL	•
ON-SITE DINING	•

Peacock Suites ★★★½
1745 S. Anaheim Blvd.
Anaheim 92805
☎ 714-535-8255
shellhospitality.com

ROOM RATING	81
COST ($=$50)	$$+
POOL	•
ON-SITE DINING	–

Portofino Inn & Suites ★★★½
1831 S. Harbor Blvd.
Anaheim 92802
☎ 714-782-7600
portofinoinnanaheim.com

ROOM RATING	82
COST ($=$50)	$$+
POOL	•
ON-SITE DINING	–

**Quality Inn & Suites
at the Park** ★★½
1166 W. Katella Ave.
Anaheim 92802
☎ 714-774-7817
qualityinn.com

ROOM RATING	56
COST ($=$50)	$$–
POOL	•
ON-SITE DINING	–

Ramada Maingate ★★★
1650 S. Harbor Blvd.
Anaheim 92802
☎ 714-772-0440
ramadamaingate.com

ROOM RATING	67
COST ($=$50)	$$
POOL	•
ON-SITE DINING	–

**Ramada Plaza Hotel–
Anaheim Resort** ★★★½
515 W. Katella Ave.
Anaheim 92802
☎ 714-991-6868
ramada.com

ROOM RATING	81
COST ($=$50)	$$$–
POOL	•
ON-SITE DINING	•

Red Lion ★★★★
1850 S. Harbor Blvd.
Anaheim 92802
☎ 714-750-2801
redlion.com

ROOM RATING	85
COST ($=$50)	$$$+
POOL	•
ON-SITE DINING	•

Sheraton Universal ★★★★
333 Universal Hollywood Dr.
Universal City 91608
☎ 818-980-1212
starwoodhotels.com

ROOM RATING	85
COST ($=$50)	$$$$+
POOL	•
ON-SITE DINING	•

**Staybridge Suites Anaheim
Resort Area** ★★★½
1855 S. Manchester Ave.
Anaheim 92802
☎ 714-748-7700
staybridge.com

ROOM RATING	82
COST ($=$50)	$$$+
POOL	•
ON-SITE DINING	–

**Super 8 Motel
Disneyland Drive** ★★
915 S. Disneyland Dr.
Anaheim 92802
☎ 714-778-0350
super8.com

ROOM RATING	55
COST ($=$50)	$+
POOL	•
ON-SITE DINING	–

**Travelodge International
Inn & Suites** ★★
2060 S. Harbor Blvd.
Anaheim 92802
☎ 714-971-9393
travelodge.com

ROOM RATING	50
COST ($=$50)	$$–
POOL	•
ON-SITE DINING	–

Tropicana Inn & Suites ★★★
1540 S. Harbor Blvd.
Anaheim 92802
☎ 714-635-4082
tropicanainn-anaheim.com

ROOM RATING	65
COST ($=$50)	$$$+
POOL	•
ON-SITE DINING	–

How the Hotels Compare

HOTEL	OVERALL QUALITY RATING	ROOM QUALITY RATING	COST ($ = $50)	PHONE
DISNEYLAND AREA				
Disney's Grand Californian Hotel & Spa	★★★★½	90	$ x 8+	☎ 714-635-2300
Disneyland Hotel	★★★★	89	$ x 6+	☎ 714-778-6600
TownePlace Suites by Marriott Anaheim	★★★★	88	$$$+	☎ 714-939-9700
Sheraton Anaheim Hotel	★★★★	87	$$$	☎ 714-778-1700
Hilton Suites Anaheim–Orange	★★★★	86	$$$–	☎ 714-938-1111
DoubleTree Guest Suites	★★★★	86	$$$	☎ 714-750-3000
Crowne Plaza Anaheim Resort	★★★★	86	$$$+	☎ 714-867-5555
Disney Paradise Pier Hotel	★★★★	86	$$$$$+	☎ 714-999-0990
Ayres Hotel	★★★★	85	$$	☎ 714-634-2106
Homewood Suites by Hilton	★★★★	85	$$+	☎ 714-740-1800
Hyatt Regency Orange County	★★★★	85	$$+	☎ 714-750-1234
Red Lion	★★★★	85	$$$+	☎ 714-750-2801
Sheraton Park Hotel	★★★★	85	$$$+	☎ 714-750-1811
Marriott Hotel Main	★★★★	85	$$$$–	☎ 714-750-8000
DoubleTree Hotel Anaheim–Orange County	★★★★	84	$$$–	☎ 714-634-4500
The Anabella	★★★★	84	$$$+	☎ 714-905-1050
Marriott Anaheim Suites	★★★★	83	$$$–	☎ 714-750-1000
Best Western Stovall's Inn	★★★½	82	$$–	☎ 714-778-1880
Greenwood Suites	★★★½	82	$$	☎ 714-808-9000
Holiday Inn Hotel & Suites Anaheim	★★★½	82	$$+	☎ 714-535-0300
Portofino Inn & Suites	★★★½	82	$$+	☎ 714-782-7600
Desert Palms Hotel & Suites	★★★½	82	$$$	☎ 714-535-1133
Staybridge Suites Anaheim Resort Area	★★★½	82	$$$+	☎ 714-748-7700
Marriott Hotel Anaheim	★★★½	82	$$$$–	☎ 714-750-8000
Desert Inn & Suites	★★★½	81	$$+	☎ 714-772-5050
Peacock Suites	★★★½	81	$$+	☎ 714-535-8255
Ramada Plaza Hotel–Anaheim Resort	★★★½	81	$$$–	☎ 714-991-6868
Residence Inn Anaheim–Maingate	★★★½	81	$$$–	☎ 714-533-3555

HOTEL	OVERALL QUALITY RATING	ROOM QUALITY RATING	COST ($ = $50)	PHONE
Hilton Anaheim	★★★½	81	$$$+	☎ 714-750-4321
Embassy Suites Anaheim– South	★★★½	81	$$$$–	☎ 714-539-3300
Holiday Inn–Anaheim Resort	★★★½	80	$$+	☎ 714-748-7777
Anaheim Camelot Inn & Suites	★★★½	80	$$$–	☎ 714-635-7275
Hilton Garden Inn	★★★½	79	$$+	☎ 714-703-9100
Candy Cane Inn	★★★½	78	$$$–	☎ 714-774-5284
Anaheim La Quinta Inn & Suites	★★★½	76	$$$–	☎ 714-635-5000
Ramada Limited	★★★½	75	$$–	☎ 714-999-0684
Anaheim Fairfield Inn	★★★½	75	$$+	☎ 714-772-6777
Howard Johnson Hotel	★★★½	75	$$$–	☎ 714-776-6120
Ramada at Anaheim Convention Center	★★★	72	$+	☎ 714-971-3553
Cortona Inn & Suites	★★★	72	$$	☎ 714-971-5000
Carousel Inn & Suites	★★★	72	$$$–	☎ 714-758-0444
Holiday Inn Express–Anaheim Maingate Hotel	★★★	72	$$$–	☎ 714-772-7755
Clarion Anaheim Hotel Resort	★★★	70	$$+	☎ 714-750-3131
Extended Stay America	★★★	69	$+	☎ 714-502-9988
Comfort Inn & Suites	★★★	69	$$	☎ 714-772-8713
Jolly Roger Hotel Anaheim	★★★	68	$$	☎ 714-782-7500
Ramada Maingate	★★★	67	$$	☎ 714-772-0440
Best Western Raffles Inn	★★★	67	$$+	☎ 714-750-6100
Ayres Inn Orange	★★★	66	$$	☎ 714-978-9168
Travelodge Anaheim on Disney Drive	★★★	65	$+	☎ 714-774-7600
Anaheim Plaza Hotel & Suites	★★★	65	$$–	☎ 714-772-5900
Best Western Park Place Inn & Mini Suites	★★★	65	$$$–	☎ 714-776-4800
Tropicana Inn & Suites	★★★	65	$$$+	☎ 714-635-4082
Alpine Inn	★★½	64	$$–	☎ 714-535-2186
Comfort Inn Maingate	★★½	64	$$–	☎ 714-703-1220
Days Inn Anaheim West	★★½	64	$$–	☎ 714-520-0101
Best Western Pavilions	★★½	63	$$–	☎ 714-776-0140

How the Hotels Compare (continued)

HOTEL	OVERALL QUALITY RATING	ROOM QUALITY RATING	COST ($ = $50)	PHONE
Hotel Menage	★★½	63	$$+	☎ 714-758-0900
Castle Inn & Suites	★★½	62	$$+	☎ 714-774-8111
America's Best Value Astoria Inn & Suites	★★½	61	$+	☎ 714-774-3882
Motel 6 Anaheim Maingate	★★½	61	$+	☎ 714-520-9696
Best Western Anaheim Inn	★★½	61	$$+	☎ 714-774-1050
Anaheim Carriage Inn	★★½	60	$+	☎ 714-740-1440
Anaheim Luxury Suites	★★½	60	$$−	☎ 714-971-9000
Anaheim del Sol Inn	★★½	60	$$	☎ 714-234-3411
Best Western Courtesy Inn	★★½	60	$$$−	☎ 714-772-2470
Park Vue Inn	★★½	59	$$+	☎ 714-772-3691
Quality Inn Maingate	★★½	58	$+	☎ 714-750-5211
America's Best Inn	★★½	58	$$−	☎ 714-533-2570
Anaheim Maingate Rodeway Inn	★★½	57	$+	☎ 714-533-2500
Anaheim Quality Inn & Suites	★★½	57	$$−	☎ 714-991-8100
Econo Lodge Maingate	★★½	57	$$−	☎ 714-535-7878
Days Inn & Suites	★★½	56	$$−	☎ 714-533-8830
Quality Inn & Suites at the Park	★★½	56	$$−	☎ 714-774-7817
Super 8 Motel Disneyland Drive	★★	55	$+	☎ 714-778-0350
Super 8 Motel Near Disneyland	★★	55	$+	☎ 714-778-6900
Alamo Inn & Suites Anaheim	★★	52	$$−	☎ 714-635-8070
Budget Inn	★★	50	$$−	☎ 714-535-5524
Travelodge International Inn & Suites	★★	50	$$−	☎ 714-971-9393
Hacienda Inn & Suites	★½	46	$+	☎ 714-750-2101
America's Best Value Fantasy Inn & Suites	★½	38	$$−	☎ 714-776-2815
Econo Lodge	★	34	$$−	☎ 714-533-4505

HOTEL	OVERALL QUALITY RATING	ROOM QUALITY RATING	COST ($ = $50)	PHONE
UNIVERSAL AREA				
Hilton Los Angeles at Universal City	★★★★	87	$$$$–	☎ 818-506-2500
Sheraton Universal	★★★★	85	$$$$+	☎ 818-980-1212
Chamberlain West Hollywood	★★★½	81	$$$$$	☎ 310-657-7400
Marriott Burbank Airport	★★★½	80	$$$+	☎ 818-843-6000
Holiday Inn Burbank Airport	★★★	68	$$$+	☎ 818-841-4770
Best Western Hollywood Plaza Inn	★★½	62	$$$$+	☎ 323-851-1800
Colony Inn	★★½	60	$$–	☎ 818-763-2787

continued from page 61

entertainment. The essence of optimum touring is to see the attractions in a series of shorter, less-exhausting visits during the cooler, less-crowded times of day, with plenty of rest and relaxation between excursions.

Because optimum touring calls for leaving and returning to the theme parks, it makes sense to stay in one of the Disney hotels or in one of the non-Disney hotels within walking distance. If you visit Disneyland during busy times, you need to get up early to beat the crowds. Short lines and stress-free touring are incompatible with sleeping in. If you want to sleep in *and* enjoy your touring, visit Disneyland when attendance is lighter.

THE CARDINAL RULES FOR SUCCESSFUL TOURING

MANY VISITORS DON'T HAVE 3 DAYS to devote to Disneyland Resort. For these visitors, efficient touring is a must. Even the most time-effective plan, however, won't allow you to cover both Disney theme parks in 1 day. Plan to allocate at least an entire day to each park. If your schedule permits only 1 day of touring, concentrate on one theme park and save the other for another visit.

1-day Touring

A comprehensive 1-day tour of Disneyland Park or Disney California Adventure is possible, but it requires knowledge of the park, good planning, and plenty of energy and endurance. One-day touring doesn't leave much time for full-service meals, prolonged shopping, or lengthy breaks. One-day touring can be fun and rewarding, but allocating 2 days per park, especially for Disneyland Park, is always preferable.

Successful touring of Disneyland Park or Disney California Adventure hinges on three rules:

I. DETERMINE IN ADVANCE WHAT YOU REALLY WANT TO SEE What rides and attractions most appeal to you? Which additional rides and attractions would you like to experience if you have any time left? What are you willing to forgo?

To help you establish your touring priorities, we have described every attraction in detail. In each description, we include the author's critical evaluation of the attraction as well as the opinions of Disneyland Resort guests expressed as star ratings. Five stars is the highest (best) rating possible.

Finally, because Disneyland Resort attractions range in scope from midway-type rides and horse-drawn trolleys to colossal, high-tech extravaganzas spanning the equivalent of whole city blocks, we have developed a hierarchy of categories for attractions to give you some sense of their order of magnitude:

SUPER-HEADLINERS The best attractions that the theme park has to offer. They are mind-boggling in size, scope, and imagination and represent the cutting edge of modern attraction technology and design.

HEADLINERS Full-blown, multimillion-dollar, full-scale, themed adventure experiences and theater presentations. They are modern in their technology and design and employ a full range of special effects.

MAJOR ATTRACTIONS Themed adventure experiences on a more modest scale but incorporating state-of-the-art technologies, or larger-scale attractions of older design.

MINOR ATTRACTIONS Midway-type rides, small-scale "dark rides" (spook-house-type rides), minor theater presentations, transportation rides, and elaborate walk-through attractions.

DIVERSIONS Exhibits, both passive and interactive. Also includes playgrounds, video arcades, and street theater.

Though not every attraction fits neatly into the above categories, the categories provide a relative comparison of attraction size and scope. Remember, however, that bigger and more elaborate does not always mean better. Peter Pan's Flight, a minor attraction, continues to be one of the park's most beloved rides. Likewise, for many small children, there is no attraction, regardless of size, that can surpass Dumbo.

2. ARRIVE EARLY! ARRIVE EARLY! ARRIVE EARLY! This is the single most important key to touring efficiently and avoiding long lines. With your admission pass in hand, be at the gate ready to go at least 30 minutes before the theme park's stated opening time. There are no lines and relatively few people first thing in the morning. The same four rides you can experience in 1 hour in the early morning will take more than 3 hours to see after 11 a.m. Have breakfast before you arrive, so you will not have to waste prime touring time sitting in a restaurant.

From a Cincinnati, Ohio, mom:

Arriving early made a tremendous difference. But I'll admit that at 6:15 in the morning when I was dragging our children out of bed, I thought we'd lost our minds. But we had so much fun that morning riding rides with no waiting in line. It was worth the early arrival.

A couple from Austin, Texas, waxed enthusiastically:

I am telling everyone about your book. It saved my girlfriend and me hours and hours of waiting in line (during spring break no less!). We were first in line for the parks every morning, and boy was it worth it.

Be aware that all park guests must pass through security, set up in open tents in the Esplanade between the two parks. If you arrive before security screening begins and go straight to the turnstiles to await admittance, you will ultimately be directed to abandon your position to go through security. If this occurs, you'll find yourself behind people who arrived 20–30 minutes after you. Therefore, if you arrive before security is set up, wait in one of the open tents for the security folks to arrive.

3. AVOID BOTTLENECKS Helping you avoid bottlenecks is what this guide is all about. Bottlenecks occur as a result of crowd concentrations and/or less-than-optimal traffic engineering. Concentrations of hungry people create bottlenecks at restaurants during the lunch and dinner hours; concentrations of people moving toward the exit near closing time create bottlenecks in the gift shops en route to the gate; concentrations of visitors at new and unusually popular rides create bottlenecks and long waiting lines; rides slow to load and unload passengers create bottlenecks and long waiting lines. Avoiding bottlenecks involves being able to predict where, when, and why they occur. To this end, we provide field-tested touring plans to keep you ahead of the crowd or out of its way (see discussion following). In addition, we provide critical data on all rides and shows that helps you estimate how long you may have to wait in line, compares rides in terms of their capacity to accommodate large crowds, and rates the rides according to our opinions and the opinions of other Disneyland visitors.

TOURING PLANS

OF UTMOST IMPORTANCE: READ THIS!

IN ANALYZING READER SURVEYS we were astonished by the percentage of readers who do not use our touring plans. Scientifically tested and proven, these plans can save you 4 entire hours or more of waiting in line. Four hours! Four fewer hours of standing, 4 hours freed up to do something fun. Our groundbreaking research that created the touring plans has been the subject of front-page articles in the *Dallas Morning News* and *The New York Times* and has been cited in numerous scholarly journals. So the question is, why would you not use them?

We get a ton of mail from both our Disneyland and Walt Disney World readers—98% of it positive—commenting on our touring plans. First, from a family of four from West Chester, Pennsylvania:

unofficial **TIP**
By using our touring plans, you can save as much as 4 hours in line per day.

This book and your touring plans, without a doubt, made the trip. We followed the adult 1-day plans almost to the letter. Probably the longest line we stood in was maybe 30 minutes max during one of the [busiest] times of the year. The key was getting to the parks 30 minutes or so before opening. The plans also saved arguing over what to do next. We simply followed the guide. We are believers!

A family from Stockton, California, descended on Disneyland Park over the Easter holiday:

We're not much for plans and regimentation, so we winged it the first day. It was so awful that the next day we gave one of your itineraries a shot as sort of a last-ditch alternative. It worked so well that I was telling strangers about it that night like [I was] some kind of Bible thumper.

A mom from Aurora, Colorado, offered this:

We went to WDW in 2007, and I didn't use the touring plans provided because, with my kids, I didn't think the extra walking would be worth it. I decided to try out the plans in Disneyland when it was just my mom and me without the kids. It was great. I was amazed that when I got to the point where it said, "Now might be a good time to grab lunch," it was 11:15 a.m. We are going to WDW in November with the kids, and I have already put together all our touring plans from your book!

From a Chicago mom:

I was caught off guard while flipping through the book at how many people were complaining about the rigidity of the daily touring plans. I feel strongly that you have to go into a Disney trip with a firm plan or else all you will remember of your vacation will be the squabbles and the long lines! The daily touring plans not only allowed me to see everything that I wanted but even allowed me time to revisit my favorite attractions multiple times! Those who complain that the touring plans are too rigid need a serious reality check. Yes they are structured but they save you mountains of time! RELAX and use the touring plans if you are going during a busy part of the year. Not only will it save you the time you are spending complaining about the plans in the first place, but it will also save you the complaining you will be doing when you are in line for Space Mountain for 90 minutes!

A family of six from Sacramento, California:

The Unofficial Guide *was a godsend! I was not so sure how the touring plans would work, but they went over and beyond my expectations. We went to Disneyland during spring break, a very busy time, very crowded, and we hardly spent any time at all in lines for rides (as long as we stuck to the touring plans)! At one point we would get off a ride and get right on another. We did six rides within a half hour. This trip was the first time EVER that my family and I got to do everything we wanted at Disneyland! (By the way our three daughters were ages 3, 9, and 15 and our son was 7 at the time, so these plans can work for anyone!)*

WHAT'S A QUEUE?

ALTHOUGH IT'S NOT COMMONLY used in the United States, *queue* (pronounced "cue") is the universal English word for a line, such as one in which you wait to cash a check at the bank or to board a ride at a theme park. There's a mathematical area of specialization within the field of operations research called queuing theory, which studies and models how lines work. Because the *Unofficial Guide* draws heavily on this discipline, we use some of its terminology. In addition to the noun, the verb *to queue* means to get in line, and a *queuing area* is a waiting area that accommodates a line. When guests decline to join a queue because they perceive the wait to be too long, they are said to *balk*.

TOURING PLANS:
WHAT THEY ARE AND HOW THEY WORK

We followed your plans to the letter—which at times was troublesome to the dad in our party . . . somewhat akin to testing the strength of your marriage by wallpapering together!
—Unofficial Guide reader and mother of two
from Milford, Connecticut

WHEN WE INTERVIEWED DISNEYLAND VISITORS who toured the theme park(s) on slow days, they invariably waxed eloquent about the sheer delight of their experience. When we questioned visitors who toured on moderate or busy days, however, they talked at length about the jostling crowds and how much time they stood in line. What a shame, they said, that so much time and energy are spent fighting crowds in a place as special as Disneyland.

Given this complaint, our researchers descended on Disneyland to determine whether a touring plan could be devised that would liberate visitors from the traffic flow and allow them to see any theme park in 1 day with minimal waiting in line. On some of the busiest days of the year, our team monitored traffic into and through Disneyland Park, noting how it filled and how patrons were distributed among the attractions. We also observed which rides and attractions were most popular and where bottlenecks were most likely to occur.

After many years of collecting data, we devised preliminary touring plans, which we tested during one of the busiest weeks of the year. Each day, our researchers would tour the park using one of the preliminary plans, noting how long it took to walk from place to place and how long the wait in line was for each attraction. Combining the information gained on trial runs, we devised a master plan that we retested and fine-tuned. This plan, with very little variance from day to day, allowed us to experience all major rides and attractions and most lesser ones in 1 day, with an average wait in line of less than 10 minutes at each.

From this master plan, we developed alternative plans that took into account the varying tastes and personal requirements of different Disneyland patrons. Each plan operated with the same logic as the master plan but addressed the special needs and preferences of its intended users.

Finally, after all of the plans were tested by our staff, we selected (using convenience sampling) Disneyland visitors to test the plans. The only prerequisite for being chosen to test the plans was that the guests must have been visiting a Disney park for the first time. A second group of patrons was chosen for a control group. These were first-time visitors who would tour the park according to their own plans but who would make notes about what they did and how much time they spent in lines.

When the two groups were compared, the results were amazing. On days when major theme-park attendance exceeded 42,000, visitors touring without our plans *averaged* 2.6 hours more waiting in line per day than the patrons touring with our plans, and they experienced 33% fewer attractions. In 2004 the application of a cutting-edge algorithm to our touring-plan software increased the waiting time saved to an average of 4 hours. We expect additional research to continue to improve the performance of the touring plans in future editions.

General Overview of the Touring Plans

Our touring plans are step-by-step guides for seeing as much as possible with a minimum of standing in line. They're designed to help you avoid crowds and bottlenecks on days of moderate to heavy attendance. On days of lighter attendance (see "Selecting the Time of Year for Your Visit," page 22), the plans still save time but aren't as critical to successful touring.

What You Can Realistically Expect from the Touring Plans

Though we present 1-day touring plans for both of the theme parks, you should understand that Disneyland Park has more attractions than you can see in 1 day, even if you never wait in line. If you must cram your visit to Disneyland Park into a single day, the 1-day touring plans will allow you to see as much as is humanly possible. Under certain circumstances you may not complete the plan, and you definitely won't be able to see everything. For Disneyland Park, the most comprehensive, efficient, and relaxing touring plans are the 2-day plans. Although Disney California Adventure has grown over the last few years, you should have no problem for the moment seeing everything in 1 day.

Variables That Will Affect the Success of the Touring Plans

How quickly you move from one ride to another; when and how many refreshment and restroom breaks you take; when, where, and how you eat meals; and your ability (or lack thereof) to find your way around will all have an impact on the success of the plans. Smaller groups almost always move faster than larger groups, and parties of adults generally can cover more ground than families with young children. Switching off (see page 150), among other things, prohibits families with little ones from moving expeditiously among attractions. Plus, some children simply cannot conform to the "early to rise" conditions of the touring plans.

A mom from Nutley, New Jersey, writes:

> [Although] the touring plans all advise getting to parks at opening, we just couldn't burn the candle at both ends. Our kids (10, 7, and 4) would not go to sleep early and couldn't be up at dawn and still stay relatively sane. It worked well for us to let them sleep a little later, go out and bring breakfast back to the room while they slept, and still get a relatively early start by not spending time on eating breakfast out. We managed to avoid long lines with an early morning, and hitting popular attractions during parades, mealtimes, and late evenings.

And a family from Centerville, Ohio, says:

> The toughest thing about your tour plans was getting the rest of the family to stay with them, at least to some degree. Getting them to pass by attractions in order to hit something across the park was no easy task (sometimes impossible).

A multigenerational family wonders how to know if you are on track or not, writing:

> It seems like the touring plans were very time dependent, yet there were no specific times attached to the plan outside of the early morning. On more than 1 day, I often had to guess as to whether we were "on track." Having small children and a grandparent in our group, we couldn't move at a fast pace.

There is no objective measurement for being on track. Each group's experience will differ to some degree. Regardless of whether your group is large or small, fast or slow, the sequence of attractions in the touring plans will allow you to enjoy the greatest number of attractions in the least possible time. Two quickly moving adults will probably take in more attractions in a specific time period than will a large group comprised of children, parents, and grandparents. However, given the characteristics of the respective groups, each will maximize their touring time and experience as many attractions as possible.

Finally, if you have young children in your party, be prepared for character encounters. The appearance of a Disney character is usually

sufficient to stop a touring plan dead in its tracks. What's more, while some characters continue to stroll the parks, it is becoming more the rule to assemble characters in some specific venue (such as at Mickey's Toontown), where families must queue up for photos of and autographs from Mickey. Meeting characters, posing for photos, and collecting autographs can burn hours of touring time. If your kids are into character-autograph collecting, you will need to anticipate these interruptions to the touring plan and negotiate some understanding with your children about when you will follow the plan and when you will collect autographs. Our advice is to either go with the flow or alternatively set aside a certain morning or afternoon for photos and autographs. Be aware, however, that queues for autographs, especially in Mickey's Toontown and Pixie Hollow at Disneyland Park, are every bit as long as the queues for major attractions. The only time-efficient way to collect autographs is to line up at the character-greeting areas first thing in the morning. Because this is also the best time to experience the more

popular attractions, you may have some tough decisions to make.

While we realize that following the touring plans is not always easy, we nevertheless recommend continuous, expeditious touring until around noon. After that hour, breaks and diversions won't affect the plans significantly.

Some variables that can profoundly affect the touring plans are beyond your control. Chief among these is the manner and timing of bringing a particular ride to capacity. For example, Big Thunder Mountain Railroad, a roller coaster in Disneyland Park, has five trains. On a given morning it may begin operation with two of the five, then add the other three if and when they are needed. If the waiting line builds rapidly before operators decide to go to full capacity, you could have a long wait, even in early morning.

Another variable relates to the time you arrive for a show. Usually your wait will be the length of time from your arrival to the end of the presentation in progress. Thus, if the *Enchanted Tiki Room* show is 15 minutes long and you arrive 1 minute after a show has begun, your wait for the next show will be 14 minutes. Conversely, if you arrive as the show is wrapping up, your wait will be only 1 or 2 minutes.

What to Do If You Lose the Thread

Anything from a blister to a broken attraction can throw off a touring plan. If unforeseen events interrupt a plan:

1. Skip one step on the plan for every 20 minutes' delay. If, for example, you lose your billfold and spend an hour finding it, skip three steps and pick up from there, or

2. Forget the plan and organize the remainder of your day using the recommended attraction visitation times included in each attraction profile.

Flexibility

The attractions included in the touring plans are the most popular attractions as determined by more than 10,000 reader surveys. Even so, your favorite attractions might be different. Fortunately, the touring plans are flexible. If the touring plan calls for an attraction that you don't wish to experience, simply skip it and move on to the next attraction on the plan. Additionally, you can substitute similar attractions in the same area of the park. If the plan calls for riding Dumbo, for example, and you're not interested but would enjoy the Mad Tea Party (which is not on the plan), then substitute the Mad Tea Party for Dumbo. As long as the substitution is a similar attraction (it won't work to substitute a show for a ride) and located pretty close to the attraction called for in the plan, you won't compromise the overall effectiveness of the touring plan.

A family of four from South Slocan, British Columbia, found they could easily tailor the touring plans to meet their needs:

> We amended your touring plans by taking out the attractions we didn't want to do and just doing the remainder in order. It worked great, and by arriving before the parks opened, we got to see everything we wanted, with virtually no waits! The best advice by far was "get there early!"

Clip-out Pocket Outlines of Touring Plans

Select the plan appropriate for your party, and then clip the pocket version from the back of this guide and carry it with you as a quick reference at the theme park.

Will the Plans Continue to Work Once the Secret Is Out?

Yes! First, all of the plans require that a patron be there when the theme parks open. Many Disneyland patrons simply refuse to get up early while on vacation. Second, less than 1% of any day's attendance has been exposed to the plans, too little to affect results. Last, most groups tailor the plans, skipping rides or shows according to personal taste.

How Frequently Are the Touring Plans Revised?

Because Disney is always adding new attractions and changing operations, we revise the touring plans every year. Most complaints we receive about them come from readers who are using out-of-date editions of the *Unofficial Guide*. Be prepared, however, for surprises. Opening procedures and showtimes, for example, may change, and you never know when an attraction might break down.

Tour Groups from Hell

We have discovered that tour groups of up to 200 people sometimes use our plans. Unless your party is as large as that tour group, this development shouldn't alarm you. Because tour groups are big, they move slowly and have to stop periodically to collect stragglers. The tour guide also has to accommodate the unpredictability of five dozen or so bladders. In short, you should have no problem passing a group after the initial encounter.

Bouncing Around

Many readers object to crisscrossing a theme park, as our touring plans sometimes require. A woman from Decatur, Georgia, said she "got dizzy from all the bouncing around" and that the "running back and forth reminded [her] of a scavenger hunt." We empathize, but here's the rub, park by park.

In Disneyland Park, the most popular attractions are positioned across the park from one another. This is no accident. It's good planning, a method of more equally distributing guests throughout the park. If you want to experience the most popular attractions in 1 day without long waits, you can arrive before the park fills and see those attractions first thing (which requires crisscrossing the park), or you can enjoy the main attractions on one side of the park first thing in the morning, then use Fastpass for the popular attractions on the other side. All other approaches will subject you to awesome waits at some attractions if you tour during busy times of the year.

The best way to minimize bouncing around at Disneyland Park is to use one of our 2-day Touring Plans, which spread the more popular attractions over 2 mornings and work beautifully even when the park closes at 8 p.m. or earlier. Using Fastpass will decrease your waiting time but will increase bouncing around because you must first go to the attraction to obtain your Fastpass and then backtrack later to the same attraction to use your pass.

Disney California Adventure is configured in a way that precludes an orderly approach to touring, or to a clockwise or counterclockwise rotation. Orderly touring is further frustrated by the limited guest capacity of the midway rides in the Paradise Pier district of the park. At DCA, therefore, you're stuck with bouncing around, whether you use the touring plan or not, if you want to avoid horrendous waits.

We suggest that you follow the touring plans religiously, especially in the mornings, if you're visiting Disneyland during busy, more crowded times. The consequence of touring spontaneity in peak season is hours of otherwise avoidable standing in line. During quieter times of year, there's no need to be compulsive about following the plans.

Touring Plan Rejection

We've discovered that you can't implant a touring plan in certain personalities without vehement rejection. Some folks just do not respond well to regimentation. If you bump into this problem with someone in your party, it's best to roll with the punches, as did this couple:

> The rest of the group was not receptive to the use of the touring plans. They all thought I was being a little too regimented about planning this vacation. Rather than argue, I left the touring plans behind as we ventured off for the parks. You can guess the outcome. We took our camcorder with us and when we returned home, watched the movies. About every 5 minutes there is a shot of us all gathered around a park map trying to decide what to do next.

Finally, as a Connecticut woman alleges, the touring plans are incompatible with some readers' bladders as well as their personalities:

> I want to know if next year when you write those "day" schedules if you could schedule bathroom breaks in there too. You expect us to be at a certain ride at a certain time and with no stops in between. In one of the letters in your book a guy writes, "You expect everyone to be theme-park commandos." When I read that, I thought, there is a man who really knows what a problem the schedules are if you are a laid-back, slow-moving, careful detail-noticer. What were you thinking when you made these schedules?

A Clamor for Customized Touring Plans

We're inundated by letters urging us to create additional touring plans. These include a plan for 9th- and 10th-graders, a plan for rainy days, a seniors' plan, a plan for folks who sleep late, a plan omitting rides that "bump, jerk, and clonk," a plan for gardening enthusiasts, and a plan for single women.

The touring plans in this book are intended to be flexible. Adapt them to your preferences. If you don't like rides that bump and jerk, skip them when they come up in a touring plan. If you want to sleep in and go to the park at noon, use the afternoon part of a plan. If you're a 9th-grader and want to ride Space Mountain three times in a row, do it. Will it decrease the touring plan's effectiveness? Sure, but the plan was created only to help you have fun. It's your day. Don't let the tail wag the dog.

WHAT TO EXPECT WHEN YOU ARRIVE AT THE PARKS

BECAUSE EACH TOURING PLAN IS BASED on being present when the theme park opens, you need to know a little about opening procedures.

Disney transportation to the parks, and the respective theme-park parking lots, open 1–2 hours before official opening time.

Each park has an entrance plaza just outside the turnstiles. Usually you will be held outside the turnstiles until 30 minutes before official opening time. If you are admitted before the official opening time, what happens next depends on the season of the year and the anticipated crowds for that day.

1. MOST DAYS You will usually be held at the turnstiles. Sometimes you might be confined in a small section of the park until the official opening time. At Disneyland Park you might be admitted to Main Street, U.S.A.; at Disney California Adventure to Buena Vista Street. If you proceed farther into a park, you will encounter a rope barrier manned by Disney cast members who will keep you from entering the remainder of the park. You will remain here until the rope drop, when the rope barrier is removed and the park and all (or most) of its attractions are opened at the official opening time.

2. HIGH SEASON AND HOLIDAYS Sometimes, when large crowds are expected, you will be admitted through the turnstiles 30 minutes before the official opening time. This time, however, the entire park will be up and running, and you will not encounter any rope barriers.

3. VARIATIONS Sometimes Disney will run a variation of the two opening procedures described above. In this situation, you will be permitted through the turnstiles and will find that one or several specific attractions are open early for your enjoyment.

A Word about the Rope Drop

Until recently, Disney cast members would dive for cover when the rope was dropped as thousands of adrenaline-charged guests stampeded to the most popular attractions. This practice occasioned the legendary Space Mountain Morning Mini-Marathon and the Splash Mountain Rapid Rampage at Disneyland Park.

Well, this scenario no longer exists—at least not in the crazed versions of years past. Recently, Disney has beefed up the number of cast members supervising the rope drop in order to suppress the mayhem. In some cases, the rope is not even dropped. Instead, it's walked back. In other words, Disney cast members lead you with the rope at a fast walk toward the attraction you're straining to reach, forcing you (and everyone else) to maintain their pace. Not until they come within close proximity of the attraction do the cast members step aside.

So, here's the scoop. If Disney persists in walking the rope back, the only way you can gain an advantage over the rest of the crowd is to arrive early enough to be one of those up front close to the rope. Be alert, though; sometimes the Disney folks will step out of the way after about 50 yards or so. If this happens, you can fire up the afterburners and speed the remaining distance to your destination.

FASTPASS

FASTPASS IS A SYSTEM for moderating the waiting time for popular attractions. Here's how it works.

Your handout park map, as well as signs at respective attractions, will tell you which attractions are included. Attractions that use Fastpass will have a regular line and a Fastpass line. A sign at the entrance will tell you how long the wait is in the regular line. If the wait is acceptable, hop in line. If the wait seems too long, you can insert your park admission pass into a special Fastpass machine and receive an appointment time (for sometime later in the day) to come back and ride. When you return at the appointed time, you will enter the Fastpass line and proceed directly to the attraction's preshow or boarding area with no further wait. There is no extra charge to use Fastpass, but you can get an appointment for only one attraction at a time. Interestingly, this procedure was pioneered by Universal Studios Hollywood many years ago and was pretty much ignored by major theme parks at first.

Fastpass works remarkably well, primarily because Fastpass holders get amazingly preferential treatment. The effort to accommodate Fastpass holders makes anyone in the regular line feel like an illegal immigrant. As a telling indication of their status, Disney (borrowing a term from the airlines) refers to those in the regular line as "standby guests." Indeed, we watched guests in the regular line stand by and stand by, shifting despondently from foot to foot while dozens and sometimes hundreds of Fastpass holders were ushered into the boarding area ahead of them. Clearly Disney is sending a message here, to wit: Fastpass is heaven; anything else is limbo at best and probably purgatory. In either event, you'll think you've been in purgatory if you get stuck in the regular line during the hot, crowded part of the day.

FASTPASS ATTRACTIONS

DISNEYLAND PARK	DISNEY CALIFORNIA ADVENTURE
Autopia	California Screamin'
Big Thunder Mountain	Goofy's Sky School*
Buzz Lightyear Astro Blasters	Grizzly River Run
Haunted Mansion holiday (operates seasonally)	Radiator Springs Racers (opens 2012)
Indiana Jones Adventure	Soarin' Over California*
Roger Rabbit's Car Toon Spin*	The Twilight Zone Tower of Terror
Space Mountain*	World of Color
Splash Mountain*	
Star Tours: The Adventures Continue*	

*Denotes rides that routinely issue Fastpasses for redemption 3–7 hours later.

Fastpass, however, doesn't eliminate the need to arrive at the theme park early. Because each park offers at most 10 Fastpass attractions, you still need to get an early start if you want to see as much as possible in a single day. Plus, as we'll discuss later, there's only a limited supply of Fastpasses available for each attraction on a given day. So, if you don't show up until the middle of the afternoon, you might discover that all the Fastpasses have been distributed to other guests. Fastpass does, happily, make it possible to see more with less waiting than ever before, and it's a great benefit to those who like to sleep late or who enjoy an afternoon or evening at the theme parks on their arrival day. It also enables you to postpone wet rides such as the Grizzly River Run at Disney California Adventure or Splash Mountain at Disneyland Park until the warmer part of the day.

Understanding the Fastpass System

The purpose of the Fastpass system is to reduce the waiting time for designated attractions by more equally distributing the arrival of guests at those attractions over the course of the day. This is accomplished by providing a shorter wait in line for guests who are willing to postpone experiencing the attraction until sometime later in the day. The system also, in effect, imposes a penalty—that is, being relegated to standby status—to those who opt not to use it (although spreading guest arrivals more equally decreases waiting time for standby guests too).

When you insert your admission pass into a Fastpass machine, it spits out a small slip of paper about two-thirds the size of a credit card, small enough to fit in your wallet (but also small enough to lose easily). Printed on the paper will be the name of the attraction and a specific 1-hour time window—for example, 1:15–2:15 p.m. You can return to enjoy the ride anytime from 1:15 p.m. until park closing. Each person in your party must have his or her own Fastpass.

When you report back to the attraction later, you'll enter a line marked FASTPASS RETURN that will route you more or less directly to the boarding area or preshow area. Each person in your party must have his or her own Fastpass and be ready to show it to the Disney cast member at the entrance of the Fastpass return line. Before you enter the boarding area, another cast member will collect your Fastpass.

You may show up at any time after the period printed on your Fastpass begins, and from our observation, no specific time is better or worse. This holds true because cast members are instructed to minimize waits for Fastpass holders. Thus, if the Fastpass return line is suddenly inundated (something that occurs more or less by chance), cast members rapidly intervene to reduce the Fastpass line. This is done by admitting as many as 25 Fastpass holders for each standby guest until the Fastpass line is down to an acceptable length. Though Fastpass will lop off as much as 80% of the wait you'd experience in the regular line, you can still expect a short wait, but usually less than 20 minutes.

You can obtain a Fastpass anytime after a park opens, though the Fastpass return lines do not begin operating until about 35–50 minutes after opening. Thus, if the attractions at Disneyland Park open at 9 a.m., the Fastpass machines will also be available at 9 a.m., and the Fastpass line will begin operating at about 9:35 a.m.

Whatever time you obtain a Fastpass, you can be assured of a period of time between when you receive your Fastpass and the beginning of your return window. The interval can be as short as 30 minutes or as long as 7 hours depending on park attendance, the popularity of the attraction, and the attraction's hourly capacity. As a general rule, the earlier in the day you secure a Fastpass, the shorter the interval between time of issue and the beginning of your return window. If on a day that the park opens at 9 a.m., you pick up a Fastpass for Splash Mountain at, say, 9:25 a.m., your recommended window for returning to ride would be something like 10–11 a.m., or perhaps 10:10–11:10 a.m. The exact time will be determined by how many other guests have obtained Fastpasses before you.

To more effectively distribute guests over the course of a day, the Fastpass machines bump the 1-hour return period back 5 minutes for a specific number of passes issued (usually the number is equal to about 6% of the attraction's hourly capacity). When Splash Mountain opens at 9 a.m., for example, the first 125 people to obtain a Fastpass will get a 10–11 a.m. recommended return window. The next 125 guests are issued Fastpasses that can be used between 10:05–11:05 a.m., with the next 125 assigned a 10:10–11:10 a.m. time slot. And so it goes, with the time window dropping back 5 minutes for every 125 guests. The fewer guests who obtain Fastpasses for an attraction, the shorter the interval between the receipt of your pass and the return window. Conversely, the more guests issued Fastpasses, the longer the interval. If an attraction is exceptionally popular and/or its hourly capacity is relatively small, the return window might be pushed back all the way to park closing time. When this happens, the Fastpass machines stop issuing passes. It would not be unusual, for example, for Goofy's Sky School at Disney California Adventure to distribute an entire day's allocation of Fastpasses by 2 p.m. When this happens, the machines simply shut down and a sign is posted saying that Fastpasses are all gone for the day.

unofficial **TIP**
Use Fastpass if the wait in the regular line is more than 30 minutes.

FASTPASS GUIDELINES

- Don't use Fastpass unless it can save you 30 minutes or more at an attraction.
- If you arrive after a park opens, obtain a Fastpass for your preferred Fastpass attraction first thing.
- Always check the Fastpass return period before obtaining your Fastpass.
- Obtain Fastpasses for Star Tours, Space Mountain, and Splash Mountain at Disneyland Park and for Soarin' Over California, *World of Color,* and Goofy's Sky School at DCA as early in the day as practical.

- Try to obtain Fastpasses for rides not mentioned above by 1 p.m.

- Don't depend on Fastpasses being available for ride attractions after 2 p.m. during busier times of the year.

- Make sure that everyone in your party has his or her own Fastpass.

- You can obtain a second Fastpass as soon as you enter the return period for your first Fastpass or after 2 hours from issuance, whichever comes first.

- Maximize efficiency by always obtaining a new Fastpass for the next attraction before using the first Fastpass you already hold.

- Be mindful of your Fastpass return time, and plan intervening activities accordingly.

- Don't sweat the ending time on your Fastpass return window; you'll be accepted at any time up until park closing.

- Rides don't dispense Fastpasses during Magic Mornings, nor while they are closed for technical difficulties or special events.

Disconnected Fastpass Attractions

Some attractions' Fastpass kiosks function independently and are not hooked up to the park-wide Fastpass distribution system. Because a "disconnected" attraction has no way of knowing if you have a Fastpass for another attraction, it will issue you a Fastpass at any time. In Disneyland Park, Roger Rabbit's Car Toon Spin is sometimes disconnected, and Grizzly River Run at DCA has been disconnected during certain periods. *World of Color*'s Fastpasses are always disconnected from the other attractions. Disney can connect and disconnect Fastpass attractions at will, so it's possible that the disconnected lineup will vary somewhat during your visit. The use of disconnected Fastpass attractions is incorporated in our touring plans. Finally, Disneyland Park's and DCA's Fastpass systems are not connected. You can obtain a Fastpass at one park and then immediately walk to the other park and obtain another Fastpass.

When to Use Fastpass

Except as discussed below, there's no reason to use Fastpass during the first 30–40 minutes a park is open. Lines for most attractions are quite manageable during this period. In addition, this is the only time of the day when the Fastpass attractions exclusively serve those in the regular line. Regardless of time of day, however, if the wait in the regular line at a Fastpass attraction is 25–30 minutes or less, we recommend joining the regular line.

Think about it. Using Fastpass requires two trips to the same attraction: one to obtain the pass and one to use it. This means that you must invest time to secure the pass (by the way, sometimes there are lines at the Fastpass machines!) and then later interrupt your touring and backtrack in order to use your Fastpass. The additional time, effort, and touring modification required, therefore, are justified only if you can save more than 30 minutes. And don't forget: Even in the Fastpass line you must endure some waiting.

Tricks of the Trade

Although Disney stipulates that you can hold a Fastpass to only one attraction at a time, it's possible to acquire a second Fastpass before using the first. Let's say you obtain a Fastpass to Star Tours at Disneyland Park with a return time slot of 10:15–11:15 a.m. Any time after your Fastpass window begins (anytime after 10:15 a.m.), you will be able to obtain another Fastpass, for Splash Mountain, for example. This is possible because the Fastpass computer system monitors only the distribution of passes, ignoring whether or when a Fastpass is used. Finally, don't forget that you can obtain a second Fastpass 2 hours after the time of issuance of the first Fastpass if that's sooner than the return time on your first Fastpass.

When obtaining Fastpasses, it's faster and more considerate of other guests if one person obtains passes for your entire party. This means entrusting one individual with both your valuable park admission passes and your Fastpasses, so choose wisely.

Fastpass Runners

If you've ever taken a walk with a dog that runs and darts all over the place while you plod along in a straight line, you'll appreciate the concept of Fastpass running. First you choose a high-energy, inexhaustible member of your party who is quick on his feet and mature and responsible enough not to lose everyone's admission passes. Second, you give him all the passes and dispatch him to the first attraction to obtain Fastpasses for the whole group. Then, about once each hour the Fastpass runner will split from the group to get the next Fastpasses. Rinse, repeat. In Disneyland Park, for example, he would speed off to Space Mountain. Because the return time is usually 1 hour or less, it won't be long until he can scoot off again to obtain Fastpasses at Splash Mountain. And so it goes. Collecting Fastpasses this way allows the group to spend the less-crowded early-morning time visiting popular slow-loading attractions that don't offer Fastpass.

SAVING TIME IN LINE BY UNDERSTANDING THE RIDES

THERE ARE MANY DIFFERENT TYPES of rides in Disneyland. Some rides, such as It's a Small World, are engineered to carry several thousand people every hour. At the other extreme, rides such as Dumbo the Flying Elephant can accommodate only around 500 people in an hour. Most rides fall somewhere in between. Lots of factors figure into how long you will have to wait to experience a particular ride: the popularity of the ride, how it loads and unloads, how many people can ride at one time, how many units (cars, rockets, boats, flying elephants, or whatever) of those available are in service at a given time, and how many staff personnel are available to operate the ride. Let's take them one by one:

1. HOW POPULAR IS THE RIDE? Newer rides such as Finding Nemo Submarine Voyage or Toy Story Midway Mania! attract a lot of people, as do longtime favorites such as the Jungle Cruise. If you know a ride is popular, you need to learn a little more about how it operates to determine when might be the best time to ride. But a ride need not be especially popular to form long lines. The lines can be the result of less-than-desirable traffic engineering; that is, it takes so long to load and unload that a line builds up. This is the situation at the Mad Tea Party and Dumbo. Only a small percentage of the visitors to Disneyland Park (mostly kids) ride Dumbo, for instance, but because it takes so long to load and unload, this ride can form long waiting lines.

2. HOW DOES THE RIDE LOAD AND UNLOAD? Some rides never stop. They are like a circular conveyor belt that goes around and around. We call these "continuous loaders." The Haunted Mansion is a continuous loader. The more cars or ships or whatever on the conveyor, the more people can be moved through in an hour. The Haunted Mansion has lots of cars on the conveyor belt and consequently can move more than 2,400 people an hour.

Other rides are "interval loaders." This means that cars are unloaded, loaded, and dispatched at certain set intervals (sometimes controlled manually and sometimes by a computer). Matterhorn Bobsleds is an interval loader. It has two separate tracks (in other words, the ride has been duplicated in the same facility). Each track can run up to 10 sleds, released at 23-second or greater intervals (the bigger the crowd, the shorter the interval). In another kind of interval loader, such as the Jungle Cruise, empty boats return to the starting point, where they line up waiting to be reloaded. In a third type of interval loader, one group of riders enters the vehicle while the last group of riders departs. We call these "in-and-out" interval loaders. Indiana Jones is a good example of an "in-and-out" interval loader. As a troop transport pulls up to the loading station, those who have just completed their ride exit to the left. At almost the same time, those waiting to ride enter the troop transport from the right. The troop transport is released to the dispatch point a few yards down the line where it is launched according to whatever second interval is being used. Interval loaders of all three types can be very efficient at moving people if (1) the release (launch) interval is relatively short and (2) the ride can accommodate a large number of vehicles in the system at one time. Because many boats can be floating through Pirates of the Caribbean at a given time and the release interval is short, almost 2,300 people an hour can see this attraction.

A third group of rides are "cycle rides." Another name for these same rides is "stop-and-go" rides; those waiting to ride exchange places with those who have just ridden. The main difference between

Cycle Rides

DISNEYLAND PARK

Fantasyland	Mickey's Toontown	Tomorrowland
Casey Jr. Circus Train	Gadget's Go Coaster	Astro Orbitor
Dumbo the Flying Elephant		
King Arthur Carrousel		
Mad Tea Party		

DISNEY CALIFORNIA ADVENTURE

a bug's land	Paradise Pier	Cars Land
Flik's Flyers	Golden Zephyr	Luigi's Flying Tires
Francis' Ladybug Boogie	Jumpin' Jellyfish	Mater's Junkyard Jamboree
Mickey's Fun Wheel	King Triton's Carousel	
Tuck and Roll's Drive 'Em Buggies	Silly Symphony Swings	

"in-and-out" interval rides and cycle rides is that with a cycle ride, the whole system shuts down when loading and unloading is in progress. While one boat is loading and unloading in It's a Small World, many other boats are proceeding through the ride. But when Dumbo the Flying Elephant touches down, the whole ride is at a standstill until the next flight is launched.

In discussing a cycle ride, the amount of time the ride is in motion is called "ride time." The amount of time that the ride is idle while loading and unloading is called "load time." Load time plus ride time equals "cycle time," or the time expended from the start of one run of the ride until the start of the succeeding run. Cycle rides are the least efficient of all the Disneyland rides in terms of traffic engineering. Disneyland Park has 6 cycle rides, while Disney California Adventure will have 10 when Cars Land opens, an astonishing number for a modern park.

3. HOW MANY PEOPLE CAN RIDE AT ONE TIME? This figure is defined in terms of "per-ride capacity" or "system capacity." Either way, the figures refer to the number of people who can ride at the same time. Our discussion above illustrates that the greater a ride's carrying capacity (all other things being equal), the more visitors it can accommodate in an hour.

4. HOW MANY "UNITS" ARE IN SERVICE AT A GIVEN TIME? A *unit* is simply a term for the vehicle you sit in during your ride. At the Mad Tea Party the unit is a teacup, and at Alice in Wonderland it's a caterpillar. On some rides (mostly cycle rides), the number of units in operation at a given time is fixed. Thus, there are always 16 flying-elephant units operating on the Dumbo ride, 72 horses on King Arthur Carrousel, and so on. What this fixed number of units means to you is that there is no way to increase the carrying capacity of the ride by adding more units. On a busy day, therefore, the only way to carry more people each hour on a fixed-unit cycle ride is to shorten the loading time (which, as we will see in number 5 below, is sometimes impossible) or by decreasing the riding time, the actual time the ride is in motion. The bottom line on a busy day for a cycle ride is that you will wait longer and be rewarded for your wait with a shorter ride. This is why we try to steer you clear of the cycle rides unless you are willing to ride them early in the morning or late at night.

Other rides at Disneyland can increase their carrying capacity by adding units to the system as the crowds build. The Big Thunder Mountain Railroad is a good example. If attendance is very light, Big Thunder can start the day by running one of five available mine trains. When lines start to build, more mine trains can be placed into operation. At full capacity, a total of five trains can carry about 2,400 people an hour. Likewise, Finding Nemo can increase its capacity by adding more submarines. Sometimes a long line will disappear almost instantly when new units are brought online. When an interval-loading ride places more units into operation, it usually shortens the dispatch interval, so more units are being dispatched more often.

5. HOW MANY CAST MEMBERS ARE AVAILABLE TO OPERATE THE RIDE? Allocation of additional staff to a given ride can allow extra units to be placed in operation, or additional loading areas or holding areas to be opened. Pirates of the Caribbean and It's a Small World can run two separate waiting lines and loading zones. The Haunted Mansion has a short preshow, which is staged in a "stretch room." On busy days a second stretch room can be activated, thus permitting a more continuous flow of visitors to the actual loading area. Additional staff make a world of difference on some cycle rides. Often, if not usually, one attendant will operate the Golden Zephyr. This single person must clear the visitors from the ride just completed, admit and seat visitors for the upcoming ride, check that all zephyrs are properly secured (which entails an inspection of each zephyr), return to the control panel, issue instructions to the riders, and finally, activate the ride (whew!). A second attendant allows for the division of these responsibilities and has the effect of cutting loading time by 25%–50%.

BEWARE OF THE DARK, WET, ROUGH, AND SCARY

 OOPS, ALMOST FORGOT: There's a member of our team you need to meet. Called a Wuffo, she's our very own character. She'll warn you when rides are too scary, too dark, or too wet. You'll bump into her throughout the book doing, well, what characters do. Pay attention to her—she knows what she's talking about.

SAVING TIME IN LINE BY UNDERSTANDING THE SHOWS

MANY OF THE FEATURED ATTRACTIONS at Disneyland are theater presentations. While they're not as complex as rides from a traffic-engineering viewpoint, a little enlightenment concerning their operation may save some touring time.

Most Disneyland theater attractions operate in three distinct phases:

1. First, there are the visitors who are in the theater viewing the presentation.

2. Next, there are the visitors who have passed through the turnstile into a holding area or waiting lobby. These people will be admitted to the theater as soon as the current presentation is concluded. Several attractions offer a preshow in their waiting lobby to entertain the crowd until they are admitted to the main show.

3. Finally, there is the outside line. Visitors waiting here will enter the waiting lobby when there is room and then move into the theater when the audience turns over (is exchanged) between shows.

The theater capacity and popularity of the presentation, along with the level of attendance in the park, determine how long the lines will be at a given theater attraction. Except for holidays and other days of especially heavy attendance, the longest wait for a show usually does not exceed the length of one complete performance.

Because almost all Disneyland theater attractions run continually, only stopping long enough for the previous audience to leave and the waiting audience to enter, a performance will already be in progress when you arrive. If the *Enchanted Tiki Room* show lasts 15 minutes, the wait under normal circumstances should be 15 minutes if you were to arrive just after the show began.

All Disneyland theaters (except the Main Street Cinema and some amphitheater productions) are very strict when it comes to controlling access. Unlike at a regular movie theater, you can't just walk in during the middle of a performance; you will always have at least a short wait.

GUIDED TOURS AT DISNEYLAND PARK AND DCA

FOUR GUIDED TOURS ARE OFFERED. All require a valid park admission in addition to the price of the tour. All four tours can be booked up to 30 days in advance by calling ☎ 714-781-4400. All tours are

Caution: *How Theater Attractions Work*

subject to change without notice. During the Halloween and Christmas seasons, special tours highlighting holiday decorations may be available in addition to the following year-round offerings.

DISCOVER THE MAGIC TOUR Kids interact with Disney characters in a sort of treasure hunt to find clues to the treasure and avoid villainous characters. Designed for ages 3–9, the frenetic, fast-paced family program lasts approximately 2½ hours and includes a frozen treat and souvenir Disney pin. Prices are $59 for the first two tickets, $49 for the third and subsequent tickets.

WELCOME TO DISNEYLAND TOUR This 2½-hour tour for first-time visitors provides a warp-speed look at pretty much the entire Disneyland Resort. Guides provide background and history of the parks, attractions, and sights as you tour both theme parks, Downtown Disney, and the Disney-owned hotels. Suffice it to say, you'll do a lot of walking. The tour includes special reserved seats for a performance at a stage show or parade (selected locations) and two Fastpasses per person for use after the tour. The tour is reasonably priced at $25.

A WALK IN WALT'S FOOTSTEPS This 3½-hour tour offers a historical perspective on both Disneyland Park and the man who created it. A Walk in Walt's Footsteps provides a lot of detail as it covers Disney's vision and the challenges in bringing the groundbreaking theme park to life. The tour includes a light lunch. Highlights of the tour are an inside look at the Disneyland Railroad and a glimpse of the lobby of Club 33, where Disney was to entertain his friends and dignitaries. Unfortunately, he died 5 months before the club was finished. Cost is $64 for all ages. (The tour is considered inappropriate for younger children and those who can't walk on their own.)

VIP TOURS For the well-heeled, exclusive VIP tours are available for an eye-popping $125 per hour ($150 if booked less than 48 hours in advance) with a 4-hour minimum; park admission is not included. VIP guides will arrange special parade and show seating, make dining reservations, and dispense Disneyland trivia, but they won't "back door" you past the attractions queues, which limits their utility.

PART TWO

ESSENTIALS

 The **BARE NECESSITIES**

CREDIT CARDS

AMERICAN EXPRESS, MASTERCARD, VISA, Discover, Japan Credit Bureau (JCB), and, of course, the Disney Visa credit card are accepted for theme-park admission. Disneyland shops, fast-food and counter-service restaurants, sit-down restaurants, and the Disneyland Resort hotels also accept all the cards listed above. Some vendor carts accept credit cards while others do not—ask before you order.

RAIN

IF IT RAINS, GO ANYWAY; the bad weather will diminish the crowds. Additionally, most of the rides and attractions at the parks are under cover. Likewise, all but a few of the waiting areas are protected from inclement weather. Some outdoor attractions—such as Tom Sawyer's Island, Mad Tea Party, Alice in Wonderland, Tarzan's Treehouse, and Gadget's Go Coaster at Disneyland Park, and Redwood Creek Challenge Trail and Golden Zephyr at DCA—may close for safety reasons in inclement weather. Roller coasters such as Big Thunder Mountain and California Screamin' can operate in a drizzle but will close down if lightning is nearby. Fireworks are rarely canceled solely due to rain but may be scuttled by strong winds, and parades may be shortened or modified for safety. A father from Petaluma, California, recommends some supplemental supplies for wet weather, writing:

> Ride operators make a token effort to use a shop vac or towels, but it's good to have your own towel even on sunny days for the water ride seats. For multiday park touring in the rain, it is good to have a second pair of shoes to switch off every night at the hotel, allowing 24 hours to dry.

If you get caught in an unexpected downpour, raingear can be purchased at a number of shops. Whatever you do, don't flee for the parking trams during a sudden thunderstorm, or you may find yourself in an unpleasant scene like this mother of two from Los Angeles:

> *It was pouring rain and the park rapidly emptied out with everyone heading for the trams that take you to the parking structure. There was complete chaos by the tram loading area [with] hundreds of people pushing and shoving—desperate to get on a tram and get out of there. The trams were arriving very sporadically and tempers were rising.*

Instead, wait out the storm inside a self-paced indoor attraction, such as *Great Moments with Mr. Lincoln,* Main Street Cinema, or Innoventions at Disneyland Park, and Blue Sky Cellar or Disney Animation at DCA.

VISITORS WITH SPECIAL NEEDS

DISABLED VISITORS Rental wheelchairs are available if needed just inside both parks' main gates. Daily wheelchair rentals are $12 (manual) or $50 (electric); a $20 refundable deposit is required. Note that wheelchairs and electric convenience vehicles (ECVs) rented inside the parks are not permitted beyond the Esplanade. A limited supply of nonelectric wheelchairs which may be taken through the Downtown Disney district are available to rent at the three Disneyland Resort hotels.

Most rides, shows, attractions, restrooms, and restaurants are engineered to accommodate the disabled. For specific inquiries call ☎ 714-781-7290. If you have an impairment that makes it difficult for you to stand in line and navigate stairs, or otherwise need special assistance, go to City Hall on Main Street in Disneyland Park or Guest Relations in the entrance plaza at Disney California Adventure (DCA) and ask for a Guest Assistance Card. These passes are free and available for the disabled visitor and up to five additional guests. You should not have to show a doctor's note or proof of disability, but the card does *not* entitle you to skip the lines at attractions, as a traveler from Santa Clara notes:

> *Keep in mind that the Guest Assistance Pass will not necessarily cut down the time that you have to wait to board a given ride, but it will provide you with a more accessible way to board.*

For guests with visual or auditory impairments, digital audio and Braille guides, assistive listening devices, captioning, and sign language services are also available through City Hall and Guest Relations. Trained service animals are welcome but must be kept on a leash at all times.

Close-in parking is available for the disabled; inquire when you pay your parking fee. Parking trams can accommodate guests who bring their own wheelchairs, and a special transportation van is also available (ask a parking lot cast member). Curbside drop-off is only available at the Harbor Boulevard entrance, near the stops for hotel shuttles and local buses. It may be challenging for disabled guests who don't bring their own wheelchairs to walk from there into the parks. If you don't think that you can travel the necessary distance, consider renting a chair or scooter for the length of your vacation from a third-party vendor who can deliver it to your hotel.

VISITORS WITH DIETARY RESTRICTIONS Guests on special or restricted diets, including those requiring kosher meals, can arrange for assistance at City Hall at Disneyland Park or at Guest Relations at DCA. These locations can also provide information on gluten-free menu options at restaurants in the resort. For special service at Disneyland Resort restaurants, call the restaurant 1 day in advance for assistance.

FOREIGN-LANGUAGE ASSISTANCE Translation services are available to guests who do not speak English. Inquire by calling ☎ 714-781-7290 or visiting City Hall at Disneyland Park or at Guest Relations at DCA.

LOST ADULTS Arrange a plan for regrouping with those in your party should you become separated. Failing this, you can leave a message at City Hall or Guest Relations for your missing person. For information concerning lost children, see page 154.

MESSAGES Messages for your fellow group members can be left at City Hall in Disneyland Park or at DCA Guest Relations.

CAR TROUBLE If you elected to decrease the chance of losing your keys by locking them in your car, or decided that your car might be easier to find if you left your lights on, you may have a little problem to deal with when you return to the parking lot. Fortunately, the security patrols that continually cruise the parking lots are equipped to handle these types of situations and can quickly put you back in business.

LOST AND FOUND The lost-and-found office is located in the Guest Services building in the Esplanade to the west of the park entrances. This location services both theme parks and the Downtown Disney complex. If you do not discover your loss until you have left the parks, call ☎ 714-817-2166.

EXCUSE ME, BUT WHERE CAN I FIND . . .

SOME PLACE TO PUT ALL THESE PACKAGES? Lockers are available at both parks for $7–$15 per day, depending on size. A more convenient solution, if you plan to spend a minimum of 2 or more hours in the park, is to have the salesperson forward your purchases to Package Pickup. When you leave the park, they will be there waiting for you.

GROCERIES? Several convenience stores are on Harbor Boulevard near Disneyland, but no supermarkets are within easy walking distance. The closest store with a good selection is **Food-4-Less** at 1616 W. Katella Ave. about a mile west of Disneyland Resort. See **food4less1.com** or call ☎ 714-539-7497. **Target** is about a 5-minute drive south of Disneyland on Harbor. The adjacent **Viva Bargain Center** dollar store is a good place for cheap snacks and supplies.

A MIXED DRINK OR BEER? If you are in Disneyland Park, you are out of luck. You will have to exit the park and try one of the hotels. At DCA alcoholic beverages are readily available.

SOME RAINGEAR? At Disneyland, raingear is available at most shops but is not always displayed. You have to ask for it. Ponchos are $7 for adults and $6 for kids, and umbrellas are $10 and up.

A CURE FOR THIS HEADACHE? Aspirin and various other sundries can be purchased on Main Street at the Emporium in Disneyland Park and at Greetings from California at the DCA entrance plaza (they keep them behind the counter, so you have to ask).

A PRESCRIPTION FILLED? Unfortunately, there is no place in Disneyland Resort to have a prescription filled.

A DOCTOR? Housecall Physicians (☎ 800-362-7911) will make house calls to your hotel room 24/7. The fee is $290 per house call plus incidentals (such as medications dispensed) payable at the time of the visit. The closest hospital to Disneyland is the **University California Irvine Medical Center,** which is about 2 miles distant at Chapman Avenue and City Drive. For dental emergencies, there is **A Plus Emergency Dental Service** at 637 N. Euclid St. in Anaheim, ☎ 714-772-2893, or for the true emergency after hours, call ☎ 714-687-6967, providing 24-hour assistance.

SUNTAN LOTION? Suntan lotion and various other sundries can be purchased in Disneyland Park on Main Street at the Emporium and at Greetings from California at the DCA entrance plaza (they keep them behind the counter, so you have to ask).

A SMOKE? You won't find cigarettes for sale at Disneyland parks, and you'll have a hard time finding a place to smoke any you bring with you. Smoking is strongly discouraged throughout the parks and resorts, though there are a few designated smoking areas.

FEMININE-HYGIENE PRODUCTS? These are available in most women's restrooms at Disneyland Resort.

CASH? Basic banking services and foreign currency exchange are provided at City Hall in Disneyland Park, Guest Relations at DCA, Travelex in Downtown Disney, and the front desks of Disneyland hotels. At Travelex you can also exchange travelers' checks or receive cash advances on MasterCard and Visa credit cards. Starcade in Tomorrowland also offers cash advances on MasterCard and Visa credit cards. If the cashier is closed, ATMs are at these locations:

AT DISNEYLAND PARK

- Outside the main entrance
- On Main Street, next to the *Disneyland Story* at the Town Square end
- At the entrance to Frontierland on the left
- Near Disney Princess Fantasy Faire
- In Tomorrowland, near Starcade

AT DOWNTOWN DISNEY

- Next to Häagen-Dazs
- At the LEGO Imagination Center

AT DISNEY CALIFORNIA ADVENTURE

- Outside the main entrance
- At the phone and locker complex just inside the main entrance and to the right
- Near the restrooms at Hollywood Pictures Backlot
- Near the restrooms on Pacific Wharf
- Near the restrooms behind Golden Vine Winery across from Paradise Bay
- Near Mickey's Fun Wheel at Paradise Pier

A PLACE TO LEAVE MY PET? Pets are not allowed in the parks (except for assistance dogs). Kennels and holding facilities are provided for the temporary care of your pets and are located at the parking garage. If you are adamant, the folks at the kennels will accept custody of just about any type of animal. Owners of pets, exotic or otherwise, must themselves place their charge in the assigned cage. Small pets (mice, hamsters, birds, snakes, turtles, alligators, and the like) must arrive in their own escape-proof quarters. Kennels cost $20 per pet per day and are located at 1313 Harbor Blvd. For more information, call ☎ 714-781-7290. There are several other details you may need to know:

- Advance reservations for animals are not accepted.
- Only cash or Disney dollars are accepted.
- Kennels' hours are the same as theme-park operating hours.
- Pets may not be boarded overnight.
- Guests leaving exotic pets should supply food for their pet.
- On busy days, there is a 1- to 2-hour bottleneck at the kennel, beginning 30 minutes before the park opens. If you need to use the kennels on such a day, arrive at least 1 hour before the park's stated opening time.
- Pets are fed on request only (yours, not your pet's), and there is no additional charge for food.
- Proof of current rabies and distemper vaccine is required.

CAMERAS AND FILM? You can buy a disposable camera, with or without a flash, in both parks. You can buy film, digital memory cards, and batteries throughout the parks. If you'd rather let professionals take the pictures, Disney PhotoPass photographers are stationed at scenic spots around the parks. They'll take your snapshot with their camera (and yours, if you request) for free, and then hand you a PhotoPass identification card, which you can continue using during your vacation. Then stop by Main Street Photo Supply in Disneyland Park or Kingswell Camera Shop in DCA (go at midafternoon to avoid long lines), or log onto **disneyphotopass.com** within 30 days of your visit to preview and purchase all your pictures. You can purchase prints individually ($15 and up) along with books, mugs, and mouse pads. Or order a photo CD with all of your high-resolution pictures for about $60, and print them at your local drugstore for less.

PART THREE

DISNEYLAND
with KIDS

The BRUTAL TRUTH *about* FAMILY VACATIONS

IT HAS BEEN SUGGESTED that the phrase *family vacation* is a bit of an oxymoron. This is because you can never take a vacation from the responsibilities of parenting if your children are traveling with you. Though you leave work and normal routine far behind, your children require as much attention, if not more, when traveling as they do at home.

Parenting on the road is an art. It requires imagination and organization. Think about it: You have to do all the usual stuff (feed, dress, bathe, supervise, teach, comfort, discipline, put to bed, and so on) in an atmosphere where your children are hyperstimulated, without the familiarity of place and the resources you take for granted while at home. Although it's not impossible—and can even be fun—parenting on the road is not something you want to learn on the fly, particularly at Disneyland.

The point we want to drive home is that preparation, or the lack thereof, can make or break your Disneyland vacation. Believe us: You don't want to leave the success of your expensive Disney vacation to chance. But don't confuse chance with good luck. Chance is what happens when you fail to prepare; good luck is when preparation meets opportunity.

Your preparation can be organized into several categories, all of which we'll help you undertake. Broadly speaking, you need to prepare yourself and your children mentally, emotionally, physically, organizationally, and logistically. You also need a basic understanding of the two theme parks and a well-considered plan for how to go about seeing them.

MENTAL *and* EMOTIONAL PREPARATION

MENTAL PREPARATION BEGINS with realistic expectations about your Disney vacation and consideration of what each adult and child in your party most wants and needs from his or her Disneyland experience. Getting in touch with this aspect of planning requires a lot of introspection and good, open family communication.

DIVISION OF LABOR

TALK ABOUT WHAT YOU AND YOUR PARTNER need and what you expect to happen on the vacation. This discussion alone can preempt some unpleasant surprises mid-trip. If you are a two-parent (or two-adult) family, do you have a clear understanding of how the parenting workload is to be distributed? We've seen some distinctly disruptive misunderstandings in two-parent households in which one parent is (pardon the legalese) the primary caregiver. Often, the other parent expects the primary caregiver to function on vacation as she (or he) does at home. The primary caregiver, on the other hand, is ready for a break. She expects her partner to either shoulder the load equally or perhaps even assume the lion's share so she can have a real vacation. However you divide the responsibility, of course, is up to you. Just make sure you negotiate a clear understanding before you leave home.

TOGETHERNESS

ANOTHER DIMENSION TO CONSIDER is how much togetherness seems appropriate to you. For some parents, a vacation represents a rare opportunity to really connect with their children, to talk, exchange ideas, and get reacquainted. For others, a vacation affords the time to get a little distance, to

> *unofficial* **TIP**
> Try to schedule some time alone with each of your children—if not each day, then at least a couple of times during the trip.

enjoy a round of golf while the kids are enjoying the theme park. The point here is to think about your and your children's preferences and needs concerning your time together. A typical day at a Disney theme park provides the structure of experiencing attractions together, punctuated by periods of waiting in line, eating, and so on, which facilitate conversation and sharing. Most attractions can be enjoyed together by the whole family, regardless of age ranges. This allows for more consensus and less dissent when it comes to deciding what to see and do. For many parents and children, however, the rhythms of a Disneyland day seem to consist of passive entertainment experiences alternated with endless discussions of where to go and what to do next. As a mother from Winston-Salem, North Carolina, reported:

> *Our family mostly talked about what to do next with very little sharing or discussion about what we had seen. [The conversation] was pretty task-oriented.*

Two observations: First, fighting the crowds and keeping the family moving along can easily escalate into a pressure-driven outing. Having a plan or itinerary eliminates moment-to-moment guesswork and decision making, thus creating more time for savoring and connecting. Second, external variables such as crowd size, noise, and weather, among others, can be so distracting as to preclude any meaningful togetherness. These negative impacts can be moderated, as previously discussed in Part One, by your being selective concerning the time of year, day of the week, the time of day you visit the theme parks, and the number of days of your visit. The bottom line is that you can achieve the degree of connection and togetherness you desire with a little advance planning and a realistic awareness of the distractions you will encounter.

LIGHTEN UP

PREPARE YOURSELF MENTALLY to be a little less compulsive on vacation about correcting small behavioral deviations and pounding home the lessons of life. Certainly, little Mildred will have to learn eventually that it's very un–Disney-like to take off her top at the pool. But there's plenty of time for that later. So what if Matt eats hamburgers for breakfast, lunch, and dinner every day? You can make him eat peas and broccoli when you get home. Roll with the little stuff, and remember when your children act out that they are wired to the max. At least some of that adrenaline is bound to spill out in undesirable ways. Coming down hard will send an already frayed little nervous system into orbit.

SOMETHING FOR EVERYONE

IF YOU TRAVEL WITH AN INFANT, toddler, or any child who requires a lot of special attention, make sure that you have some energy and time remaining for the rest of your brood. In the course of your planning, invite each child to name something special to do or see at Disneyland with Mom or Dad alone. Work these special activities into your trip itinerary. Whatever else, if you commit, write it down so that you don't forget. Remember: A casually expressed willingness to do this or that may be perceived as a promise.

WHOSE IDEA WAS THIS, ANYWAY?

THE DISCORD THAT MANY VACATIONING families experience arises from the kids being on a completely different wavelength from Mom and Dad. Parents and grandparents are often worse than children when it comes to conjuring fantasy scenarios of what a Disneyland vacation will be like. It can be many things, but believe us when we tell you that there's a lot more to it than just riding Dumbo and seeing Mickey.

In our experience, most parents and nearly all grandparents expect children to enter a state of rapture at Disneyland, bouncing from attraction to attraction in wide-eyed wonder, appreciative beyond words to their adult benefactors. What they get, more often than not, is not even in the same ballpark. Preschoolers will, without a doubt, be wide-eyed, often with delight but also with a general sense of being overwhelmed by noise, crowds, and Disney characters as big as toolsheds. We've substantiated through thousands of interviews and surveys that the best part of a Disney vacation for a preschooler is the hotel swimming pool. With some grade-schoolers and pre-driving-age teens, you get near-manic hyperactivity coupled with periods of studied nonchalance. This last phenomenon, which relates to the importance of being "cool at all costs," translates into a maddening display of boredom and a "been there, done that" attitude. Older teens are frequently the exponential version of the younger teens and grade-schoolers, except without the manic behavior.

As a function of probability, you may escape many—but most likely not all—of the above behaviors. Even in the event that they are all visited on you, however, take heart; there are antidotes.

For preschoolers, you can keep things light and happy by limiting the time you spend in the theme parks. The most critical point is that the overstimulation of the parks must be balanced by adequate rest and more-mellow activities. For grade-schoolers and early teens, you can moderate the hyperactivity and false ennui by enlisting their help in planning the vacation, especially by allowing them to take a leading role in determining the itinerary for days at the theme parks. Putting them in charge of specific responsibilities that focus on the happiness of other family members also

unofficial **TIP**
The more information your kids have before arriving at Disneyland, the less likely they'll be to act out.

works well. For example, one reader turned a 12-year-old liability into an asset by asking him to help guard against attractions that might frighten his 5-year-old sister. Knowledge enhances anticipation and at the same time affords a level of comfort and control that helps kids understand the big picture. The more they feel in control, the less they will act out of control.

BASIC CONSIDERATIONS:
Is Disneyland for You?

ALMOST ALL VISITORS ENJOY Disneyland on some level and find things to see and do that they like. In fact, for many, the theme-park attractions are just the tip of the iceberg. The more salient question, then (since this is a family vacation), is whether the members of your family basically like the same things. If you do, fine. If not, how will you handle the differing agendas?

A mother from Toronto wrote a couple of years ago describing her husband's aversion to Disney's (in his terms) "phony, plastic, and idealized version of life." Touring the theme parks, he was a real cynic and managed to diminish the experience for the rest of the family. As it happened, however, Dad's pejorative point of view didn't extend to the area golf courses. So Mom packed him up and sent him golfing while the family enjoyed the theme parks.

If you have someone in your family who doesn't like theme parks or, for whatever reason, doesn't care for Disney's brand of entertainment, it helps to get the attitude out in the open. We recommend dealing with the person up front. Glossing over or ignoring the contrary opinion and hoping that "Tom will like it once he gets there" is naive and unrealistic. Either leave Tom at home or help him discover and plan activities that he will enjoy, resigning yourself in the process to the fact that the family won't be together at all times.

DIFFERENT FOLKS, DIFFERENT STROKES

IT'S NO SECRET THAT WE at the *Unofficial Guides* believe that thorough planning is an essential key to a successful Disneyland vacation. It's also no secret that our emphasis on planning rubs some folks the wrong way. My sister and her husband, for example, are spontaneous people and do not appreciate the concept of detailed planning or, more particularly, following one of our touring plans when they visit the theme parks. To them the most important thing is to relax, take things as they come, and enjoy the moment. Sometimes they arrive at 10:30 in the morning (impossibly late for us *Unofficial Guide* types), walk around enjoying the landscaping and architecture, and then sit with a cup of espresso, watching other guests race around the park like maniacs. They would be the first to admit that they don't see many attractions, but experiencing attractions is not what lights their sparklers.

Not coincidentally, most of our readers are big on planning. When they go to the theme park, they want to experience the attractions, and the shorter the lines, the better. In a word, they are willing to sacrifice some spontaneity for touring efficiency.

We want you to have the best possible time, whatever that means to you, so plan (or not) according to your preference. The point here is that most families (unlike my sister and her husband) are not entirely in agreement on this planning versus spontaneity issue. If you are a serious planner and your oldest daughter and husband are free spirits, you've got the makings of a problem. In practice, the way this and similar scenarios shake out is that the planner (usually the more assertive or type-A person) just takes over. Sometimes daughter and husband go along and everything works out, but just as often they feel resentful. There are as many ways of developing a win-win compromise as there are well-intentioned people on different sides of this situation. How you settle it is up to you. We're simply suggesting that you examine the problem and work out the solution before you go on vacation.

THE NATURE OF THE BEAST

THOUGH MANY PARENTS DON'T REALIZE IT, there is no law that says you must take your kids to Disneyland or Walt Disney World. Likewise, there's no law that says you will enjoy Disneyland. And although we will help you make the most of any visit, we can't change the basic nature of the beast—er, mouse. A Disneyland vacation is an active and physically demanding undertaking. Regimentation, getting up early, lots of walking, waiting in lines, fighting crowds, and (often) enduring the hot California sun are as intrinsic to a Disneyland vacation as stripes are to a zebra. Especially if you're traveling with children, you'll need a sense of humor, more than a modicum of patience, and the ability to roll with the punches.

KNOW THYSELF AND NOTHING TO EXCESS

unofficial **TIP**
You can have a perfectly wonderful time at Disneyland if you're realistic, organized, and prepared.

THIS GOOD ADVICE WAS MADE AVAILABLE to ancient Greeks courtesy of the oracle of Apollo at Delphi, who gave us permission to pass it along to you. First, concerning the "know thyself" part, we want you to do some serious thinking concerning what you want in a vacation. We also want you to entertain the notion that having fun and deriving pleasure from your vacation may be very different indeed from doing and seeing as much as possible.

Because Disneyland Resort is expensive, many families confuse "seeing everything" in order to "get our money's worth" with having a great time. Sometimes the two are compatible, but more often they're not. So if sleeping in, relaxing with the paper over coffee, sunbathing by the pool, or taking a nap rank high on your vacation hit parade, you need to accord them due emphasis on your Disney visit (are you listening?), even if it means you see less of the theme parks.

Which brings us to the "nothing to excess" part. At the Disneyland parks, especially if you're touring with children, less is definitely more. Trust us: It's tough to go full-tilt from dawn to dusk in the theme parks. First you'll get tired, then you'll get cranky, and then you'll adopt a production mentality ("we've got three more rides and then we can go back to the hotel"). Finally, you'll hit the wall because you just can't maintain the pace.

This mom had a great vacation, but not exactly the vacation she had been expecting:

unofficial **TIP**
Get a grip on your needs and preferences before you leave home, and develop an itinerary that incorporates all the things that make you happiest.

> *Unfortunately, I was unprepared for traveling with a 2-year-old. All the indoor rides were deemed too dark and scary, and all she wanted to do was see the characters (which I thought she'd be petrified of!). We had a great trip once I threw all my maps and plans out the window and just went with the flow! Also, 3 nights was not enough to have a leisurely trip. We were running around way too much. We all would have appreciated more pool time. It was a great trip overall, but I would definitely warn people to think twice before bringing a 2-year-old. It is one exhausting trip!*

Plan on seeing the Disneyland parks in bite-size chunks with plenty of sleeping, swimming, napping, and relaxing in between. Most Disneyland vacations are short. Even if you have to stay an extra day to build in some relaxation, you'll be happier while you're there and more rested when you get home. Ask yourself over and over in both the planning stage and while you are at Disneyland: What will contribute the greatest contentedness, satisfaction, and harmony? Trust your instincts. If stopping for ice cream or returning to the hotel for a dip feels like more fun than seeing another attraction, do it—even if it means wasting the remaining hours of an expensive admissions pass.

The AGE THING

THERE'S A LOT OF SERIOUS COGITATION among parents and grandparents in regard to how old a child should be before embarking on a trip to Disneyland. The answer, not always obvious, stems from the personalities and maturity of the children, and the personalities and parenting style of the adults.

Disneyland for Infants and Toddlers

We believe that traveling with infants and toddlers is a great idea. Developmentally, travel is a stimulating learning experience for even the youngest of children. Infants, of course, won't know Mickey Mouse from a draft horse but will respond to sun and shade, music, bright colors, and the extra attention they receive from you. From first steps to full mobility, toddlers respond to the excitement and spectacle of the Disneyland parks, though of course in a much different way than you do. Your toddler will prefer splashing in fountains and clambering over curbs and benches to experiencing most attractions, but no matter: He or she will still have a great time.

An Iowa City, Iowa, mother of three says, "Get over it!":

> *Get over it!! In my opinion, people think too much about the age thing. If taking your 3-year-old would make you happy, that's all that counts. End of story. It doesn't matter if the trip is really for you or your child—it's all good. You shouldn't have to jump through a bunch of hoops to give yourself permission to go.*

*uno**fficial* **TIP**
Traveling with infants and toddlers sharpens parenting skills and makes the entire family more mobile and flexible, resulting in a richer, fuller life for all.

Somewhere between 4 and 6 years of age, your child will experience the first vacation that he or she will remember as an adult. Though more likely to remember the coziness of the hotel room than the theme parks, the child will be able to experience and comprehend many attractions and will be a much fuller participant in your vacation. Even so, his or her favorite activity is likely to be swimming in the hotel pool.

As concerns infants and toddlers, there are good reasons and bad reasons for vacationing at Disneyland. A good reason for taking your little one to Disneyland Resort is that you want to go and there's no one available to care for your child during your absence. Philosophically, we are very much against putting your life (including your vacation) on hold until your children are older.

Especially if you have children of varying ages (or plan to, for that matter), it's better to take the show on the road than to wait until the youngest reaches the perceived ideal age. If your family includes a toddler or infant, you will find everything from private facilities for breast-feeding to changing tables in both men's and women's restrooms to facilitate baby's care. Your whole family will be able to tour together with fewer hassles than on a day's picnic outing at home.

An illogical reason, however, for taking an infant or toddler to Disneyland Resort is that you think Disneyland is the perfect vacation destination for babies. It's not, so think again if you are contemplating Disneyland Resort primarily for your child's enjoyment. For starters, attractions are geared more toward older children and adults. Even designer play areas such as the Pirate's Lair on Tom Sawyer Island in Disneyland Park are developed with older children in mind.

By way of example, Bob has a friend who bought a video camera when his first child was born. He delighted in documenting his son's reaction to various new experiences on video. One memorable night when the baby was about 18 months old, he recorded the baby eating a variety of foods (from whipped cream to dill pickles) that he had never tried before. While some of the taste sensations elicited wild expressions and animated responses from the baby, the exercise was clearly intended for the amusement of Dad, not junior.

That said, let us stress that for the well prepared, taking a toddler to Disneyland Resort can be a totally glorious experience. There's truly nothing like watching your child respond to the color, the sound, the festivity, and, most of all, the characters. You'll return home with scrapbooks of photos that you will treasure forever. Your little one won't remember much, but never mind. Your memories will be unforgettable.

unofficial **TIP** Baby supplies—including disposable diapers, formula, and baby food— are for sale, and rockers and special chairs are available for nursing mothers.

Along similar lines, remember when you were little and you got that nifty electric train for Christmas, the one with which Dad wouldn't let you play? Did you ever wonder for whom that train was really? Ask yourself the same question about your vacation to Disneyland Resort. Whose dream are you trying to make come true: yours or your child's?

If you elect to take your infant or toddler to Disneyland Resort, rest assured that their needs have been anticipated. The theme parks have centralized facilities for infant and toddler care. Everything necessary for changing diapers, preparing formula, and warming bottles and food is available. At the Disneyland Park, the Baby Center is next to the Plaza Inn at the end of Main Street and to the right. At DCA the Baby Center is tucked out of the way next to the Ghirardelli Chocolate Factory (opening in 2012) in the Pacific Wharf area of the park. Dads in charge of little ones are welcome at the centers and can use most services offered. In addition, men's rooms in the theme parks have changing tables.

Infants and toddlers are allowed to experience any attraction that doesn't have minimum height or age restrictions. But as a Minneapolis mother reports, some attractions are better for babies than others:

> Theater and boat rides are easier for babies (ours was almost 1 year old, not yet walking). Rides where there's a bar that comes down are doable, but harder. Peter Pan was our first encounter with this type, and we had barely gotten situated when I realized that he might fall out of my grasp. The [3-D] films are too intense; the noise level is deafening, and the images inescapable. You don't have a rating system for babies, and I don't expect to see one, but I thought you might want to know what a baby thought (based on his reactions).
>
> At the Park: Jungle Cruise—didn't get into it. Pirates—slept through it. Riverboat—the horn made him cry. Small World—wide-eyed, took it all in. Peter Pan—couldn't really sit on the seat. A bit dangerous. He didn't get into it. Railroad—liked the motion and scenery. Tiki Room—loved it. Danced, clapped, sang along.

The same mom also advises:

> We used a baby sling on our trip and thought it was great when standing in the lines—much better than a stroller, which you have to park before getting in line (and navigate through crowds). My baby was still nursing when we went. It is impractical to go to the baby station every time, so a nursing mom had better be comfortable about nursing in very public situations.

unofficial **TIP**
In addition to providing an alternative to carrying your child, a stroller serves as a handy cart for diaper bags, water bottles, and other necessary items.

Two points in our reader's comment warrant elaboration. First, the rental strollers at the theme parks are designed for toddlers and children up to 4 and 5 years old, but they're definitely not for infants. Still, if you bring pillows and padding, these strollers can be made to work. You can alternatively bring your own stroller, but unless it's collapsible, you will not be able to take it on Disney parking lot trams.

Even if you opt for a stroller (your own or a rental), we nevertheless recommend that you also bring a baby sling or baby/child backpack. Simply put, there will be many times in the theme parks when you will have to park the stroller and carry your child. As an aside, if you haven't checked out baby slings and packs lately, you'll be amazed by some of the technological advances made in these products.

The second point that needs addressing is our reader's perception that there are not many good places in the theme parks for breast-feeding unless you are accustomed to nursing in public. Many nursing moms recommend breast-feeding during a dark Disney theater presentation. This only works, however, if the presentation is long enough for the baby to finish nursing. Shows at the Hyperion Theater at DCA are long enough at about 45 minutes, but the theater is not as dark as those that show films. *Captain EO* at Disneyland Park is way too loud, as is *Muppet-Vision 3-D* at DCA.

Many Disney shows run back to back with only 1 or 2 minutes in between to change the audience. If you want to breast-feed and require more time than the length of the show, tell the cast member on entering that you want to breast-feed and ask if you can remain in the theater while your baby finishes.

If you can adjust to nursing in more public places with your breast and the baby's head covered with a shawl or some such, nursing will not be a problem at all. Even on the most crowded days, you can always find a back corner of a restaurant or a comparatively secluded park bench or garden spot to nurse.

unofficial **TIP**
Infants are easy travelers. As long as they are fed and comfortable, there is really no limit to what you can do when on the road with little ones. Food plus adequate rest is the perfect formula for happy babies.

Disneyland for 4-, 5-, and 6-year-olds

Kids in this age group vary immensely in their capacity to comprehend and enjoy Disneyland Resort. With this age group, the go/no-go decision is a judgment call. If your child is sturdy, easygoing, fairly adventuresome, and demonstrates a high degree of independence, the trip will probably work. On the other hand, if your child tires easily, is temperamental, or is a bit timid or reticent in embracing new experiences, you're much better off waiting a few years. Whereas the travel and sensory-overload problems of infants and toddlers can be addressed and (usually) remedied on the go, discontented 4- to 6-year-olds have the ability to stop a family dead in its tracks, as this mother of three from Cape May, New Jersey, attests:

My 5-year-old was scared pretty badly on Snow White's Scary Adventures our first day. From then on for the rest of the trip, we had to coax and reassure her before each and every ride before she would go. It was like pulling teeth.

If you have a retiring, clinging, and/or difficult 4- to 6-year-old who, for whatever circumstances, will be part of your group, you can sidestep or diminish potential problems with a bit of preparation. Even if your preschooler is plucky and game, the same prep measures (described later in this section) will enhance his or her experience and make life easier for the rest of the family.

Parents who understand that a visit with 4- to 6-year-old children is going to be more about the cumulative experience than about seeing it all will have a blast and wonderful memories of their children's amazement.

The Ideal Age

Although our readers report both successful trips as well as disasters with children of all ages, the consensus is that children's ages ideal for family compatibility and togetherness at Disneyland are 8–12 years. This age group is old enough, tall enough, and sufficiently stalwart to experience, understand, and appreciate practically all Disney attractions. Moreover, they are developed to the extent that they can get around the parks on their own steam without being carried or collapsing. Best of all, they are still young enough to enjoy being with Mom and Dad. From our experience, ages 10–12 are better than 8–9, though what you gain in maturity is at the cost of that irrepressible, wide-eyed wonder so prevalent in the 8- and 9-year-olds.

Disneyland for Teens

Teens love Disneyland, and for parents of teens, Disneyland Resort is a nearly perfect, albeit expensive, vacation choice. Although your teens might not be as wide-eyed and impressionable as their younger sibs, they are at an age where they can sample, understand, and enjoy practically everything Disneyland Resort has to offer.

For parents Disneyland Resort is a vacation destination where you can permit your teens an extraordinary amount of freedom. The entertainment is wholesome, the venues are safe, and the entire complex of hotels, theme parks, restaurants, and shopping is easily accessible on foot. Because most adolescents relish freedom, you may have difficulty keeping your teens with the rest of the family. Thus, if one of your objectives is to spend time with your teenage children during your Disneyland vacation, you will need to establish some clear-cut guidelines regarding togetherness and separateness before you leave home. Make your teens part of the discussion and try to meet them halfway in crafting a decision with which everyone can live. For your teens, touring on their own at Disneyland is tantamount to being independent in an exotic city. It's intoxicating, to say the least, and can be an excellent learning experience, if not a rite of passage. In any event, we're not suggesting that you just turn them loose. Rather, we are just attempting to sensitize you to the fact that for your teens, some transcendent issues are involved.

Most teens crave the company of other teens. If you have a solitary teen in your family, do not be surprised if he or she wants to invite a friend on your vacation. If you are invested in sharing intimate, quality time with your solitary teen, the presence of a friend will make this more difficult, if not impossible. However, if you turn down the request to bring a friend, be prepared to go the extra mile to be a companion to your teen at Disneyland. If you're a teen, it's not much fun to ride Space Mountain by yourself.

One specific issue that absolutely should be addressed before you leave home is what assistance (if any) you expect from your teen in regard to helping with younger children in the family. Once again, try to carve out a win-win compromise. Consider the case of the mother from Indiana who had a teenage daughter from an earlier marriage and two children under age 10 from a second marriage. After a couple of vacations where she thrust the unwilling teen into the position of being a surrogate parent to her stepsisters, the teen declined henceforth to participate in family vacations.

Some parents have written the *Unofficial Guide* asking if there are unsafe places at Disneyland Resort or places where teens simply should not be allowed to go. Although the answer depends more on your family values and the relative maturity of your teens than on Disneyland Resort, the basic answer is no. Though it's true that teens (or adults, for that matter) who are looking for trouble can find it anywhere, there is absolutely nothing at Disneyland Resort that could be construed as a precipitant or a catalyst. Be advised, however, that adults consume alcohol at most Disneyland Resort restaurants. Also, be aware that some of the movies available at the cinemas at Downtown Disney demand the same discretion you exercise when allowing your kids to see movies at home.

About INVITING *Your* CHILDREN'S FRIENDS

IF YOUR CHILDREN WANT TO INVITE FRIENDS on your Disneyland vacation, give your decision careful thought. There's more involved here than might be apparent. First, consider the logistics of numbers. Is there room in the car? Will you have to leave something at home that you had planned on taking to make room in the trunk for the friend's luggage? Will additional hotel rooms or a larger suite be required? Will the increased number of people in your group make it hard to get a table at a restaurant?

If you determine that you can logistically accommodate one or more friends, the next step is to consider how the inclusion of the friend will affect your group's dynamics. Generally speaking, the presence of a friend will make it harder to really connect with your own children. So if one of your vacation goals is an intimate bonding experience with your children, the addition of friends will possibly frustrate your attempts to realize that objective.

If family relationship building is not necessarily a primary objective of your vacation, it's quite possible that the inclusion of a friend will make life easier for you. This is especially true in the case of only children, who may otherwise depend exclusively on you to keep them happy and occupied. Having a friend along can take the pressure off and give you some much-needed breathing room.

If you decide to allow a friend to accompany you, limit the selection to children you know really well and whose parents you also know. Your Disneyland vacation is not the time to include "my friend Eddie from school" whom you've never met. Your children's friends who have spent time in your home will have a sense of your parenting style, and you will have a sense of their personality, behavior, and compatibility with your family. Assess the prospective child's potential to fit in well on a long trip. Is he or she polite, personable, fun to be with, and reasonably mature? Does he or she relate well to you and to the other members of your family?

Because a Disneyland vacation is not, for most of us, a spur-of-the-moment thing, you should have adequate time to evaluate potential candidate friends. A trip to the mall including a meal in a sit-down restaurant will tell you volumes about the friend. Likewise, inviting the friend to share dinner with the family and then spend the night will provide a lot of relevant information. Ideally this type of evaluation should take place early on in the normal course of family events, before you discuss the possibility of a friend joining you on your vacation. This will allow you to size things up without your child (or the friend) realizing that an evaluation is taking place.

By seizing the initiative, you can guide the outcome. Ann, a Redding, California, mom, for example, anticipated that her 12-year-old son would ask to take a friend on their vacation. As she pondered the various friends her son might propose, she came up with four names. One, an otherwise sweet child, had a medical condition that Ann felt unqualified to monitor or treat. A second friend was overly aggressive with younger children and was often socially inappropriate for his age. Two other friends, Chuck and Marty, with whom she had had a generally positive experience, were good candidates for the trip. After orchestrating some opportunities to spend time with each of the boys, she made her decision and asked her son, "Would you like to take Marty with us to Disneyland?" Her son was delighted, and Ann had diplomatically preempted having to turn down friends her son might have proposed.

unofficial **TIP**
We suggest that you arrange for the friend's parents to reimburse you after the trip for things such as restaurant meals and admissions. This is much easier than trying to balance the books after every expenditure.

We recommend that you do the inviting, instead of your child, and that the invitation be extended parent to parent (to avoid disappointment, you might want to sound out the friend's parent before broaching the issue with your child). Observing this recommendation will allow you to query the friend's parents concerning food preferences, any medical conditions, how discipline is administered in the friend's family, how the friend's parents feel about the way you administer discipline, and the parents' expectation regarding religious observations while their child is in your care.

Before you extend the invitation, give some serious thought to who pays for what. Make a specific proposal for financing the trip a part of your invitation, for example: "There's room for Marty in the hotel room, and transportation's no problem because we're driving. So we'll just need you to pick up Marty's meals, theme-park admissions, and spending money."

A **FEW WORDS** *for* **SINGLE PARENTS**

BECAUSE SINGLE PARENTS GENERALLY are also working parents, planning a special getaway with your children can be the best way to spend some quality time together. But remember, the vacation is not just for your child—it's for you too. You might invite a grandparent or a favorite aunt or uncle along; the other adult provides nice company for you, and your child will benefit from the time with family members. You might likewise consider inviting an adult friend.

Though bringing along an adult friend or family member is the best option, the reality is that many single parents don't have friends, grandparents, or favorite aunts or uncles who can make the trip. And while spending time with your child is wonderful, it is very difficult to match the energy level of your child if you are the sole focus of his or her world.

One alternative: Try to meet other single parents at Disneyland. It may seem odd, but most of them are in the same boat as you; besides, all you have to do is ask. Another option, albeit expensive, is to take along a trustworthy babysitter (18 or up) to travel with you.

The easiest way to meet other single parents is to hang out at the hotel pool. Make your way there on the day you arrive, after traveling by car or plane and without enough time to blow a full admission ticket at a theme park. In any event, a couple of hours spent poolside is a relaxing way to start your vacation.

If you visit Disneyland Resort with another single parent, get adjoining rooms; take turns watching all the kids; and, on at least one night, get a sitter and enjoy an evening out.

Throughout this book we mention the importance of good planning and touring. For a single parent, this is an absolute must. In addition, make sure that every day you set aside downtime back at the hotel.

Finally, don't try to spend every moment with your children on vacation. Instead, plan some activities for your children with other children. Then take advantage of your free time to do what you want to do: Read a book, have a massage, take a long walk, or enjoy a catnap.

"He Who Hesitates Is Launched!"
TIPS *and* WARNINGS
for GRANDPARENTS

SENIORS OFTEN GET INTO PREDICAMENTS caused by touring with grandchildren. Run ragged and pressured to endure a blistering pace, many seniors just concentrate on surviving Disneyland rather than enjoying it. The theme parks have as much to offer older visitors as they do children, and seniors must either set the pace or dispatch the young folks to tour on their own.

An older reader writes:

> *The main thing I want to say is that being a senior is not for wussies. At Disney [parks] particularly, it requires courage and pluck. Things that used to be easy take a lot of effort, and sometimes your brain has to wait for your body to catch up. Half the time, your grandchildren treat you like a crumbling ruin, amd then turn around and trick you into getting on a roller coaster in the dark. What you need to tell seniors is that they have to be alert and not trust anyone. Not their children or even the Disney people, and especially not their grandchildren. When your grandchildren want you to go on a ride, don't follow along blindly like a lamb to the slaughter. Make sure you know what the ride is all about. Stand your ground and do not waffle. He who hesitates is launched!*

If you don't get to see much of your grandchildren, you might think that Disneyland is the perfect place for a little bonding and togetherness. Wrong! Disneyland can potentially send children into system overload and precipitates behaviors that pose a challenge even to adoring parents, never mind grandparents. You don't take your grandchildren straight to Disneyland for the same reason you don't buy your 16-year-old son a Ferrari: Handling it safely and well requires some experience.

Begin by spending time with your grandchildren in an environment that you can control. Have them over one at a time for dinner and to spend the night. Check out how they respond to your oversight and discipline. Most of all, zero in on whether you are compatible, enjoy each other's company, and have fun together. Determine that you can set limits and that they will accept those limits. When you reach this stage, you can contemplate some outings to the zoo, the movies, the mall, or the state fair. Gauge how demanding your grandchildren are when you are out of the house. Eat a meal or two in a full-service restaurant to get a sense of their social skills and their ability to behave appropriately. Don't expect perfection, and be prepared to modify your behavior a little too. As a senior friend of mine told her husband (none too decorously), "You can't see Disneyland sitting on a stick."

If you have a good relationship with your grandchildren and have had a positive one-on-one experience taking care of them, you might consider a trip to Disneyland. If you do, we have two recommendations. Visit Disneyland without them to get an idea of what you're getting into. A scouting trip will also provide you an opportunity to enjoy some of the attractions that won't be on the itinerary when you return with the grandkids.

Tips for Grandparents

1. It's best to take one grandchild at a time, two at the most. Cousins can be better than siblings because they don't fight as much. To preclude sibling jealousy, try connecting the trip to a child's milestone, such as finishing the 6th grade.

2. Let your grandchildren help plan the vacation, and keep the first one short. Be flexible, and don't overplan.

3. Discuss mealtimes and bedtime. Fortunately, many grandparents are on an early dinner schedule, which works nicely with younger children.

4. Gear plans to your grandchildren's age levels, because if they're not happy, you won't be happy.

5. Create an itinerary that offers some supervised activities for children in case you need a rest.

6. If you're traveling by car, this is the one time we highly recommend earphones or earbuds. Kids' musical tastes are vastly different from most grandparents'. It's simply more enjoyable when everyone can listen to his or her own preferred style of music, at least for some portion of the trip.

7. Take along a night-light.

8. Carry a notarized statement from parents for permission for medical care in case of an emergency. Also be sure that you have insurance information and copies of any prescriptions for medicines the kids may take. Ditto for eyeglass prescriptions.

9. Tell your grandchildren about any medical problems you may have, so they can be prepared if there's an emergency.

10. Many attractions and hotels offer discounts for seniors, so be sure to check ahead of time for bargains.

11. Plan your evening meal early to avoid long waits. And make Priority Seatings if you're dining in a popular spot, even if it's early. Take some crayons and paper to keep kids occupied. If planning a family-friendly trip seems overwhelming, try a tour operator–travel agent aimed at kids and their grandparents.

HOW *to* CHILDPROOF *a* HOTEL ROOM

TODDLERS AND SMALL CHILDREN up to 3 years of age (and sometimes older) can wreak mayhem if not outright disaster in a hotel room. They're mobile, curious, and amazingly fast, and they have a penchant for turning the most seemingly innocuous furnishing or decoration into a lethal weapon. Chances are that you're pretty experienced when it comes to spotting potential dangers, but just in case you need a refresher course, here's what to look for.

Always begin by checking the room for hazards that you cannot neutralize, such as balconies, chipping paint, cracked walls, sharp surfaces, shag carpeting, and windows that can't be secured shut. If you encounter anything that you don't like or is too much of a hassle to fix, ask for another room.

If you use a crib supplied by the hotel, make sure that the mattress is firm and covers the entire bottom of the crib. If there is a mattress cover, it should fit tightly. Slats should be 2⅜ inches (about the width of a soda can) or less apart. Test the drop sides to ensure that they work properly and that your child cannot release them accidentally. Examine the crib from all angles (including from underneath) to make sure that it has been assembled correctly and that there are no sharp edges. Check for chipping paint and other potentially toxic substances that your child might ingest. Wipe down surfaces your child might touch to diminish the potential of infection transmitted from a previous occupant. Finally, position the crib away from drape cords, heaters, wall sockets, and air conditioners.

If your infant can turn over, we recommend changing him or her on a pad on the floor. Likewise, if you have a child seat of any sort, place it where it cannot be knocked over, and always strap your child in.

If your child can roll, crawl, or walk, you should bring about eight electrical outlet covers and some cord to tie cabinets shut and to bind drape cords and the like out of reach. Check for appliances, lamps, ashtrays, ice buckets, and anything else that your child might pull down on him- or herself. Have the hotel remove coffee tables with sharp edges, and both real and artificial plants that are within your child's reach. Round up items from table and countertops such as matchbooks, courtesy toiletries, and drinking glasses and store them out of reach.

If the bathroom door can be accidentally locked, cover the locking mechanism with duct tape or a doorknob cover. Use the security chain or upper latch on the room's entrance door to ensure that your child doesn't open it without your knowledge.

Inspect the floor and remove pins, coins, and other foreign objects that your child might find. Don't forget to check under beds and furniture. One of the best tips we've heard came from a Fort Lauderdale, Florida, mother who crawls around the room on her hands and knees in order to see possible hazards from her child's perspective.

If you rent a suite, you'll have more territory to childproof and will have to deal with the possible presence of cleaning supplies, a stove, a refrigerator, cooking utensils, and low cabinet doors, among other things. Sometimes the best option is to seal off the kitchen with a folding safety gate.

PHYSICAL PREPARATION

YOU'LL FIND THAT SOME PHYSICAL CONDITIONING, coupled with a realistic sense of the toll that Disneyland takes on your body, will preclude falling apart in the middle of your vacation. As one of our readers put it, "If you pay attention to eat, heat, feet, and sleep, you'll be OK."

As you contemplate the stamina of your family, it's important to understand that somebody is going to run out of steam first, and when they do, the whole family will be affected. Sometimes a cold drink or a snack will revive the flagging member. Sometimes, however, no amount of cajoling or treats will work. In this situation it's crucial that you recognize that the child, grandparent, or spouse is at the end of his or her rope. The correct decision is to get them back to the hotel. Pushing the exhausted beyond their capacity will spoil the day for them—and you. Accept that stamina and energy levels vary and be prepared to administer to members of your family who poop out. One more thing: no guilt trips. "We've driven 300 miles to take you to Disneyland and now you're going to ruin everything!" is not an appropriate response.

THE AGONY OF THE FEET

HERE'S A LITTLE FACTOID TO CHEW ON: If you spend a day at Disneyland Park, you will walk 3–6 miles! If you walk to the theme park from your hotel, you can add 1–2 miles, and tack on another couple of miles if you park hop over to DCA. The walking, however, will be nothing like a 5-mile hike in the woods. At Disneyland Park and DCA you will be in direct sunlight most of the time, have to navigate through huge jostling crowds, be walking on hot pavement, and have to endure waits in line between bursts of walking. The bottom line,

unofficial **TIP**
If your children (or you, for that matter) think that wearing socks isn't cool, get over it! Bare feet, whether encased in Nikes, Weejuns, Docksides, or Crocs, will turn into lumps of throbbing red meat if you tackle a Disney park without socks.

if you haven't figured it out, is that Disney theme parks (especially in the summer) are not for wimps!

Though most children are active, their normal play usually doesn't condition them for the exertion of touring a Disney theme park. We recommend starting a program of family walks 6 weeks or more before your trip. A Pennsylvania mom who did just that offers the following:

We had our 6-year-old begin walking with us a bit every day 1 month before leaving—when we arrived, her little legs could carry her and she had a lot of stamina.

A father of two had this to say:

My wife walked with my son to school every day when it was nice. His stamina was outstanding.

The first thing you need to do, immediately after making your hotel reservation, is to get thee to a footery. Take the whole family to a shoe store and buy each member the best pair of walking, hiking, or running shoes you can afford. When trying on the shoes, wear exactly the kind of socks that you will wear when using them to hike. Do not under any circumstances attempt to tour Disneyland shod in plastic sandals, cheap flip-flops, loafers, or any kind of high heel or platform shoe (though one of our authors swears by high-quality leather sandals or river-rafting footwear, especially for water rides).

Good socks are as important as good shoes. When you walk, your feet sweat like a mule in a peat bog, and moisture increases friction. To minimize friction, wear a pair of Smart-Wool or CoolMax hiking socks, available at most outdoor retail (camping equipment) stores, as well as Kmart and online retailers. To further combat moisture, dust your feet with some antifungal talcum powder.

unofficial **TIP**
Be sure to give your kids adequate recovery time between training walks (48 hours will usually be enough), however, or you'll make the problem worse.

Now that you have some good shoes and socks, the next thing to do is to break the shoes in. You can accomplish this painlessly by wearing the shoes in the course of normal activities for about 3 weeks.

Once the shoes are broken in, it's time to start walking. The whole family will need to toughen up their feet and build endurance. As you begin, remember that little people have little strides, and though your 6-year-old may create the appearance of running circles around you, consider that (1) he won't have the stamina to go at that pace very long, and (2) more to the point, he probably has to take two strides or so to every one of yours to keep up.

Start by taking short walks around the neighborhood, walking on pavement, and increasing the distance about 0.25 mile on each outing.

unofficial **TIP**
If your child is age 8 or younger, we recommend regular foot inspections whether he or she understands the hot-spot idea or not. Even the brightest and most well-intentioned child will fail to sound off when distracted.

Older children will shape up quickly. Younger children should build endurance more slowly and incrementally. Increase distance until you can manage a 6- or 7-mile hike without requiring CPR. And remember, you're not training to be able to walk 6–7 miles just once; at Disneyland you will be hiking 5–7 miles or more almost every day of your visit. So unless you plan to crash after the first day, you need to prepare your feet to walk long distances for 3–5 consecutive days.

Let's be honest and admit up front that not all feet are created equal. Some folks are blessed with really tough feet, whereas the feet of others sprout blisters if you look at them sideways. Assuming that there's nothing wrong with either shoes or socks, a few brisk walks will clue you in to what kind of feet the members of your family have. If you have a tenderfooted family member, walks of incrementally increased distances will usually toughen up his or her feet to some extent. For those whose feet refuse to toughen, your only alternative is preventive care. After several walks, you will know where your tenderfoot tends to develop blisters. If you can anticipate where blisters will develop, you can cover sensitive spots in advance with moleskin, a friction-resistant adhesive dressing.

When you initiate your walking program, teach your children to tell you if they feel a hot spot on their feet. This is the warning that a blister is developing. If your kids are too young, too oblivious, too preoccupied, or don't understand the concept, your best bet is to make regular foot checks. Have your children remove their shoes and socks and present their feet for inspection. Look for red spots and blisters, and ask if they have any places on their feet that hurt.

unofficial **TIP**
If you have a child who will physically fit in a stroller, rent one, no matter how well conditioned your family is.

During your conditioning, and also at Disneyland, carry a foot emergency kit in your day pack or hip pack. The kit should contain gauze, Betadine antibiotic ointment, moleskin and an assortment of Band-Aid Blister Bandages, scissors, a sewing needle or some such to drain blisters, as well as matches to sterilize the needle. An extra pair of dry socks and talc are optional.

If you discover a hot spot, dry the foot and cover the spot immediately with moleskin. Cut the covering large enough to cover the skin surrounding the hot spot. If you find that a blister has fully or partially developed, first air out and dry the foot. Next, using your sterile needle, drain the fluid but do not remove the top skin. Clean the area with your Betadine, and place a Band-Aid Blister Bandage over the blister. If you do not have moleskin or Band-Aid Blister Bandages, do not try to cover the hot spot or blister with regular Band-Aids. Regular Band-Aids slip and wad up.

A stroller will provide the child the option of walking or riding, and, if he poops out, you won't have to carry him. Even if your child hardly uses the stroller, it serves as a convenient place for water bottles and other stuff you may not feel like carrying. Strollers at Disneyland are covered in detail on pages 137–139.

SLEEP, REST, AND RELAXATION

OK, WE KNOW THAT THIS DISCUSSION is about physical preparation before you go, but this concept is so absolutely critical that we need to tattoo it on your brain right now.

Physical conditioning is important but is not a substitute for rest. Even marathon runners need recovery time. If you push too hard and try to do too much, you'll either crash or, at a minimum, turn what should be fun into an ordeal. Rest means plenty of sleep at night and,

unofficial **TIP**
If your kids are little and don't mind a hairdo change, consider getting them a short haircut before you leave home. Not only will they be cooler and more comfortable, but—especially with your girls—you'll save them (and yourselves) the hassle of tangles and about 20 minutes of foo-fooing a day.

if possible, naps during the afternoon and planned breaks in your vacation itinerary. And don't forget that the brain needs rest and relaxation as well as the body. The stimulation inherent in touring a Disney theme park is enough to put many children and some adults into system overload. It is imperative that you remove your family from this unremitting assault on the senses and do something relaxing and quiet such as swimming or reading.

The theme parks are pretty big, so don't try to see everything in 1 day. Even during the off-season, when the crowds are smaller and the temperatures more pleasant, the size of the theme parks will exhaust most children under age 8 by lunchtime. A Texas family underscores the importance of naps and rest:

Despite not following any of your "tours," we did follow the theme of visiting a specific park in the morning, leaving midafternoon for either a nap back at the room or a trip to the pool, and then returning to one of the parks in the evening. On the few occasions when we skipped your advice, I was muttering to myself by dinner. I can't tell you what I was muttering. . . .

When it comes to naps, this mom does not mince words:

One last thing for parents of small kids—take the book's advice and get out of the park and take the nap, take the nap, TAKE THE NAP! Never in my life have I seen so many parents screaming at, ridiculing, or slapping their kids. (What a vacation!) Disney [parks are] overwhelming for kids and adults.

A mom from Rochester, New York, was equally adamant:

[You] absolutely must rest during the day. Kids went from 8 a.m.– 9 p.m. in the park. Kids did great that day, but we were all completely worthless the next day. Definitely must pace yourself.

If you plan to return to your hotel at midday and would like your room made up, let housekeeping know.

Routines That Travel

If when at home you observe certain routines—for example, reading a book before bed or having a bath first thing in the morning—try to incorporate these familiar activities into your vacation schedule. They will provide your children with a sense of security and normalcy.

Maintaining a normal routine is especially important with toddlers, as a mother of two from Lawrenceville, Georgia, relates:

The first day, we tried an early start, so we woke the children (ages 2 and 4) and hurried them to get going. BAD IDEA with toddlers. This put them off schedule for naps and meals the rest of the day. It is best to let young ones stay on their regular schedule and see Disney at their own pace, and you'll have much more fun.

DEVELOPING *a* GOOD PLAN

ALLOW YOUR CHILDREN to participate in the planning of your time at Disneyland. Guide them diplomatically through the options, establishing advance decisions about what to do each day and how the day will be structured. Begin with your trip to Disneyland, deciding what time to depart, who sits by the window, whether to stop for meals or eat in the car, and so on. For the Disneyland part of your vacation, build consensus for wake-up call, bedtime, and building naps into the itinerary, and establish ground rules for eating, buying refreshments, and shopping. Determine the order for visiting the two theme parks and make a list of must-see attractions. To help you fill in the blanks of your days, and especially to prevent you from spending most of your time standing in line, we offer a number of field-tested touring plans. The plans are designed to minimize your waiting time at each park by providing step-by-step itineraries that route you counter to the flow of traffic. The plans are explained in greater detail starting on page 73.

Generally, it's better to just sketch in the broad strokes on the master plan. The detail of what to do when you actually arrive at the park can be decided the night before you go, or with the help of one of our touring plans once you get there. Above all, be flexible. One important caveat: Make sure that you keep any promises or agreements that you make when planning. They may not seem important to you, but they will to your children, who will remember for a long, long time that you let them down.

The more you can agree to and nail down in advance, the less potential you'll have for disagreement and confrontation once you arrive. Because children are more comfortable with the tangible than the conceptual, and also because they sometimes have short memories, we recommend typing up all of your decisions and agreements and providing a copy to each child. Create a fun document, not a legalistic one. You'll find that your children will review it in anticipation of all the things they will see and do, will consult it often, and will even read it to their younger siblings.

unofficial **TIP**
To keep your thinking fresh and to adequately cover all bases, develop your plan in two or three family meetings no longer than 40 minutes each. You'll discover that all members of the family will devote a lot of thought to the plan both in and between meetings. Don't try to anticipate every conceivable contingency, or you'll end up with something as detailed and unworkable as the tax code.

By now you're probably wondering what one of these documents looks like, so we've provided a sample on pages 122–123. Incidentally, this itinerary reflects the preferences of its creators, the Shelton family, and is not meant to be offered as an example of an ideal itinerary. It does, however, incorporate many of our most basic and strongly held recommendations, such as setting limits and guidelines in advance, getting enough rest, getting to the theme parks early, and

SHELTON FAMILY ITINERARY

DAY 1: FRIDAY

6:30 p.m.	Dinner
After dinner	Pack car
10 p.m.	Lights out

DAY 2: SATURDAY

7 a.m.	Wake up!
7:15 a.m.	Breakfast
8 a.m.	Depart Portland for Hampton Inn Oakland–Hayward; Confirmation #DE56432; Lynn rides shotgun
About noon	Stop for lunch; Jimmy picks restaurant
7 p.m.	Dinner
9:30 p.m.	Lights out

DAY 3: SUNDAY

7 a.m.	Wake up!
7:30 a.m.	Breakfast
8:15 a.m.	Depart Oakland for Disneyland, Disneyland Hotel; Confirmation #L124532; Jimmy rides shotgun
About noon	Stop for lunch; Lynn picks restaurant
5 p.m.	Check in, buy park admissions, and unpack
6–7 p.m.	Mary and Jimmy shop for breakfast food for cooler
7:15 p.m.	Dinner at Rainforest Cafe at Downtown Disney
After dinner	Explore Downtown Disney
10 p.m.	Lights out

DAY 4: MONDAY

7 a.m.	Wake up! Cold breakfast from cooler in room
8 a.m.	Depart room for Disneyland Park
Noon	Lunch at park
1 p.m.	Return to hotel for swimming and a nap
5 p.m.	Return to park for touring, dinner, and *Fantasmic!*
9:30 p.m.	Return to hotel
10:30 p.m.	Lights out

DAY 5: TUESDAY

7 a.m.	Wake up! Cold breakfast from cooler in room
7:45 a.m.	Depart room for DCA
Noon	Lunch at park
2:30 p.m.	Return to hotel for swimming and a nap

DAY 5: TUESDAY (CONTINUED)

6 p.m.	Drive to dinner at Outback Steakhouse
7:30 p.m.	Return to DCA for touring
10 p.m.	Return to hotel
11 p.m.	Lights out

DAY 6: WEDNESDAY

ZZZZZZ!	Lazy morning—sleep in!
10:30 a.m.	Late-morning swim
Noon	Check out of Disneyland Hotel
1 p.m.	Fast food lunch
1:45 p.m.	Depart Anaheim for Hollywood; Sheraton Universal; Confirmation #3542986X; Lynn rides shotgun
7:30 p.m.	Dinner at Universal CityWalk
9:15 p.m.	Return to hotel
10:30 p.m.	Lights out

DAY 7: THURSDAY

7 a.m.	Wake up! Cold breakfast from cooler in room
7:45 a.m.	Depart for Universal Studios
11:30 a.m.	Lunch at park
4:45 p.m.	Return to hotel for downtime
7:30 p.m.	Dinner at Asakuma Rice, 14543 Ventura Blvd., Sherman Oaks
10 p.m.	Return to hotel
11:45 p.m.	Lights out

DAY 8: FRIDAY

7:30 a.m.	Wake up!
8:30 a.m.	After fast-food breakfast, depart for Vagabond Inn Executive, Old Town Sacramento; Confirmation #SD234; Jimmy rides shotgun
About noon	Stop for lunch; Lynn picks restaurant
7 p.m.	Dinner
10 p.m.	Lights out

DAY 9: SATURDAY

7 a.m.	Wake up!
7:45 a.m.	Depart for home after fast-food breakfast; Lynn rides shotgun
About noon	Stop for lunch; Jimmy picks restaurant
5:30 p.m.	Home sweet home!

saving time and money by having a cooler full of food for breakfast. As you will see, the Sheltons go pretty much full-tilt without much unstructured time and will probably be exhausted by the time they get home, but that's their choice. One more thing—the Sheltons visited Disneyland in late June, when all of the theme parks stay open late.

Notice that the Sheltons' itinerary on pages 122–123 provides minimum structure and maximum flexibility. It specifies which park the family will tour each day without attempting to nail down exactly what the family will do there. No matter how detailed your itinerary is, be prepared for surprises at Disneyland, both good and bad. If an unforeseen event renders part of the plan useless or impractical, just roll with it. And always remember that it's your itinerary; you created it, and you can change it. Just try to make any changes the result of family discussion and be especially careful not to scrap an element of the plan that your children perceive as something you promised them.

THE GREAT DISNEYLAND EXPEDITION

CO-CAPTAINS Mary and Jack Shelton

TEAM MEMBERS Lynn and Jimmy Shelton

EXPEDITION FUNDING The main Expedition Fund will cover everything except personal purchases. Each team member will receive $40 for souvenirs and personal purchases. Anything above $40 will be paid for by team members with their own money.

EXPEDITION GEAR Each team member will wear an official expedition T-shirt and carry a hip pack.

PRE-DEPARTURE Jack makes Priority Seating arrangements at Disneyland restaurants. Mary, Lynn, and Jimmy make up trail mix and other snacks for the hip packs.

LOGISTIC PREPARATION

WHEN WE RECENTLY LAUNCHED into our spiel about good logistic preparation for a Disneyland vacation, a friend from Phoenix said, "Wait, what's the big deal? You pack clothes, a few games for the car, then go!" So OK, we confess, that will work, but life can be sweeter and the vacation smoother (as well as less expensive) with the right gear.

CLOTHING

LET'S START WITH CLOTHES. We recommend springing for vacation uniforms. Buy for each child several sets of jeans (or shorts) and T-shirts, all matching, and all the same. For a 1-week trip, for example, get each child three pairs of khaki shorts, three light-yellow T-shirts, and three pairs of SmartWool or CoolMax hiking socks. What's the point? First, you don't have to play fashion designer, coordinating a week's worth of stylish combos. Each morning the kids put on their uniform. It's simple, it saves time, and there are no decisions to make or arguments about what to wear. Second, uniforms make your children easier to spot and keep together in the theme parks. Third, the uniforms give your family, as well as the vacation itself, some added identity. If you're like the Shelton family who created the sample itinerary in the previous section, you might go so far as to create a logo for the trip to be printed on the shirts.

When it comes to buying your uniforms, we have a few suggestions. Purchase well-made, durable shorts or jeans that will serve your children well beyond the vacation. Active children can never have too many pairs of shorts or jeans. As far as the T-shirts go, buy short-sleeve shirts in light colors for warm weather, or long-sleeve, darker-colored T-shirts for cooler weather. We suggest that you purchase your colored shirts from a local T-shirt printing company. Cleverly listed under "T-shirts" (sometimes under "Screen Printing") in the Yellow Pages, these firms will be happy to sell you either printed T-shirts or unprinted T-shirts (called "blanks") with long or short sleeves. You can select from a wide choice of colors not generally available in retail clothing stores and will not have to worry about finding the sizes you need. Plus, the shirts will cost a fraction of what a clothing retailer would charge. Most shirts come in the more durable 100% cotton or in the more wrinkle-resistant 50% cotton and 50% polyester (50–50s). The cotton shirts are a little cooler and more comfortable in hot, humid weather. The 50–50s dry a bit faster if they get wet.

unofficial **TIP**
Give your teens the job of coming up with the logo for your shirts. They will love being the family designers.

LABELS A great idea, especially for younger children, is to attach labels with your family name, hometown, the name of your hotel, the dates of your stay, and your cell phone number inside the shirt—for example:

HODDER FAMILY OF DENVER, CO.; CAMELOT INN; MAY 5–12; 303-662-2108

Instruct your smaller children to show the label to an adult if they get separated from you. Elimination of the child's first name (which most children of talking age can articulate in any event) allows you to order labels that are all the same, that can be used by anyone in the family, and that can also be affixed to such easily lost items as caps, hats, jackets, hip packs, ponchos, and umbrellas. If fooling with labels sounds like too much of a hassle, check out "Lost Children" (see page 154) for some alternatives.

DRESSING FOR COOLER WEATHER Southern California experiences temperatures all over the scale November–March, so it could be a bit chilly if you visit during those months. Our suggestion is to layer: for example, a breathable, waterproof or water-resistant Windbreaker over a light, long-sleeved polypro shirt over a long-sleeved T-shirt. As with the baffles of a sleeping bag or down coat, it is the air trapped between the layers that keeps you warm. If all the layers are thin, you won't be left with something bulky to cart around if you want to pull off one or more. Later in this section, we'll advocate wearing a hip pack. Each layer should be sufficiently compatible to fit easily in that hip pack along with whatever else is in it.

ACCESSORIES

I (BOB) WANTED TO CALL THIS PART "Belts and Stuff," but our editor (who obviously spends a lot of time at Macy's) thought "Accessories" put a finer point on it. In any event, we recommend pants for your children with reinforced elastic waistbands that eliminate the need to wear a belt (one less thing to find when you're trying to leave). If your children like belts or want to carry an item suspended from their belts, buy them military-style 1½-inch-wide web belts at any Army–Navy surplus or camping-equipment store. The belts weigh less than half as much as leather, are cooler, and are washable.

SUNGLASSES Smog notwithstanding, the California sun is so bright and the glare so blinding that we recommend sunglasses for each family member. For children and adults of all ages, a good accessory item is a polypro eyeglass strap for spectacles or sunglasses. The best models have a little device for adjusting the amount of slack in the strap. This allows your child to comfortably hang sunglasses from his or her neck when indoors or, alternately, to secure them fast to his or her head while experiencing a fast ride outdoors.

HIP PACKS AND WALLETS Unless you are touring with an infant or toddler, the largest thing anyone in your family should carry is a hip pack, or fanny pack. Each adult and child should have one. They should be large enough to carry at least a half-day's worth of snacks as well as other items deemed necessary (lip balm, bandanna, antibacterial hand gel, and so on) and still have enough room left to stash a hat, poncho, or light Windbreaker. We recommend buying full-size hip packs at outdoor retailers as opposed to small, child-size hip packs. The packs are light; can be made to fit any child large enough to tote a hip pack; have slip-resistant, comfortable, wide belting; and will last for years.

unofficial **TIP**
Equip each child with a big bandanna. Although bandannas come in handy for wiping noses, scouring ice cream from chins and mouths, and dabbing sweat from the forehead, they can also be tied around the neck to protect from sunburn.

Do not carry billfolds or wallets, car keys, Disney Resort IDs, or room keys in your hip packs. We usually give this advice because hip packs are vulnerable to thieves (who snip them off and run), but pickpocketing and theft are not all that common at Disneyland. In this instance, the advice stems from a tendency of children to inadvertently drop their wallet in the process of rummaging around in their hip packs for snacks and other items.

You should weed through your billfold and remove to a safe place anything that you will not need on your vacation (family photos, local library card, department store credit cards, business cards, movie-rental ID cards, and so on). In addition to having a lighter wallet to lug around, you will decrease your exposure in the event that your wallet is lost or stolen. When we are working at Disneyland, we carry a small profile billfold with a driver's license, a credit card, our room key, and a small amount of cash. Think about it: You don't need anything else.

DAY PACKS   We see a lot of folks at Disneyland carrying day packs (that is, small, frameless backpacks) and/or water bottle belts that strap around your waist. Day packs might be a good choice if you plan to carry a lot of camera equipment or if you need to carry baby supplies on your person. Otherwise, try to travel as light as possible. Packs are hot, cumbersome, not very secure, and must be removed every time you get on a ride or sit down for a show. Hip packs, by way of contrast, can simply be rotated around the waist from your back to your abdomen if you need to sit down. Additionally, our observation has been that the contents of one day pack can usually be redistributed to two or so hip packs (except in the case of camera equipment).

CAPS   Kids pull caps on and off as they enter and exit attractions, restrooms, and restaurants, and—big surprise—they lose them. In fact, they lose them by the thousands. You could provide a ball cap for every Little Leaguer in California from the caps that are lost at Disneyland each summer.

If your children are partial to caps, a device sold at ski and camping supply stores might increase the likelihood of the cap returning home with the child. Essentially, it's a short, light cord with little alligator clips on both ends. Hook one clip to the shirt collar and the other to the hat. It's a great little invention. Bob uses one when he skis in case his ball cap blows off.

RAINGEAR   Rain is a fact of life, though persistent rain day after day is unusual. Check out the Weather Channel or weather forecasts on the Internet for 3 or so days before you leave home to see if there are any major storm systems heading for Southern California. Weather forecasting has improved to the extent that predictions concerning systems and fronts 4–7 days out are now pretty reliable. If it appears that you might see some rough weather during your visit, you're better off bringing raingear from home. If, however, nothing big is on the horizon weatherwise, you can take your chances.

We at the *Unofficial Guides* usually do not bring raingear. Raingear is pretty cheap at Disneyland, especially the ponchos for about $7 adults, $6 child, available in seemingly every retail shop, and it's even cheaper at local discount stores (such as Kmart). Moreover, in the theme parks, a surprising number of attractions and queuing areas are under cover. Finally, we prefer to travel light.

Respect for the Sun

Health and science writer **Avery Hurt** sheds some light on the often confusing products and methods for avoiding sunburn.

No matter what time of year you make your trip, don't make the mistake of underestimating the Southern California sun. Even in winter, it can be a problem. And in the summer, old Sol can be wicked, indeed.

The most obvious precaution is to slather on the sunscreen. But when you get to the drugstore to load up, you may discover that choosing a product is anything but simple. Cream? Lotion? Spray? Waterproof or not? And what's this SPF number all about anyway?

The problem of making sense of sunscreens is so complex that it has precipitated lawsuits, required the amendment (and re-amendment) of FDA regulations, and confused officials almost as much as consumers. Sunscreen manufacturers, the FDA, and all of the lawyers may have plenty of time to duke it out, but you have a trip planned! Don't worry. It's not as complicated as it seems. Here's the basic advice from the medical experts.

Choose a sunscreen that is convenient for you to use. Some prefer sprays, others lotions. The form of the sunscreen doesn't matter as much as the technique of applying it. Apply sunscreen 30 minutes before going out, and be sure to get enough on you. One ounce per application is recommended—that means a full shot glass worth each time you apply. The 1-ounce amount was calculated for average adults in swimsuits; larger adults will need proportionately more. For a 1-year-old child wearing a bathing suit, figure about one-third of an ounce (10 cc) per application. An average 7-year-old will probably take two-thirds of an ounce (20 cc). It's a good idea to measure that ounce in your hands (at home, when an ounce measure—shot glass or whatever—is handy), so that you will be familiar with what an ounce looks like in your palms. It really is far more sunscreen than you tend to think.

Don't miss any spots. A few years ago, a group of researchers from Berlin journeyed to the beach to measure how well covered beachgoers really

If you do find yourself in a big storm, however, you'll want to have both a poncho and an umbrella. As one *Unofficial* reader puts it, "Umbrellas make the rain much more bearable. When rain isn't beating down on your ponchoed head, it's easier to ignore."

And consider this tip from a Memphis, Tennessee, mom:

Scotchgard your shoes. The difference is unbelievable.

MISCELLANEOUS ITEMS

MEDICATION Some parents of hyperactive children on medication discontinue or decrease the child's normal dosage at the end of the school year. If you have such a child, be aware that the Disneyland parks might were. It turned out that even the most dedicated sunscreen users did an abysmal job of applying their chosen brand. Most areas of skin were only sparsely covered, and areas such as the ears and the tops of feet were hardly covered at all. Be sure and get a generous covering on all exposed skin. Then reapply (another full shot glass) every 2 hours or after swimming or sweating. No matter what it says on the label, no sunscreen is waterproof, and water resistance is limited. And none of them last all day.

MAKING SENSE OF SPF

SPF stands for "sun protection factor" and is a measure of how long the protection will last. Geniuses in lab coats come up with this number by calculating how long it will take a person to burn without sunscreen (please don't volunteer me for that study) and comparing that to how long the same person takes to burn with sunscreen. Theoretically, a sunscreen with an SPF of 15 will protect you 15 times longer than if you wore no sunscreen at all.

This might make it sound like the higher the SPF the better, but studies have not borne that out. The effect diminishes as the number gets higher, and the initial estimate doesn't take into account the fact that during the day your sunscreen rubs off, washes off, and sweats off. In actual practice, there is very little difference in protection between 15 or so SPF and 45 or 50 or greater. There is no need to spend more for higher SPF numbers. In fact, it is much safer to choose a lower (and typically less expensive) SPF (as long as it is at least 15) and apply it more often. The American Academy of Dermatology (AAD) recommends an SPF of at least 30. Paying more for a higher SPF will give you very little more protection, and the false sense of security that comes with a 45 or 50 SPF may do more harm than the slight increase in protection. However, do be sure to choose a product that has broad-spectrum coverage, meaning that it filters out both UVA and UVB rays.

(continued on next page)

overly stimulate him or her. Consult your physician before altering your child's medication regimen. Also, if your child has attention-deficit disorder, remember that especially loud sounds can drive him or her right up the wall. Unfortunately, some Disney theater attractions are almost unbearably loud.

SUNSCREEN Overheating and sunburn are among the most common problems of younger children at Disneyland. Carry and use sunscreen of SPF 15 or higher. Be sure to put some on kids in strollers, even if the stroller has a canopy. Some of the worst cases of sunburn we've seen were on the

unofficial **TIP**
Often little ones fall asleep in their strollers (hallelujah!). Bring a large lightweight cloth to drape over the stroller to cover your child from the sun. A few clothespins will keep it in place.

Respect for the Sun (continued)

CHILDREN AND THE SUN

It is best to keep babies under 6 months covered and out of the sun. However, the American Academy of Pediatrics condones a small amount of sunscreen on vulnerable areas, such as the nose and chin, when you have your baby out. Be very careful to monitor your baby even if he is wearing a hat and sitting under an umbrella. The sun moves. A spot that was shady when you ordered your funnel cake might be baking by the time you've finished eating it. If your child develops a rash while using sunscreen, get the baby out of the sun, stop using the sunscreen, and call your doctor.

With older children, slather liberally and often. Don't make the mistake of thinking that because you've coated your children in a bazillion-SPF-water-resistant-all-day-protection-top-of-the-line brand sunscreen that you don't have to worry until dinnertime. Reapply and check for redness often. Sunburn can be sneaky. Children aren't likely to notice the mild discomfort of impending sunburn, especially when they are having fun. Check them often and get them out of the sun as soon as you see even slight redness. You don't have to pay extra for special formulas made for children. As long as the SPF is at least 30 and offers broad-spectrum protection, one brand can serve the whole family.

NOT JUST SKIN DEEP

It is just as important to protect the eyes and lips as the skin. Using a lip gloss with an SPF of 15 is pretty easy to do but also easy to forget. Keep several tubes

exposed foreheads and feet of toddlers and infants in strollers. Protect skin from overexposure. To avoid overheating, rest regularly in the shade or in an air-conditioned restaurant or show.

WATER BOTTLES Don't count on keeping young children hydrated with soft drinks and stops at water fountains. Long lines may impede buying refreshments, and fountains may not be handy. Furthermore, excited children may not realize or tell you that they're thirsty or hot. We recommend renting a stroller for children age 6 and younger and carrying plastic bottles of water and sports drinks. Bottled water runs about $3 in all major parks, or bring your own water bottle and strap from home.

unofficial **TIP**
About 2 weeks before arriving, ship a box to your hotel containing food, plastic cutlery, and toiletries, plus pretty much any other consumables that might come in handy during your stay. If you fly, this helps avoid overweight fees and problems with liquid restrictions for carry-on luggage.

COOLERS AND MINI-FRIDGES If you drive to Disneyland, bring two coolers: a small one for drinks in the car and a large one for the hotel room. If you fly and rent a car, stop and purchase a large Styrofoam cooler, which can be discarded at the end of the trip. If you will be without a car, book a hotel with mini-fridges in in your bag or pocket and reapply often to your own lips and those of your kids. Again, the brand is less important than choosing something that you will use—and remembering to use it.

Sunglasses are also a must. Too much sun exposure can contribute to age-related macular degeneration (among other things). This may not seem much of an issue when you are young and healthy, but when you get old and go blind, you'll wish that you had remembered to put on some shades. Not all sunglasses filter out damaging rays. Be sure to choose shades (for adults and kids) that have 99% UV protection. Large lenses and wraparound styles might not look as cool, but they offer much better protection. You may have to spend a little more to be sure that you are getting adequate protection, but you don't want to skimp on this. Much of the damage to the eyes from too much sun is irreversible and, like sun damage to the skin, it starts accumulating in childhood.

If you do slip up and get a burn, cool baths, aloe gels, and ibuprofen (or for adults, aspirin) usually help ease the suffering. Occasionally sunburns can be as dangerous in the short-term as they are in the long-term. If you or your child experience nausea, vomiting, high fever, severe pain, confusion, or fainting, seek medical care immediately.

All of the above is important—and sunscreen is a must if you are headed to Disneyland after a nice, cushy winter indoors in less-sun-drenched climes—but don't let that little bottle with its inscrutable numbers get you off your guard. You still need to wear a hat and stay well-hydrated.

each room. If mini-fridges aren't provided, rent one from the hotel.

Coolers and mini-fridges allow you to have breakfast in your hotel room, store snacks and lunch supplies to take to the theme parks, and supplant expensive vending machines for snacks and beverages at the hotel. To keep the contents of your cooler cold, freeze a 2-gallon milk jug full of water before you head out. In a good cooler, it will take the jug 5 or more days to thaw. If you buy a Styrofoam cooler, you can use bagged ice and ice from the ice machine at your hotel. Even if you have to rent a mini-fridge, you will save a bundle of cash as well as significant time by reducing dependence on restaurant meals and expensive snacks and drinks purchased from vendors.

FOOD-PREP KIT If you plan to make sandwiches, bring along your favorite condiments and seasonings from home. A typical travel kit will include mayonnaise, ketchup, mustard, salt and pepper, and packets of sugar or artificial sweetener. Also throw in some plastic knives and spoons, paper napkins, plastic cups, and a box of zip-top plastic bags. For breakfast you will need some plastic bowls for cereal. Of course, you can buy this stuff in Anaheim, but you probably won't consume it all, so why waste the money? If you drink bottled beer or wine, bring a bottle opener and corkscrew.

ENERGY BOOSTERS Kids get cranky when they're hungry, and when that happens, your entire group has a problem. Like many parents you might, for nutritional reasons, keep a tight rein on snacks available to your children at home. At Disneyland, however, maintaining energy and equanimity trumps between-meal snack discipline. For maximum zip and contentedness, give your kids snacks containing complex carbohydrates (fruits, crackers, nonfat energy bars, and the like) before they get hungry or show signs of exhaustion. You should avoid snacks that are high in fats and proteins because these foods take a long time to digest and will tend to unsettle your stomach if it's a hot day.

ELECTRONICS Regardless of your children's ages, always bring a night-light. Flashlights are also handy for finding stuff in a dark hotel room after the kids are asleep.

MP3 players and iPods with earphones, as well as some electronic games, are often controversial gear for a family outing. We recommend compromise. Earphones allow kids to create their own space even when they're with others, and that can be a safety valve. That said, try to agree before the trip on some earphone parameters, so you don't begin to feel as if they're being used to keep other family members and the trip itself at a distance. If you're traveling by car, take turns choosing the radio station or CD for part of the trip.

Likewise, mobile phones are a mixed blessing. On the one hand, they can be invaluable in an emergency or if your party wants to split up, and if you have a smartphone, you can use our Lines app to see current wait times throughout the parks. Unfortunately, they also lead to guests missing out on what's around them and bumping into each other because they're glued to a tiny screen. If you bring yours, consider disabling high-speed Internet to save on batteries since public charging locations are few and far between.

DON'T FORGET THE TENT This is not a joke and has nothing to do with camping. When Bob's daughter was preschool age, he almost went crazy trying to get her to sleep in a shared hotel room. She was accustomed to having her own room at home and was hyperstimulated whenever she traveled. Bob tried makeshift curtains and room dividers and even rearranged the furniture in a few hotel rooms to create the illusion of a more private, separate space for her. It was all for naught. It wasn't until she was around 4 years old and Bob took her camping that he seized on an idea that had some promise. She liked the cozy, secure, womblike feel of a backpacking tent and quieted down much more readily than she ever had in hotel rooms. So the next time the family stayed in a hotel, he pitched his backpacking tent in the corner of the room. In she went, nested for a bit, and fell asleep.

Since the time of Bob's daughter's childhood, there has been an astounding evolution in tent design. Responding to the needs of climbers and paddlers who often have to pitch tents on rocks (where it's impossible to drive stakes), tent manufacturers developed a broad range of tents with self-supporting frames that can be erected virtually any-where without ropes or stakes. Affordable and sturdy, many are as simple to put up as opening an umbrella. So if your child is too young for a room of his or her own or you can't afford a second hotel room, try pitching a small tent. Modern tents are self-contained with floors and an entrance that can be zipped up (or not) for privacy but cannot be locked. Kids appreciate having their own space and enjoy the adventure of being in a tent, even one set up in the corner of a hotel room. Sizes range from children's "play tents" with a 2- to 3-foot base to models large enough to sleep two or three husky teens. Light and compact when stored, a two-adult-size tent in its own storage bag (called a "stuff sack") will take up about one-tenth or less of a standard overhead bin on a commercial airliner. Another option for infants and toddlers is to drape a sheet over a portable crib or playpen to make a tent.

THE BOX Bob here: On one memorable Disneyland excursion when my children were younger, we began each morning with an immensely annoying, involuntary scavenger hunt. Invariably, seconds before our scheduled departure to the theme park, we discovered that some combination of shoes, billfolds, sunglasses, hip packs, or other necessities were unaccountably missing. For the next 15 minutes we would root through the room like pigs hunting truffles in an attempt to locate the absent items. Now I don't know about your kids, but when my kids lost a shoe or something, they always searched where it was easiest to look, as opposed to where the lost article was most likely to be. I would be jammed under a bed feeling around while my children stood in the middle of the room intently inspecting the ceiling. As my friends will tell you, I'm as open to a novel theory as the next guy, but we never did find any shoes on the ceiling. Anyway, here's what I finally did: I swung by a local store and mooched a big empty box. From then on, every time we returned to the room, I had the kids deposit shoes, hip packs, and other potentially wayward items in the box. After that the box was off-limits until the next morning, when I doled out the contents.

PLASTIC GARBAGE BAGS At the Grizzly River Run raft ride at DCA and Splash Mountain in Disneyland Park, you are certain to get wet and possibly soaked. If it's really hot and you don't care, then fine. But if it's cool or you're just not up for a soaking, bring a large plastic trash bag or a cheap poncho to the park. By cutting holes in the top and on the sides, you can fashion a sack poncho that will keep your clothes from getting wet. On the raft ride, you will also get your feet wet. If you're not up for walking around in squishing, soaked shoes, bring a second, smaller plastic bag to wear over your feet while riding.

SUPPLIES FOR INFANTS AND TODDLERS

BASED ON RECOMMENDATIONS from hundreds of *Unofficial Guide* readers, here's what we suggest that you carry with you when touring with infants and toddlers:

- A disposable diaper for every hour you plan to be away from your hotel
- A cloth diaper or kitchen towel to put over your shoulder for burping
- Two receiving blankets: one to wrap the baby, one to lay the baby on or to drape over you when you nurse
- Ointment for diaper rash
- A package of wipes
- Prepared formula in bottles if you are not breast-feeding
- A washable bib, baby spoon, and baby food if your infant is eating solids
- For toddlers, a small toy for comfort and to keep them occupied during attractions

Baby-care centers at the theme parks will sell you just about anything that you forget or run out of. Like all things Disney, prices will be higher than elsewhere, but at least you won't need to detour to a drugstore in the middle of your touring day.

REMEMBERING *Your* TRIP

1. Purchase a notebook for each child and spend time each evening recording the day's events. If your children have trouble getting motivated or don't know what to write about, start a discussion; otherwise, let them write or draw whatever they want to remember from the day.

2. Collect mementos along the way and create a treasure box in a small tin or cigar box. Months or years later, it's fun to look at postcards, pins, seashells, or ticket stubs to jump-start a memory.

3. Add inexpensive postcards to your photographs to create an album; then write a few words on each page to accompany the images.

4. Give each child a disposable camera to record his or her version of the trip. One 5-year-old snapped an entire series of photos that never showed anyone above the waist—his view of Disneyland (and the photos were priceless).

5. Nowadays, many families travel with a video camera, digital camera, or camera phone, though we recommend using one sparingly—parents end up viewing the trip through the lens rather than being in the moment. If you must, take it along, but only record a few moments of major sights (too much is boring anyway). And let the kids record and narrate. On the topic of narration, speak loudly so as to be heard over the not insignificant background noise of the parks. Make use of lockers at all of the parks when the camera becomes a burden or when you're going to experience an attraction that might damage it or get it wet. Unless you have a camera designed for underwater shots or a waterproof carrying case, leave it behind on Splash Mountain, the Grizzly River Run, and any other ride where water is involved. Don't forget extra batteries.

6. Another inexpensive way to record memories is a palm-size tape recorder. Let all family members describe their experiences. Hearing

a small child's voice years later is so endearing, and those recorded descriptions will trigger an album's worth of memories, far more focused than what many novices capture with a camcorder.

7. Consider using Disney's PhotoPass service for some professional-quality pictures; it's free to use and you only pay for the images you want to keep (see page 99 for details).

Finally, when it comes to taking photos and collecting mementos, don't let the tail wag the dog. You are not going to Disneyland to build the biggest scrapbook in history. Or as this Houston mom put it:

Tell your readers to get a grip on the photography thing. We were so busy shooting pictures that we kind of lost the thread. We had to get our pictures developed when we got home to see what all we did [while on vacation].

TRIAL RUN

IF YOU GIVE THOUGHTFUL CONSIDERATION to all areas of mental, physical, organizational, and logistical preparation discussed in this chapter, what remains is to familiarize yourself with the Disneyland parks and, of course, to conduct your field test. Yep, that's right, we want you to take the whole platoon on the road for a day to see if you are combat ready. No joke—this is important. You'll learn who tuckers out first, who's prone to developing blisters, who has to pee every 11 seconds, who keeps losing her cap, and, given the proper forum, how compatible your family is in terms of what you like to see and do.

For the most informative trial run, choose a local venue that requires lots of walking, dealing with crowds, and making decisions on how to spend your time. Regional theme parks and state fairs are your best bets, followed by large zoos and museums. Devote the whole day. Kick off the morning with an early start, just like you will at Disneyland, paying attention to who's organized and ready to go and who's dragging his or her butt and holding up the group. If you have to drive 1 or 2 hours to get to your test venue, no big deal. You may have to do some commuting at Disneyland too. Spend the whole day, eat a couple of meals, and stay late.

Don't bias the sample (that is, mess with the outcome) by telling everyone that you are practicing for Disneyland. Everyone behaves differently when they know that they are being tested or evaluated. Your objective is not to run a perfect drill but to find out as much as you can about how the individuals in your family, as well as the family as a group, respond to and deal with everything they experience during the day. Pay attention to who moves quickly and who is slow; who is adventuresome and who is reticent; who keeps going and who needs frequent rest breaks; who sets the agenda and who is content to follow; who is easily agitated and who stays cool; who tends to dawdle or wander off; who is curious and who is bored; who is demanding and who is accepting. You get the idea.

Discuss the findings of the test run with your spouse the next day. Don't be discouraged if your test day wasn't perfect; few (if any) are. Distinguish between problems that are remediable and problems that are intrinsic to your family's emotional or physical makeup (no amount of hiking, for example, will toughen up some people's feet).

Establish a plan for addressing remediable problems (further conditioning, setting limits before you go, trying harder to achieve family consensus) and develop strategies for minimizing or working around problems that are a fact of life (waking sleepyheads 15 minutes early, placing moleskin on likely blister sites before setting out, or packing familiar food for the toddler who balks at restaurant fare). If you are an attentive observer, a fair diagnostician, and a creative problem solver, you'll be able to work out a significant percentage of the problems you're likely to encounter at Disneyland before you leave home.

ABOUT THE *UNOFFICIAL GUIDE* TOURING PLANS Parents who embark on one of our touring plans are often frustrated by the various interruptions and delays occasioned by their small children. In case you haven't given the subject much thought, here is what to expect:

1. Many small children will stop dead in their tracks whenever they see a Disney character. Our advice: Live with it. An attempt to haul your children away before they have satisfied their curiosity is likely to precipitate anything from whining to a full-scale revolt.

2. The touring plans call for visiting attractions in a specified sequence, often skipping certain attractions along the way. Children do not like skipping *anything*! If they see something that attracts them, they want to experience it *now*. Some children can be persuaded to skip attractions if parents explain things in advance. Other kids severely flip out at the threat of skipping something, particularly something in Fantasyland. A mom from Charleston, South Carolina, had this to say:

   Following the touring plans turned out to be a train wreck. The main problem with the plan is that it starts in Fantasyland. When we were on Dumbo, my 5-year-old saw eight dozen other things in Fantasyland she wanted to see. The long and the short is that after Dumbo, there was no getting her out of there.

3. Children seem to have a genetic instinct when it comes to finding restrooms. We have seen perfectly functional adults equipped with all manner of maps search interminably for a restroom. Small children, on the other hand, including those who cannot read, will head for the nearest restroom with the certainty of a homing pigeon. While you may skip certain attractions, you can be sure that your children will ferret out (and want to use) every restroom in the theme park.

STROLLERS

STROLLERS ARE AVAILABLE to guests for about $15 per day for a single, $25 per day for two, at Disneyland and DCA. The rental covers the entire day and is good at both parks. If you rent a stroller and later decide to go back to your hotel for lunch, a swim, or a nap, turn in your stroller but hang on to your rental receipt. When you return to either park later in the day, present your receipt. You will be issued another stroller with no additional charge. The rental procedure is fast and efficient, especially since a new central stroller rental facility opened in the Main Entrance Plaza between Disneyland and DCA. Likewise, returning the stroller is a breeze. Even in the evening, when several hundred strollers are turned in following the laser-and-fireworks show, there is no wait or hassle. *Note:* Rented strollers are not permitted in Downtown Disney.

The strollers come with sun canopies and small cargo compartments under the seat. For infants and toddlers, strollers are a must, and we recommend taking a small pillow or blanket with you to help make them more comfortable for your child during what may be long periods in the seat. We have also observed many sharp parents renting strollers for somewhat older children. Strollers prevent parents from having to carry children when they run out of steam and provide an easy, convenient way to carry water, snacks, diaper bags, and the like.

When you enter a show or board a ride, you will have to park your stroller, usually in an open, unprotected area. If it rains before you return, you'll need a cloth, towel, or spare diaper to dry off the stroller.

Bringing Your Own Stroller

You are allowed to bring your own stroller to the theme parks. However, only collapsible strollers are allowed on the monorail and parking-lot trams. Your stroller is unlikely to be stolen, but mark it with your name. We strongly recommend bringing your own stroller. In addition to the parks there is the walk from and to your hotel, the parking-lot tram, or the bus/hotel-shuttle boarding area, not to mention many other occasions at your hotel or during shopping when you will be happy to have a stroller handy.

If you do not want to bring your own stroller, you may consider buying one of the umbrella-style collapsible strollers. You may even consider ordering online at places such as **walmart.com, toysrus.com,** or **sears.com** and shipping it right to your hotel. Make sure you leave enough time between your order and arrival dates.

Having her own stroller was indispensable to this mother of two toddlers:

How I was going to manage to get the kids from the parking [garage] to the park was a big worry for me before I made the trip. I didn't read anywhere that it was possible to walk to the entrance of the parks instead of taking the tram, so I wasn't sure I could do it.

I found that for me personally, since I have two kids ages 1 and 2, it was easier to walk to the entrance of the park from the parking [garage] with the kids in [my own] stroller than to take the kids out of the stroller, fold the stroller (while trying to control the two kids and associated gear), load the stroller and the kids onto the tram, etc. . . . . No matter where I was parked, I could always just walk to the entrance. . . . It sometimes took a while, but it was easier for me.

An Oklahoma mom, however, reports a bad experience with bringing her own stroller:

The first time we took our kids we had a large stroller (big mistake). It is so much easier to rent one in the park. The large [personally owned] strollers are nearly impossible to get on [airport shuttle] buses and are a hassle at the airport. I remember feeling dread when a bus pulled up that was even semi-full of people. People look at you like you have a cage full of live chickens when you drag heavy strollers onto the bus.

Stroller Wars

Sometimes strollers disappear while you are enjoying a ride or a show. Do not be alarmed. You won't have to buy the missing stroller, and you will be issued a new stroller for your continued use. Lost strollers can be replaced at the main rental facility near the respective park entrances.

While replacing a ripped-off stroller is not a big deal, it is an inconvenience. One family complained that their stroller had been taken six times in one day. Even with free replacements, larceny on this scale represents a lot of wasted time. Through our own experiments and suggestions from readers, we have developed several techniques for hanging on to your rented stroller:

1. Write your name in permanent marker on a 6- by 9-inch card, put the card in a transparent freezer bag, and secure the bag to the handle of the stroller with masking or duct tape.

2. Affix something personal (but expendable) to the handle of the stroller. Evidently most strollers are pirated by mistake (since they all look the same) or because it's easier to swipe someone else's stroller (when yours disappears) than to troop off to the replacement center. Since most stroller theft is a function of confusion, laziness, or revenge, the average pram-pincher will balk at hauling off a stroller bearing another person's property. After trying several items, we concluded that a bright, inexpensive scarf or bandanna tied to the handle works well, and a sock partially stuffed with rags or paper works even better (the weirder and more personal the object, the greater the deterrent). Best of all is a dead mackerel dangling from the handle, though in truth, the

kids who ride in the stroller prefer the other methods.

We receive quite a few letters from readers debating the pros and cons of bringing your own stroller versus renting one of Disney's. A mother with two small children opted for her own pram:

I took my own stroller because the rented strollers aren't appropriate for infants (we had a 5-year-old and a 5-month-old). No one said anything about me using a bike lock to secure our brand-new Aprica stroller. However, an attendant came over and told us not to lock it anywhere because it's a fire hazard! (Outside?) When I politely asked the attendant if she wanted to be responsible for my $300 stroller, she told me to go ahead and lock it but not tell anyone! I observed the attendants constantly moving the strollers. This seems very confusing—no wonder people think their strollers are getting ripped off!

As the reader mentioned, Disney cast members often rearrange strollers parked outside an attraction. Sometimes this is done simply to "tidy up." At other times the strollers are moved to make additional room along a walkway. In any event, do not assume that your stroller is stolen because it is missing from the exact place you left it. Check around. Chances are it will be "neatly arranged" just a few feet away.

BABYSITTING

CHILD-CARE SERVICES ARE UNAVAILABLE in the Disney parks. The services of Pinocchio's Workshop, a child-care facility at the Grand Californian Hotel, are available only to guests of the three Disneyland Resort hotels. Children ages 5–12 can be left for up to 4 hours at a cost of $13 per hour, per child. Pinocchio's Workshop requires a minimum of 2 hours, and its hours are 5 p.m.–midnight. Dinner is available for an additional fee. Fullerton Childcare Agency, an independent organization, provides in-room sitting for infants and children. If you pay the tab, Fullerton sitters will even take your kids to Disneyland.

All sitters are experienced and licensed to drive, and the Fullerton Childcare Agency is fully insured. The basic rate for in-room sitting for one or two children is $48 for the first 4 hours, with a 4-hour minimum, and $10 each hour thereafter. The charge for each additional child varies with the sitter. There is no transportation fee, but the client is expected to pay for parking when applicable. All fees and charges must be paid in cash at the end of the assignment. To reserve a sitter, 1 or 2 days' advance notice is requested. They fill up quickly, so a couple of weeks' notice is ideal. You can reach the Fullerton Childcare Agency by calling ☎ 714-528-1640.

DISNEY, KIDS, & SCARY STUFF

DISNEYLAND PARK and Disney California Adventure are family theme parks. Yet some of the Disney adventure rides can be intimidating to small children. On certain rides, such as Splash Mountain and the roller coasters (California Screamin', Space Mountain, Matterhorn Bobsleds, and Big Thunder Mountain Railroad), the ride itself may be frightening. On other rides, such as The Haunted Mansion and Snow White's Scary Adventures, it is the special effects. We recommend a little parent-child dialogue coupled with a "testing the water" approach. A child who is frightened by Pinocchio's Daring Journey should not have to sit through The Haunted Mansion. Likewise, if Big Thunder Mountain Railroad is too much, don't try Space Mountain or California Screamin'.

Disney rides and shows are adventures. They focus on the substance and themes of all adventure, and indeed of life itself: good and evil, beauty and the grotesque, fellowship and enmity, quest, and death. As you sample the variety of attractions at the Disney parks, you transcend the mundane spinning and bouncing of midway rides to a more thought-provoking and emotionally powerful entertainment experience. Though the endings are all happy, the impact of the adventures, with Disney's gift for special effects, is often intimidating and occasionally frightening to small children.

There are rides with menacing witches, rides with burning towns, and rides with ghouls popping out of their graves, all done tongue-in-cheek and with a sense of humor, provided you are old enough to understand the joke. And there are bones, lots of bones—human bones, cattle bones, and whole skeletons are everywhere you look. There have to be more bones at Disneyland Park than at the Smithsonian and the UCLA Medical School combined. A stack of skulls is at the headhunter's camp on the Jungle Cruise; a veritable platoon of skeletons sail ghost ships in Pirates of the Caribbean; a macabre assemblage of skulls and skeletons are in The Haunted Mansion; and more skulls, skeletons, and bones punctuate Snow White's Scary Adventures, Peter Pan's Flight, and Big Thunder Mountain Railroad.

One reader wrote us after taking his preschoolers on Star Tours:

We took a 4-year-old and a 5-year-old and they had the *#%^! scared out of them at Star Tours. We did this first thing in the morning, and it took hours of Tom Sawyer Island and It's a Small World to get back to normal.

Our kids were the youngest by far in Star Tours. I assume that either other adults had more sense or were not such avid readers of your book. Preschoolers should start with Dumbo and work up to the Jungle Cruise in the late morning, after being revved up and before getting hungry, thirsty, or tired. Pirates of the Caribbean is out for preschoolers. You get the idea.

The reaction of young children to the inevitable system overload of Disney parks should be anticipated. Be sensitive, alert, and prepared for almost anything, even behavior that is out of character for your child at home. Most small children take Disney's variety of macabre trappings in stride, and others are quickly comforted by an arm around the shoulder or a little squeeze of the hand. For parents who have observed a tendency in their kids to become upset, we recommend taking it slowly and easily by sampling more benign adventures such as the Jungle Cruise, gauging reactions, and discussing with children how they felt about the things they saw.

Sometimes, small children will rise above their anxiety in an effort to please their parents or siblings. This behavior, however, does not necessarily indicate a mastery of fear, much less enjoyment. If children come off a ride in ostensibly good shape, we recommend asking if they would like to go on the ride again (not necessarily right now, but sometime). The response to this question will usually give you a clue as to how much they actually enjoyed the experience. There is a lot of difference between having a good time and mustering the courage to get through something.

Evaluating a child's capacity to handle the visual and tactile effects of the Disney parks requires patience, understanding, and experimentation. Each of us, after all, has his own demons. If a child balks at or is frightened by a ride, respond constructively. Let your children know that lots of people, adults as well as children, are scared by what they see and feel. Help them understand that it is OK if they get frightened and that their fear does not lessen your love or respect. Take pains not to compound the discomfort by making a child feel inadequate; try not to undermine self-esteem, impugn courage, or subject a child to ridicule. Most of all, do not induce guilt, as if your child's trepidation is ruining the family's fun. When older siblings are present, it is sometimes necessary to restrain their taunting and teasing.

A visit to a Disney park is more than an outing or an adventure for a small child. It is a testing experience, a sort of controlled rite of passage. If you help your little one work through the challenges, the time can be immeasurably rewarding and a bonding experience for both of you.

The Fright Factor

While each youngster is different, there are essentially seven attraction elements that alone or combined can push a child's buttons:

I. THE NAME OF THE ATTRACTION Small children will naturally be

Small-child Fright-potential Chart

As a quick reference, we provide this chart to warn you which attractions to be wary of and why. Remember that the chart represents a generalization and that all kids are different. The chart relates specifically to kids 3–7 years of age. On average, as you would expect, children at the younger end of the age range are more likely to be frightened than children in their 6th or 7th year.

Disneyland Park

MAIN STREET, U.S.A.

Disneyland Railroad Tunnel with dinosaur display frightens some small children.

The Disneyland Story, presenting *Great Moments with Mr. Lincoln* Brief battle sound effects may surprise small children.

Main Street Cinema Not frightening in any respect.

Main Street Vehicles Not frightening in any respect.

ADVENTURELAND

Enchanted Tiki Room A small thunderstorm momentarily surprises very young children.

Indiana Jones Adventure Visually intimidating, with intense effects and a jerky ride. Switching-off option (see page 150).

Jungle Cruise Moderately intense, with some macabre sights; a good test attraction for little ones.

Tarzan's Treehouse Not frightening in any respect.

NEW ORLEANS SQUARE

Haunted Mansion Name of attraction raises anxiety, as do sights and sounds of waiting area. An intense attraction with humorously presented macabre sights. The ride itself is gentle.

Pirates of the Caribbean Slightly intimidating queuing area; an intense boat ride with gruesome (though humorously presented) sights and two short, unexpected slides down flumes.

apprehensive about something called The Haunted Mansion or Snow White's Scary Adventures.

2. THE VISUAL IMPACT OF THE ATTRACTION FROM OUTSIDE Splash Mountain, The Twilight Zone Tower of Terror, and Big Thunder Mountain Railroad look scary enough to give even adults second thoughts. To many small kids, the rides are visually terrifying.

3. THE VISUAL IMPACT OF THE INDOOR QUEUING AREA Pirates of the Caribbean with its dark bayou scene and The Haunted Mansion, with its "stretch rooms" are capable of frightening small children before they even board the ride.

4. THE INTENSITY OF THE ATTRACTION Some attractions are so intense as to be overwhelming; they inundate the senses with sights, sounds,

CRITTER COUNTRY

Davy Crockett's Explorer Canoes Not frightening in any respect.

The Many Adventures of Winnie the Pooh Not frightening in any respect.

Splash Mountain Visually intimidating from the outside. Moderately intense visual effects. The ride itself is somewhat hair-raising for all ages, culminating in a 52-foot plunge down a steep chute. Switching-off option (see page 150).

FRONTIERLAND

Big Thunder Mountain Railroad Visually intimidating from the outside; moderately intense visual effects. The roller coaster may frighten many adults, particularly seniors. Switching-off option (see page 150).

Frontierland Shootin' Exposition Not frightening in any respect.

Golden Horseshoe Stage Not frightening in any respect.

Mark Twain **Riverboat** Not frightening in any respect.

Pirate's Lair on Tom Sawyer Island Some very small children are intimidated by dark walk-through tunnels that can be easily avoided.

Sailing Ship *Columbia* Not frightening in any respect.

FANTASYLAND

Alice in Wonderland Pretty benign but frightens a small percentage of preschoolers.

Casey Jr. Circus Train Not frightening in any respect.

Dumbo the Flying Elephant A tame midway ride; a great favorite of most small children.

It's a Small World Not frightening in any respect.

King Arthur Carrousel Not frightening in any respect.

Mad Tea Party Midway-type ride can induce motion sickness in all ages.

Matterhorn Bobsleds The ride itself is wilder than Big Thunder Mountain Railroad but not as wild as Space Mountain. Switching-off option (see page 150).

continued on next page

movement, and even smell. *Captain EO, Muppet-Vision 3-D,* and *It's Tough to Be a Bug!,* for instance, combine loud music, tactile effects, lights, and 3-D cinematography to create a total sensory experience. For some preschoolers, this is two or three senses too many.

5. THE VISUAL IMPACT OF THE ATTRACTION ITSELF As previously discussed, the sights in various attractions range from falling boulders to lurking buzzards, from underwater volcanoes to attacking hippos. What one child calmly absorbs may scare the owl poop out of another child the same age.

6. DARK Many Disneyland attractions are "dark" rides—that is, they operate indoors in a dark environment. For some children, this fact alone is sufficient to trigger significant apprehension. A child who is

Fright-potential Chart (continued)

Disneyland Park (continued)

FANTASYLAND (CONTINUED)

Mr. Toad's Wild Ride Name of ride intimidates some. Moderately intense spook-house-genre attraction with jerky ride. Frightens only a small percentage of preschoolers.

Peter Pan's Flight Not frightening in any respect.

Pinocchio's Daring Journey Less frightening than Alice in Wonderland but scares a few very young preschoolers.

Snow White's Scary Adventures Moderately intense spook-house-genre attraction with some grim characters. Absolutely terrifying to many preschoolers.

Storybook Land Canal Boats Not frightening in any respect.

MICKEY'S TOONTOWN

Chip 'n Dale Treehouse Not frightening in any respect.

Gadget's Go Coaster Tame as far as coasters go; frightens some small children.

Goofy's Playhouse Not frightening in any respect.

Mickey's House Not frightening in any respect.

Minnie's House Not frightening in any respect.

Miss Daisy, Donald Duck's Boat Not frightening in any respect.

Roger Rabbit's Car Toon Spin Intense special effects, coupled with a dark environment and wild ride; frightens many preschoolers.

TOMORROWLAND

Astro Orbitor Waiting area is visually intimidating to preschoolers. The ride is a lot higher, but just a bit wilder, than Dumbo.

Autopia The noise in the waiting area slightly intimidates preschoolers; otherwise, not frightening.

Buzz Lightyear Astro Blasters Intense special effects plus a dark environment frighten some preschoolers.

Disneyland Monorail Not frightening in any respect.

---

frightened on one dark ride, for example Snow White's Scary Adventures, may be unwilling to try other indoor rides.

7. THE RIDE ITSELF; THE TACTILE EXPERIENCE Some Disney rides are downright wild—wild enough to induce motion sickness, wrench backs, and generally discombobulate patrons of any age.

A Bit of Preparation

We receive many tips from parents relating how they prepared their small children for the Disneyland experience. A common strategy is to acquaint children with the characters and the stories behind the attractions by reading Disney books and watching Disney DVDs at home.

Finding Nemo Submarine Voyage Being enclosed, as well as certain ride effects, may frighten preschoolers.

Captain EO Extremely intense visual effects and the loud volume scare many preschoolers.

Space Mountain Very intense roller coaster in the dark; Disneyland's wildest ride and a scary roller coaster by anyone's standards. Switching-off option (see page 150).

Star Tours: The Adventures Continue Extremely intense visually for all ages; the ride is one of the wildest in Disney's repertoire. Switching-off option (see page 150).

Disney California Adventure

A BUG'S LAND

Flik's Fun Fair Rides and Playground Not frightening in any respect.

It's Tough to Be a Bug! Loud and extremely intense with special effects that will terrify children under 8 years or anyone with a fear of insects.

GOLDEN STATE

Boudin Bakery Not frightening in any respect.

Ghirardelli Chocolate Factory Not frightening in any respect.

Grizzly River Run Frightening to guests of all ages. Wet too!

Redwood Creek Challenge Trail is a bit overwhelming to preschoolers but not frightening.

Soarin' Over California Frightens some children 7 years and under. Really a very sweet ride.

HOLLYWOOD PICTURES BACKLOT

Disney Animation Not frightening in any respect.

Disney Junior Not frightening in any respect.

Hollywood Backlot Stage Not frightening in any respect.

Hyperion Theater Some productions are both very intense and loud.

continued on next page

Thanks to half the population of California walking around the parks with video cameras, you can view a clip of every attraction and show on **youtube.com.** Videos of dark rides aren't stellar but are good enough to get a sense of what you're in for. The mother of a 7-year-old found YouTube quite effective:

> We watched every ride and show on YouTube before going so my timid 7-year-old daughter would be prepared, and we cut out all the ones that looked too scary to her. She still did not like, and cried at, Honey, I Shrunk the Audience *and also did not like* It's Tough to Be a Bug.

Fright-potential Chart (continued)

Disney California Adventure (continued)

HOLLYWOOD PICTURES BACKLOT

Monsters, Inc. Mike and Sulley to the Rescue May frighten children under 7 years of age.

Muppet-Vision 3-D Intense and loud with a lot of special effects. Frightens some preschoolers.

The Twilight Zone Tower of Terror Frightening to guests of all ages.

PARADISE PIER

California Screamin' Frightening to guests of all ages.

Golden Zephyr Frightening to a small percentage of preschoolers.

Goofy's Sky School Frightening to the under-8 crowd.

Jumpin' Jellyfish The ride's appearance frightens some younger children. The ride itself is exceedingly tame.

King Triton's Carousel Not frightening in any respect.

The Little Mermaid: Ariel's Undersea Adventure Moderately intense effects; Ursula may frighten children under 7 years of age.

Mickey's Fun Wheel The ride in the stationary cars is exceedingly tame. The ride in the swinging cars is frightening to guests of all ages.

Silly Symphony Swings Height requirement keeps preschoolers from riding. Moderately intimidating to younger grade-schoolers.

Toy Story Midway Mania! Loud and intense but not frightening.

CARS LAND

Luigi's Flying Tires Not frightening in any respect.

Mater's Junkyard Jamboree Midway-type ride can induce motion sickness in all ages.

Radiator Springs Racers Moderately intense effects, with high-speed sections that may frighten younger children.

A mother from Gloucester, Massachusetts, handled her son's preparation a bit more extemporaneously:

The 3½-year-old liked It's a Small World [but] was afraid of The Haunted Mansion. We just pulled his hat over his face and quietly talked to him while we enjoyed [the ride].

A Word about Height Requirements

A number of attractions require children to meet minimum height and age requirements, usually 40 inches tall to ride with an adult, or at least 40 inches and 7 years of age or older to ride alone. If you have children too short or too young to ride, you have several options, including switching off (described on page 150). Although the alternatives may resolve some practical and logistical issues, be forewarned that your smaller children might nonetheless be resentful of their

older (or taller) siblings who qualify to ride. A mom from Virginia bumped into just such a situation, writing:

> You mention height requirements for rides but not the intense sibling jealousy this can generate. Frontierland was a real problem in that respect. Our very petite 5-year-old, to her outrage, was stuck hanging around while our 8-year-old went on Splash Mountain and [Big] Thunder Mountain with Grandma and Granddad, and the nearby alternatives weren't helpful [too long a line for rafts to Tom Sawyer Island, and so on]. If we had thought ahead, we would have left the younger kid back in Mickey's Toontown with one of the grown-ups for another roller-coaster ride or two and then met up later at a designated point. The best areas had a playground or other quick attractions for short people near the rides with height requirements.

The reader makes a valid point, though splitting the group and then meeting later can be more complicated in practical terms than she might imagine. If you choose to split up, ask the Disney greeter at the entrance to the height-restricted attraction(s) how long the wait is. If you tack 5 minutes for riding onto the anticipated wait, and then add 5 or so minutes to exit and reach the meeting point, you'll have an approximate sense of how long the younger kids (and their supervising adult) will have to do other stuff. Our guess is that even with a long line for the rafts, the reader would have had more than sufficient time to take her daughter to Tom Sawyer Island while the sibs rode Splash Mountain and Big Thunder Mountain with the grandparents. For sure she had time to tour Tarzan's Treehouse in adjacent Adventureland.

Attractions that Eat Adults

You may spend so much energy worrying about Junior's welfare that you forget to take care of yourself. If the ride component of the attraction (that is, the actual motion and movement of the conveyance itself) is potentially disturbing, persons of any age may be adversely affected. Several attractions likely to cause motion sickness or other problems for older children and adults are listed in the chart below. Fast, jerky rides are also noted with icons in the attraction profiles.

POTENTIALLY PROBLEMATIC ATTRACTIONS FOR ADULTS

DISNEYLAND PARK

Adventureland	Indiana Jones Adventure
Critter Country	Splash Mountain
Fantasyland	Mad Tea Party and Matterhorn Bobsleds
Frontierland	Big Thunder Mountain Railroad
Tomorrowland	Space Mountain and Star Tours

DISNEY CALIFORNIA ADVENTURE

Cars Land	Mater's Junkyard Jamboree Radiator Springs Racers
Golden State	Grizzly River Run
Hollywood Pictures Backlot	The Twilight Zone Tower of Terror
Paradise Pier	California Screamin' and Goofy's Sky School

WAITING-LINE STRATEGIES *for* ADULTS *with* SMALL CHILDREN

CHILDREN HOLD UP BETTER through the day if you minimize the time they have to spend in lines. Arriving early and using the touring plans in this guide will reduce waiting time immensely. There are, however, additional measures you can employ to reduce stress on little ones.

1. LINE GAMES It is a smart parent who anticipates how restless children get waiting in line and how a little structured activity can relieve the stress and boredom. In the morning, kids handle the inactivity of waiting in line by discussing what they want to see and do during the course of the day. Later, however, as events wear on, they need a little help. Watching for, and counting, Disney characters is a good diversion. Simple guessing games such as 20 Questions also work well. Lines for rides move so continuously that games requiring pen and paper are cumbersome and impractical. Waiting in the holding area of a theater attraction, however, is a different story. Here, tic-tac-toe, hangman, drawing, and coloring can really make the time go by.

2. LAST-MINUTE ENTRY If a ride or show can accommodate an unusually large number of people at one time, it is often unnecessary to stand in line. The *Mark Twain* riverboat in Frontierland is a good example. The boat holds about 450 people, usually more than are waiting in line to ride. Instead of standing uncomfortably in a crowd with dozens of other guests, grab a snack and sit in the shade until the boat arrives and loading is well under way. After the line has all but disappeared, go ahead and board.

In large-capacity theaters, such as the one showing *Captain EO* in Tomorrowland, ask the entrance greeter how long it will be until guests are admitted to the theater for the next show. If the answer is 15 minutes or more, use the time for a restroom break or to get a snack; you can return to the attraction just a few minutes before the show starts. You will not be permitted to carry any food or drink into the attraction, so make sure you have time to finish your snack before entering.

To help you determine which attractions to target for last-minute entry, we provide the chart below.

ATTRACTIONS YOU CAN USUALLY ENTER AT THE LAST MINUTE		
DISNEYLAND PARK		
Frontierland	*Mark Twain* Riverboat	Sailing Ship *Columbia*
Main Street, U.S.A.	*Disneyland Story*, presenting *Great Moments with Mr. Lincoln*	
Tomorrowland	*Captain EO*	
DISNEY CALIFORNIA ADVENTURE		
Hollywood Pictures Backlot	*Muppet-Vision 3-D*	Disney Animation

3. THE HAIL-MARY PASS Certain waiting lines are configured in such a way that you and your smaller children can pass under the rail to join your partner just before boarding or entry. This technique allows the kids and one adult to rest, snack, cool off, or tinkle, while another adult or older sibling does the waiting. Other guests are understanding when it comes to using this strategy to keep small children content. You are likely to meet hostile opposition, however, if you try to pass older children or more than one adult under the rail. Attractions

---

ATTRACTIONS WHERE YOU CAN USUALLY COMPLETE A HAIL-MARY PASS

DISNEYLAND PARK

Adventureland	Jungle Cruise	Tarzan's Treehouse
Fantasyland	Casey Jr. Circus Train	Dumbo the Flying Elephant
	King Arthur Carrousel	Mad Tea Party
	Mr. Toad's Wild Ride	Peter Pan's Flight
	Snow White's Scary Adventures	Storybook Land Canal Boats
Tomorrowland	Autopia	

DISNEY CALIFORNIA ADVENTURE

Paradise Pier	Golden Zephyr	Jumpin' Jellyfish
	King Triton's Carousel	

---

where it is usually possible to complete a Hail Mary pass are listed on the chart above.

4. SWITCHING OFF (ALSO KNOWN AS THE BABY SWAP) Several attractions have minimum height and/or age requirements; children usually 40 inches tall or under must ride with an adult, or be at least 7 years of age *and* 40 inches tall to ride alone. Some couples with children too small or too young forgo these attractions, while others split up and take turns riding separately. Missing out on some of Disney's best rides is an unnecessary sacrifice, and waiting in line twice for the same ride is a tremendous waste of time.

A better way to approach the problem is to take advantage of an option known as "switching off" or "the baby swap." Switching off requires at least two adults. Everybody waits in line together, both adults and children. When you reach a Disney attendant (known as a "greeter"), say you want to switch off. The greeter will allow everyone, including the small children, to enter the attraction. When you reach the loading area, one adult will ride while the other stays with the kids. The riding adult then disembarks and takes responsibility for the

---

ATTRACTIONS WHERE SWITCHING OFF IS COMMON

DISNEYLAND PARK

Adventureland	Indiana Jones Adventure	
Critter Country	Splash Mountain	
Fantasyland	Matterhorn Bobsleds	
Frontierland	Big Thunder Mountain Railroad	
Tomorrowland	Space Mountain	Star Tours

DISNEY CALIFORNIA ADVENTURE

Cars Land	Radiator Springs Racers	
Golden State	Grizzly River Run	Soarin' Over California
Hollywood Pictures Backlot	The Twilight Zone Tower of Terror	
Paradise Pier	California Screamin'	Goofy's Sky School

children while the other adult rides. A third adult in the party can ride twice, once with each of the switching-off adults, so they do not have to experience the attraction alone. The 12 attractions where switching off is routinely practiced are listed on the chart on the opposite page.

Disney has been experimenting with a new switching-off procedure for certain Fastpass attractions. Here the cast member gives two Fastpasses to the parent who will be waiting with the child. That parent and the child then leave the queue and are free to do other things while the riding parent is waiting in line and experiencing the attraction. When the family regroups, the nonriding parent can use her Fastpasses to ride, taking another member of the family with her if she desires.

An Ada, Michigan, mother discovered that the procedure for switching off varies from attraction to attraction and offered this suggestion:

Parents need to tell the very first attendant they come to that they would like to switch off. Each attraction has a different procedure for this. Tell every other attendant too because they forget quickly.

Finally, you don't have to be a baby to utilize the baby swap; it works just as well for older children and adults who are unable or unwilling to ride an attraction but still want to experience the queue with their party.

5. HOW TO RIDE TWICE IN A ROW WITHOUT WAITING Many small children like to ride a favorite attraction two or more times in succession. Riding the second time often gives the child a feeling of mastery and accomplishment. Unfortunately, repeat rides can be time-consuming, even in the early morning. If you ride Dumbo as soon as Disneyland Park opens, for instance, you will only have a 1- or 2-minute wait for your first ride. When you come back for your second ride, your wait will be about 12 minutes. If you want to ride a third time, count on a 20-minute or longer wait.

The best way for getting your child on the ride twice (or more) without blowing your whole morning is by using the Chuck-Bubba Relay (named in honor of a reader from Kentucky):

1. Mom and little Bubba enter the waiting line.
2. Dad lets a certain number of people go in front of him (32 in the case of Dumbo) and then gets in line.
3. As soon as the ride stops, Mom exits with little Bubba and passes him to Dad to ride the second time.
4. If everybody is really getting into this, Mom can hop in line again, no less than 32 people behind Dad.

The Chuck-Bubba Relay will not work on every ride because of differences in the way the waiting areas are configured (that is, it is impossible in some cases to exit the ride and make the pass). The rides where the Chuck-Bubba Relay does work appear on the chart along with the number of people to count off.

When practicing the Chuck-Bubba Relay, if you are the second adult in line, you will reach a point in the waiting area that is obviously the easiest place to make the handoff. Sometimes this point is where those exiting the ride pass closest to those waiting to board. In any event, you will know it when you see it. Once there, if the first parent has not arrived with little Bubba, just let those behind you slip past until Bubba shows up.

ATTRACTIONS WHERE THE CHUCK-BUBBA RELAY USUALLY WORKS

DISNEYLAND PARK	Number of people between adults
Alice in Wonderland (tough, but possible)	38 people
Casey Jr. Circus Train	34 people, if 2 trains are operating
Davy Crockett's Explorer Canoes	94 people, if 6 canoes are operating
Dumbo the Flying Elephant	32 people
King Arthur Carrousel	70 people
Mad Tea Party	53 people
Mr. Toad's Wild Ride	32 people
Peter Pan's Flight	25 people
Snow White's Scary Adventures	30 people
DISNEY CALIFORNIA ADVENTURE	
Golden Zephyr	64 people
Jumpin' Jellyfish	16 people
King Triton's Carousel	64 people

6. LAST-MINUTE COLD FEET If your small child gets cold feet at the last minute after waiting for a ride (where there is no age or height requirement), you can usually arrange with the loading attendant for a switch-off; see the chart on page 150. This situation arises frequently at Pirates of the Caribbean—small children lose their courage en route to the loading area.

There is no law that says you have to ride. If you get to the boarding area and someone is unhappy, just tell a Disney attendant that you have changed your mind, and one will show you the way out.

7. THROW YOURSELF ON THE GRENADE, MILDRED! For by-the-book, do-the-right-thing parents determined to sacrifice themselves on behalf of their children, we provide a 1-day Touring Plan for Disneyland Park called the Dumbo-or-Die-in-a-Day Touring Plan for Parents with Small Children. This touring plan, detailed starting on page 364, will ensure that you run yourself ragged. Designed to help you forfeit everything of personal interest for the sake of your children's pleasure, the plan is guaranteed to send you home battered and exhausted with extraordinary stories of devotion and heroic perseverance. By the way, the plan really works. Anyone under 8 years old will love it.

8. DISNEY CALIFORNIA ADVENTURE This is not a great park for little ones. With the exception of Flik's Fun Fair, three play areas, and a carousel, the remaining attractions will be either boring or too frightening for most preschoolers. Elementary school–age children will fare better but will probably be captivated by the low-capacity/long-line rides at the Paradise Pier district of the park. Although designed to be appealing to the eye, these attractions are simply gussied-up versions of midway rides your kids can enjoy less expensively and with a fraction of the wait at a local amusement park or state fair.

9. AUTOPIA Though the Autopia at Disneyland Park is a great treat for small children, they are required to be 54 inches tall in order to drive unassisted. To work around the height requirement issues, go on the ride with your small child. After getting into the car, shift your child over behind the steering wheel. From your position you will still be able to control the foot pedals. To your child, it will feel like driving. Because the car travels on a self-guiding track, there is no way your child can make a mistake while steering.

LOST CHILDREN

LOST CHILDREN NORMALLY do not present much of a problem at Disneyland Resort. All Disney employees are schooled in handling such situations should they arise. If you lose a child while touring, report the situation to a Disney employee; then check in at City Hall (Disneyland Park) or Guest Relations (DCA) where lost-children logs are maintained. In an emergency, an alert can be issued throughout the park through internal communications. If a Disney cast member encounters a lost child, the cast member will escort the child immediately to the Baby Care Center located at the central-hub end of Main Street in Disneyland Park and at the entrance plaza in DCA. Guests age 11 or under are taken to the Baby Care Center in the Pacific Wharf Area at Disney California Adventure park. Guests age 12 and older may leave a written message at City Hall or the Guest Relations lobby or wait there.

It is amazingly easy to lose a child (or two) at a Disney park. It is a good idea to sew a label into each child's shirt that states his or her name, your name, and the name of your hotel. The same task can be accomplished less elegantly by writing the information on a strip of masking tape; hotel security professionals suggest that the information be printed in small letters, and that the tape be affixed to the outside of the child's shirt 5 inches or so below the armpit.

unofficial **TIP**
We suggest that children younger than 8 years be color coded by dressing them in purple T-shirts or equally distinctive clothes.

HOW KIDS GET LOST

CHILDREN GET SEPARATED from their parents every day at the Disney parks under circumstances that are remarkably similar (and predictable).

1. PREOCCUPIED SOLO PARENT In this scenario the only adult in the party is preoccupied with something such as buying refreshments, loading the camera, or using the restroom. Junior is there one moment and gone the next.

2. THE HIDDEN EXIT Sometimes parents wait on the sidelines while allowing two or more young children to experience a ride together. As it usually happens, the parents expect the kids to exit the attraction in

- Same-colored T-shirts for the whole family will help you gather your troops in an easy and fun way. You can opt for just a uniform color or go the extra mile and have the T-shirts printed with a logo such as "The Brown Family's Assault on the Mouse." You might also include the date or the year of your visit. Your imagination is the limit. Light-colored T-shirts can even be autographed by the Disney characters.

- Clothing labels are great, of course. If you don't sew, buy labels that you can iron on the garment. If you own a cell phone, be sure to include the number on the label. If you do not own a cell phone, put in the phone number of the hotel where you'll be staying.

- In pet stores you can have name tags printed for a very reasonable price. These are great to add to necklaces and bracelets, or attach to your child's shoelaces or a belt loop.

- When you check into the hotel, take a business card of the hotel for each member in your party, especially those old enough to carry wallets and purses.

- Always agree on a meeting point before you see a parade, fireworks, and nighttime spectacles such as *Fantasmic!* Make sure the meeting place is in the park (as opposed to the car or some place outside the front gate).

- If you have a digital camera or camera phone, you may elect to take a picture of your kids every morning. If they get lost, the picture will show what they look like and what they are wearing.

- If all members of your party have cell phones, it's easy to locate each other. Be aware, however, that the noise in the parks is so loud that you probably won't hear your cell phone ring. Carry your phone in a front pants pocket and program the phone to vibrate. Or communicate via text message. If any of your younger kids carry cell phones, secure the phones with a strap.

- Save key tags and luggage tags for use on items you bring to the parks, including your stroller, diaper bag, and backpack or hip pack.

- Don't underestimate the power of the permanent marker, such as a Sharpie. They are great for labeling pretty much anything. Mini-Sharpies are great for collecting character autographs. The Sharpie will also serve well for writing down the location of your car in the parking lot.

one place, and, lo and behold, the young ones pop out somewhere else. The exits of some Disney attractions are considerably distant from the entrances. Make sure that you know exactly where your children will emerge before letting them ride by themselves.

3. AFTER THE SHOW At the completion of many shows and rides, a Disney staffer will announce, "Check for personal belongings and take small children by the hand." When dozens, if not hundreds, of people leave an attraction at the same time, it is easy for parents to temporarily lose contact with their children unless they have them directly in tow.

4. RESTROOM PROBLEMS Mom tells 6-year-old Tommy, "I'll be sitting on this bench when you come out of the restroom." Three situations: One, Tommy exits through a different door and becomes disoriented (Mom may not know there is another door). Two, Mom decides belatedly that she will also use the restroom, and Tommy emerges to find her absent. Three, Mom pokes around in a shop while keeping an eye on the bench but misses Tommy when he comes out. A restroom adjacent to the Rancho del Zocalo Restuarante in Frontierland accounts for many lost children. Because it's located in a passageway connecting Frontierland and the central hub, children can wander into a totally different area of the park from where they came by simply making a wrong turn out of the restroom.

If you can't be with your child in the restroom, make sure that there is only one exit. Designate a meeting spot more distinctive than a bench, and be specific in your instructions: "I'll meet you by this flagpole. If you get out first, stay right here." Have your child repeat the directions back to you.

5. PARADES There are many special parades and shows at the theme park during which the audience stands. Children, because they are small, tend to jockey around for a better view. By moving a little this way and a little that way, it is amazing how much distance kids can put between themselves and you before anyone notices.

6. MASS MOVEMENTS Another situation to guard against is when huge crowds disperse after shows, fireworks, parades, or at park closing. With between 5,000 and 12,000 people suddenly moving at once, it is very easy to get separated from a small child or others in your party. Extra caution is recommended following the evening parades, fireworks, and *Fantasmic!* Families should develop specific plans for what to do and where to meet in the event they are separated.

7. CHARACTER GREETINGS A fair amount of activity and confusion is commonplace when the Disney characters are on the scene. See the next section on meeting the Disney characters.

The DISNEY CHARACTERS

FOR YEARS THE COSTUMED, walking versions of Mickey, Minnie, Donald, Goofy, and others have been a colorful supporting cast at Disneyland and Walt Disney World. Known unpretentiously as the "Disney characters," these large and friendly figures help provide a link between Disney animated films and the Disney theme parks.

Audiences, it has been observed, cry during the sad parts of Disney animated films and cheer when the villain is vanquished. To the emotionally invested, the characters in these features are as real as next-door neighbors; never mind that they are simply drawings on plastic. In recent years, the theme-park personifications of Disney characters have likewise become real to us. For thousands of visitors, it is not just some person in a mouse costume they see—it is really Mickey. Similarly, running into Goofy or Snow White in Fantasyland is a memory to be treasured, an encounter with a real celebrity.

About 250 of the Disney animated-film characters have been brought to life in costume. Of these, a relatively small number (about 50) are greeters (the Disney term for characters who mix with the patrons). The remaining characters are relegated exclusively to performing in shows or participating in parades. Some appear only once or twice a year, usually in Christmas parades or Disney anniversary celebrations.

CHARACTER ENCOUNTERS

CHARACTER WATCHING has developed into a pastime. Where families were once content to stumble across a character occasionally, they now relentlessly pursue them armed with autograph books and cameras. For those who pay attention, some characters are much more frequently encountered than others. Mickey, Minnie, and Goofy, for example, are seemingly everywhere, while Thumper comes out only on rare occasions. Other characters are seen regularly, but limit themselves to a specific location.

The fact that some characters are seldom seen has turned character watching into character collecting. Mickey Mouse may be the best-known and most-loved character, but from a collector's perspective he is also the most common. To get an autograph from Mickey is no big deal, but Daisy Duck's signature is a real coup. Commercially tapping into the character-collecting movement, Disney sells autograph books throughout the parks.

Unofficial Guide friend and contributor Ken Warhola offers this suggestion regarding character autographs:

> *Young children learn very quickly! If they see another child get an autograph, then they will want an autograph book as well. I recommend buying an autograph book right away. My 4-year-old daughter saw a child get Goofy's autograph, and right away she wanted to join the fun.*

PREPARING YOUR CHILDREN TO MEET THE CHARACTERS Because most small children are not expecting Minnie Mouse to be the size of a forklift, it's best to discuss the characters with your kids before you go. Almost all of the characters are quite large, and several, such as Br'er Bear, are huge! All of them can be extremely intimidating to a preschooler.

On first encounter, it is important not to thrust your child upon the character. Allow the little one to come to terms with this big thing from whatever distance the child feels safe. If two adults are present, one should stay close to the youngster while the other approaches the character and demonstrates that the character is safe and friendly. Some kids warm to the characters immediately, while some never do. Most take a little time, and often require several different encounters.

There are two kinds of characters: those whose costume includes a face-covering headpiece (animal characters plus some human characters such as Captain Hook), and face characters, or actors who resemble the cartoon characters to such an extent that no mask or headpiece is necessary. Face characters include Mary Poppins, Ariel, Jasmine, Aladdin, Cinderella, Mulan, Tarzan, Jane, Belle, Snow White, and Prince Charming, to name a few.

Only the face characters are allowed to speak. Headpiece characters, called "furs" in Disney-speak, do not talk or make noises of any kind. Because the cast members could not possibly imitate the distinctive voice of the characters, the Disney folks have determined that it is more effective to keep them silent. Lack of speech notwithstanding, the headpiece characters are extremely warm and responsive, and they communicate very effectively with gestures. As with the characters' size, children need to be forewarned that the characters do not talk. The exception is a new "living character"

> *unofficial* **TIP**
> Don't underestimate your child's excitement at meeting the Disney characters—but also be aware that very small kids may find the large, costumed characters a little frightening.

interactive Mickey Mouse with articulated facial features who can converse with guests, much as in *Turtle Talk with Crush* at DCA. At press time he has only been seen in Disneyland Park for sporadic testing (usually in Toontown), but if he's greeting guests during your visit, the effect is startling, and well worth the wait.

Parents need to understand that some of the character costumes are very cumbersome and that cast members often suffer from very poor visibility. You have to look closely, but the eye holes are frequently in the mouth of the costume or even down on the neck. What this means in practical terms is that the characters are sort of clumsy and have a limited field of vision. Children who approach the character from the back or the side may not be noticed, even if the child is touching the character. It is perfectly possible in this situation for the character to accidentally step on the child or knock him or her down. The best way for a child to approach a character is from the front, and occasionally not even this works. For example, the various duck characters (Donald, Daisy, Uncle Scrooge, and so on) have to peer around their bills. If it appears that the character is ignoring your child, pick your child up and hold her in front of the character until the character responds.

It is OK to touch, pat, or hug the character if your child is so inclined. Understanding the unpredictability of children, the characters will keep their feet very still, particularly refraining from moving backward or to the side. Most of the characters will sign autographs or pose for pictures. Once again, be sure to approach from the front so that the character will understand your intentions. If your child collects autographs, it is a good idea to carry a big, fat pen about the size of a Magic Marker. The costumes make it exceedingly difficult for the characters to wield a smaller pen, so the bigger the better.

THE BIG HURT Many children expect to bump into Mickey the minute they enter a park and are disappointed when he is not around. If your children are unable to settle down and enjoy things until they see Mickey, simply ask a Disney cast member where to find him. If the cast member does not know Mickey's whereabouts, he or she can find out for you in short order.

"THEN SOME CONFUSION HAPPENED" Be forewarned that character encounters give rise to a situation during which small children sometimes get lost. There is usually a lot of activity around a character, with both adults and children touching the character or posing for pictures. In the most common scenario, the parents stay in the crowd while their child marches up to get acquainted. With the excitement of the encounter, all the milling people, and the character moving around, a child may get turned around and head off in the wrong direction. In the words of a Salt Lake City mom:

Milo was shaking hands with Dopey one moment, then some confusion happened and he [Milo] was gone.

Families with several small children, and parents who are busy fooling around with cameras, can lose track of a youngster in a heartbeat. Our recommendation for parents of preschoolers is to stay with the kids when they meet the characters, stepping back only long enough to take a picture, if necessary.

MEETING CHARACTERS You can *see* the Disney characters in live shows and in parades. For times, consult your *Times Guide.* If you have the time and money, you can share a meal with the characters (more about this later). But if you want to *meet* the characters, get autographs, and take photos, it's helpful to know where the characters hang out.

Responding to guest requests, Disneyland Resort has added a lot of information about characters to its handout park maps and entertainment *Times Guide.* A listing specifies where and when certain characters will be available and also provides information on character dining. On the maps of the parks themselves, Mickey's gloved hand is used to denote locations where characters can be found.

At DCA, look for characters in Hollywood Pictures Backlot near the Animation Building, in parades, and in shows at the Hyperion Theater. Elsewhere around the park, characters will be less in evidence than at Disneyland Park, but they will make periodic appearances at Flik's Fun Fair and Buena Vista Street (the central hub).

*un*official **TIP**
Explain to your children that the headpiece characters do not talk. Keep in mind, too, that the characters are clumsy and have a limited field of vision.

The last few years have seen a number of Disney initiatives aimed at satisfying guests' inexhaustible desire to meet the characters. At Disneyland Park, Disney relegated four (Mickey, Minnie, Pluto, and Donald) of the "fab five" to all-day tours of duty in Mickey's Toontown. The fifth "fab," Goofy, works a similar schedule most days in Frontierland but also spends plenty of time in Toontown. Likewise, Pooh and Tigger can usually be found in Critter Country, Belle and Beast in Fantasyland, and Aladdin and Jasmine in Adventureland. Tinkerbell and her fairy friends draw long lines at their Pixie Hollow area off the central hub between Tomorrowland and the Matterhorn. Characters less in demand roam the "lands" consistent with their image (Br'er Bear and Br'er Fox in Critter Country, for example).

While making the characters routinely available has taken the guesswork out of finding them, it has likewise robbed character encounters of much of their surprise and spontaneity. Instead of chancing on a character as you turn a corner, it is much more common now to wait in a queue in order to meet the character. Speaking of which, be aware that lines for face characters move *m-u-c-h* more slowly than do lines for nonspeaking characters, as you might surmise. Because face characters are allowed to talk, they do, often engaging children in lengthy conversations, much to the consternation of the families stuck in the queue.

unofficial **TIP**
Characters make appearances in all the "lands" but are especially thick in Fantasyland, Mickey's Toontown, and Town Square on Main Street.

If you believe that there are already quite enough lines in Disneyland Park, and, furthermore, if you prefer to bump into your characters on the run, here's a quick rundown of where the bears and chipmunks roam. There will almost always be a character in Town Square on Main Street and often at the central hub. Snow White, Cinderella, and Princess Aurora hang out in the courtyard of the castle; the aforementioned Br'ers cruise Critter Country; and Pocahontas meets and greets in Frontierland. Any characters whom we haven't specifically mentioned generally continue to turn up randomly throughout the park.

Characters are also featured in the afternoon and evening parades, Frontierland waterfront shows, *Fantasmic!*, and Disney Princess Fantasy Faire. Performance times for all of the shows and parades are listed in the Disneyland Park's daily *Times Guide* entertainment listings. After the shows, characters will sometimes stick around to greet the audience.

Mickey Mouse is available to meet guests and pose for photos all day long in his dressing room at Mickey's Movie Barn in Mickey's Toontown. To reach the Movie Barn, proceed through the front door of Mickey's House and follow the crowd. If the line extends back to the entrance of Mickey's House, it will take you about 25–30 minutes to actually reach Mickey. When you finally get to his dressing room, one or two families at a time are admitted for a short personal audience with Mickey.

Many children are so excited about meeting Mickey that they cannot relax to enjoy the other attractions. If Mickey looms large in your child's day, board the Disneyland Railroad at the Main Street Station as soon as you arrive at the park, and proceed directly to Mickey's Toontown (half a circuit). If you visit Mickey before 10 a.m., your wait will be short.

Minnie receives guests at her house in Toontown most of the day as well, and Donald and Pluto are frequently available for photographs and autographs in the gazebo situated in front of the Toontown Town Hall. There is, of course, a separate line for each character. Also, be aware that the characters bug out for parades and certain other special performances. Check the daily *Times Guide* entertainment listings for performance times and plan your visit to Toontown accordingly.

CHARACTER DINING

FRATERNIZING WITH DISNEY CHARACTERS has become so popular that Disney offers character breakfasts, brunches, and dinners where families can dine in the presence of Minnie, Goofy, and other costumed versions of animated celebrities. Besides grabbing customers from Denny's and McDonald's, character meals provide a familiar, controlled setting in which young children can warm gradually to the characters. All meals are attended by several characters. Adult prices apply to persons age 10 or older, children's prices to ages 3–9. Little ones under age 3 eat free.

Because character dining is very popular, we recommend that you arrange Priority Seating as far in advance (up to 60 days) as possible. Priority Seating is Disney's version of a reservation—you arrive at an appointed time and the restaurant will be expecting you, but no specific table will be set aside. Instead, you will be seated at the first available table. The "priority" part simply means that you will be seated ahead of walk-ins. In practice the system works reasonably well, and your wait for a table will usually be less than 15 minutes.

unofficial **TIP**
Arrange Priority Seating as far in advance as possible. Your wait for a table will usually be less than 15 minutes.

CHARACTER DINING: WHAT TO EXPECT Character meals are bustling affairs, held in hotels' or theme parks' largest table-service or "buffeteria" restaurants. Character breakfasts (there are five) offer a fixed menu served family-style or as a buffet. The typical family-style breakfast includes scrambled eggs; bacon, sausage, and ham; hash browns; waffles, pancakes, or French toast; biscuits, rolls, or pastries; and fruit. The meal is served in large skillets or platters at your table. If you run

"Casting! This is George at the character breakfast. There's been a mistake. We were supposed to get the Assorted Character Packages with one Mickey, one Goofy, one Donald, one Pluto. . . ."

out of something, you can order seconds (or thirds) at no additional charge. Buffets offer much the same fare, but you have to fetch it yourself. The only character dinner at Disneyland Resort is a buffet serving standard American fare.

Whatever the meal, characters circulate around the room while you eat. During your meal, each of the three to five characters present will visit your table, arriving one at a time to cuddle the kids (and sometimes the adults), pose for photos, and sign autographs. Keep autograph books (with pens) and loaded cameras handy. For the best photos, adults should sit across the table from their children. Always seat the children where characters can reach them most easily. If a table is against a wall, for example, adults should sit with their backs to the wall and children should sit nearest the aisle.

You will not be rushed to leave after you've eaten. Feel free to ask for seconds on coffee or juice, and stay as long as you wish. Remember, however, lots of eager children and adults might be waiting not so patiently to be admitted.

You can dine with Disney characters at the Plaza Inn in Disneyland Park, at Goofy's Kitchen at the Disneyland Hotel, at Ariel's Grotto at DCA, at the Storytellers Café at the Grand Californian Hotel, and at

Disney's PCH Grill at the Paradise Pier Hotel. For information about character meals and to make Priority Seatings up to 60 days in advance, call ☎ 714-781-DINE (3463).

ARIEL'S DISNEY PRINCESS CELEBRATION Overlooking Paradise Bay, Ariel's Grotto restaurant hosts a breakfast and lunch with Ariel and friends daily until 1 hour before park closing. The breakfast admission costs are $35 for adults and $19 for children, and for lunch it's $37 for adults and $21 for children. Priority Seating is recommended.

DISNEY'S PCH (PACIFIC COAST HIGHWAY) GRILL PCH Grill at the Paradise Pier Hotel serves a Surf's Up! Breakfast with Mickey & Friends buffet 7–11 a.m. that features traditional Mexican breakfast items such as *chilaquiles* in addition to the usual American fare. Prices are $26 for adults and $14 for kids. Mickey (wearing beach togs) entertains you, along with Stitch, Minnie, and Pluto. This is usually the least crowded of the hotel character meals. Priority Seating is recommended.

GOOFY'S KITCHEN Located at the Disneyland Hotel, Goofy's Kitchen serves a character breakfast buffet 7 a.m.–noon (2 p.m. weekends) and a character dinner buffet 5–9 p.m. Breakfast is $30 for adults and $16 for kids. Dinners run $36 and $16, respectively. Goofy, of course, is the head character, but he's usually joined by Minnie, Pluto, and others. Priority Seating is recommended.

PLAZA INN Located at the end of Main Street and to the right, the Plaza Inn character buffet is usually packed because it hosts character breakfasts that are included in vacation packages sold by the Disney Resort Travel Sales Center. Served from opening until 11 a.m., the buffet costs $24 for adults and $12 for children. Characters present usually include Minnie, Goofy, Pluto, and Chip 'n' Dale. Priority Seating is recommended.

STORYTELLERS CAFÉ Storytellers Café, located at the Grand Californian Hotel, is the most attractive of the character-meal venues. A breakfast buffet is served 7–11 a.m. Cost is $24 for adults and $12 for children. Chip 'n Dale, the featured characters, are usually assisted by Pluto. Priority Seating is recommended.

PART FOUR

DINING *and* SHOPPING *in and around* DISNEYLAND

DINING *in* DISNEYLAND RESORT

IN THIS SECTION, we aim to help you find good food without going broke or tripping over one of Disneyland Resort's many culinary land mines. More than 50 restaurants operate in Disneyland Resort, including about 25 full-service restaurants, several of which are inside the theme parks. Collectively, Disney restaurants offer reasonable variety, serving everything from Louisiana Creole to Texas barbecue, but sadly, international cuisines other than Mexican, Asian, and Italian are not represented.

On the upside, we've never seen as dramatic an improvement in Disneyland restaurant quality as we have in the last few years. Some establishments have undergone complete menu makeovers, with terrific results. The selections are more varied and exciting, the fare is fresher, and the care in preparation and service has improved tenfold. Unlike other attractions and shops inside the resort, the food and beverage operation remains in constant flux. Venues open and close, add and delete menu items, and change decor throughout the year. We strive to provide you with the most accurate information possible; however, we do eventually have to go to press with the most current information we have at the time. Keep this in mind when using the guide.

You can expect to pay heavy prices for food within Disneyland Resort. Every meal, snack, and drink is anywhere from 100%–400% more inside the parks than outside (not counting Downtown Disney).

With the introduction of fine dining inside California Adventure, you can enjoy a glass of wine, a mug of beer, or even a cocktail inside the resorts without having to exit the park. Downtown Disney offers a wide variety of dining options, from mediocre to awesome, from intimate and adult to wild and kid-friendly. The Grand Californian

Hotel is home to **Napa Rose,** one of the finest dining spots in all of Anaheim, and even character meals at eateries such as **Ariel's Grotto** and **Disney's PCH Grill** offer better, healthier food than ever before.

Note: Priority Seating is the Disney-restaurant equivalent of Fastpass. This feature is available where noted and gives you the option of picking a time and cutting to the head of the line. You may still have to wait, but it's from the front of the line instead of the back.

GETTING IT RIGHT

ALTHOUGH WE WORK HARD to be objective and accurate, many readers think that we're too critical of the restaurants at Disneyland. One Charleston, West Virginia, woman came out swinging:

> *Get a life! It's crazy and unrealistic to be so snobbish about restaurants at a theme park. Considering the number of people Disney feeds each day, I think they do a darn good job. Also, you act so surprised that the food is expensive. Have you ever eaten at an airport? HELLO IN THERE? . . . Surprise, you're a captive! It's a theme park!*

And a mom from Erie, Pennsylvania, struck a practical note:

> *Most of the food is OK. In our experience, more of it is good than bad. If you pay attention to what other visitors say and what's in the guidebooks, you can avoid the yucky places. You pay more than you should, but it's more convenient [to eat Disney food] than to try to find cheaper restaurants somewhere else.*

As you might infer from the reader comments above, getting our dining coverage right is a bit of a challenge. While researching and reviewing restaurants may appear to be a straightforward endeavor, we can assure you that it is fraught with

unofficial **TIP**
It's necessary, we believe, to present both an expert and a popular opinion of each restaurant.

peril. We've read dining reviews by writers who turn up their noses at anything except four-star French restaurants (of which there are a whole lot fewer than people think). Likewise, we've seen reviewers who totally avoid Thai and Indian restaurants (among others) because they don't understand those cuisines, and we've read critiques absolutely devoid of criticism, written by "experts" unwilling to risk offending the sources of their free meals. Finally, we've seen reviews that are wholly based on surveys submitted by diners whose credentials for evaluating fine dining are mysterious at best and questionable at least.

How, then, do we go about presenting the best possible dining coverage? What is the best way to get it right? We at the *Unofficial Guide* have elected to begin with highly qualified culinary experts and then balance their opinions with those of our readers.

The expert opinion is essential because it's important to be able to differentiate what the restaurant really serves from what it purports to serve. Many years ago in Lexington, Kentucky, by way of example, there was only one Chinese restaurant. It was wildly successful even though it was Chinese in name only. Still, its specialty dishes, essentially American vegetable casseroles smothered in cornstarch, were happily consumed by patrons who had never been exposed to real Chinese cooking. The food wasn't bad, mind you, but it wasn't Chinese either. Visitors from out of town, inquiring about a good local Chinese restaurant, were often directed to this place. As you would expect, they were routinely horrified by the fare.

In this guide, we think you deserve to know whether or not you're getting the real thing. If we recommend, say, the shrimp remoulade (shrimp served cold in a mayonnaise-based sauce with chopped onion, Creole mustard, and paprika) at Blue Bayou, it's pretty essential that our dining critics know what shrimp remoulade is, how it should be prepared, how it should be served, and how it should taste. In our opinion, it's almost impossible to publish a creditable restaurant review without the help of a knowledgeable, professional dining critic.

The ultimate test of success for a restaurant, however, is not the authenticity of its dishes but the satisfaction of its patrons. If diners have a bad experience and don't come back, the restaurant will fail. Thus, we regard our experts' opinions and our readers' feedback as two halves of a whole: Both are necessary to inform your dining decisions.

Our experts are knowledgeable, seasoned professionals who have studied culinary arts around the world and who have written cookbooks or columns. They are well versed in ethnic dishes and have no prejudice about high or low cuisine. Our experts also conduct their reviews anonymously and always pay full menu prices for their meals. Additionally, many of our experts spent years working in the industry; they empathize with the operators and recognize how difficult it is to prove themselves worthy with every plate many times over every day.

We encourage you to fill out the dining survey in the back of this guide or on **touringplans.com.** If you want to share your dining experience in depth, write to us at the address listed on page 9, or send us an e-mail at **unofficialguides@menasharidge.com.**

DISNEY DINING 101

DISNEYLAND RESORT RESTAURANT RESERVATIONS: WHAT'S IN A NAME

DISNEY TINKERS CEASELESSLY with its restaurant-reservations policy. Priority Seating issues reservations that aren't exactly reservations. When you call Disney Dining at ☎ 714-781-3463, option 4, your name and essential information are taken, well, as if you were making a reservation. The Disney representative then tells you that you have Priority Seating for the restaurant on the date and time you requested, usually explaining that "priority" means you will be seated ahead of walk-ins—that is, those guests without Priority Seating.

BEHIND THE SCENES AT
DISNEYLAND RESORT DINING

DISNEY RESTAURANTS OPERATE on what they call a "template system." Instead of scheduling Priority Seating for actual tables, reservationists fill time slots. The number of slots available is based on the average observed length of time that guests occupy a table at a particular restaurant, adjusted for seasonality.

Here's a rough example of how it works: Let's say the Blue Bayou Restaurant at Disneyland Park has 38 tables for four and 10 tables for six, and that the average length of time for a family to be seated, order, eat, pay, and depart is 40 minutes. Add 5 minutes to bus the table and set it up for the next guests, and the tables are turning every 45 minutes. The restaurant provides Disneyland Resort Dining (DRD) with a computer template of its capacity, along with the average time the table is occupied. Thus, when DRD makes Priority Seatings for four people at 6:15 p.m., the system removes one table for four from overall capacity for 45 minutes. The template on the reservationist's computer indicates that the table will not be available for reassignment until 7 p.m. (45 minutes later). And so it goes for all the tables in the restaurant, each being subtracted from overall capacity for 45 minutes, then listed as available again, then assigned to other guests and subtracted again, and so on, throughout the meal period. DRD tries to fill every time slot for every seat in the restaurant, or come as close to filling every slot as possible. No seats—repeat, none—are *reserved* for walk-ins, though all restaurants accommodate such customers on a space-available basis.

unofficial **TIP**
Priority Seating is available to all Disneyland visitors—not just guests of the resort hotels. In the theme parks, you can make Priority Seatings for later in the day at the door of the restaurant.

Templates are filled differently depending on the season. During slower times of year, when Priority Seatings are easier to get, DRD will overbook a restaurant for each time slot, assuming that there will be a lot of no-shows. During busy times of year, when Priority Seatings are harder to come by, there are very few no-shows, so the restaurant is booked according to its actual capacity.

With Priority Seating, your waiting time will almost always be less than 20 minutes during peak hours, and often less than 10 minutes. If you just walk in, especially during busier seasons, expect to wait 40–75 minutes.

GETTING YOUR ACT TOGETHER

IF YOU WANT TO PATRONIZE any of the Disneyland Resort full-service restaurants, especially buffets or character-dining eateries, you should consider Priority Seating (call ☎ 714-781-3463, option 4, up to 60 days in advance). DRD handles Priority Seatings for both Disney-owned and independent restaurants at the theme parks, Disney hotels, and Downtown Disney. The sole exception is the

Rainforest Cafe at Downtown Disney, which makes its own reservations at ☎ 714-772-0413.

If you fail to make Priority Seatings before you leave home, or if you want to make your dining decisions spontaneously, your chances of getting a table at the restaurant of your choice are good. Blue Bayou at Disneyland Park, Napa Rose at the Grand Californian Hotel, and the various character-meal venues are the most likely to sell out. If, however, you visit Disneyland during a very busy time of year, it's to your advantage to make Priority Seatings.

If you poop out at the theme park and you don't feel like using your Priority Seating, there's no penalty. Also be aware that if you're a no-show for a particular Priority Seating, it won't affect any other such seatings you may have made. If you're running late, however, the restaurant will void your Priority Seating 15 minutes after the scheduled time. If you've lined up many seatings, it's a good idea to phone DRD a few days before you arrive to make sure that everything is in order. If you stay at a Disney resort, Guest Services can print out a summary of all your Priority Seatings. If you have a seating for a theme-park restaurant at a time before park opening, as is sometimes the case for a character breakfast, simply proceed to the turnstiles and inform a cast member, who will admit you to the park.

unofficial **TIP**
Disney kids' meals are now for ages 3–9; the cutoff used to be age 11.

DRESS

DRESS IS INFORMAL at all theme-park restaurants, but dressy casual is appropriate for resort restaurants such as Napa Rose. That means dress slacks (or dress shorts) with a collared shirt for men and slacks, skirts, or dress shorts with a blouse or sweater (or a dress) for women. You may be surprised how comfortable you feel when you're dressed appropriately.

FOOD ALLERGIES AND SPECIAL REQUESTS

IF YOU HAVE FOOD ALLERGIES or follow a specific type of diet (such as kosher or gluten-free), make your needs known when you arrange your Priority Seating. Does it work? Well, a Phillipsburg, New Jersey, mom reports her family's experience:

My 6-year-old has many food allergies, and we often have to bring food with us to restaurants when we go out to eat. I was able to make reservations at the Disney restaurants in advance and indicate these allergies to the reservation clerk. When we arrived at the restaurants, the staff was already aware of my child's allergies and assigned our table a chef who double-checked the list of allergies with us. Each member of the waitstaff was also informed of the allergies. The chefs were very nice and made my son feel very special (to the point where my other family members felt a little jealous).

A FEW CAVEATS

BEFORE YOU BEGIN eating your way through Disneyland, take our advice:

1. However creative and enticing the menu descriptions, avoid fancy food at full-service restaurants in the theme parks. Order dishes that the kitchen is unlikely to botch. Stick with what's familiar in most cases and you won't be disappointed.

2. Don't order baked, broiled, poached, or grilled seafood unless the restaurant specializes in seafood or rates at least ★★★½ in our dining profiles.

3. Theme-park restaurants rush their customers in order to make room for the next group of diners. Eating at high speed may appeal to a family with young, restless children, but for people wanting to relax, it's more like dining in a pressure chamber.

   If you want to linger over your expensive meal, don't order your entire dinner at once. Order drinks, study the menu while you sip, and then order appetizers. Tell the waiter you need more time to decide among entrées. Order your main course only after appetizers have been served. Dawdle over coffee and dessert.

4. If you're dining in a theme park and cost is an issue, make lunch your main meal. Entrées are similar to those on the dinner menu, but prices are significantly lower.

DISNEYLAND RESORT RESTAURANT CATEGORIES

IN GENERAL, food and beverage offerings at Disneyland Resort are defined by service, price, and convenience:

FULL-SERVICE RESTAURANTS Full-service restaurants are in all Disneyland Resort hotels, both theme parks, and Downtown Disney. Disney operates most of the restaurants in the theme parks and its hotels; contractors or franchisees operate those at Downtown Disney. The restaurants accept Visa, MasterCard, American Express, Discover, Diners Club, and the Disney Credit Card.

BUFFETS AND FIXED-PRICE MEALS With set-price character meals such as Ariel's Grotto at DCA, you can choose one item each from a limited selection of appetizers, salads, main courses, and desserts. Character buffets such as the one at Goofy's Kitchen in the Disneyland Hotel have a separate children's menu featuring grub such as hot dogs, burgers, chicken nuggets, pizza, macaroni and cheese, and spaghetti and meatballs. Priority Seating is highly recommended for all character meals.

COUNTER SERVICE Counter-service fast food is available at both theme parks and Downtown Disney. The food compares in quality with McDonald's, Captain D's, Pizza Hut, or Taco Bell but is more expensive, though it's often served in larger portions.

HARD CHOICES

DINING DECISIONS will definitely affect your Disneyland Resort experience. If you're short on time and you want to see the theme parks, avoid full service. Ditto if you're short on funds. If you want to try a Disney full-service restaurant, arrange Priority Seating—this won't reserve you a table, but it will minimize your wait.

Integrating Meals into the *Unofficial Guide* Touring Plans

Arrive before the park of your choice opens. Tour expeditiously, using your chosen plan (taking as few breaks as possible), until about 11–11:30 a.m. Once the park becomes crowded around midday, meals and other breaks won't affect the plan's efficiency. If you intend to stay in the park for evening parades, fireworks, or other events, eat dinner early enough to be finished in time for the festivities.

Character Dining

A number of restaurants, primarily those that serve all-you-can-eat buffets and family-style meals, offer character dining. At character meals, you pay a fixed price and dine in the presence of one to five Disney characters who circulate throughout the restaurant, hugging children, posing for photos, and signing autographs. Character breakfasts, lunches, and dinners are served at restaurants in and out of the theme parks. For an extensive discussion of character dining, see page 161.

FULL-SERVICE DINING FOR FAMILIES WITH YOUNG CHILDREN

NO MATTER HOW FORMAL a restaurant appears, the staff is accustomed to wiggling, impatient, and often boisterous children. In Disneyland Resort's finest dining rooms, it's not unusual to find at least two dozen young diners attired in basic black . . . mouse ears.

Almost all Disney restaurants offer children's menus, and all have booster seats and high chairs. Waiters will supply little ones with crackers and rolls and serve your dinner much faster than in comparable restaurants elsewhere. In fact, letters from readers suggest that being served too quickly is much more common than having a long wait.

QUIET, ROMANTIC PLACES TO EAT

RESTAURANTS WITH GOOD FOOD *and* a couple-friendly ambience are rare in the theme parks. Only one Disneyland dining spot satisfies both requirements: **Blue Bayou** at Disneyland Park. In Disney California Adventure, the **Wine Country Trattoria** offers one of the quietest and more relaxed environments, along with a California wine country–inspired menu that ranks as one of the best, if not *the* best, food in both theme parks. Among the hotels at the resort, **Napa Rose** at the Grand Californian Hotel & Spa is the leading candidate for a

unofficial **TIP**
Bottom line: Young children are the rule, not the exception, at Disney restaurants.

romantic adult dining experience. At Downtown Disney, try **Ralph Brennan's Jazz Kitchen**; ask for a quiet table, though, if you're not interested in the jazz music. **Catal** in Downtown Disney also offers an exceptionally quiet ambience and an ambitious gourmet menu geared mostly to adults.

Eating later in the evening and choosing a restaurant we've mentioned will improve your chances for intimate dining; nevertheless, know that children, well behaved or otherwise, are everywhere at Disneyland, and you can't escape them.

FAST FOOD IN THE THEME PARKS

BECAUSE MOST MEALS during a Disneyland vacation are consumed on the run while touring, we'll tackle counter-service and vendor foods first. Plentiful at all theme parks are hot dogs, hamburgers, chicken sandwiches, salads, and pizza. They're augmented by special items that relate to the park's theme or the part of the park you're touring. In the Alpine village setting of Fantasyland, for example, counter-service bratwurst and apple strudel are sold; in New Orleans Square, Cajun and Creole dishes are available. Counter-service prices are fairly consistent from park to park. Expect to pay the same amount for your coffee or hot dog at DCA that you would at Disneyland Park.

Getting your act together in regard to counter service is more a matter of courtesy than necessity. Rude guests rank fifth among reader complaints. A mother from Fort Wayne, Indiana, points out that indecision can be as maddening as outright discourtesy, especially when you're hungry:

> *Every fast-food restaurant has menu signs the size of billboards, but do you think anybody reads them? People waiting in line spend enough time in front of these signs to memorize them and still don't have a clue what they want when they finally get to the order taker. Tell your readers PULEEEZ get their orders together ahead of time!*

Another reader offers a tip about counter-service food lines:

> *[Many] counter-service registers serve two queues each, one to the left and one to the right of each register. People are not used to this and will instinctively line up in one queue per register. We had register operators wave us up to the front several times to start a left queue instead of waiting behind others on the right.*

Healthful Food at Disneyland Resort

One of the most commendable developments in food service at Disneyland has been the introduction of healthier foods and snacks. Diabetics, vegetarians, weight watchers, those requiring kosher meals, and guests on restricted diets should have no trouble finding something to eat. The same goes for anyone seeking wholesome, nutritious food. Health-conscious choices are available at most fast-food counters and even from vendors.

Cutting Your Dining Time at the Theme Parks

Even if you confine your meals to vendor and counter-service fast food, you lose a lot of time getting sustenance in the theme parks. At Disneyland Park and DCA, everything begins with a line and ends with a cash register. When it comes to fast food, "fast" may apply to the time you spend eating it, not the time invested in obtaining it.

Here are suggestions for minimizing the time you spend hunting and gathering food:

1. Don't waste touring time on breakfast at the parks. Restaurants outside Disneyland offer some outstanding breakfast specials. Many hotels furnish small refrigerators in their guest rooms, or you can rent one. If you can get by on cold cereal, rolls, fruit, and juice, having a fridge in your room will save a ton of time. If you can't get a fridge, bring a cooler.

2. After a good breakfast, buy snacks from vendors in the parks as you tour, or stuff some snacks in a hip pack. This is very important if you're on a tight schedule and can't spend a lot of time waiting in line for food.

3. All theme-park restaurants are busiest between 11:30 a.m.–2:15 p.m. for lunch and 6–9 p.m. for dinner. For shorter lines and faster service, don't eat during these hours, especially 12:30–1:30 p.m.

4. Many counter-service restaurants sell cold sandwiches. Buy a cold lunch (except for drinks) before 11:30 a.m., and carry it until you're ready to eat. Ditto for dinner. Bring small plastic bags in which to pack the food; purchase drinks at the appropriate time from any convenient vendor.

5. Most fast-food eateries have more than one service window. Regardless of the time of day, check the lines at all windows before queuing. Sometimes a window that's staffed but out of the way will have a much shorter line or none at all. Note, however, that some windows may offer only certain items.

6. If you're short on time and the park closes early, stay until closing and eat dinner outside Disneyland before returning to your hotel. If the park stays open late, eat dinner about 4 or 4:30 p.m. at the restaurant of your choice. You should miss the last wave of lunchers and sneak in just ahead of the dinner crowd. Be warned, however, that most eateries at Downtown Disney and the Disneyland Resort hotels stop serving at 10 p.m., even when the parks are open until midnight.

Beyond Counter Service: Tips for Saving Money on Food

Though buying food from counter-service restaurants and vendors will save you time and money compared with full-service dining, additional strategies can bolster your budget and maintain your waistline. Here are some suggestions that our readers have offered over the years:

1. Go to Disneyland during a period of fasting and abstinence. You can save a fortune *and* save your soul!

2. Wear clothes that are slightly too small and make you feel like dieting. (No spandex allowed!)

3. Whenever you're feeling hungry, ride the Mad Tea Party, California Screamin', or other attractions that can induce motion sickness.

4. Leave your cash and credit cards at your hotel. Buy food only with money your children fish out of fountains and wishing wells.

Cost-conscious readers also have volunteered ideas for stretching food dollars. A Missouri mom writes:

unofficial **TIP**
Restaurants with a Disney's Munch Inc. logo on their menu boards (showing three red cogwheels in the shape of Mickey's head) offer special meals for kids ages 3–9. Menu items frequently available include mini-pizzas, mac and cheese, chicken tenders, and PB&J.

We shopped and arrived with our steel Coleman cooler well stocked with milk and sandwich fixings. I froze a block of ice in a milk bottle, and we replenished it daily from the resort ice machine. I also froze small packages of deli-type meats for later in the week. We ate cereal, milk, and fruit each morning, with boxed juices. I also had a hot pot to boil water for instant coffee, oatmeal, and soup.

Each child had a belt bag of his own, which he filled from a special box of goodies each day. I made a great mystery of filling that box in the weeks before the trip. Some things were actual food, [such as] packages of crackers and cheese [and] packets of peanuts and raisins. Some were worthless junk, [such as] candy and gum. They grazed from their bags at will throughout the day, with no interference from Mom and Dad. Each also had a small, rectangular plastic water bottle that could hang on the belt. We filled these at water fountains before getting into lines and were the envy of many.

We left the park before noon; ate sandwiches, chips, and soda in the room; and napped. We purchased our evening meal in the park at a counter-service eatery. We budgeted for both morning and evening snacks from a vendor but often did not need them. It made the occasional treat all the more special. Our cooler had been pretty much emptied by the end of the week, but the block of ice was still there.

A mom from Whiteland, Indiana, who purchases drinks in the parks, offers this suggestion:

One must-take item if you're traveling with younger kids is a supply of small paper or plastic cups to split drinks, which are both huge and expensive.

We interviewed one woman who brought a huge picnic for her family of five packed in a large diaper–baby paraphernalia bag. She stowed the bag in a locker on Main Street and retrieved it when the family was hungry.

Note: Disney has a rule against bringing your own food and drink into the parks. Although since 9/11 all packs, purses, diaper bags, and such have been searched, security usually does not enforce the ban.

Why Our Friend Ken Weighs 500 Pounds

Really, our friend Ken Warhola doesn't weigh 500 pounds, but if he ate all the stuff listed below, he might. A self-appointed goodies probe, Ken shares his snacking insights on keeping your tummy happy at The Happiest Place on Earth. Call ☎ 714-781-0112 for a recorded message that reveals what candy will be made that week.

> *From Ken:*
> *I recommend adding to the **Unofficial Guide** a list of some of the great snacks and tasty things that can found in DLR. The following list is some food for thought (pardon the pun). It's a tough assignment, but you'll probably want to taste everything on this list, just to make sure that it's correct.*

DISNEYLAND PARK

Bacon-wrapped asparagus
  (Bengal Barbecue)

Blended mocha *(Blue Ribbon Bakery)*

Caramel apple pie *(Plaza Inn)*

Chicken on a stick *(Bengal Barbecue)*

Chimichangas *(vending cart)*

Chocolate-caramel pretzel rods
  (Pooh's Hunny Spot)

Chocolate-dipped Oreos
  (Pooh's Hunny Spot)

Churros *(vending carts)*

Cinnamon-roll French toast
  (breakfast at Carnation Café)

Cinnamon twists *(Blue Ribbon Bakery)*

Coconut macaroons drizzled with
  chocolate *(Blue Ribbon Bakery)*

Cream cheese pretzels *(IASW Snack Shop)*

DL Tigger tails *(Pooh's Hunny Spot)*

English toffee *(Candy Palace)*

Flying Dutchman cookie-boat dessert
  (Blue Bayou)

French fries *(Golden Horseshoe,
  Stage Door Café)*

Fritter trio *(New Orleans Square)*

Frozen lemonade *(vending cart)*

Granola-yogurt parfait
  (Blue Ribbon Bakery)

Honey-pot caramel apple
  (Pooh's Hunny Spot)

Honey-pot krispie *(Pooh's Hunny Spot)*

Hot chocolate *(Carnation Café)*

Hot fudge sundae *(Golden Horseshoe)*

Ice cream in a freshly made, chocolate-
dipped waffle cone
  (Gibson Girl)

THEME-PARK COUNTER-SERVICE RESTAURANT
Mini-profiles

TO HELP YOU FIND PALATABLE FAST-SERVICE FOODS that suit your taste, we've developed mini-profiles of Disneyland Park and DCA counter-service restaurants. The restaurants are listed alphabetically by park. Detailed profiles of all Disneyland full-service restaurants follow this section.

Mickey Mouse pancakes
(breakfast at River Belle Terrace)

Mickey Mouse waffles
(breakfast at Carnation Café)

Mickey-shaped beignets (Café Orléans)

Mint juleps (nonalcoholic—Mint Julep Bar)

Mozzarella cheese sticks with marinara
dipping sauce (Golden Horseshoe)

Peanut brittle (Main Street)

Pecan nettles (Candy Palace)

Pickles (fruit cart near Hungry Bear)

Pineapple—Dole whips, Dole whip
floats, pineapple spears
(Tiki Juice Bar, near Tiki Room)

Pomme frites (Café Orléans)

Popcorn (vending cart)

Pretzels stuffed with jalapeño cheese
(Refreshment Corner, Bengal Barbecue)

Snickerdoodles (Pooh's Hunny Spot)

Strawberry shortcake
(Blue Ribbon Bakery)

Sugar cookies (Pooh's Hunny Spot)

Taffy (Candy Palace)

Turkey legs (vending cart)

Waffle bowl ice cream sundaes
(Gibson Girl)

White chocolate—raspberry cookie
(Pooh's Hunny Spot)

DISNEY CALIFORNIA ADVENTURE

Full-throttle criss-cut fries
(Taste Pilots' Grill)

Mango madness (Schmoozies)

Orange sorbet (Wine Country Trattoria)

DOWNTOWN DISNEY

Beignets (Ralph Brennan's
Jazz Kitchen Express)

Belgian chocolate ice cream
(Häagen-Dazs)

Brownie sundae (ESPN Zone)

Candy that is unique to DL (Marceline's)

Chocolate-chip cookie sundae
(ESPN Zone)

Chunky strawberry (Jamba Juice)

Coconut ice cream with hot fudge
(Häagen-Dazs)

Excellent cup of coffee (Compass Books)

Fried shrimp po'boy (Ralph Brennan's
Jazz Kitchen Express)

RESORT RESTAURANTS

Bananas Foster French toast
(breakfast character meal at Storytellers
Café at Grand Californian)

Beef nachos (White Water Snacks at
Grand Californian)

Disney Dining's response to the recession is to whittle down portions while maintaining or raising prices. Disney claims that it was accommodating the desires of health-conscious guests. Give us a break. Especially hard hit are salads and pasta dishes with chicken, where the chicken is largely AWOL.

It should be noted that the Disneyland Hotel has recently undergone an extensive renovation and remodeling. New dining and lounge experiences have been introduced in the former locations of Hook's Pointe, Croc's Bits 'n' Bites, the Wine Cellar, and Lost Bar. **Tangaroa Terrace,** a new smart casual dining area, takes its architectural cue from the original Tahitian Terrace restaurant in Disneyland Park and the Polynesian architecture popular during the early era of the hotel. **Trader Sam's,** a new bar themed after the Jungle Cruise, features specialty drinks and surprises for guests.

When Cars Land opens, guests can enjoy fruit smoothies at **Fillmore's Taste-in,** chili and corn at the **Cozy Cone Motel,** and burgers and milk shakes at **Flo's V8 Café.** Also, with the transformation of Sunshine Plaza into Buena Vista Street, the **Fiddler Fifer and Practical Cafe** will replace Baker's Field Bakery. All are scheduled to open in the second half of 2012.

The restaurants profiled in the following pages are rated for quality and portion size as well as value. The value rating ranges from A to F as follows:

A = *Exceptional value; a real bargain*

B = *Good value*

C = *Fair value; you get exactly what you pay for*

D = *Somewhat overpriced*

F = *Extremely overpriced*

Note: Because of special or unusual offerings, the following counter-service restaurants are profiled in full and are listed with the full-service restaurants:

The French Market *Disneyland Park*	Rancho del Zocalo Restaurante *Disneyland Park*
Pacific Wharf Café *DCA*	River Belle Terrace *Disneyland Park*

DISNEYLAND PARK

Bengal Barbecue

QUALITY Good–Excellent	VALUE B	PORTION Small	LOCATION Adventureland

Selections Beef, chicken, and vegetable skewers; jalapeño cheese–stuffed pretzels.

Comments Skewers are small, but nothing costs more than $10. The bacon-wrapped asparagus and hot-and-spicy Banyan beef skewers are best, proving the old adage that everything tastes better on a stick.

Daisy's Diner

QUALITY Good	VALUE C	PORTION Medium	LOCATION Mickey's Toontown

Selections Pepperoni and cheese pizzas.

Comments Fine for eating on the run—there's no place convenient to sit.

Golden Horseshoe

QUALITY Fair	VALUE C	PORTION Medium	LOCATION Frontierland

Selections Chicken tenders, fish-and-chips, mozzarella strips, chili-cheese fries, and ice-cream sundaes.

Comments The Golden Horseshoe hosts the best live entertainment in the park. Meaty chili is a tribute to Walt and available in an unadvertised side portion perfect for a snack. Service is very slow, so get drinks here and eat elsewhere. Gazebo-style seating next to the stage is best.

Harbour Galley

QUALITY Good	VALUE B–	PORTION Medium	LOCATION Critter Country

Selections Broccoli and Cheddar cheese soup, clam chowder, or vegetarian chili, all served in a sourdough bread bowl; also steak salad or grilled salmon salad. Kids' meal includes string cheese, yogurt, and fruit.

Comments The broccoli and cheese soup is really good on cool days. Limited seating, but other seats are available along the dock around the back of the restaurant. The quality of the offerings here (and from around the park) have improved, sometimes dramatically.

Hungry Bear Restaurant

QUALITY Fair–Good	VALUE B+	PORTION Medium–large	LOCATION Critter Country

Selections A new menu here includes a huge, one-third-pound chili cheeseburger topped with a fried onion ring (skip the chili; it's pasty and bland), a fried green tomato sandwich with a side of jicama cole-slaw (some of the best greens in the park), and a fried chicken sandwich with honey mustard. Healthier choices include a turkey and provolone sandwich on a multigrain roll and Big Al's smoked chicken salad with lettuce, watermelon, candied pecans, dried cherries, and pickled red onions with a sweet-tart honey-lime vinaigrette. Kids can feast on healthier meals with string cheese, nonfat yogurt, sliced apples, and whole-grain fish crackers.

Comments The sweet potato fries are really tasty. Popular and crowded during busier times of the year. During slower times, grab a snack and sit on the deck overlooking the Rivers of America. We highly recommend the heirloom tomato sandwich (with Havarti and remoulade on hearty whole grain) to ovo-lacto vegetarians and carnivores alike.

Pluto's Dog House

QUALITY Good	VALUE C	PORTION Medium	LOCATION Mickey's Toontown

Selections Mini–hot dogs, knockwurst, bratwurst, and mac and cheese.
Comments Food's not bad, but there's really no place to sit and eat it.

Redd Rockett's Pizza Port

QUALITY Good	VALUE C	PORTION Medium–large	LOCATION Tomorrowland

Selections Redd Rockett's is set up cafeteria-style, typically with two or three kinds of pasta available, as well as pizzas and salads. All hot items sit under heat lamps until someone grabs them, but servers will be happy to mix up a fresh bowl of pasta or a pizza on request (a much better choice). Try the Asian chicken salad if it's available—slightly spicy with good flavor. Free drink refills are available.

Comments The cafeteria-style set-up usually means less waiting. The A/C system is on steroids, making it a really cool place on a really hot day.

Refreshment Corner

QUALITY Good	VALUE C	PORTION Medium	LOCATION Main Street, U.S.A.

Selections Hot dogs, chili-cheese dogs, and chili in a bread bowl.
Comments Not much of a selection, but dogs are good. Limited seating.

Royal Street Veranda

QUALITY Good	VALUE C	PORTION Medium	LOCATION New Orleans Square

Selections Steak gumbo, vegetarian gumbo, and clam chowder, all served in a sourdough bread bowl; coffee, espresso, cappuccino, and fritters (fried dough balls) for dessert.
Comments Usually not crowded. Veggie gumbo and clam chowder are the best, though all are seasoned well. You have to look hard to find any steak in the steak gumbo. Don't miss the fritters with fruit dipping sauce.

Stage Door Café

QUALITY Good	VALUE C	PORTION Medium	LOCATION Frontierland

Selections Chicken tenders, fish-and-chips, funnel cakes, and corn dogs.
Comments The stand on Main Street has better corn dogs, but the fish-and-chips are decent. Try the funnel cakes if you like those (who doesn't?).

Tomorrowland Terrace

QUALITY Fair	VALUE C+	PORTION Large	LOCATION Tomorrowland

Selections Turkey, roast beef, grilled veggie, and grilled chicken sandwiches; burgers; fresh salads; grilled mahi wrap.
Comments The food isn't anything special, although the bread is fresh. The grilled veggie sandwich or any of the salads may be your best choice. Seating is available outdoors overlooking the Tomorrowland Terrace stage, which hosts live music and the popular Jedi Training Academy.

Troubadour Tavern

QUALITY Good–Fair	VALUE C+	PORTION Medium	LOCATION Fantasyland

Selections Bratwurst with sauerkraut; top-your-own baked potatoes, sweet corn on the cob, decorate-your-own castle cookie kits.
Comments Built as a concession stand for the adjoining Fantasyland Theatre, the former Enchanted Cottage (now Troubadour Tavern) is overwhelmed during shows but often overlooked the rest of the day. This is the only quick-service sausage vendor that serves spicy brown mustard.

Vendor Treats

LOCATIONS Throughout the park

Selections Popcorn, French fries, smoked turkey legs, ice cream, churros, chimichangas, and more.
Comments We love the smoked turkey legs—big enough for a whole meal and only $6. Plus, there's something delightfully Neanderthal and exhibitionist about tucking into a huge, meaty bone as you stroll the park.

Village Haus

QUALITY Good	VALUE B–	PORTION Medium	LOCATION Fantasyland

Selections Premium cheeseburger, chicken sausage sandwich, veggie burger, pepperoni and cheese pizzas, apple Cheddar salad, and mac-and-cheese kids' meals. Black Forest cupcake or apple strudel for dessert.

Comments "Never eat in Fantasyland" used to be a rule we lived by, but the Village Haus's new menu and redone decor may have just changed all that. The flatbread pizzas and heart-stopping pastrami cheeseburger are actually pretty good. Kids will love the Pinnochio-themed seating area. Try the fresh salad with fruit and cheese in a tangy yogurt-honey dressing.

DISNEY CALIFORNIA ADVENTURE
Award Wieners

QUALITY Fair–Good	VALUE B	PORTION Medium	LOCATION Hollywood Pictures Backlot

Selections Chili-cheese dogs, grilled sausages, and hot dogs; grilled mushroom, onion, and pepper sandwich.

Comments The grilled sausages are moderately spicy and good.

Boardwalk Pizza & Pasta

QUALITY Good	VALUE A	PORTION Medium	LOCATION Paradise Pier

Selections Flatbread pizzas run the gamut from a traditional cheese or pepperoni to a portobello mushroom and spinach. Pasta offerings include spaghetti and meatballs, chicken pasta in a sun-dried tomato cream sauce, or pesto ravioli. Freshly tossed salads include a chicken Caesar and a Mediterranean chef salad with provolone, salami, fresh mozzarella, ham, roasted peppers, and olives in a red-wine vinaigrette.

Comments Formerly known as Pizza Oom Mow Mow, it has been rethemed as part of Paradise Garden, a Victorian-era outdoor dining courtyard. Freestanding beer and corn dog stands share the plaza.

Cocina Cucamonga Mexican Grill

QUALITY Good	VALUE C+	PORTION Large	LOCATION Pacific Wharf

Selections Tacos, burritos, tamales, grilled chicken, fajita salad, and chicken Caesar salad. Kids' choices include *arroz con pollo* (chicken with rice), bean and cheese burrito, and chicken tacos.

Comments Salads are a safe and solid choice. The chicken is marinated with cumin, garlic, cilantro, and citrus, and it comes with flour tortillas. Very tasty. Skip the carne asada; it's dry and virtually tasteless. The burritos include a lot of beans.

Lucky Fortune Cookery

QUALITY Fair–Good	VALUE C–	PORTION Medium	LOCATION Pacific Wharf

Selections Steamed rice bowls with vegetables and your choice of chicken, beef, or tofu, all with your choice from a variety of pan-Asian sauces, including a popular teriyaki and a sweet, tangy Korean sauce; edamame; mango slices; teriyaki chicken and rice for kids.

Comments The tofu bowl is good, the chicken and beef are average, and the coconut curry sauce is bland. Edamame makes a nice side to share, especially dipped in spicy *sriracha* sauce.

Paradise Garden Grill

QUALITY Good	VALUE A	PORTION Medium	LOCATION Paradise Pier

Selections Variety of skewers (beef, chicken, and tofu) served with rice pilaf and a pita, and fresh salads, including a classic Greek. For kids, there's a grilled chicken or beef skewer, served with choice of sauce.

Comments This new open-air dining venue, themed to a Victorian beer garden, shares seating with Boardwalk Pizza. The backstory is about an immigrant family whose humble roadside grill grew into a dining empire.

Taste Pilots' Grill

QUALITY Good	VALUE B–	PORTION Medium–large	LOCATION Condor Flats

Selections Choose from American comfort food such as burgers, pork ribs, chicken sandwiches, and grilled chicken salad.

Comments The pork ribs are decent. The burgers come with a variety of toppings and sauces, and a separate toppings bar is available in case you need to stack on more.

DISNEYLAND RESORT RESTAURANTS: *Rated and Ranked*

TO HELP YOU MAKE YOUR DINING CHOICES, we've developed profiles of full-service restaurants at Disneyland Resort. Each profile lets you quickly check the restaurant's cuisine, location, star rating, cost range, quality rating, and value rating. Profiles are listed alphabetically by restaurant. In addition to all full-service restaurants, we also list and profile a couple of delis and several self-serve restaurants in the theme parks that transcend basic burgers, hot dogs, and pizza.

STAR RATING The star rating represents the entire dining experience: style, service, and ambience, in addition to taste, presentation, and food quality. Five stars, the highest rating, indicates that the restaurant offers the best of everything. Four-star restaurants are above average, and three-star restaurants offer good, though not necessarily memorable, meals. Two-star restaurants serve mediocre fare, and one-star restaurants are below average. Our star ratings don't correspond to ratings awarded by AAA, Mobil, Zagat, or other restaurant reviewers.

COST RANGE The next rating tells how much a complete meal will cost: a main dish with vegetable or side dish and a choice of soup or salad. Appetizers, desserts, drinks, and tips aren't included. We've rated the cost as inexpensive, moderate, or expensive.

Inexpensive	$12 or less per person
Moderate	$13–$23 per person
Expensive	More than $23 per person

QUALITY RATING The food quality is rated on a scale of one to five stars, five being the best. The quality rating is based on the taste, freshness of ingredients, preparation, presentation, and creativity of food. There is no consideration of price. If you want the best food available and cost is no issue, look no further than the quality ratings.

VALUE RATING If, on the other hand, you are looking for both quality and value, check the value rating, also expressed as stars.

★★★★★	Exceptional value; a real bargain
★★★★	Good value
★★★	Fair value; you get exactly what you pay for
★★	Somewhat overpriced
★	Significantly overpriced

PAYMENT All Disney restaurants accept American Express, Master-Card, Visa, Diners Club, Discover, the Disney Credit Card, and JCB (Japanese Credit Bureau).

BEER, WINE, AND MIXED DRINKS Available at most restaurants except those at Disneyland Park.

Ariel's Grotto ★★★

CHARACTER DINING/AMERICAN   EXPENSIVE   QUALITY ★★★   VALUE ★★★½

Disney California Adventure; ☎ 714-781-DINE

Priority Seating Recommended. **When to go** Anytime. **Entrée range** Fixed-price meals, $29–$40. **Service** ★★★★. **Friendliness** ★★★★★. **Bar** The Cove bar is upstairs. **Dress** Casual. **Disabled access** Yes. **Hours** Daily, 9 a.m.–10 p.m.

SETTING AND ATMOSPHERE You're "under the sea" with bright 3-D ocean-themed murals, jellyfish lanterns, and seashell tables, all with views of the wharf, Paradise Bay, and Paradise Pier. The overstuffed semi-circular booths along the back wall are the best seats in the house and well worth waiting for.

HOUSE SPECIALTIES The menu has been revamped again. Now serving slow-roasted tri-tip steak, a seafood "soup" that's more like a cioppino, and some of the same rich pasta dishes from the previous menu.

OTHER RECOMMENDATIONS Herb-crusted chicken and a kids' menu featuring chicken skewered on sugarcane and spaghetti.

SUMMARY AND COMMENTS Ariel's Grotto is *fun* but very pricey. Kids will love the fact that Ariel and two to four other Disney princesses—Snow White, Cinderella, Aurora, or Belle—are on hand for pictures and autographs during breakfast and lunch. One set price buys adults an antipasto starter and salad, main course, and dessert, or a kids' appetizer of

Disneyland Resort Restaurants by Cuisine

CUISINE	LOCATION	OVERALL RATING	COST	QUALITY RATING	VALUE RATING
AMERICAN					
The River Belle Terrace*	Disneyland Park	★★★½	Mod	★★★½	★★★½
Tangaroa Terrace*	Disneyland Hotel	★★★½	Mod	★★★½	★★★½
Big Thunder Ranch Barbecue	Disneyland Park	★★★½	Exp	★★★	★★★
Ariel's Grotto*	DCA	★★★	Exp	★★★	★★★½
Carnation Café*	Disneyland Park	★★½	Mod	★★½	★★½
Disney's PCH Grill*	Paradise Pier Hotel	★★½	Mod	★★½	★★½
ESPN Zone	Downtown Disney	★★½	Mod	★★	★★
Rainforest Cafe*	Downtown Disney	★★½	Mod	★★	★½
Goofy's Kitchen*	Disneyland Hotel	★★	Exp	★★	★★
Plaza Inn*	Disneyland Park	★½	Mod	★★½	★★½
CALIFORNIA/FUSION					
Napa Rose	Grand Californian	★★★★½	V. Exp	★★★★½	★★★★
Wine Country Trattoria	DCA	★★★★	Mod	★★★★	★★★½
Storytellers Café*	Grand Californian	★★★★	Exp	★★★★	★★★
CAJUN/CREOLE					
Ralph Brennan's Jazz Kitchen*	Downtown Disney	★★★★	Mod	★★★★½	★★★
Café Orléans	Disneyland Park	★★★½	Mod	★★★½	★★★
Blue Bayou	Disneyland Park	★★★½	Exp	★★★½	★★½
House of Blues	Downtown Disney	★★	Mod	★★	★★
CHARACTER DINING					
Storytellers Café*	Grand Californian	★★★★	Exp	★★★★	★★★
Ariel's Grotto*	DCA	★★★	Exp	★★★	★★★½
Disney's PCH Grill*	Paradise Pier Hotel	★★½	Mod	★★½	★★½

CUISINE	LOCATION	OVERALL RATING	COST	QUALITY RATING	VALUE RATING
CHARACTER DINING					
Goofy's Kitchen*	Disneyland Hotel	★★	Exp	★★	★★
Plaza Inn*	Disneyland Park	★½	Mod	★★½	★★½
DELI/BAKERY					
La Brea Bakery Café*	Downtown Disney	★★★	Inexp	★★½	★★★*
Napolini*	Downtown Disney	★★½	Inexp	★★½	★½
HEALTHY/VEGETARIAN					
Pacific Wharf Café*	DCA	★★★	Inexp	★★★	★★★★
ITALIAN					
Naples Ristorante Pizzeria	Downtown Disney	★★½	Mod	★★½	★★½
Napolini*	Downtown Disney	★★½	Inexp	★★½	★½
MEDITERRANEAN					
Catal Restaurant & Uva Bar*	Downtown Disney	★★★	Mod/Exp	★★★½	★★★
MEXICAN					
Tortilla Jo's	Downtown Disney	★★★	Mod/Exp	★★½	★★½
Rancho del Zocalo Restaurante	Disneyland Park	★★	Mod	★★	★★½
POLYNESIAN					
Tangaroa Terrace*	Disneyland Hotel	★★★½	Mod	★★★½	★★★½
SOUTHERN					
The French Market	Disneyland Park	★★★	Mod	★★★★	★★★
STEAK HOUSE					
Steakhouse 55*	Disneyland Hotel	★★★★★	V. Exp	★★★★½	★★★★½

Serves breakfast.

celery and carrot sticks with ranch dressing, a main course, and dessert (slices of Granny Smith apples and caramel dipping sauce or fruit parfait). Even toddlers will enjoy the bright surroundings and nonthreatening character visits. Adults can escape upstairs to The Cove, the only full bar in the park, for a cocktail, glass of wine, or bottle of beer. Each diner receives a Preferred Viewing ticket to see *World of Color*. Demand is high here for obvious reasons, so book your Priority Seating early.

Big Thunder Ranch Barbecue ★★½

| AMERICAN | EXPENSIVE | QUALITY ★★★ | VALUE ★★★ |

Disneyland Park; ☎ 714-781-DINE

Priority seating Accepted. **When to go** Lunch or dinner. **Entrée range** $10–$25. **Service** ★★★★. **Friendliness** ★★★★. **Dress** Casual. **Disabled access** Yes. **Hours** Daily, 8 a.m.–10 p.m.

SETTING AND ATMOSPHERE Outdoor, family-style seating on long wooden tables and benches with lots of Western Americana touches such as hurricane lamps and checkered tablecloths.

HOUSE SPECIALTIES Family-style, all-you-can-eat barbecue featuring buckets of pork ribs and chicken in an overly sweet barbecue sauce, coleslaw, smoked sausages, and corn bread. The skillet chocolate-chip cookie with vanilla ice cream and hot fudge will definitely put you over the edge.

OTHER RECOMMENDATIONS Vegetarians can request a barbecue skewer with potatoes, squash, bell peppers, mushrooms, and tofu.

SUMMARY AND COMMENTS Prices may surprise you at first, but if the family is ready to pound some serious grub, this never-ending, all-you-can-eat palace to excess is just the spot. Drinks and dessert are à la carte. The dinner menu is the same as lunch, plus smoked sausage and corn cob wheels. A band of honky-tonk musicians belts out country favorites from Stephen Foster to the latest country tunes.

Blue Bayou ★★★½

| CAJUN/CREOLE | EXPENSIVE | QUALITY ★★★½ | VALUE ★★½ |

Disneyland Park; ☎ 714-781-DINE

Priority Seating Required. **When to go** Early or late lunch, early evening. **Entrée range** $22–$40. **Service** ★★★. **Friendliness** ★★★. **Dress** Casual. **Disabled access** Yes. **Hours** Daily, 11 a.m.–4 p.m. and 5:30–10 p.m.

SETTING AND ATMOSPHERE The Blue Bayou overlooks Pirates of the Caribbean and maintains an appropriately dark, moist ambience. The best tables ring the perimeter and afford a view of the faux bayou, replete with fireflies flickering among the weeping willows and mangroves, dilapidated houseboats, and soft lantern lights. If you're not lucky enough to get a table bayou-side, there's still enough wrought iron, uneven lighting, and twilight allure to soften the most hardened soul.

HOUSE SPECIALTIES Mahimahi, New York strip steak, and Le Special de Monte Cristo sandwich.

OTHER RECOMMENDATIONS Jambalaya or Tesoro Island chicken.

SUMMARY AND COMMENTS Easily the best restaurant in Disneyland Park, Blue Bayou is as close to fine dining as you'll get here. The restaurant fills quickly and stays busy, so make Priority Seatings before you leave home (up to 60 days in advance) or obtain a same-day Priority Seating at the restaurant door as soon as you get to the park. Although there's a children's menu, this isn't the place to bring wound-up or tired kids for a leisurely meal; they'll be bored. Tables are tightly packed, and nothing disrupts the busy servers more than wild kids up and out of their seats. Blue Bayou is more of a place where adults can escape the noise and happy chaos in the rest of the park without having to exit the gates. For lunch, we love the Monte Cristo sandwich, a deep-fried turkey, ham, and cheese creation that you don't find on many menus these days. Side dishes—including the Blue Bayou potatoes, a house gratin, and fresh vegetables—are quite good as well. The crème brûlée is also a crowd-pleaser. Servers are Disney-pleasant, if a tad harried, but they're more than happy to accommodate the random request. And the dinner rolls are great!

La Brea Bakery Café ★★★

BAKERY/DELI	INEXPENSIVE	QUALITY ★★½	VALUE ★★★

Downtown Disney; ☎ 714-490-0233 or 714-781-DINE; labreabakery.com

Priority Seating Available. **When to go** Breakfast. **Entrée range** $15–$36. **Service** ★★. **Friendliness** ★★. **Bar** Limited. **Dress** Casual. **Disabled access** Yes. **Hours** Sunday–Friday, 8 a.m.–10 p.m., Saturday, 8 a.m.–11 p.m. Open 1 hour later in summer.

SETTING AND ATMOSPHERE This indoor-outdoor space is rich with the yeasty aromas of breads and cakes, plus whiffs of herbs and spices. Hardwood floors and large glass display counters distinguish the dining room. A pleasant patio with colorful umbrellas fronting the café is the perfect perch for a quick cappuccino and pastry while you people-watch.

HOUSE SPECIALTIES For breakfast, nothing beats a crumbly maple-walnut scone or a big, yeasty fruit muffin and your coffee drink of choice. The panini at lunch and dinner are better than the ones at Napolini.

OTHER RECOMMENDATIONS Take home one or more loaves of the artisanal breads to snack on later. Or try this sandwich on for size: thick sourdough layered with warm shaved Parmesan and Gruyère cheeses and grilled, marinated white asparagus.

SUMMARY AND COMMENTS It's all about the bread . . . and the muffins, pastries, desserts, and anything else containing baked flour and yeast. Breakfast is the obvious time to enjoy La Brea (they serve a mean cup of joe), and if you must supplement your carbohydrate fix, add an egg dish (the omelets are good) and a side of bacon or sausage. At lunch and dinner, the salads and sandwiches take over. Service has improved markedly since our last visit; servers are more attentive and pleasant. Get there early—it's the first eatery at the east end of the resort entrance, and a popular starting (and ending) place for tourists and locals alike.

Café Orléans ★★★½

| CAJUN/CREOLE | MODERATE | QUALITY ★★★½ | VALUE ★★★ |

Disneyland Park; ☎ 714-781-DINE

Priority Seating Recommended. **When to go** Early or late lunch, early evening. **Entrée range** $15–$40. **Service** ★★★★. **Friendliness** ★★★★. **Dress** Casual. **Disabled access** Yes. **Hours** Daily, 11 a.m.–midnight.

SETTING AND ATMOSPHERE Across the alley from Blue Bayou, Café Orléans overlooks the Rivers of America. There's a small patio and limited inside seating, but the table-side service offers a nice break from the serve-yourself and buffet options in the same price range. After a day of traipsing around the park, it's nice to kick back amid the wrought-iron and scrolled-wood accents.

HOUSE SPECIALTIES The chef's *pommes frites* have to be among the best sides in the park: traditional thick-cut French fries tossed with Parmesan cheese, garlic, and parsley and served with a mildly spicy Cajun remoulade sauce. Mickey-shaped beignets are also a treat for dessert.

OTHER RECOMMENDATIONS A decent French onion soup with melted Gruyère cheese; an artery-clogging Monte Cristo sandwich in two versions, traditional and three-cheese; and a nice selection of sweet and savory crêpes.

SUMMARY AND COMMENTS The *pommes frites* are worth the price of admission. If you don't eat anything else in the park your entire visit, try these. We like to hit Café Orléans for a midafternoon break, kick our feet up for a soda or iced tea, and pick through a plate of the fries while we people-watch. The small menu makes ordering easy, provided you bring a big appetite and aren't afraid of a little cholesterol and trans fat. The Monte Cristo sandwiches are as good as Blue Bayou's and a few bucks cheaper. Kids will love the three-cheese version: Swiss, mozzarella, and double-cream Brie between thick slices of deep-fried egg-battered bread. The gumbo is passable, if a little bland, while the salads, including a blackened-chicken Caesar and the Crescent City salad (a mix of baby spinach, field greens, caramelized pecans, roasted corn, grapes, orange slices, and pan-seared salmon in an orange-cilantro vinaigrette), are very good. For something different, try the crêpes—paper-thin pancakes stuffed with a variety of fillings, including chicken gumbo and seafood. A Dixieland jazz band periodically provides lively entertainment.

Carnation Café ★★½

| AMERICAN | MODERATE | QUALITY ★★½ | VALUE ★★½ |

Disneyland Park; ☎ 714-781-DINE

Priority Seating Recommended. **When to go** Breakfast or late lunch. **Entrée range** $10–$20. **Service** ★★★★. **Friendliness** ★★★★. **Dress** Casual. **Disabled access** Yes. **Hours** Daily, 8 a.m.–2 p.m.

SETTING AND ATMOSPHERE A Main Street staple since the park opened in 1955, the Carnation Café serves up an American menu heavy with traditional favorites—chicken potpie and pot roast, pancakes and Mickey-shaped waffles, and butcher-block sandwiches—in a parlor circa 1890. There's lots of brass, marble, and bright white accents, plus a terrific patio for people-watching.

HOUSE SPECIALTIES Chicken potpie, on the menu since forever, is a favorite, with chunks of white-meat chicken, chopped veggies, and potato swimming in thick, creamy gravy and baked into a buttery, flaky piecrust.

OTHER RECOMMENDATIONS A nice selection of deli-style sandwiches, featuring ham, roast beef, or turkey piled on slabs of thick-cut shepherd's bread; dressed with mayo, lettuce, and tomato; and served with a dill pickle slice and a choice of sides.

SUMMARY AND COMMENTS The Carnation Café is another compromise spot—a place where the adults can find a decent plate, the kids can choose from their favorites, and it's easy on the wallet. Because of its location along Main Street, close to bathrooms and across from the locker facility, it gets busy—expect to see waiting lines stretching down the street. Service is friendly and unusually patient; someone's briefed these young cast members on how an hour's wait and low blood sugar can quickly erode a diner's mood. Once you're seated, the order comes quickly and with a smile. This place also serves one of the best cups of coffee in the Land.

Catal Restaurant & Uva Bar ★★★

| MEDITERRANEAN | MODERATE–EXPENSIVE | QUALITY ★★★½ | VALUE ★★★ |

Downtown Disney; ☎ 714-774-4442; patinagroup.com/catal

Priority Seating Recommended. **When to go** Dinner. **Entrée range** $19–$37. **Service** ★★★. **Friendliness** ★★★. **Bar** Full bar and extensive wine list. **Dress** Dressy casual. **Disabled access** Yes. **Hours** *Catal:* Daily, 8 a.m.–11 p.m. *Uva Bar:* Daily, 11 a.m.–10 p.m.

SETTING AND ATMOSPHERE Uva Bar, a circular open-air lounge, sits immediately outside the restaurant and is a good place for a quick bite (sans line) or a leisurely cocktail while you watch the crowds go by. Inside is an elegant Art Deco–inspired restaurant with hardwood floors, spacious dining areas, and fine accoutrements. There are two fireplaces and a large central bar; a narrow balcony with tables wraps around the entire top floor.

HOUSE SPECIALTIES Tapas, marinated Mediterranean-olive plate, and various small plates outside at the bar; rotisserie chicken in a sweet garlic au jus reduction and bone-in New York steak with béarnaise sauce inside.

OTHER RECOMMENDATIONS A huge and very tasty plate of paella with bay scallops, clams, mussels, shrimp, chicken, chorizo sausage, saffron rice, and garlic aioli; a Moroccan-inspired lamb shank with olive potatoes and lemon confit. The short rib sliders and lamb burgers at the bar are tender and tasty, and the enormous Prince Edward Islands mussels come steamed in a delicious white wine sauce.

SUMMARY AND COMMENTS Catal & Uva Bar are a Patina Group pairing, one in a chain of eateries operated by celebrity chef Joachim Splichal. Despite overblown descriptions, the menu is pretty straightforward. The small plates—mainly appetizers, salads, and a few pasta dishes—are better than the rest of the menu and a real value for the money. When the weather cooperates, Uva is the better of the two venues. Be cautious when ordering some of the more complex or unusual offerings, including the duck and rabbit: They can be very inconsistent and terribly fatty. Side dishes shine though. Price notwithstanding, this is a very adult experience.

Disney's PCH Grill ★★½

CHARACTER DINING/AMERICAN	MODERATE	QUALITY ★★½	VALUE ★★½

Disneyland Paradise Pier Hotel; ☎ 714-781-DINE

Priority Seating Available. **When to go** Breakfast and dinner. **Entrée range** $15–$36. **Service** ★★★★. **Friendliness** ★★★★. **Bar** Wine and beer. **Dress** Casual. **Disabled access** Yes. **Hours** Daily, 6:30–10:30 a.m. and 5–11 p.m.

SETTING AND ATMOSPHERE A taste of Southern California beach life: bright primary colors, potted palms, and decorative elements such as surfboards, oversize kites, and beach chairs.

HOUSE SPECIALTIES Wood-fired flatbread pizzas and burgers.

OTHER RECOMMENDATIONS The steaks and salads are actually quite good, if a little pricey. Breakfasts are your best bet with an omelet station for the grown-ups and a kids' buffet. What kid doesn't like choosing his or her own dining destiny?

SUMMARY AND COMMENTS If you can take one more character breakfast, this time with Mickey and friends, get the kids up early and hit the "beach." Since reopening in 2010 with a revamped menu, the food has improved.

ESPN Zone ★★½

AMERICAN	MODERATE	QUALITY ★★	VALUE ★★

Downtown Disney; ☎ 714-781-DINE; espnzone.com

Priority Seating Recommended. **When to go** Lunch or dinner. **Entrée range** $15–$36. **Service** ★★★. **Friendliness** ★★★. **Bar** Full bar. **Dress** Casual. **Disabled access** Yes. **Hours** Sunday–Thursday, 11 a.m.–11 p.m.; Friday–Saturday, 11 a.m.–midnight.

SETTING AND ATMOSPHERE Maybe the most entertaining place outside the park walls, with a little something for everyone except the very youngest, the ESPN Zone is a massive, two-story sports enthusiast's dream. Huge flat-panel TVs are everywhere, and there's not a bad seat in the house. There's also a TV and radio broadcast facility inside as well as a massive game and interactive sports arcade.

HOUSE SPECIALTIES A variety of sliders (three little sandwiches such as cheeseburgers and barbecued pork) and the barbecued baby back ribs.

OTHER RECOMMENDATIONS Keep it simple. Most of what comes off the grill or as a sandwich or appetizer is a safe bet. The more complicated the dish, the more likely it won't measure up to expectations. Wings, burgers, sliders, and a surprisingly good mahimahi tostada rank as your best options.

SUMMARY AND COMMENTS The ESPN Zone is a three-ring circus—food and beverages oozing from every corner, more televised sports feeds than you can count, and an interactive game zone. Kids will love the manic pace and endless ways to spend more of your money, as well as the kid-friendly fare. Even teens will have a reason to smile here (hoops, a batting cage, and a climbing wall). And adults won't feel guilty over letting the youngsters run amok while they soak up quite possibly the largest televised sports feed on the planet. The food's OK, the service is steady, and you may find yourself in the studio audience for one of the many taped and live sports broadcasts produced right in front of you.

The French Market ★★★

SOUTHERN	MODERATE	QUALITY ★★★★	VALUE ★★★

Disneyland Park; ☎ 714-781-DINE

Priority Seating Not accepted. **When to go** Lunch and dinner. **Entrée range** $12–$14. **Service** ★★★. **Friendliness** ★★★. **Dress** Casual. **Disabled access** Yes. **Hours** Daily, 11 a.m.–10 p.m.

SETTING AND ATMOSPHERE In the heart of New Orleans Square, The French Market suggests a laid-back Southern vibe with lots of wrought iron under the shade of large, mature ficus trees. There's a small indoor-dining area, but the best seating is outdoors on a large patio, covered with umbrellas and shadowed further by the trees.

HOUSE SPECIALTIES The menu features roasted chicken breast with citrus and Cajun spices, herb and garlic salmon Creole, and roast beef with Cognac. The jambalaya is a hearty, savory alternative that hits the spot on cooler winter days. Most meals come with a side of rice or mashed potatoes and corn bread.

OTHER RECOMMENDATIONS Hearty soups; a few fresh and flavorful salads (including a decent fried-chicken salad). The cheesecake may be one of the best desserts in Disneyland.

SUMMARY AND COMMENTS The French Market features comfort food with a Cajun-Creole flair.

Goofy's Kitchen ★★

CHARACTER DINING/AMERICAN	EXPENSIVE	QUALITY ★★	VALUE ★★

Disneyland Hotel; ☎ 714-781-DINE

Priority Seating Available. **When to go** Breakfast. **Entrée range** $16–$36. **Service** ★★★★. **Friendliness** ★★★★. **Bar** Wine, beer, and cocktails. **Dress** Casual. **Disabled access** Yes. **Hours** Daily, 7–11 a.m. and 5–10 p.m.

SETTING AND ATMOSPHERE Goofy's was also redone as part of the hotel renovation, but aside from some fresh paint, new furniture, and your typical Disney artistic touches, it feels very much like the old Goofy's.

HOUSE SPECIALTIES It's a buffet . . . which should tell you everything you need to know. Breakfast features Mickey-shaped waffles, sausages, pancakes, bacon, scrambled eggs, and other traditional breakfast items. Dinner offers everything from prime rib to premium salads.

OTHER RECOMMENDATIONS Kids seem to love Goofy's peanut butter pizza.

SUMMARY AND COMMENTS You come for two reasons: 1) It's easy and convenient, especially if you're staying at the resort, and 2) the youngsters haven't yet had their fill of dining with a rotating cast of Disney characters. Goofy and all his friends always put a smile to kids' faces.

House of Blues ★★

CAJUN/CREOLE	MODERATE	QUALITY ★★	VALUE ★★

Downtown Disney; ☎ 714-778-BLUE; hob.com/venues/clubvenues/anaheim

Priority Seating Recommended. **When to go** Dinner. **Entrée range** $15–$36. **Service** ★★★. **Friendliness** ★★★. **Bar** Wine list and full bar. **Dress** Casual. **Disabled access** Yes. **Hours** Daily, 11 a.m.–1:30 a.m.

SETTING AND ATMOSPHERE Think rustic-but-trendy blues club somewhere along the Mississippi River, maybe St. Louis. It's dark except for outside patios and a second-story terrace, with hardwood floors, small intimate tables, and indirect lighting.

HOUSE SPECIALTIES The finger food is always safe, and the sandwiches, especially the Blues burger and the shrimp po'boy, are worth a taste.

OTHER RECOMMENDATIONS The Elwood blackened-chicken sandwich, jambalaya, and red beans and rice with sausage.

SUMMARY AND COMMENTS The House of Blues is first and foremost a major concert site, with marquee names, up-and-comers, and strong local talent taking the stage every night. Food is a secondary thought. Tables are small and scrunched close together for maximum capacity. It's best to stick with the basics: finger foods, sandwiches, and salads. Some of the decidedly Southern fare, such as the jambalaya and fried chicken with country gravy, is pretty good, but you won't leave raving about the food. And unless stated otherwise, this is strictly an adult venue (18 and older).

Napa Rose ★★★★½

CALIFORNIA/FUSION	VERY EXPENSIVE	QUALITY ★★★★½	VALUE ★★★★

Grand Californian Hotel; ☎ 714-781-DINE

Priority Seating Recommended. **When to go** Dinner. **Entrée range** $37–$45; $85 for four courses. **Service** ★★★★★. **Friendliness** ★★★★. **Bar** Impressive wine list. **Dress** Dressy casual. **Disabled access** Yes. **Hours** Daily, 5–10 p.m.

SETTING AND ATMOSPHERE Napa Rose is Disneyland Resort's flagship fine-dining experience. The Grand Californian's Craftsman theme is carried into this premier room with sweeping views of Disney California Adventure from virtually every table. A large, open demonstration kitchen lets you watch the magic happen, and wine, in all of its glory, is displayed at every turn. Fine linens, china, and flatware are the norm. This is an absolutely gorgeous room with food and service to match.

HOUSE SPECIALTIES The menu, rotated seasonally, focuses on the cuisine of California's wine region, ranchlands, farm belts, and coastline. Wine finds its way onto most of the menu in sauces, reductions, infusions, and dressings. Dishes include sautéed portobello mushroom ravioli in truffled sage brown butter; Zinfandel-braised Angus beef short rib; citrus-seared ahi sashimi; and s'mores popover (a scrumptious dessert with toasted marshmallows, peanut butter ice cream, and chocolate sauce).

OTHER RECOMMENDATIONS Game meat, ranch and free-range beef and poultry, and the chef's prix fixe Vintner's Table are constantly changing and always exciting.

SUMMARY AND COMMENTS Napa Rose may be the best restaurant in Anaheim (lauded by many as the best restaurant in Orange County) and has been at the top of most critics' lists since its debut. Top talent in the kitchen and in the dining room—a beautiful space with panoramic views and a wine cellar second to none—make this an incomparable gustatory experience. Every server has earned sommelier status, a designation that takes years of study and practical experience with wine and winemaking, easing the chore of choosing a wine from their cellar of more than 16,000 bottles. Look for unusual ingredients (Tahitian vanilla, smoked sturgeon, truffled quail eggs, lemongrass, almond oil) married to top-notch staples (Colorado lamb, Berkshire pork, pheasant breast), all deftly handled by a world-class kitchen crew. And although staff are very accommodating in the usual Disney manner, this is definitely not an adventure for the kids.

Naples Ristorante e Pizzeria ★★½

ITALIAN	MODERATE	QUALITY ★★½	VALUE ★★½

Downtown Disney; ☎ **714-776-6200 or 714-781-DINE; patinagroup.com/naples**

Priority Seating Recommended. **When to go** Late lunch or early dinner. **Entrée range** $14–$46. **Service** ★★. **Friendliness** ★★★. **Bar** Extensive wine list and full bar. **Dress** Casual. **Disabled access** Yes. **Hours** Sunday–Thursday, 11 a.m.–10 p.m.; Friday–Saturday, 11 a.m.–11 p.m.

SETTING AND ATMOSPHERE Food aside, this is a really fun restaurant: modern, colorful, and spacious, with tile floors, an open demonstration kitchen, and whimsical design touches that mirror nearby Disneyland. It's also noisy and crowded, typically filled with families. During peak hours, it's difficult to hear yourself think, let alone carry on a meaningful conversation. Nonetheless, it's a great gathering place, and there's something to appeal to everyone from small children to adults.

HOUSE SPECIALTIES Wood-fired Neapolitan-style pizzas: thin, crispy crusts with a hearty, almost spicy red sauce; handmade mozzarella cheese; and fresh toppings of choice.

OTHER RECOMMENDATIONS The family-style dinners give you a choice of salads, soups, and pasta (think tubs of spaghetti and four-cheese ravioli) served en masse and, if everyone can agree, make a great bargain.

SUMMARY AND COMMENTS Another Patina–Joachim Splichal venture where most of the effort went into the design. While the menu seems sophisticated, the recipes are rather bland and uninspired with a few exceptions. Some of the nonpasta entrées—pan-roasted white fish with fennel-and-tomato vinaigrette and a citrus-and-herb-rubbed chicken, for example—are the real highlights. The kids will enjoy the colorful decor and activities; adults can get a good glass of wine or a cocktail and feed the entire crew for less than $100.

Napolini ★★½

ITALIAN/DELI	INEXPENSIVE	QUALITY ★★½	VALUE ★½

Downtown Disney; ☎ 714-781-DINE

Priority Seating Not accepted. **When to go** Lunch or a quick dinner. **Entrée range** $7–$12. **Service** ★★★. **Friendliness** ★★★. **Bar** Wine and beer only. **Dress** Casual. **Disabled access** Yes. **Hours** Sunday–Thursday, 11 a.m.–10 p.m.; Friday–Saturday, 11 a.m.–midnight.

SETTING AND ATMOSPHERE This is next-door Naples's cousin—a quick-in, quick-out deli with most of what you'd expect, from swinging salamis to large jars of peppers. Counter and table service have improved since our last visit.

HOUSE SPECIALTIES Wood-fired Neapolitan-style pizzas, panini, and salads.

OTHER RECOMMENDATIONS The pastas are hit or miss—the angel hair with pesto was terrific, while the rigatoni in marinara was a gooey mess.

SUMMARY AND COMMENTS Don't set your expectations too high and you won't be disappointed here. Best bets are the panini—grilled sandwiches on thick Italian bread, loaded to order with salami, veggies, peppers, onions, and such. Servers get flustered easily, and order mistakes are common (our guess is that Napolini serves as a training ground for Naples). Noise spills over from Naples on busy nights, as do impatient diners who don't want to wait for a table next door, making for a volatile mix that can have you feeling very uncomfortable in a hurry. But maybe that's the plan: to get you in with the sweet, spicy aromas of Italian cooking and then out quickly.

Pacific Wharf Café ★★★

HEALTHY/VEGETARIAN	INEXPENSIVE	QUALITY ★★★	VALUE ★★★★

Disney California Adventure; ☎ 714-781-DINE

Priority Seating Not accepted. **When to go** Breakfast, lunch, and dinner. **Entrée range** $8–$9. **Service** ★★. **Friendliness** ★★★. **Bar** Beers on tap; substantial wine list. **Dress** Casual. **Disabled access** Yes. **Hours** Daily, 10 a.m.–6 p.m.

SETTING AND ATMOSPHERE A little slice of pier life, San Francisco–style, with wooden floors, large wooden-framed windows amid blue-and-white trim, and hurricane lamps.

HOUSE SPECIALTIES Fresh soups and salads served in hollowed-out sourdough loaves from the famous Boudin bakery for grown-ups, and turkey wraps and string cheese for the kids. The Carmel roast beef sandwich and the vegetarian chili are very popular, as is the Santa Rosa corn chowder.

OTHER RECOMMENDATIONS The clam chowder is actually quite good, with heaps of clams in a creamy, slightly salty base.

SUMMARY AND COMMENTS This is another great compromise restaurant, with food and ambience that adults will appreciate as well as a very kid-friendly menu (nonfat yogurt, sliced apples, and whole-grain fish crackers). A full view of Paradise Bay (and a decent seat for *World of Color*) and friendly Disney service make this an easy place to gather for a snack, a full-blown meal, or a dessert that won't bankrupt you.

Plaza Inn ★½

CHARACTER DINING/AMERICAN	MODERATE	QUALITY ★★½	VALUE ★★½

Disneyland Park; ☎ 714-781-DINE

Priority Seating Recommended. **When to go** When you need a compromise, the kids insist, or you arrive right at the meal switch. **Entrée range** $10–$22. **Service** ★★★. **Friendliness** ★★. **Dress** Casual. **Disabled access** Yes. **Hours** Daily, 8 a.m.–midnight.

SETTING AND ATMOSPHERE Probably the high point of your meal at the Plaza Inn is the gorgeous Victorian B&B ambience—comfortable, widely spaced tables in a spacious dining room with lots of brocade and brass. A pleasant patio with huge umbrellas rings the east end of the circle at the top of Main Street.

HOUSE SPECIALTIES The menu has been revamped with new items, but it's still a buffeteria that can be hit or miss; see if you can catch something being freshly delivered. Best bets are the pot roast or the roasted chicken, two items that rarely suffer from sitting on the steam table.

OTHER RECOMMENDATIONS The little ones will love the character breakfast hosted by Minnie Mouse and two to four other characters. Adults will suffer through rubbery pancakes and soggy bacon.

SUMMARY AND COMMENTS Don't expect fine dining when you eat at the Plaza Inn, but some strides have been made in the quality of the food and the steam table's maintenance. Hit this place right when everything comes fresh, during the transitions from breakfast to lunch and from lunch to dinner, but it's still your basic been-in-the-steam-table-too-long scenario. Kosher meals are also available; call in advance to make arrangements.

Rainforest Cafe ★★½

AMERICAN	MODERATE	QUALITY ★★	VALUE ★½

Downtown Disney; ☎ 714-772-0413; rainforestcafe.com

Priority Seating Not accepted. **When to go** Lunch or dinner. **Entrée range** $13–$32. **Service** ★★. **Friendliness** ★★★. **Bar** Full bar. **Dress** Casual. **Disabled access** Yes. **Hours** Sunday–Thursday, 8 a.m.–10:30 p.m.; Friday–Saturday, 8 a.m.–midnight.

SETTING AND ATMOSPHERE Couldn't get enough of the Jungle Cruise next door *and* you're starving? Exit the park and head to the Rainforest Cafe, a lush tropical experience that attracts a few thousand of your fellow diners on a daily basis. Take a safari through the winding sections of greenery, faux wildlife, and piped-in jungle sounds, and wade through a menu as large as the Orinoco Basin.

HOUSE SPECIALTIES Stick to the basics: burgers, simple sandwiches, and salads. The Jungle Chopped Salad—a huge mix of romaine and iceberg greens, olives, cucumbers, cranberries, candied pecans, red cabbage, carrots, crumbled blue cheese, and grilled chicken in a raspberry vinaigrette—is arguably the best one on the menu.

OTHER RECOMMENDATIONS The Mojo Bones (barbecued baby back ribs) are tasty; the Volcano chocolate dessert (complete with sparkler top) is gargantuan but irresistible. The sandwich wraps are also a good alternative with some tasty meat and sauce mixes.

SUMMARY AND COMMENTS If the Adventureland experience just doesn't satisfy your lust for all things green and lush, this is the place for you. The menu is massive (maybe a little too large) and mostly palatable, but none of it is truly great. They do make up in quantity for any lack of quality; plates are enough for two in most circumstances. Children love the rain forest theme, and you can count on any number of the chain's signature animal characters to show up during the meal for photo ops and a little interaction with the kiddies. All in all, a bit distracting—but maybe that's the point.

Ralph Brennan's Jazz Kitchen ★★★★

| CAJUN/CREOLE | MODERATE | QUALITY ★★½ | VALUE ★★★ |

Downtown Disney; ☎ 714-776-5200; rbjazzkitchen.com

Priority Seating Available. When to go Lunch or dinner. Entrée range $18–$33. Service ★★★. Friendliness ★★½. Bar Full bar. Dress Casual. Disabled access Yes. Hours Daily, 8–10 a.m. and 11 a.m.–4 p.m.; Sunday–Thursday, 4:30–10 p.m., Friday–Saturday, 4:30 p.m.–11 p.m.; Sunday (zydeco jazz brunch), 10 a.m.–3 p.m.

SETTING AND ATMOSPHERE Take a step back in time and space to the 19th-century French Quarter of New Orleans. Almost half the seating area is an open-air courtyard surrounded by wrought iron, hanging ferns, and milled hardwood. Above a small stage where live jazz plays daily, there's a pounded-copper ceiling; to stage left is a beautiful enamel-finished grand piano. You can people-watch from a balcony dining area, but no matter where you sit, you're going to enjoy the ambience.

HOUSE SPECIALTIES We loved the blackened-chicken ravioli: white-meat chicken blackened on the grill and served on top of deep-fried pillows of cheese-stuffed pasta in a pumpkin-pesto sauce. The pecan-crusted catfish—a fillet crusted with pecan flour and panfried—is served with sweet-potato dirty rice and spaghetti squash.

OTHER RECOMMENDATIONS Shrimp Creole, filet mignon with Creole spice rub, and pasta jambalaya are all good.

SUMMARY AND COMMENTS This used to be one of our favorite restaurants in or immediately around the resort, but it seems to have suffered a little through the recession. The Brennan family is still intimately involved with every aspect of the menu, but both quality and presentation suffered between visits. Servers, including actual Southerners and even a smattering of Louisiana natives, exude a laid-back (sometimes too laid-back), gracious attitude most of the time but have been known to get a little testy and impatient during the restaurant's rush. Add live jazz to the mix (the zydeco brunch is really fun), and, all things considered, you have one of Disneyland's better dining experiences. Small children (and probably even preteens and teens) aren't going to appreciate the finer qualities here—this is a dining experience best suited to adults. For a quick early breakfast, the sugar-dusted beignets and chicory coffee from the adjoining quick-service counter can't be beat.

Rancho del Zocalo Restaurante ★★

MEXICAN	MODERATE	QUALITY ★★	VALUE ★★½

Disneyland Park; ☎ 714-781-DINE

Priority Seating Not accepted. **When to go** Early lunch or early dinner. **Entrée range** $9–$20. **Service** ★★★. **Friendliness** ★★★. **Dress** Casual. **Disabled access** Yes. **Hours** Daily, 11 a.m.–10 p.m.

SETTING AND ATMOSPHERE Welcome to the hacienda! Faux adobe, wooden beams, and Mexican tilework ring a dark interior and covered outdoor patio. Tucked away from the throngs and major thoroughfares in the northeast area of Frontierland, this can be a nice, quiet place for a meal.

HOUSE SPECIALTIES The enchiladas are quite good, probably because they lend themselves to the buffet-style dining here.

OTHER RECOMMENDATIONS Hit or miss: If you can catch a tray of soft tacos, burritos, or grilled chicken fresh from the commissary, you score.

SUMMARY AND COMMENTS Three words sum up the Zocalo: Mexican, cafeteria style. On the bright side, most of the cuisine holds up well under the heat lamps and over the steam tables, the enchiladas and grilled chicken in particular. The rest of the menu—the typical tacos, burritos, Mexican rice, and refried beans—is resolutely average, except at opening or right before the dinner rush, when the food is fresh and uncorrupted. The tortillas, both corn and flour, are pretty tasty. Anybody not intimately familiar with really good Mexican cuisine may rate this place higher. Zocalo is also a great choice when you've brought the kids along and you can't possibly choke down another hot dog, burger, or pizza slice.

The River Belle Terrace ★★★½

AMERICAN	MODERATE	QUALITY ★★★½	VALUE ★★★½

Disneyland Park; ☎ 714-781-DINE

Priority Seating Not accepted. **When to go** Breakfast and lunch. **Entrée range** $12–$20. **Service** ★★★. **Friendliness** ★★★. **Dress** Casual. **Disabled access** Yes. **Hours** Daily, 9 a.m.–10 p.m.

SETTING AND ATMOSPHERE Situated between New Orleans Square and Frontierland, The River Belle Terrace has an Old South–style exterior replete with wrought iron and wood siding. Large shuttered windows belie a small indoor-dining area; most of the seating is outdoors on a large patio covered with colorful umbrellas.

HOUSE SPECIALTIES Mickey-shaped pancakes, country potatoes, and bacon are breakfast diner favorites. Little kids love the Mickey-shaped peanut-butter-and-jelly sandwiches.

OTHER RECOMMENDATIONS The freshly carved prime-rib, turkey, and barbecued-pork sandwiches are very good, served on fresh baguettes with a choice of tasty sides; a fixin's bar includes sautéed mushrooms and onions, red onions, sauces, tomatoes, and pickles.

SUMMARY AND COMMENTS This 1955 Disneyland original seems to survive by keeping the menu fresh and flexible, and the new Carver menu has truly proved itself. Disney lore places Walt here every morning for breakfast for Mickey pancakes, scrambled eggs, bacon and sausage, and large, buttery cinnamon rolls dripping with buttercream frosting (a staff favorite). We like this place for light lunches or dinners when you don't want to take a lot of time for a formal sit-down meal. Grab a hot sandwich, a PB&J or a couple of mini–corn dogs for the kids, and a tall lemonade, and people-watch from the patio awhile.

Steakhouse 55 ★★★★★

STEAK HOUSE	VERY EXPENSIVE	QUALITY ★★★★½	VALUE ★★★★½

Disneyland Hotel; ☎ 714-781-DINE

Priority Seating Recommended. **When to go** Dinner. **Entrée range** $25–$65. **Service** ★★★★. **Friendliness** ★★★★. **Bar** Wine list and full bar. **Dress** Business casual. **Disabled access** Yes. **Hours** Daily, 7–11 a.m. and 5–10 p.m.

SETTING AND ATMOSPHERE Steakhouse 55 has recently reopened with new decor (as part of the Disneyland Hotel's entire renovation) with an update on classic American steak house. The big, overstuffed red leather booths are gone and in their place are stylishly Art Deco–inspired hardwood tables, sleek leather chairs, and smaller banquettes. The indirect lighting casts a warm glow over everything, including an impressive collection of black-and-white photographs from Disney's storied past.

HOUSE SPECIALTIES It's all about the meat—grilled certified Angus beef seasoned with the restaurant's signature rub—but you can also order one of the fresh seafood choices or delectable lamb, pork, or chicken. Order a glass of wine from an impressive wine cellar, or simply engage one of the numerous sommeliers to choose a wine to complement your meal.

OTHER RECOMMENDATIONS The lobster and steak combination is actually very good, but the price can catch you by surprise; always ask up front before ordering unless you have very deep pockets.

SUMMARY AND COMMENTS This underrated eatery has been a well-kept secret for years and matches many of the more well-known steak houses in the area (Morton's and Ruth Chris's) steak for steak. The recent renovation has only made the place more alluring and comfortable, a perfect place to spend a grown-up evening over a leisurely meal matched to premium wines. Leave the kids behind for this experience; they'll bore easily and may disrupt what could be one of the best adult nights you're likely to have during your stay.

Storytellers Café ★★★★

| CALIFORNIA/CHARACTER DINING   EXPENSIVE   QUALITY ★★★★   VALUE ★★★ |

Grand Californian Hotel; ☎ 714-781-DINE

Priority Seating Recommended. **When to go** Breakfast or dinner. **Entrée range** $15–$36. **Service** ★★★★★. **Friendliness** ★★★★. **Bar** Extensive wine list and full bar. **Dress** Casual. **Disabled access** Yes. **Hours** Daily, 8 a.m.–10 p.m.

SETTING AND ATMOSPHERE The Storytellers Café carries the Grand Californian's Arts and Crafts theme throughout with large, open beams; natural wood and wood carvings; milled stone; and stained glass. The walls are adorned with impressive murals depicting the state's rich literary history, from Mark Twain's "The Celebrated Jumping Frog of Calaveras County" to Scott O'Dell's *Island of the Blue Dolphins.*

HOUSE SPECIALTIES Children under age 10 will love the character breakfast. Hosted by Chip 'n Dale, a complement of woodland friends visit the tables, sing songs, and pose for photos between bites of omelets, waffles, and hotcakes. The Sonoma braised chicken and lemon prawns are lunch and dinner favorites.

OTHER RECOMMENDATIONS Health-conscious diners will love the café's salads, such as the Storytellers Salad (baby greens, white asparagus, and orange slices topped with a white-balsamic vinaigrette). The chicken melt is one of the best sandwiches on the planet, and if you like barbecue, don't miss the rack of Santa Maria–style baby back ribs.

SUMMARY AND COMMENTS You may experience a little sticker shock at first, but there's real value here. It's not quite on par with Napa Rose across the way, but the same dedication to quality and originality is evident from the menu to the service. Kids will find lots to like about the menu, along with enough distractions between the colorful menus, murals, and character visits to let the adults enjoy a wide range of California wine country–inspired menu options (from pastas to steaks to fresh fish) and a leisurely cocktail or glass of wine. You'll want to save some room for dessert too—who could pass up warm seasonal-fruit cobbler heaped with vanilla ice cream or a chocolate fondue for two (or more) with pound cake, biscotti, assorted chopped fruit, and banana fritters?

Tangaroa Terrace ★★★½

| AMERICAN/POLYNESIAN   MODERATE   QUALITY ★★★½   VALUE ★★★½ |

Disneyland Hotel; ☎ 714-781-DINE

Priority Seating Available. **When to go** Anytime. **Entrée range** $6–$15. **Service** ★★★★. **Friendliness** ★★★★. **Bar** Beer, wine, and cocktails. **Dress** Casual. **Disabled access** Yes. **Hours** Daily, 7 a.m.–10 p.m.

SETTING AND ATMOSPHERE This is Disneyland Hotel's poolside tropical retreat. Tiki torches and South Seas music are a dead giveaway that they want to evoke that island feeling.

HOUSE SPECIALTIES Breakfast starts with French toast with bacon and banana-caramel sauce or grilled cinnamon-spiced oatmeal cakes. Lunch and dinner feature a one-third-pound Hawaiian cheeseburger with teriyaki sauce, bacon, and grilled pineapple served on a multigrain roll, or try the Asian chicken salad with red and yellow peppers tossed in sesame vinaigrette.

OTHER RECOMMENDATIONS Dinner gets a little more involved with different Island Plate Dinners, such as miso-crusted salmon, tamarind-glazed island pork shanks, or katsu-style panko-crusted chicken.

SUMMARY AND COMMENTS Recently remodeled along with the rest of the Disneyland Hotel, this poolside eatery has something for everyone, as long as everyone enjoys food with an Asian/Polynesian flare. Adults can enjoy a cocktail (maybe something a little exotic with fruit garnish and little pink umbrellas) while kids frolic in the nearby pool in between bites. The adjoining Trader Sam's Enchanted Tiki Bar serves exotic cocktails and Asian-inspired appetizers in an intimate and elaborately decorated environment reminiscent of Walt Disney World's extinct Adventurers Club. Order an Uh Oa, Krakatoa Punch, or Shipwreck on the Rocks to see some explosive special effects.

Tortilla Jo's ★★★

| MEXICAN | MODERATE–EXPENSIVE | QUALITY ★★½ | VALUE ★★½ |

Downtown Disney; ☎ 714-535-5000; patinagroup.com/tortillajos

Priority Seating Available. **When to go** Lunch or dinner. **Entrée range** $15–$36. **Service** ★★★. **Friendliness** ★★★. **Bar** Full bar. **Dress** Casual. **Disabled access** Yes. **Hours** Sunday–Thursday, 11 a.m.–10 p.m., Friday–Saturday, 11 a.m.–11 p.m.; *taqueria:* Sunday–Thursday, 11 a.m.–11:30 p.m., Friday–Saturday, 11 a.m.–1 a.m.

SETTING AND ATMOSPHERE Old-world Mexico meets California modern. Mexican touchstones such as glazed tiles; thick, crude glass; and wrought iron accent an open dining room with modern, eclectic touches. You can grab a quick bite on the run at the taqueria, and the bartender pours from a huge selection of more than 100 premium and super-premium tequilas at an outdoor cantina. The place goes crazy on the weekends, so gird yourself for a raucous, booze-shooting, beer-chasing good time.

HOUSE SPECIALTIES Start with *queso fundido,* a pot of melted cheese plumped up with diced tomatoes and poblano chilies, and/or a bowl of the guacamole. The Yucatan chicken, a rotisserie half-bird with a red-chile glaze and caramelized pineapple, is still the best thing on the menu.

OTHER RECOMMENDATIONS Try the *tortas,* Mexican-style sandwiches served on traditional *telera* bread. The chicken torta is made with sliced chicken breast, homemade mango-banana salsa, and chipotle mayonnaise; the steak version comes with grilled carne asada, fresh Mexican soft cheese, red onion, tomato, avocado, and lettuce.

SUMMARY AND COMMENTS Another Patina Group eater
Joachim Splichal, Tortilla Jo's is upscale Mexican wit
You can customize any taco or burrito. The eclectic,
the loosey-goosey crowd) may be too much for the ki
appreciate a shot of Sauza Silver tequila and a tall
Corona beer.

Wine Country Trattoria ★★★★

CALIFORNIA NOUVELLE	MODERATE	QUALITY ★★★★	VALUE ★★★½

Disney California Adventure; ☎ 714-781-DINE

Priority Seating Recommended. **When to go** Lunch or dinner. **Entrée range**
$15–$36. **Service** ★★. **Friendliness** ★★. **Bar** Wine and beer. **Dress** Casual. **Disabled access** Yes. **Hours** Daily, 11 a.m.–9:30 p.m.

SETTING AND ATMOSPHERE Arguably one of the best dining options at either
park, the trattoria is a leisurely place to park yourself and family away
from the frenetic crowds. Whether you choose one of three themed
patios outside or the "patio" inside, this spacious bistro captures the
California-casual mood. The park recently redesigned both interior and
exterior patios with plenty of tile, wood, and trellised greenery, whisking you away from downtown Anaheim and positing you in the middle
of California wine country.

HOUSE SPECIALTIES Try the pasta your way: your choice of pasta styles
including spaghetti, penne, or rotelle with a choice of both cream-based
white sauces and tomato-based red sauces.

OTHER RECOMMENDATIONS Wine country shrimp on polenta with lemon
caper butter sauce and the herb-roasted chicken breast.

SUMMARY AND COMMENTS With a revamped menu, the redesigned trattoria
is a popular spot for a Mediterranean-style or California-inspired
meal, paired with a glass of wine from its extensive cellar. The trattoria
is the dining focal point of the resort, with the sporadic opening and
closing of the Vineyard Room. Braised lamb shank and sustainable fish
with citrus pesto is delicious. The Wine Country shrimp and fritto
misto qualify as full-blown entrées. And to finish: Authentic tiramisu
with sweetened Italian mascarpone is an exotic treat for adults among
the more kid-friendly sweets that dominate in the rest of the resort.
Wine Country Trattoria appeals more to adults without children,
though an improved kids' menu and *World of Color* fixed-price dining
packages has made this a more attractive option for families. Note
that *World of Color* dinner patrons each receive a Preferred Viewing
ticket, while lunchtime packages only grant standard *World of Color*
Fastpasses. Also note that the fixed-price *World of Color* menu is separate from the posted à la carte selections. The soup or salad and dessert sampler included in the viewing package are all excellent, but the
entrées are disappointingly reminiscent of banquet food; avoid the
tenderloin if you like your beef rare.

NING *outside* DISNEYLAND RESORT

UNOFFICIAL GUIDE RESEARCHERS LOVE GOOD FOOD and invest a fair amount of time scouting new places to eat. And because food at Disneyland Resort (all of the Disney complex including the theme parks, hotels, and Downtown Disney) is so expensive, we (like you) have an economic incentive for finding palatable meals off campus. Unfortunately, the area surrounding Disneyland is not exactly a culinary nirvana. If you thrive on fast food and the fare at chain restaurants, you'll be as happy as a honeybee on an orange blossom. If, however, you want a superlative dining experience, the pickings are slim. That said, the average Disneyland visitor only stays for 2–4 nights, and there are more than enough fine-dining venues outside Disneyland Resort to keep you happy for that amount of time. Good ethnic dining, however, is woefully underrepresented. Especially hard to find are high-quality Thai, Chinese, Mexican, Japanese, Korean, and Greek restaurants. We've confined our coverage to restaurants you can reach by car or cab in 15 minutes or less. If you're willing to range farther afield, your choices increase exponentially.

Among specialty restaurants in and out of Disneyland Resort, location and price will determine your choice. There is, for example, a decent Italian restaurant in Downtown Disney and several independent Italian eateries within 5 miles of the Disney complex. Which one you select depends on how much you want to spend and how convenient the place is.

Better restaurants outside Disneyland Resort cater primarily to adults and aren't as well equipped to deal with children. This is a plus, however, if you're looking to escape children and eat in peace and quiet.

The opening of the Garden Walk retail and entertainment complex immediately east of the park is notable. Popular chains such as **The Cheesecake Factory, Roy's Hawaiian Fusion Cuisine, Fire + Ice,** and the **Yardhouse** are doing brisk business. The best of the lot is the Yardhouse, a limited chain of medium-priced eateries with a fusion menu with pan-Pacific influences and a bar with more than 200 beers on tap featuring microbrews from around the world.

BUFFETS AND MEAL DEALS OUTSIDE DISNEYLAND RESORT

BUFFETS, RESTAURANT SPECIALS, AND DISCOUNT DINING abound in the area surrounding Disneyland Resort, especially on Harbor Boulevard and Katella Avenue. The local visitor magazines, which are distributed free at non-Disney hotels, among other places, are packed with advertisements and discount coupons for seafood feasts, buffets (Chinese, Indian, and the like), and a host of combination specials for everything from lobster to barbecue. For a family trying to economize on meals, some of the come-ons are mighty attractive. But are these places any good? Is the food fresh, tasty, and appealing? Are the restaurants clean and inviting? Armed with little more than a roll of Tums, the *Unofficial* research team tried all the eateries that advertise heavily in the tourist publications. Here's what we discovered.

Chinese Super Buffets

Whoa! Talk about an oxymoron. If you've ever tried preparing Chinese food, especially a stir-fry, you know that split-second timing is required to avoid overcooking. So it should come as no big surprise that Chinese dishes languishing on a buffet lose their freshness, texture, and flavor in a hurry. On the bright side, however, the super buffets are so cheap that you really can't go wrong. So what if it's not the best Chinese food you've ever had if you can scarf down all you want for $10? All the Chinese buffets serve chicken prepared a dozen different ways but also offer such goodies as peel-and-eat shrimp, various fish and shellfish, the occasional carved meat, salads, soups, and sometimes sushi. Desserts are usually lackluster, but most folks are too stuffed to eat them anyway. The best Chinese buffet within a 15-minute drive of Disneyland Resort is as follows:

HARBOR SEAFOOD BUFFET 12761 Harbor Blvd., Ste. I1, Garden Grove; ☎ 714-636-3338; **www.theharborseafoodbuffet.net.** Dinner: $14.49 adults, $1.20 per year old for children ages 3–10, free for children under age 3, Monday–Thursday; $15.49 adults, $1.20 per year old for children ages 3–10, free for children under age 3, Friday–Sunday. Seniors receive 10% off. Discount coupons available. Features barbecue, Japanese food, and Mongolian barbecue in addition to Chinese dishes.

Indian Buffets

Indian food works much better on a buffet than Chinese food. The mainstays of Indian buffets are curries. *Curry,* you may be surprised to know, is essentially the Indian word for "stew." Curry powder, as sold in the United States, is nothing more than a blend of spices prepackaged to flavor a stew. In India each curry is prepared with a different combination of spices (dominated by cumin), and no self-respecting cook would dream of using an off-the-shelf mix. The salient point about Indian buffets is that curries, unlike stir-fries, actually improve with a little aging. If you've ever reheated a leftover stew at home and noticed that it tasted better the second time around, it's because the flavors and ingredients continued to marry during the storage period, making the stew richer and tastier.

In the Disneyland Resort area, most Indian restaurants offer buffets at lunch only—not too convenient if you plan on spending your day at the theme parks. If you're out shopping or taking a day off, here are some Indian buffets worth trying:

GANDHI PALACE Ramada Plaza Hotel, 515 W. Katella Avenue;

☎ 714-808-6777; **gandhipalace.com.** Lunch buffet: Monday–Saturday, $11; breakfast buffet: $9. Discount coupons available.

PUNJABI TANDOOR 327 S. Anaheim Blvd., Ste. A, Anaheim; ☎ 714-635-3155; **punjabitandoor.com.** Lunch buffet: Monday–Saturday, $9; Sunday brunch: $11. Discount coupons available. Original recipes and a superior tandoori menu with an incredible garlic naan.

Salad Buffets

The most popular of these in the Disneyland Resort area is **Souplantation** (5939 W. Chapman Ave., Garden Grove; ☎ 714-895-1314). The buffet features prepared salads and an extensive array of ingredients to build your own. In addition to the rabbit food, Souplantation offers a variety of soups, a modest pasta bar, a baked-potato bar, an assortment of fresh fruit, and ice-cream sundaes. Dinner runs $8.39 for adults, $4.99 for children ages 6–12, and $1.69 for children ages 3–5. Lunch is $8.19 for adults; kids eat for the same price as at dinner.

ANAHEIM-AREA FULL-SERVICE RESTAURANTS

SOUTHERN CALIFORNIA IS A MOTHER LODE of wonderful dining, and if we directed you to Newport Beach, La Jolla, or LA, we could guarantee you a fantastic eating experience every night. In that you've chosen Disneyland as your destination, however, we've elected to profile only solid restaurants that you can reach by car or cab in 15 minutes or less. That said, here are our picks.

Anaheim White House ★★★★½

ITALIAN	EXPENSIVE	QUALITY ★★★★½	VALUE ★★★½

887 S. Anaheim Blvd., Anaheim; ☎ 714-772-1381; anaheimwhitehouse.com

Reservations Recommended. **When to go** Dinner. **Entrée range** $27–$42. **Service** ★★★★★. **Friendliness** ★★★★. **Bar** Full bar; plentiful wine list. **Dress** Business casual. **Disabled access** Yes. **Hours** Monday–Friday, 11:30 a.m.–2:30 p.m. and 5–10 p.m.; Sunday brunch, 11 a.m.–3 p.m.

SETTING AND ATMOSPHERE Local institution the Anaheim White House sits in a restored Victorian originally built in 1909. It has nine different dining rooms, all with thick gold-and-white drapes and bright-gold accents against a bright-white background. Tables are set with fine bone china and the best flatware. Service is extremely gracious and knowledgeable.

HOUSE SPECIALTIES Italian seafood recipes from northern Italy highlight an extensive menu, each dish sporting the name of a famous Italian or Italian American celebrity—for example, the Gwen Stefani Ravioli (little pasta pillows stuffed with lobster in a ginger-citrus sauce), named for the

Anaheim-born pop star, and the Fendi Prawns (giant shrimp baked in their shells and served over pasta with fresh herbs and a sautéed-scallop garnish), a culinary tribute to the ultra-glam Milan fashion house.

OTHER RECOMMENDATIONS Chicken stuffed with ham and Fontina cheese in a light mushroom sauce.

SUMMARY AND COMMENTS The White House only seems to get better. The menu of northern Italian recipes is kept fresh and timely, and service is spot-on. This is an elegant restaurant—leave the kids with a sitter.

Carolina's Italian Restaurant ★★★

SOUTHERN ITALIAN	INEXPENSIVE	QUALITY ★★★	VALUE ★★★½

12045 Chapman Ave., Garden Grove; ☎ 714-971-5551; carolinasitalianrestaurant.com

Reservations Recommended. **When to go** Dinner. **Entrée range** $9–$21. **Service** ★★½. **Friendliness** ★★★½. **Bar** Extensive beer and wine lists. **Dress** Casual. **Disabled access** Yes. **Hours** Daily, 11 a.m.–10 p.m.

SETTING AND ATMOSPHERE Classic Italian family restaurant replete with wall murals depicting the motherland, comfortable seating, and the overwhelming aroma of garlic and olive oil.

HOUSE SPECIALTIES You can't go wrong with any one of more than three dozen hearty pasta dishes, from a very traditional meat sauce to an outstanding lasagna. The kitchen's showcase is a slab of fresh Atlantic salmon in a butter-garlic-mustard sauce.

OTHER RECOMMENDATIONS The Taste of Italy features a massive plate of shrimp fettuccine alfredo, chicken penne pesto, and spaghetti with meatballs. The house-made tiramasu, if you can manage more food after their large plates, is a treat.

SUMMARY AND COMMENTS Family owned and operated for three generations, we can't believe we missed this place all these years. Carolina's also features more than 200 beers from around the globe and a rather well-selected wine list for such a place. Portions tend toward the gigantic, so bring your appetite. On a side note, it seems that they've earned the endorsement of the local firefighters . . . who show up in packs virtually every day of the week.

The Catch ★★★½

SEAFOOD/STEAK	EXPENSIVE	QUALITY ★★★★	VALUE ★★★½

2100 E. Katella Ave., Anaheim; ☎ 714-935-0101; catchanaheim.com

Reservations Recommended. **When to go** Lunch or dinner. **Entrée range** $13–$70. **Service** ★★★. **Friendliness** ★★★½. **Bar** Full bar. **Dress** Business casual. **Disabled access** Yes. **Hours** Monday–Friday, 11:30 a.m.–10 p.m.; Saturday–Sunday, 11:30 p.m.–4 p.m. and 5 p.m.–10 p.m.

SETTING AND ATMOSPHERE Clean, contemporary take on a steak house classic, The Catch exudes urban chic with a comfortable blend of hardwood,

Anaheim-area Restaurants by Cuisine

CUISINE	OVERALL RATING	COST	QUALITY RATING	VALUE RATING
AMERICAN				
Mr. Stox, E. Katella Ave.	★★★½	Exp	★★★½	★★★
Clancy's Clubhouse S. Harbor Blvd.	★★★	Mod	★★★	★★★
CHINESE/NORTHERN				
Mas' Chinese Islamic Restaurant E. Orangethorpe Ave.	★★★½	Mod	★★★	★★★½
CONTEMPORARY				
Mr. Stox, E. Katella Ave.	★★★½	Exp	★★★½	★★★
GERMAN				
The Phoenix Club, S. Sanderson Dr.	★★★	Mod	★★★½	★★★
ITALIAN				
Anaheim White House S. Anaheim Blvd.	★★★★½	Exp	★★★★½	★★★½
Luigi's D'Italia S. State College Blvd.	★★★½	Inexp/ Mod	★★★½	★★★★
Carolina's Italian Restaurant Chapman Ave.	★★★	Inexp	★★★	★★★½
MEXICAN				
Gabbi's Mexican Kitchen S. Glassell St.	★★★	Mod	★★★★	★★★½
SEAFOOD				
The Catch, E. Katella Ave.	★★★½	Exp	★★★★	★★★½
McCormick & Schmick's Grille W. Katella Ave.	★★★	Mod	★★★	★★★
STEAK				
Park Avenue Steaks & Chops Beach Blvd.	★★★★½	Exp	★★★★	★★★★
JW's Steakhouse Anaheim Marriott	★★★★	Exp	★★★★	★★★★
Morton's, S. Harbor Blvd.	★★★★	Exp	★★★½	★★★½
The Catch, E. Katella Ave.	★★★½	Exp	★★★★	★★★½
Prime Cut Café & Wine Bar W. Katella Ave.	★★★	Mod	★★★	★★★½

glass, and tile. Expect to see dozens of young urban professionals; old, diehard loyalists; and even a smattering of professional athletes who play for the local Angels baseball and Anaheim Ducks hockey teams.

HOUSE SPECIALTIES Grilled fresh fish, premium meats, and chops dominate the menu. The drunken mahimahi, a lightly blackened fresh fillet splashed with tequila, is as good as it is simple. And for steak lovers, a rare baseball-cut top sirloin may be the best cut you're likely to see anywhere.

OTHER RECOMMENDATIONS The lunch menu features butcher-block sandwiches: piles of thinly sliced meats and fish piled high on fresh slabs of shepherd's bread, accompanied by all the usual condiments and some not-so-common spreads such as chipotle mayo. For dinner, try the terrific bone-in rib eye called the Tomahawk chop.

SUMMARY AND COMMENTS Resurrected from the demolition ball that was part of Anaheim's urban renewal project, The Catch reopened in 2010 under new leadership and in a brand-new location. Yes, the place is very expensive, but you're not likely to find a more beautiful yet comfortable room, attentive service, or quality food prepared with love and care anywhere close by. It has a vibrant bar scene favored by local luminaries, a beautiful dining room, and even a nicely appointed patio.

Clancy's Clubhouse ★★★

AMERICAN	MODERATE	QUALITY ★★★	VALUE ★★★

2191 S. Harbor Blvd., Anaheim; ☎ 714-750-7500; clancysclubhouse.com

Reservations Not accepted. When to go Lunch; dinner. Entrée range $8–$28. Service ★★. Friendliness ★★★. Bar Full bar. Dress Casual. Disabled access Yes. Hours Monday–Tuesday, 4 p.m.–midnight; Wednesday–Sunday, 11:30 a.m.–midnight.

SETTING AND ATMOSPHERE Pure sports bar with full, high-definition flat-panel TVs in every direction, a few booths, and several rooms of tables, all with a view of the televised action.

HOUSE SPECIALTIES Wings marinated, baked, fried, and broiled to perfection with all the usual sauces, as well as a very different mango habañero. The pulled pork sandwich swims in a signature barbecue sauce.

OTHER RECOMMENDATIONS Prime rib and steaks, including a baseball-cut top sirloin (a ball of meat with all the flavor of a sirloin and the tenderness of a filet mignon), are surprisingly good for a sports bar.

SUMMARY AND COMMENTS Just a few clicks down the road from the resort, Clancy's is a great alternative to the crammed insanity of the ESPN Zone in Downtown Disney. The menu is expansive and covers a lot of bases from sports bar staples such as chicken wings to a decent cut of beef. Lots of locals and a friendly vibe that sometimes consumes the staff (that is, service can be sporadic).

Gabbi's Mexican Kitchen ★★★

GOURMET MEXICAN	MODERATE	QUALITY ★★★★	VALUE ★★★½

141 S. Glassell St., Orange; ☎ 714-633-3038; gabbimex.com

Reservations Recommended. When to go Lunch or dinner. Entrée range

Great Eats in and around Anaheim

BEST BURGER

In-N-Out Burger 600 S. Brookhurst St., Anaheim; ☎ 800-786-1000; **in-n-out.com.** This small family-owned chain is the gold standard for burgers. Hamburgers, cheeseburgers, fries, and shakes are all they do—and nobody does them better. Ask for the Double-Double (double meat, double cheese), "animal style" (heavy on all the condiments).

BEST CHINESE

Grand China Restaurant 575 W. Chapman Ave., Anaheim; ☎ 714-740-1888. Really outstanding service differentiates this spot from its nearby competitors. The menu's pretty standard, but what they do, they do well—and with a big smile. The broccoli with beef and sweet-and-sour chicken are first-rate.

BEST FAMILY/ICE CREAM

Tiffy's Family Restaurant 1060 W. Katella Ave., Anaheim; ☎ 714-635-1801. Tiffy's has been serving up solid breakfasts, lunches, and dinners since Disneyland was built. Great Belgian waffles and homemade ice cream are their hallmarks. Quality and service can be sketchy at times, but Tiffy's has an entrenched and fiercely loyal following.

BEST INDIAN

Punjabi Tandoor 327 S. Anaheim Blvd., Ste. A, Anaheim; ☎ 714-635-3155; **punjabitandoor.com.** The lunch buffet is good, but the fresh tandoori in the evening is exceptional. Offers original dishes and excellent naan.

BEST JAPANESE

Koisan Japanese Cuisine 1132 E. Katella Ave., Orange; ☎ 714-639-2330; **koisanjapanesecuisine.com.** Cozy and intimate, it's perfect for theme-park decompression, and the menu is pretty extensive.

BEST MEDITERRANEAN

Zankou Chicken 2424 W. Ball Rd., Anaheim; ☎ 714-229-2060; **zankouchicken.com.** Forget that this place is a chain, disregard the cheesy ambience, and go for the spit-roasted chicken, hummus, and *shwarma* beef. Inexpensive and delicious.

BEST MEXICAN

La Casa Garcia 531 W. Chapman Ave., Anaheim; ☎ 714-740-1108. An Anaheim institution with an authentic Tex-Mex twist on traditional Mexican food. *Carnitas, barbacoa* (beef slow-cooked in a red-chile sauce), and three-flavor chimichangas are not to be missed.

Los Sanchez 11906 Garden Grove Blvd., Garden Grove; ☎ 714-590-9300; **lossanchez.com.** This locals-only gem serves authentic Sonoran cuisine at ridiculously reasonable prices. Fish ceviche, *lengua* (tongue) tacos, seafood soup, and the best chicken mole you've ever had, served in an authentically unpretentious environment, with all the fresh radishes and cilantro you can eat.

$8–$21. **Service** ★★★. **Friendliness** ★★★. **Bar** Full bar. **Dress** Casual. **Disabled access** Yes. **Hours** Daily, 11 a.m.–11 p.m.

SETTING AND ATMOSPHERE Locals flock to Gabbi's rustically hip vintage storefront that has no sign (look for the *poquito* patio next door to the Army surplus store). Just steps south of Orange's beloved plaza in charming Old Town, Gabbi's tall ceilings, exposed brick, and giant, colorful Mexican urns add style to the narrow space.

HOUSE SPECIALTIES Mayan Puerco-Chuc; quesadilla cuitlacoche; squash blossom chile rellenos.

OTHER RECOMMENDATIONS Enchiladas suizas and any of the signature margaritas made from a tequila collection that would make a desperado blush.

SUMMARY AND COMMENTS In this county teeming with taco stands and burrito counters, chef-owner Gabbi Patrick stands apart with her more refined, regional takes on Mexican food that reflect both her Napa training and her Latino family's roots in the restaurant business.

JW's Steakhouse ★★★★

STEAK HOUSE	EXPENSIVE	QUALITY ★★★★	VALUE ★★★★

Anaheim Marriott, 700 W. Convention Way; ☎ 714-703-3187; marriottanaheimhotel.com

Reservations Recommended. **When to go** Dinner. **Entrée range** $18–$56. **Service** ★★★★. **Friendliness** ★★★★. **Bar** Wine list and full bar. **Dress** Dressy casual. **Disabled access** Yes. **Hours** Daily, generally 5–10 p.m. (hours vary according to hotel occupancy; there's no set schedule).

SETTING AND ATMOSPHERE The restaurant is, in a word, gorgeous. Minimalist modern with an Asian touch.

HOUSE SPECIALTIES Steak . . . almost any of the featured cuts are outstanding. Try the Kobe flatiron, rubbed with spices and pepper, grilled to order, and served as a cutlet. It's an underrated cut that's as lean as most filets and more flavorful than a sirloin.

OTHER RECOMMENDATIONS Wedge salad: one quarter head of iceberg lettuce with Gorgonzola-cheese dressing and maple bacon.

SUMMARY AND COMMENTS Right around the corner and down the street from Morton's, JW's actually serves a better steak in a nicer room with better service. The room is absolutely stunning (ask for the cozy, private nook behind the fireplace), the meat nearly flawless, and the service sharp and warm. The trick is to catch the restaurant open: The hotel closes it when occupancy falls, so operating hours can be erratic.

Luigi's D'Italia ★★★½

ITALIAN	INEXPENSIVE–MODERATE	QUALITY ★★★½	VALUE ★★★★

801 S. State College Blvd., Anaheim; ☎ 714-490-0990; luigisditaliaoc.com

Reservations Recommended. **When to go** Lunch or dinner. **Entrée range** $11–$25. **Service** ★★★. **Friendliness** ★★★. **Bar** Wine and beer. **Dress** Casual. **Disabled access** Yes. **Hours** Monday–Friday, 11 a.m.–10 p.m.; Saturday–Sunday, noon–10 p.m.

SETTING AND ATMOSPHERE Classic tacky Italian, reminiscent of just about every neighborhood mom-and-pop pizzeria in America (think faux grapevines, funky murals, and Chianti-bottle candleholders). But there is something homey and comforting in this, and the service is generally warm and friendly.

HOUSE SPECIALTIES Better-than-average hand-tossed pizzas with all the familiar toppings (pepperoni, mushroom, sausage, and such); a very tasty (and hearty) eggplant Sorrentino.

OTHER RECOMMENDATIONS The pastas, including a superb spaghetti Bolognese, are commendable.

SUMMARY AND COMMENTS When the pocketbook can't take another huge hit no matter how good the menu looks, head to Luigi's. Old-fashioned Italian fare, a welcoming (if kitschy) ambience, and friendly smiles await. The pizzas and pastas, Italian staples, are all familiar, hearty, and tasty, if not overly generous in their portions. The kids will love watching the pizzas get tossed, and your credit card will breathe a sigh of relief.

Mas' Chinese Islamic Restaurant ★★★½

NORTHERN CHINESE	MODERATE	QUALITY ★★★	VALUE ★★★½

601 E. Orangethorpe Ave., Anaheim; ☎ 714-446-9553

Reservations Recommended. When to go Lunch or dinner. Entrée range $10–$26. Service ★★★. Friendliness ★★★½. Bar None. Dress Casual but modest (no shorts). Disabled access Yes. Hours Monday and Wednesday–Saturday, 11 a.m.–3 p.m.; Monday and Wednesday–Thursday, 5–9 p.m.; Friday–Saturday, 5–10 p.m.

SETTING AND ATMOSPHERE One of a small chain of Islamic Chinese restaurants, this is the real deal. Mas' Islamic's dining room is spacious, with comfortable booths and large tables. The decor blends Middle Eastern and Chinese motifs with lots of tile, repetitive patterned mosaics, and lofty arches.

HOUSE SPECIALTIES Get the thick sesame bread with green onions as a starter. Any lamb dish is a sure bet, especially the one served with *sa cha,* a spicy brown sauce.

OTHER RECOMMENDATIONS The warm pots—northern-Chinese stews—are great, as is the beef with green onions.

SUMMARY AND COMMENTS This is a veritable institution among local Muslims (Arabs and East and Southeast Asians), so expect to see women in veils and burkas and men dressed very conservatively; also, note that no alcohol is served. Service is gracious, if a bit English-challenged. Stick to the northern-Chinese specialties—the more familiar Chinese side of the menu is less exciting.

McCormick & Schmick's Grille ★★★

SEAFOOD	MODERATE	QUALITY ★★★	VALUE ★★★

321 W. Katella Ave., Anaheim; ☎ 714-535-9000; mccormickandschmicks.com

Reservations Recommended. **When to go** Lunch or dinner. **Entrée range** $15–$56. **Service** ★★★. **Friendliness** ★★★★. **Bar** Full bar and extensive wine list. **Dress** Business casual. **Disabled access** Yes. **Hours** Monday–Wednesday and Sunday, 11:30 a.m.–10 p.m.; Thursday–Saturday, 11:30 a.m.–11 p.m.

SETTING AND ATMOSPHERE This large chain of seafood eateries designs each of its units differently to match its local surroundings. In addition to lots of dark hardwoods and spacious booths, the decor here takes its cues from the rich agricultural history of the area.

HOUSE SPECIALTIES Fish . . . fresh and infinitely variable. Each chef is free to choose from among 80 different preparations, and there's an abundance of fresh selections. You can't miss with king crab, lobster, fresh salmon, or killer fresh swordfish.

SUMMARY AND COMMENTS This is a very popular spot with local business types, and waits without reservations can be long. The menu can be overwhelming; on the other hand, there's something for everyone, even folks who don't eat fish.

Morton's ★★★★

STEAK HOUSE	EXPENSIVE	QUALITY ★★★½	VALUE ★★★½

1895 S. Harbor Blvd., Anaheim; ☎ 714-621-0101; mortons.com

Reservations Recommended. **When to go** Dinner. **Entrée range** $35–$85. **Service** ★★★★. **Friendliness** ★★★★. **Bar** Extensive wine list and full bar. **Dress** Dressy casual. **Disabled access** Yes. **Hours** Monday–Saturday, 4:30–11 p.m.; Sunday, 4:30–10 p.m.

SETTING AND ATMOSPHERE Classic steak house with overstuffed booths, soft lighting, and dark hardwoods.

HOUSE SPECIALTIES Go for the double-cut filet mignon with béarnaise sauce.

OTHER RECOMMENDATIONS The double-cut bone-in rib eye is a Chicago staple and beef-eater's dream: 22 ounces of prime steak, grilled to order.

SUMMARY AND COMMENTS Morton's is a carnivore's delight . . . beef, lamb, pork, and chicken dominate the menu. Of course, there's a smattering of fish options, including shrimp in several different iterations, but this place is really about the beef. Lots of classic recipes, such as steak Diane and veal Oscar.

Mr. Stox ★★★½

AMERICAN/CONTEMPORARY	EXPENSIVE	QUALITY ★★★½	VALUE ★★★

1105 E. Katella Ave., Anaheim; ☎ 714-634-2994; mrstox.com

Reservations Recommended. **When to go** Dinner. **Entrée range** $20–$40. **Service** ★★★★. **Friendliness** ★★★. **Bar** Extensive wine list and full bar. **Dress** Business casual. **Disabled access** Yes. **Hours** Monday–Friday, 11:30 a.m.–2:30 p.m. and daily, 5:30–10 p.m.

SETTING AND ATMOSPHERE One of the oldest restaurants under continuous ownership in Orange County, Mr. Stox is a beacon of tradition and continuity. Founded and owned by local foodies and wine aficionados Chick, Debbie, and Tom Marshall, the restaurant is a timeless experience in good taste, comfort, and warmth. The dining rooms and lounge exude a simple, contemporary air reflective of the California experience, with works by local artists adorning the walls.

HOUSE SPECIALTIES Chef Scott Razeck does a seasonal menu, heavy on local flavors with a contemporary twist. The duck, a mesquite-grilled breast and confit of leg, is outstanding, as are the Maryland blue-crab cakes with Dijon-mustard sauce and spicy peanut coleslaw.

OTHER RECOMMENDATIONS The prime rib is always good—reliably tender.

SUMMARY AND COMMENTS The Marshalls are Orange County's first family of haute cuisine and their flagship, Mr. Stox, is a virtual landmark among epicureans. They have one of the largest and deepest wine cellars in the county and regularly sponsor cooking and demonstration events. This is where you'll find the area's chefs dining on their night off.

Park Avenue Steaks & Chops ★★★★½

STEAK HOUSE	EXPENSIVE	QUALITY ★★★★	VALUE ★★★★

11200 Beach Blvd., Stanton; ☎ 714-901-4400; parkavedining.com

Reservations Recommended. When to go Dinner. Entrée range $19–$39. Service ★★★. Friendliness ★★★½. Bar Full bar. Dress Dressy casual/business. Disabled access Yes. Hours Tuesday–Friday, 11 a.m.–midnight; Saturday–Sunday, 4 p.m.–midnight.

SETTING AND ATMOSPHERE From the flagstone walls and Sputnik-like lighting to red leather booths, this place exudes 1950s modern chic. The original Brat Pack would feel right at home here. There's also an expansive terrace and meticulously maintained grounds where the chef grows his own herbs, vegetables, and fruit.

HOUSE SPECIALTIES Delmonico bone-in rib eye and the five-spiced baked salmon drizzled with honey.

OTHER RECOMMENDATIONS The chef does a marvelous job with a marinated skirt steak, dripping with a ginger, molasses, and soy sauce. The lobster mac-and-cheese appetizer is a real palette pleaser.

SUMMARY AND COMMENTS Park Avenue is a throwback to all things mid-20th century—except the menu. The proprietors have managed to avoid the kitsch and concentrate on those things that evoke a simpler, less complicated era—down to a friendly bar shaking up some of the meanest martinis in Orange County. The food is exceptionally good (award winning) but service gets a little sloppy, especially on slower nights. They've also opened a more casual garden restaurant on the same grounds, offering a compact menu of Italian classics.

The Phoenix Club ★★★

GERMAN	MODERATE	QUALITY ★★★½	VALUE ★★★

1340 S. Sanderson Dr., behind Honda Arena, Anaheim;
☎ 714-563-4166; thephoenixclub.com

Reservations Recommended. **When to go** Lunch or dinner. **Entrée range** $9–$30. **Service** ★★★. **Friendliness** ★★★★. **Bar** Wine list, extensive draft-beer offerings, and full bar. **Dress** Casual. **Disabled access** Yes. **Hours** Sunday, 5–9 p.m.; Tuesday–Thursday, 11:30 a.m.–1:30 p.m. and 5–9 p.m.; Friday–Saturday, 11:30 a.m.–1:30 p.m. and 5–10 p.m.

SETTING AND ATMOSPHERE Once a private club reserved for family members of the original German settlers of Anaheim and more recent émigrés, this famous landmark is now open to the public (members are still welcome and enjoy a few extra privileges). Choose from the formal, elegantly appointed Loreley dining room or the boisterous Bierstube, with more than a half-dozen German beers on tap. The Bierstube's menu is more limited than the Loreley's, trending toward less-fancy preparations, but it's these basic dishes that keep folks coming back. Where the Loreley is quiet and peaceful, the Bierstube is conducive to raucous eating, drinking, and carousing. Live music seems omnipresent, from local and guest polka bands to renowned accordion artists.

HOUSE SPECIALTIES Wursts, kraut, pork roast, mixed platters, wiener schnitzel, and sauerbraten are the best in a 100-mile radius.

OTHER RECOMMENDATIONS Pork in creamy Champagne-mushroom sauce.

SUMMARY AND COMMENTS The bastion of Anaheim's founding families and subsequent waves of German immigrants, The Phoenix Club offers a little taste of the *mutterland* far from home. The food is good, occasionally great; the beer is always cold; and the help is always ready to show you a good time, German or not. During Oktoberfest, the place rocks. The kids will love the early reminders of a rough and rural Anaheim and the oompah bands, Mom and Dad will love the German beers, and everyone will love the sweet-and-sour flavors of German cuisine.

Prime Cut Café & Wine Bar ★★★

| STEAK HOUSE | MODERATE | QUALITY ★★★ | VALUE ★★★½ |

1547 W. Katella Ave. (Stadium Promenade Center), Orange;
☎ **714-532-4300; primecutcafe.com**

Reservations Recommended. **When to go** Lunch or dinner. **Entrée range** $8–$29. **Service** ★★★. **Friendliness** ★★★. **Bar** Wine and cocktails. **Dress** Casual. **Disabled access** Yes. **Hours** Sunday–Thursday, 11 a.m.–10 p.m.; Friday–Saturday, 11 a.m.–midnight.

SETTING AND ATMOSPHERE Polished but laid-back, this dapper newcomer is a welcome independent in a sea of chain operations. A massive granite bar anchors the attractive space that also offers a roomy patio overlooking the center's water fountain.

HOUSE SPECIALTIES Slow-roasted prime rib is offered in three sizes, all partnered with good Yorkshire pudding and rich creamed spinach. A huge pork "prime rib" chop is another winner, paired with corn bread stuffing and braised spiced apples. For starters, don't miss the terrific house-smoked salmon with fennel and horseradish.

OTHER RECOMMENDATIONS Prime rib may hog the spotlight, but steaks, burgers, and entrée salads often outshine the showy star of the menu. Sides such as iron-skillet corn bread, potato gratin, or mascarpone polenta are scene-stealers, as are from-scratch desserts.

SUMMARY AND COMMENTS Prime Cut Café does a good job of making first-rate dining affordable and approachable. Eighty-plus wines sold by the glass, taste, or bottle is an attraction for wine lovers, though wine snobs might find the list a bit lowbrow. The menu offers lots of appetizers and snacks that pair well with wine, making this a swell option for a quick bite or grown-up get-together. The central location means crowds swell or recede according to events at nearby Anaheim Stadium, Honda Pond, or even what's hot at the adjacent multiplex cinema.

SHOPPING *at* DISNEYLAND

SHOPS ADD REALISM AND ATMOSPHERE to the various theme settings and offer souvenirs, clothing, novelties, jewelry, decorator items, and more. Much of the merchandise displayed (with the exception of Disney trademark souvenir items), though, is available back home and elsewhere, so we recommend bypassing the shops on a 1-day visit. If you have 2 or more days to spend at Disneyland Resort, browse in the early afternoon, when many attractions are crowded.

Our recommendations notwithstanding, we realize that for many guests, Disney souvenirs and memorabilia are irresistible. One of our readers writes:

> People have a compelling need to buy Disney stuff at Disneyland. When you get home, you wonder why you ever got a cashmere sweater with Mickey Mouse embroidered on the breast, or a tie with tiny Goofys all over it. Maybe they put something in the food?

If you don't want to lug your packages around, you can leave them at the information stand just inside the front gate and pick them up as you exit the park. Retrieving your purchases might take a while if you depart after a parade or fireworks show or at closing, when guests exit en masse. If you're staying at a Disneyland Resort hotel, your loot will be delivered directly to your resort's bellhop desk (by 7a.m. the following day) on request. If you have a problem with your purchases or need to make a return, call Disneyland Exclusive Merchandise at ☎ 800-760-3566, Monday–Friday, 8 a.m.–5 p.m. PST. If you return home and realize that you forgot to buy those Rastafarian mouse ears or some similarly essential tchotchke, a large selection of park-exclusive merchandise is now available to order online at **disneyparks.com/store.**

DOWNTOWN DISNEY

DOWNTOWN DISNEY, verdant and landscaped by day, pops alive with neon and glitter at night. The complex offers more than 300,000 square feet of specialty shopping, clubs, restaurants, and movie theaters. Many of the restaurants offer entertainment in addition to dining, including **House of Blues** and **Ralph Brennan's Jazz Kitchen.** The **ESPN Zone** is a

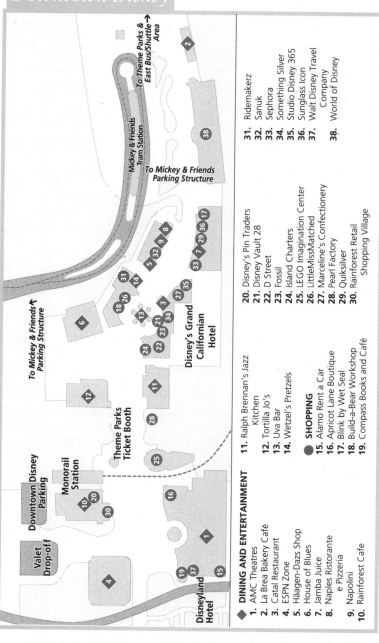

Downtown Disney

◆ DINING AND ENTERTAINMENT

1. AMC Theatres
2. La Brea Bakery Café
3. Catal Restaurant
4. ESPN Zone
5. Häagen-Dazs Shop
6. House of Blues
7. Jamba Juice
8. Naples Ristorante e Pizzeria
9. Napolini
10. Rainforest Cafe
11. Ralph Brennan's Jazz Kitchen
12. Tortilla Jo's
13. Uva Bar
14. Wetzel's Pretzels

● SHOPPING

15. Alamo Rent a Car
16. Apricot Lane Boutique
17. Blink by Wet Seal
18. Build-a-Bear Workshop
19. Compass Books and Café
20. Disney's Pin Traders
21. Disney Vault 28
22. D Street
23. Fossil
24. Island Charters
25. LEGO Imagination Center
26. LittleMissMatched
27. Marceline's Confectionery
28. Pearl Factory
29. Quiksilver
30. Rainforest Retail Shopping Village
31. Ridemakerz
32. Sanuk
33. Sephora
34. Something Silver
35. Studio Disney 365
36. Sunglass Icon
37. Walt Disney Travel Company
38. World of Disney

sports bar and restaurant with dozens of giant TV screens. Other restaurant options include the **Naples Ristorante e Pizzeria, Tortilla Jo's** Mexican restaurant, and jungle-themed dining at the **Rainforest Cafe.**

If you're not hungry, there's always shopping and a 12-theater **AMC Movieplex** to keep you occupied. A 40,000-square-foot **World of Disney** store, the second largest on the planet, anchors the shopping scene. Other retailers include **Compass Books; Sanuk,** a shoe store; **LittleMiss-Matched,** selling socks that don't match (for more than you'd pay for socks that do); **Apricot Lane,** for fashion apparel, jewelry, handbags, and accessories; **Studio Disney 365,** offering hairstyling and braiding for girls who are a little too old for a princess makeover at Bibbidi Bobbidi Boutique in Disneyland Park; cosmetics at **Sephora;** and **Something Silver,** specializing in jewelry. The **LEGO Imagination Center** features interactive play tables with LEGO bricks. At **Build-A-Bear Workshop,** you can customize a teddy bear, starting from scratch with the bearskin, stuffing it, and then accessorizing it.

Our map of Downtown Disney, listing storefronts and restaurants, appears on page 213.

ANAHEIM GARDEN WALK

ANAHEIM GARDEN WALK is a shopping, dining, and entertainment venue that stretches from West Katella Avenue to Disney Way. Built on three levels and nicely landscaped, the Garden Walk effectively doubles the restaurant, lounge, and shopping choices for Disneyland Resort visitors and attendees of conventions at nearby Anaheim Convention Center. Restaurants include **Bar Louie, Bubba Gump Shrimp Co., California Pizza Kitchen, The Cheesecake Factory, Fire + Ice, McCormick & Schmick's Grille, P.F. Chang's Chinese Bistro, Pop the Cork Wine Bar,** and **Roy's Hawaiian Fusion Cuisine.**

For entertainment, there's a 14-screen movie theater, a 41-lane bowling complex and nightspot combo, a wine bar, and an ultra lounge. Among the 20 retailers are **Harley-Davidson, Hollister, LUSH Cosmetics,** and **White House/Black Market.** For additional information, see **anaheimgardenwalk.com** or call ☎ 714-635-7410.

PART FIVE

DISNEYLAND PARK

ARRIVING *and* GETTING ORIENTED

IF YOU DRIVE, you will probably be directed to the massive Mickey and Friends parking garage on West Street near Ball Road. Parking costs $15 for cars, $20 for RVs, and $25 for buses. Be sure to make a note of your section, row, and space. A tram will transport you to a loading/unloading area connected to the entrance by a pedestrian corridor. Many locals prefer to to park in the Toy Story surface lot on Harbor Boulevard south of Katella Avenue, which offers shuttle service to the east side of the resort entrance esplanade. Because security screening is conducted just before passing through the turnstiles, the lines to enter the park are often quite lengthy. Two entrance gates, 14 and 19, are blocked by trees situated in the entrance plaza about 10 feet from the security checkpoint. The trees sometimes inhibit the formation of a line in front of both of the obstructed gates. These gates (14 and 19) are staffed nonetheless and draw guests from adjacent lines 13 or 15 and 18 or 20. When this happens, it significantly speeds up the entry process for guests waiting in lines 13 and 20. Our advice on arriving, therefore, is to inspect the lines leading to gates 14 and 19 and join whichever looks to be shortest. Later in the day, the outside gates (1 and 32) tend to be fastest for re-entry. Stroller and wheelchair rentals are available in the Main Entrance Plaza between Disneyland and DCA. As you enter Main Street, City Hall is to your left, serving as the center for general information, lost and found, and entertainment information.

Be sure to pick up a park map as you pass through the turnstiles. Maps are also available in the passages connecting the park entrance to Main Street, U.S.A.; at City Hall; and at a number of shops throughout the park. Also, pick up a *Times Guide*. This pamphlet contains the daily entertainment schedule for live shows, parades,

Disneyland Park

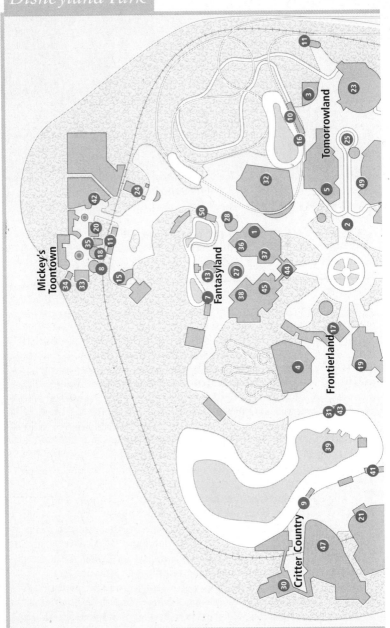

Mickey's
Toontown

Fantasyland

Tomorrowland

Frontierland

Critter Country

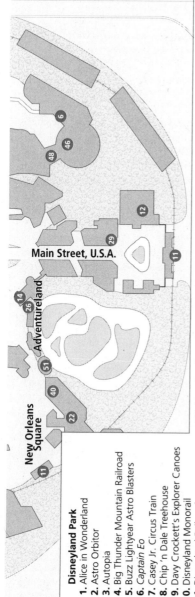

Main Street, U.S.A.

Adventureland

New Orleans Square

Disneyland Park

1. Alice in Wonderland
2. Astro Orbitor
3. Autopia
4. Big Thunder Mountain Railroad
5. Buzz Lightyear Astro Blasters
6. Captain Eo
7. Casey Jr. Circus Train
8. Chip 'n Dale Treehouse
9. Davy Crockett's Explorer Canoes
10. Disneyland Monorail
11. Disneyland Railroad
12. *The Disneyland Story,*
    presenting Great Moments
    with Mr. Lincoln
13. Dumbo the Flying Elephant
14. *Enchanted Tiki Room*
15. Fantasyland Theatre/
    Disney Princess Fantasy Faire
16. Finding Nemo Submarine Voyage
17. Frontierland Shootin' Exposition
18. Gadget's Go Coaster
19. The Golden Horseshoe
20. Goofy's Playhouse
21. The Haunted Mansion
22. Indiana Jones Adventure
23. Innoventions

24. It's a Small World
25. Jedi Training Academy
26. Jungle Cruise
27. King Arthur Carrousel
28. Mad Tea Party
29. Main Street Cinema
30. The Many Adventures
    of Winnie the Pooh
31. *Mark Twain Riverboat*
32. Matterhorn Bobsleds
33. Mickey's House and Meet Mickey
34. Minnie's House
35. *Miss Daisy, Donald's Boat*
36. Mr. Toad's Wild Ride
37. Peter Pan's Flight
38. Pinocchio's Daring Journey

39. Pirate's Lair on Tom Sawyer Island
40. Pirates of the Caribbean
41. Raft to Tom Sawyer Island
42. Roger Rabbit's Car Toon Spin
43. Sailing Ship *Columbia*
44. Sleeping Beauty Castle
45. Snow White's Scary Adventures
46. Space Mountain
47. Splash Mountain
48. Starcade
49. Star Tours: The Adventures Continue
50. Storybook Land Canal Boats
51. Tarzan's Treehouse

NOT TO BE MISSED AT DISNEYLAND PARK

ADVENTURELAND
- Indiana Jones Adventure

CRITTER COUNTRY
- Splash Mountain

FRONTIERLAND
- Big Thunder Mountain Railroad
- Golden Horseshoe

NEW ORLEANS SQUARE
- The Haunted Mansion
- Pirates of the Caribbean

TOMORROWLAND
- Space Mountain
- Star Tours: The Adventures Continue

LIVE ENTERTAINMENT
- *Fantasmic!*

fireworks, and other events and tells you where you can find the characters. If a *Times Guide* is not available for the day you visit (a very rare occurrence), the daily entertainment schedule will be included in the park map. The park map lists all the attractions, shops, and eateries and provides helpful information about first aid, baby care, assistance for the disabled, and more.

Notice on your map that Main Street ends at a central hub from which branch the entrances to four other sections of Disneyland: **Adventureland, Frontierland, Fantasyland,** and **Tomorrowland.** Two other "lands," **New Orleans Square** and **Critter Country,** can be reached through Adventureland and Frontierland. **Mickey's Toontown** is located on the far side of the railroad tracks from It's a Small World in Fantasyland. **Sleeping Beauty Castle,** the entrance to Fantasyland, is a focal landmark and the visual center of the park. The castle is a great place to meet if your group decides to split up for any reason during the day, and it can serve as an emergency meeting place if you are accidentally separated. Keep in mind, however, that the castle covers a lot of territory, so be specific about *where* to meet at the castle. Also be forewarned that parades and live shows sometimes make it difficult to access the entrance of the castle fronting the central hub. Another good meeting spot is the *Partners* statue of Mickey and Walt in the central hub.

STARTING THE TOUR

EVERYONE WILL SOON FIND his or her own favorite and not-so-favorite attractions in Disneyland Park. Be open-minded and adventuresome. Don't dismiss a particular ride or show as not being for you until *after* you have tried it. Our personal experience as well as our research indicates that each visitor is different in terms of which Disney offerings he or she most enjoys. So don't miss seeing an attraction because a friend from home didn't like it; that attraction may turn out to be your favorite.

We do recommend that you take advantage of what Disney does best—the fantasy adventures such as Indiana Jones Adventure and The Haunted Mansion, and the audio-animatronic (talking robots, that is) attractions such as Pirates of the Caribbean. Unless you have almost unlimited time, don't burn a lot of daylight browsing through the shops. Except for some special Disney souvenirs, you can find much of the same merchandise elsewhere. Try to minimize the time you spend on midway-type rides, as you probably have an amusement park, carnival, or state fair close to your hometown. Don't, however, mistake rides such as Splash Mountain and the Big Thunder Mountain Railroad for amusement-park rides. They may be of the flume-ride or the roller-coaster genre, but they represent pure Disney genius. Similarly, do not devote a lot of time to waiting in line for meals. Eat a good early breakfast before you come, snack on vendor-sold foods during the touring day, or follow the suggestions for meals incorporated into the various touring plans presented.

SINGLES LINES

YOU CAN OFTEN SAVE TIME WAITING IN LINE by taking advantage of singles lines, a separate line for people who are alone or don't mind riding alone or with a stranger. The objective of singles lines is to fill odd spaces left by groups who don't quite fill the entire ride vehicle. Because there aren't many singles and most groups aren't willing to split up, singles lines are usually much shorter than the regular line. In Disneyland Park, Indiana Jones Adventure and Splash Mountain have singles lines.

MAIN STREET, U.S.A.

THIS SECTION OF DISNEYLAND PARK is where you'll begin and end your visit. We have already mentioned that assistance and information are available at City Hall. The Disneyland Railroad stops at the Main Street Station, and you can board here for a grand circle tour of the park, or you can get off the train in New Orleans Square, Mickey's Toontown/Fantasyland, or Tomorrowland.

Main Street is an idealized version of a turn-of-the-20th-century American small-town street. Many visitors are surprised to discover that all the buildings are real, not elaborate props. Attention to detail is exceptional—interiors, furnishings, and fixtures conform to the period. As with any real Main Street, the Disney version is essentially a collection of shops and eating places, with a city hall, a fire station, and an old-time cinema. A mixed-media attraction combines static exhibits recalling the life of Walt Disney with a patriotic remembrance of Abraham Lincoln. Horse-drawn trolleys, fire engines, and horseless carriages give rides along Main Street and transport visitors to the central hub.

Disneyland Railroad ★★★

| APPEAL BY AGE | PRESCHOOL ★★★★★ | GRADE SCHOOL ★★★★ | TEENS ★★ |
| YOUNG ADULTS ★★★★ | OVER 30 ★★★½ | | SENIORS ★★★½ |

What it is Scenic railroad ride around the park's perimeter; also transportation to New Orleans Square, Mickey's Toontown, Fantasyland, and Tomorrowland.

Main Street Services

Most of the park's service facilities are centered in the Main Street section, including the following:

Baby Center/Baby-Care Needs At the central-hub end of Main Street

Banking Services/Currency Exchange At City Hall at the railroad-station end of Main Street

Disneyland and Local Attraction Information At City Hall

First Aid First Aid Center two doors from Plaza Inn at the central-hub end of Main Street

Live Entertainment and Parade Information At City Hall at the railroad-station end of Main Street

Lost Adults and Messages At City Hall

Lost and Found Lost and Found for the entire resort is located west of the entrance to Disneyland Park

Lost Children At the central-hub end of Main Street

Storage Lockers Down Main Street one block (as you walk toward the castle) and to the right

Scope and scale Major attraction. **When to go** After 11 a.m. or when you need transportation. **Special comments** The Main Street and Mickey's Toontown/Fantasyland stations are usually the least-congested boarding points. **Duration of ride** About 22 minutes for a complete circuit. **Average wait in line per 100 people ahead of you** 8 minutes. **Assumes** 3 trains operating. **Loading speed** Fast.

Thumbs Up for the Whole Family

DESCRIPTION AND COMMENTS A transportation ride that blends an eclectic variety of sights and experiences with an energy-saving way of getting around the park. In addition to providing a glimpse of all the lands except Adventureland, the train passes through the Grand Canyon Diorama (between Tomorrowland and Main Street), a three-dimensional replication of the canyon, complete with wildlife, as it appears from the southern rim. Another sight on the train circuit is Primeval World, a depiction of a prehistoric peat bog and rain forest populated by audio-animatronic (robotic) dinosaurs. Opened in 1966 Primeval World uses animatronics recycled from the Disney-designed Ford's Magic Skyway pavilion for the 1964 World's Fair, and was a precursor to a similar presentation at Epcot's Universe of Energy.

TOURING TIPS Save the train ride until after you have seen the featured attractions, or use it when you need transportation. It can also be a helpful way to relax during the peak times of the day when the crowds are swelling. You can get a good estimate of how long you'll wait for the next train by using the posted wait time sign outside each station. It will either list 5 minutes (three trains operating), 10 minutes (two trains), or 20 minutes (only one train). If you have small children who are hell-bent to see Mickey first thing in the morning, you might consider taking the train to Mickey's Toontown (a half circuit) and visiting Mickey in his dressing room as soon as you enter the park. Many families find that this tactic puts the kids in a more receptive frame of mind for the other attractions. On busy days, lines form at the New Orleans Square and Tomorrowland stations but rarely at the Main Street or Mickey's Toontown/Fantasyland stations.

The Disneyland Story, presenting Great Moments with Mr. Lincoln ★★★½

| APPEAL BY AGE | PRESCHOOL ★★★ | GRADE SCHOOL ★★ | TEENS ★★★★ |
| YOUNG ADULTS ★★★ | OVER 30 ★★★½ | | SENIORS ★★★★★ |

What it is Nostalgic exhibits documenting the Disney success story followed by an audio-animatronic patriotic presentation. **Scope and scale** Minor attraction. **When to go** During the hot, crowded period of the day. **Duration of show** 15 minutes including preshow. **Preshow** Disney exhibits. **Probable waiting time** Usually no wait.

Thumbs Up for the Whole Family

DESCRIPTION AND COMMENTS A warm and well-presented remembrance of the man who started it all. Well worth seeing; especially touching for those old enough to remember Walt Disney himself. The attraction consists of a museum of Disney memorabilia. Especially interesting are displays illustrating the construction and evolution of Disneyland, including a beautiful scale model of the park as it looked on opening day. A short film starring comedian (and former Disneyland cast member) Steve Martin and Donald Duck, originally created to celebrate the park's 50th anniversary in 2005, screens in the lobby as a preshow. Beyond the Disney memorabilia, guests are admitted to a large theater where Great Moments with Mr. Lincoln is presented. A patriotic performance, Great Moments stars an extremely lifelike and sophisticated audio-animatronic Abe Lincoln delivering an amalgamation of his notable speeches (though the over-familiar Gettysburg Address is not recited in full) as originally recorded by Royal Dano for the 1964 World's Fair. Lincoln's recently upgraded head is stunningly emotive, capable of wrinkling his brow and pursing his lips with unrivaled realism. New surround sound effects and songs borrowed from Epcot's American Adventure add to this brief but inspiring biography of America's 16th president.

DISNEY DISH WITH JIM HILL

FOUR SCORE AND SEVEN BALLOONS AGO In December 2009, the Imagineers were programming the new, improved version of Abraham Lincoln. They wanted this next-generation audio-animatronic to scan the audience and pick out guests to talk to. But how do you program for something like that when nobody is actually seated inside the hall? It's simple, really. You buy a couple of Mickey Mouse balloons, tie them to seats on different sides of the auditorium, and have the Abe figure focus its attention on those.

TOURING TIPS You usually do not have to wait long for this show, so see it during the busy times of day when lines are long elsewhere or as you are leaving the park. Sit up close to best see the detail on the Lincoln figure, or a few rows back for a more comfortable view of the screen.

Main Street Cinema ★★

APPEAL BY AGE	PRESCHOOL ★★½	GRADE SCHOOL ★★	TEENS ★★
YOUNG ADULTS ★½		OVER 30 ★★½	SENIORS ★★

What it is Vintage Disney cartoons. Scope and scale Diversion. When to go Whenever you want. Special comments Wonderful selection of old-time flicks. Duration of show Runs continuously. Preshow None. Probable waiting time No waiting.

DESCRIPTION AND COMMENTS An opening-day attraction, this small theater shows six classic Disney cartoons simultaneously. Early black-and-white Mickey Mouse shorts such as "Steamboat Willie" and "Plane Crazy" are screened, along with the celebrity caricature–stocked oddity "Mickey's Polo Team." The films have sound, but are played at low enough volume that the theater remains a quiet respite from the rest of the park.

TOURING TIPS Good place to get out of the sun or rain or to kill time while others in your group shop on Main Street. Fun, but not something you can't afford to miss. No seats; viewers stand.

Transportation Rides

DESCRIPTION AND COMMENTS Trolleys, buses, and the like that add color to Main Street. One-way only.

TOURING TIPS The rides will save you a walk to the central hub. Not worth waiting in line.

ADVENTURELAND

ADVENTURELAND IS THE FIRST "LAND" to the left of Main Street and somehow manages to seamlessly combine South Pacific island, Middle Eastern bazaar, and African safari themes. Transitions from one part of Adventureland to another feel quite natural, and the identity crisis inherent in the mixed-theme cocktail never registers in the minds of most guests. Space is tight in Adventureland, however, making for some of the worst pedestrian congestion in any of the Disney theme parks. If you're just passing through Adventureland, say on your way to Splash Mountain, you can avoid the congestion by transiting Frontierland instead.

Enchanted Tiki Room ★★★½

APPEAL BY AGE	PRESCHOOL ★★★★	GRADE SCHOOL ★★★½	TEENS ★★★
YOUNG ADULTS ★★★		OVER 30 ★★★★	SENIORS ★★★★½

What it is Audio-animatronic Pacific Island musical show. Scope and scale Minor attraction. When to go Anytime. Special comments Very, very unusual. Duration of show 14½ minutes. Preshow Talking totem poles. Probable waiting time 11 minutes.

DESCRIPTION AND COMMENTS An unusual sit-down theater performance in which more than 200 birds, flowers, and tiki-god statues sing and whistle through a Polynesian-style musical program. One of Walt's first large-scale uses of audio-animatronics, *Tiki Room* might be more impressive for the technology it took to get the show (ahem) flying in 1963. Beloved by Disneyland fans for its detail and immersive setting, the current version of the show is only slightly altered from the original.

TOURING TIPS One of the most bizarre (yet endearing) of the Disneyland Park entertainments and rarely very crowded. We like it in the late afternoon, when we can especially appreciate sitting for a bit in an air-conditioned theater. Back row seats provide the broadest view with the least neck strain.

Indiana Jones Adventure (Fastpass) ★★★★★

APPEAL BY AGE	PRESCHOOL ★★	GRADE SCHOOL ★★★★	TEENS ★★★★★
YOUNG ADULTS ★★★★★		OVER 30 ★★★★½	SENIORS ★★★★

What it is Motion-simulator dark ride. **Scope and scale** Super-headliner. **When to go** Before 9:30 a.m. or use Fastpass. **Special comments** Not to be missed; must be 46" tall to ride; switching-off provided (see page 150). **Duration of ride** 3 minutes and 20 seconds. **Average wait in line per 100 people ahead of you** 3 minutes. **Assumes** Full-capacity operation with 18-second dispatch interval. **Loading speed** Fast.

DESCRIPTION AND COMMENTS This is a combination track ride and motion simulator. You ride a military troop–transport vehicle; in addition to moving along its path, the vehicle bucks and pitches (the simulator part) in sync with the visuals and special effects. Though the plot is complicated and not altogether clear, the bottom line is that if you look into the Forbidden Eye, you're in big trouble. The Forbidden Eye, of course, stands out like Rush Limbaugh in a diaper, and *everybody* stares at it. The rest of the ride consists of a mad race to escape the temple as it collapses around you. In the process, you encounter snakes, spiders, lava pits, rats, swinging bridges, and the house-size granite bowling ball that everyone remembers from *Raiders of the Lost Ark*.

The Indiana Jones ride is a Disney masterpiece—nonstop action from beginning to end with brilliant visual effects. Elaborate even by Disney standards, the attraction provides a level of detail and variety of action that make use of the entire Imagineering arsenal of high-tech gimmickry. Combining a setting as rich as Pirates of the Caribbean with a ride that rivals Star Tours, Indiana Jones is a powerhouse. Recently, the ride was upgraded with new animatronic Indys that bear a remarkable likeness to Harrison Ford.

Sophisticated in its electronic and computer applications, Indiana Jones purports to offer a different experience on each ride. According to the designers, there are veritable menus of special effects that the computer can mix and match. In practice, however, we could not see much difference from ride to ride. There are, no doubt, subtle variations, but the ride is so wild and frenetic that it's hard to apprehend subtlety. Between explosions and falling rocks, your poor fried brain simply does not register nuance. If you ride twice and your date says, "The rat on the beam winked at me that time," it's probably a good idea to get away from Disneyland for a while.

The adventure begins in the queue, which sometimes extends out the entrance of the attraction and over the bridge leading to Adventureland! When you ultimately work your way into the attraction area, you find yourself at the site of an archaeology expedition with the Temple of the Forbidden Eye entrance beckoning only 50 feet away. After crossing a wooden bridge, you finally step into the temple. The good news is that you are out of the California sun. The bad news is that you have just entered Indiana Jones's indoor queuing area, a system of tunnels and passageways extending to within 50 yards of the Santa Monica pier.

Fortunately, the queuing area is interesting. You wind through caves, down the interior corridors of the temple, and into subterranean rotundas where the archaeologists have been hard at work. Along the way there are various surprises (be sure to disregard any DO NOT TOUCH signs you see on supporting poles or safety ropes), as well as a succession of homilies etched in an "ancient" language on the temple walls. During our first visit we decoded the messages with feverish intensity, hoping to find one that translated to "restrooms." Trust us on this one: Do *not* chug down Diet Cokes before you get in line for this attraction.

If you are dazed from spending what seems like half of your life in this line and are not up to deciphering the Disney hieroglyphics, not to worry. You will eventually stumble into a chamber where a short movie will explain the plot. From there it's back into the maze and finally on to the loading area. The ride itself is memorable. If you ride with a full bladder, it's absolutely unforgettable.

TOURING TIPS Indiana Jones stays fairly mobbed all day. Try to ride during the first hour the park is open or use Fastpass. Another alternative, if you don't mind riding alone, is to take advantage of the singles line. Guests from the singles lines are tapped, one at a time, to fill any odd seats remaining in the ride vehicles before they are dispatched. Generally the wait for guests in the singles line is about one-third that of guests in the regular queue. Be forewarned that the singles line at Indiana Jones is a bit of a maze, requiring you to negotiate your way up the exit ramp, up one elevator, across a walkway over the track, and then down another elevator to the loading area.

During the first hour or so the park is open, Indiana Jones cast members often employ a line management technique known as stacking. Simply stated, they allow the line for Indiana Jones to form outside of the attraction, leaving the cavernous inside queuing area virtually empty. Guests, of course, assume that the attraction is packed to the gills and that the outside line is overflow. Naturally, this discourages guests from getting in line. The reality is that the wait is not nearly as bad as it looks, and that it is probably as short as it will be all day. If you arrive in the park early and the Indiana Jones line appears huge, have the rest of your party get in line while you enter Indiana Jones *through the attraction exit* and check out the inside queue. If it is empty or sparsely populated, stacking is being practiced. Join your party in line and enjoy the attraction; your wait will be comparatively short. If the inside queue is bumper to bumper, try Indiana Jones later or use Fastpass or the singles line. Stacking is also sometimes practiced during the hour just before the park closes.

There is one other thing you should know. Indiana Jones, because it is high-tech, breaks down a lot. The Disney people will announce that the ride is broken but usually will not estimate how long repairs will take. From our experience, most glitches are resolved in approximately 15–30 minutes, and probably the best advice is to stick it out.

If you miss Indiana Jones in the early morning and the Fastpasses are all gone, use the singles line or try again during a parade or *Fantasmic!*, or during the hour before the park closes. Regarding the latter, the Disney folks will usually admit to the attraction anyone in line at closing time. During a recent visit to Indiana Jones, Disneyland Park closed at 8 p.m. We hopped in the line for Indiana Jones at 7:45 p.m. and actually got on the ride at 8:30 p.m.

Though the Indiana Jones ride is wild and jerky, it is primarily distinguished by its visual impact and realistic special effects. Thus, we encourage the over-50 crowd to give it a chance: We think you'll like it. As for children, most find the ride extremely intense and action-packed but not particularly frightening. We encountered very few children who met the 46-inch minimum-height requirement who were in any way intimidated.

Jungle Cruise ★★★

APPEAL BY AGE PRESCHOOL ★★★★½ GRADE SCHOOL ★★★★½ TEENS ★★★
YOUNG ADULTS ★★★½ OVER 30 ★★★½ SENIORS ★★★★½

What it is A Disney outdoor-adventure boat ride. **Scope and scale** Major attraction. **When to go** Before 10 a.m. or after 6 p.m. **Special comments** A Disney standard. **Duration of ride** 7½ minutes. **Average wait in line per 100 people ahead of you** 3½ minutes. **Assumes** 10 boats operating. **Loading speed** Moderate–slow.

Thumbs Up for the Whole Family

DESCRIPTION AND COMMENTS A boat ride through jungle waterways. Passengers encounter elephants, lions, hostile natives, and a menacing hippo. A long-enduring Disney favorite with the boatman's spiel adding measurably to the fun.

As more technologically advanced attractions have been added to the park over the years, the Jungle Cruise has, by comparison, lost some of its luster. Though still a good attraction, it offers few thrills and no surprises for Disneyland Park veterans, many of whom can rattle off the ride's narration right along with the guide. For park first-timers, however, the Jungle Cruise continues to delight.

TOURING TIPS This ride loads slowly, and long lines form as the park fills. To compound problems, guests exiting Indiana Jones tend to head for the

DISNEY DISH WITH JIM HILL

HANK-ERING FOR SOME NEW SHOW SCENES It's been several years now since the Imagineers last added any elements to the Jungle Cruise. But given that Walt Disney Studios has a movie with Tom Hanks and Tim Allen in the works, which will be built around the general premise and specific show scenes featured in this Adventureland attraction, the Imagineers are now planning on seriously juicing up the Jungle in 2013. The Imagineers are looking to add dimensional sound to this ride, so it will sound as though animals are actually moving through the brush along the shoreline, as well as incorporating some new physical effects. Which—at least in the case of the ride's hippo pool sequences—will make it seem as though the animals are attacking your boat from below.

Jungle Cruise. Go early, or during a parade or *Fantasmic!* Be forewarned that the Jungle Cruise has an especially deceptive line: Just when you think that you are about to board, you are shunted into yet another queuing maze (not visible outside the ride). Regardless of how short the line *looks* when you approach the Jungle Cruise, inquire about the length of the wait—at least you will know what you are getting into. When the queue splits before the loading dock, the left lane is often quicker. Finally, many readers consider the Jungle Cruise much better at night.

Tarzan's Treehouse ★★★

APPEAL BY AGE	PRESCHOOL ★★★★	GRADE SCHOOL ★★★½	TEENS ★★
YOUNG ADULTS ★★½		OVER 30 ★★	SENIORS ★★★

What it is Walk-through treehouse exhibit. **Scope and scale** Minor attraction. **When to go** Anytime. **Special comments** Requires climbing a lot of stairs; a very creative exhibit. **Duration of tour** 8–12 minutes. **Average wait in line per 100 people ahead of you** 7 minutes.

Thumbs Up for the Whole Family

DESCRIPTION AND COMMENTS Inspired by Disney's 1999 animated film *Tarzan*, Tarzan's Treehouse replaced the venerable Swiss Family Treehouse that had been an Adventureland icon for 37 years. To enter the attraction, you climb a rustic staircase and cross a suspension bridge. From there, as they say, it's all downhill. Pages from Jane's sketchbook scattered about tell the Tarzan story and provide insights into the various rooms and levels of the treehouse. At the base of the tree is an interactive play area where characters from Disney's *Tarzan* drop in for photos and autographs.

TOURING TIPS A self-guided, walk-through tour that involves a lot of climbing up and down stairs but with no ropes or ladders or anything fancy. People stopping during the walk-through to look extra-long or to rest sometimes create bottlenecks that slow crowd flow. We recommend visiting this attraction in the late afternoon or early evening if you are on a 1-day tour schedule.

NEW ORLEANS SQUARE

ACCESSIBLE VIA ADVENTURELAND AND FRONTIERLAND, New Orleans Square is one of three lands that does not emanate from the central hub. The architecture and setting are Caribbean colonial, like New Orleans itself, with exceptional attention to detail.

Disneyland Railroad

DESCRIPTION AND COMMENTS The Disneyland Railroad stops in New Orleans Square on its circle tour around the park. See the description on pages 219–220 for additional details regarding the sights en route.

TOURING TIPS This is a pleasant and feet-saving way to commute to Mickey's Toontown/Fantasyland, Tomorrowland, or Main Street. Be advised, however, that the New Orleans Square station is usually the most congested.

The Haunted Mansion ★★★★

APPEAL BY AGE PRESCHOOL ★★★½ GRADE SCHOOL ★★★★½ TEENS ★★★★
YOUNG ADULTS ★★★★★ OVER 30 ★★★★½ SENIORS ★★★★½

What it is Indoor haunted-house ride. **Scope and scale** Major attraction. **When to go** Before 11:30 a.m. or after 6:30 p.m. **Special comments** Not to be missed; frightens some small children; some of Disneyland's best special effects. **Duration of ride** 5½-minute ride plus a 2-minute preshow. **Average wait in line per 100 people ahead of you** 2½ minutes. **Assumes** Both stretch rooms operating. **Loading speed** Fast.

Dark Scary

DESCRIPTION AND COMMENTS With new characters (an ax-murdering bride), scenes, and effects added in 2006, The Haunted Mansion is a fun attraction more than a scary one. An ingenious preshow serves as a vehicle to deliver guests to the ride's boarding area, where they board "doom buggies" for a ride through the mansion's parlor, dining room, library, halls, and attic before descending to an uncommonly active graveyard. Disney employs almost every special effect in its repertoire in The Haunted Mansion, making it one of the most inventive and different of all Disney attractions. Be warned that some youngsters build a lot of anxiety concerning what they think they will see. The actual attraction scares almost nobody.

The Haunted Mansion is one of veteran *Unofficial Guide* writer Eve Zibart's favorite attractions. She warns:

> Don't let the childishness of the old-fashioned Haunted Mansion put you off: This is one of the best attractions [in the park]. It's jam-packed with visual puns, special effects, hidden Mickeys, and really lovely Victorian-spooky sets. It's not scary, except in the sweetest of ways, but it will remind you of the days before ghost stories gave way to slasher flicks.

Usually beginning in September, The Haunted Mansion substitutes a special holiday version of the attraction that runs through early January. Inspired by Tim Burton's 1993 stop-motion musical *The Nightmare Before Christmas,* the overlay features characters such as Jack Skellington and Oogie Boogie cavorting among the familiar mansion haunts to songs from Danny Elfman's classic score. Though the Haunted Mansion is not normally a Fastpass attraction, the holiday version is usually included in the Fastpass lineup.

TOURING TIPS   This attraction would be more at home in Fantasyland, but no matter—it's Disney at its best: another not-to-be-missed attraction. Because The Haunted Mansion is in an especially high-traffic corridor (between Pirates of the Caribbean and Splash Mountain), it stays busy all day. Try to see The Haunted Mansion before 11:30 a.m., after 6:30 p.m., or during a parade. In the evening, crowds for *Fantasmic!* gather in front of The Haunted Mansion, making it very difficult to access.

Pirates of the Caribbean   ★★★★★

| APPEAL BY AGE   PRESCHOOL ★★★½   GRADE SCHOOL ★★★★½   TEENS ★★★★★ |
| YOUNG ADULTS ★★★★★   OVER 30 ★★★★½   SENIORS ★★★★★ |

What it is A Disney indoor-adventure boat ride. **Scope and scale** Major attraction. **When to go** Before 11:30 a.m. or after 4:30 p.m. **Special comments** Frightens some small children; our pick as one of Disneyland's very best. **Duration of ride** Approximately 14 minutes. **Average wait in line per 100 people ahead of you** 3 minutes. **Assumes** 42 boats operating. **Loading speed** Fast.

Dark   Loud   Scary

DESCRIPTION AND COMMENTS   Another boat ride, this time indoors, through a series of sets depicting a pirate raid on an island settlement, from the bombardment of the fortress to the debauchery that follows the victory. Pirates of the Caribbean was the target of a much-publicized political-correctness controversy relating to the objectification of women and the "boys will be boys" way in which the pirates' debauchery was depicted. Ultimately, Disney was pressured into revamping the attraction (though not much). More recently, the attraction underwent an extensive rehab that included the addition of characters (Jack Sparrow and Barbossa in animatronic form, and a high-tech mist projection of Davy Jones) from the *Pirates of the Caribbean* movies.

TOURING TIPS   Another not-to-be-missed attraction. Undoubtedly one of the most elaborate and imaginative attractions in Disneyland Park. Though engineered to move large crowds, this ride sometimes gets overwhelmingly busy in the early and midafternoon. Try to ride before noon or while a parade or *Fantasmic!* is in progress. If you have only experienced the Walt Disney World version of Pirates, don't bypass Disneyland's version thinking that it's more of the same: The original ride is far longer, more detailed, and better maintained than its Floridian cousin.

CRITTER COUNTRY

CRITTER COUNTRY, situated at the end of a cul-de-sac and accessible via New Orleans Square, sports a pioneer appearance not unlike that of Frontierland.

Davy Crockett's Explorer Canoes ★★★
(open seasonally)

APPEAL BY AGE   PRESCHOOL ★★   GRADE SCHOOL ★★★½   TEENS ★★★★½
YOUNG   ADULTS   ★   OVER 30   ★★★   SENIORS   ★

What it is Scenic canoe ride. **Scope and scale** Minor attraction. **When to go** As soon as it opens, usually 11 a.m. **Special comments** Skip if the lines are long; closes at dusk. **Special comments** Most fun way to see Rivers of America. **Duration of ride** 8–10 minutes, depending on how fast you paddle. **Average wait in line per 100 people ahead of you** 12½ minutes. **Assumes** 6 canoes operating. **Loading speed** Slow.

DESCRIPTION AND COMMENTS   Paddle-powered ride (you do the paddling) around Tom Sawyer Island and Fort Wilderness. Runs·the same route with the same sights as the steamboat and the sailing ship. According to newspaper accounts, when the entire 9-million-gallon river was drained in 2010 for refurbishment, workers found half a canoe, scores of Mickey Mouse ears, and hundreds of cell phones at the bottom. The lesson here is to always keep a tight grip on your canoe. The canoes operate only on busier days and close at dusk. The sights are fun and the ride is a little different in that the patrons paddle the canoe. We think that this is the most fun of any of the various river trips. Long lines from about 11 a.m. on reflect the popularity of this attraction.

TOURING TIPS   The canoes represent one of three ways to see the same waterways. Since the canoes are slower in loading, we usually opt for the larger steamboat or sailing ship. If you are not up for a boat ride, a different view of the same sights can be had by hoofing around Tom Sawyer Island. Try to ride at 11 a.m. or shortly thereafter. The canoes operate on selected days and seasonal periods only. If the canoes are a big deal to you, call ahead to make sure they are operating.

The Many Adventures of Winnie the Pooh   ★★★½

APPEAL BY AGE   PRESCHOOL ★★★★★   GRADE SCHOOL ★★★★½   TEENS ★★★
YOUNG   ADULTS   ★★   OVER 30   ★★★½   SENIORS   ★★★½

What it is Indoor track ride. **Scope and scale** Minor attraction. **When to go** Before 11 a.m. or during the late afternoon and evening. **Special comments** Critter Country's newest ride. **Duration of ride** About 3 minutes. **Average wait in line per 100 people ahead of you** 5 minutes. **Loading speed** Moderate.

Thumbs Up for the Whole Family

DESCRIPTION AND COMMENTS   Opened in the summer of 2003, this addition to Critter Country replaced the alternately praised and maligned Country Bear Playhouse. Pooh is sunny, upbeat, and fun—more in the image of Peter Pan's Flight or Splash Mountain. You ride a "hunny pot" through the pages of a huge picture book into the Hundred Acre Wood, where you encounter Pooh, Eeyore, Owl, Rabbit, Tigger, Kanga, Roo, and Piglet too as they contend with a blustery day. There's even a dream sequence with Heffalumps and Woozles, a favorite of this 30-something couple from Lexington, Massachusetts, who think Pooh has plenty to offer adults:

DISNEY DISH WITH JIM HILL

WHERE TO LOOK IF YOU WANT TO SEE-O THE TRIO Many Disneyland fans still miss *The Country Bear Jamboree*, the audio-animatronic extravaganza that used to occupy the building that now houses The Many Adventures of Winnie the Pooh. But if you know just where to look while you're riding through Pooh, you can still see a few members of the *Jamboree* cast. As you exit this ride's Heffalumps and Woozles scene, turn around and look up. There, on the wall above you, you'll see Max the buck, Buff the buffalo, and Melvin the moose, which the Imagineers hid inside this Critter Country attraction as a tribute to the *Country Bear Jamboree.*

The attention to detail and special effects on this ride make it worth seeing even if you don't have children in your party. The Pooh dream sequence was great!

TOURING TIPS Try to ride before 11 a.m., during a parade, or in the late afternoon or evening. Though well done, The Many Adventures of Winnie the Pooh is not wildly popular. Even so, it stays relatively busy, thanks in large part to the steady stream of guests exiting nearby Splash Mountain.

Splash Mountain (Fastpass) ★★★★½

APPEAL BY AGE	PRESCHOOL †	GRADE SCHOOL ★★½	TEENS ★★★★★
YOUNG ADULTS ★★★	OVER 30 ★★★★★		SENIORS ★★★★

† *Many preschoolers are too short to meet the height requirement, while others are intimidated by watching the ride while standing in line. Of those preschoolers who actually ride, most give the attraction high marks;* ★★★½

What it is Water-flume adventure boat ride. **Scope and scale** Headliner. **When to go** Before 9:45 a.m. or use Fastpass. **Special comments** A wet winner, not to be missed; must be 40" tall to ride; those age 7 or younger must ride with an adult; switching-off provided (see page 150). **Duration of ride** About 10 minutes. **Average wait in line per 100 people ahead of you** 3½ minutes. **Assumes** Operation at full capacity. **Loading speed** Moderate.

Scary   Lose Things   Queasy

DESCRIPTION AND COMMENTS Splash Mountain is a Disney-style amusement-park flume ride. The ride combines steep chutes with a variety of Disney's best special effects. Covering more than 0.5 mile, the ride splashes through swamps, caves, and backwoods bayous before climaxing in a 52-foot plunge and Br'er Rabbit's triumphant return home. The entire ride is populated by more than 100 audio-animatronic characters, including Br'er Rabbit, Br'er Bear, and Br'er Fox, all regaling riders with songs, including "Zip-A-Dee-Doo-Dah."

TOURING TIPS This is the most popular ride in Disneyland Park for patrons of all ages—happy, exciting, and adventuresome all at once. Though eclipsed somewhat by the Indiana Jones attraction, Splash Mountain nevertheless builds crowds quickly during the morning, and waits of more than 2 hours are not uncommon once Disneyland Park fills up on a busy day. Lines persist throughout the day until a few minutes before closing.

There are five ways to experience Splash Mountain without a long wait. The first is to be on hand when the park opens and to sprint over and get in line before anyone else. The second way is to allow the initial mob of Splash cadets to be processed through and to arrive at Splash Mountain about 20–40 minutes after the park opens or after riding Finding Nemo Submarine Voyage and/or Space Mountain. A third strategy is to get in line for Splash Mountain during a parade and/or a performance of *Fantasmic!* Be advised, however, that huge crowds gathering along the New Orleans Square and Frontierland waterfronts for *Fantasmic!* make getting to Splash Mountain very difficult (if not impossible) just before, during, and just after performances. Fourth, use Fastpass, and fifth, use the singles line.

Disneyland veteran Ken Warhola offers this suggestion:

Use Fastpass to experience Splash. Using Fastpass lets you visit non-Fastpass, slow-loading attractions in the golden early morning. Also, who wants to get wet first thing in the morning?

A Suffolk, Virginia, mom contends that there are more important considerations than beating crowds:

The only recommendation I do have is to definitely wait to do Splash Mountain at the end of the day. We were seated in the front of the ride and needless to say we were drenched to the bone. If we had ridden the ride [first thing in the morning] according to your plan, I personally would have been miserable for the rest of the day. Parents, beware! It says you will get wet, not drowned.

It is almost a certainty that you will get wet, though probably not drenched, riding Splash Mountain. During the summer months, the water jets are cranked up to 11, practically guaranteeing that you'll get soaked. If you visit on a cool day, you may want to carry a plastic garbage bag. By tearing holes in the bottom and sides, you can fashion a sort of raincoat. Be sure to tuck the bag under your bottom. Though you can get splashed regardless of where you sit, riders in the front seat generally get the worst of it. If you have a camera, either leave it with a nonriding member of your party or wrap it in a plastic bag.

One final word: This is not just a fancy flume ride—it is a full-blown Disney adventure. The scariest part by far is the big drop into the pool (visible from the sidewalk in front of Splash Mountain), and even this plunge looks worse than it really is. Despite reassurances, however, many children wig out after watching it from the sidewalk. A Grand Rapids, Michigan, mother recalls her kids' rather unique reaction:

We discovered after the fact that our children thought they would go underwater after the five-story drop and tried to hold their breath throughout the ride in preparation. They were really too preoccupied to enjoy the clever Br'er Rabbit story.

Flash Mountain

What it is Water-flume adventure strip show. **Scope and scale** Eye-popper. **When to go** Spring break; weekend nights. **Special comments** A liberating experience. **Duration of show** About 2 seconds.

DESCRIPTION AND COMMENTS It was reported by the Associated Press that certain female Splash Mountain riders (though we're sure that male riders, not to be outdone, will soon follow their female compatriots in similar fashion) are behaving in a most un–Disney-like manner by "flinging their blouses open" as they plummet down the climactic plunge at the end of the ride. (Fully visible, we might add, to dozens of guests waiting in line in front of the attraction.)

Indeed, automatic cameras shooting souvenir photographs of participants have documented an astounding array of feminine anatomy in free fall. The practice is apparently too spontaneous for Disneyland, which reports that it "has no plans at this time to change the theme of the attraction." Though, ever mindful of guest safety, management has concerns about "undue congestion" in front of the ride and the "possibility of guests catching cold." Some years ago, Disney initiated what it called its "nipple policy," which decreed that photos of offending guests were vaporized immediately. Thanks to budget cuts, the cast members who formerly spent their days screening snapshots for contraband skin have been reassigned, leaving the images free for all to enjoy again. This development has been roundly applauded by nearly everyone except the reassigned employees, some of whom had collected veritable scrapbooks of the floating strippers.

TOURING TIPS During spring break or weekend nights, spectators should stand on the walkway directly in front of Splash Mountain. Be sure to bring a sign denouncing such unchaste exhibitionist behavior, or, depending on your point of view, a camera with a telescopic lens. If you are a participant, you will have approximately 2 minutes following the big plunge to get yourself back together before you arrive at the unloading area.

FRONTIERLAND

FRONTIERLAND ADJOINS NEW ORLEANS SQUARE as you move clockwise around the theme park. The focus here is on the Old West, with log stockades and pioneer trappings. In addition to the attractions listed below, there is the Big Thunder Ranch—featuring pungent pygmy petting goats and Miss Chris's cabin of coloring activities and equestrian Disney memorabilia—on the walkway to Fantasyland.

Big Thunder Mountain Railroad (Fastpass) ★★★★

APPEAL BY AGE	PRESCHOOL ★★★	GRADE SCHOOL ★★★★	TEENS ★★★★★
YOUNG ADULTS ★★★★½	OVER 30 ★★★★½		SENIORS ★★★½

What it is Tame roller coaster with exciting special effects. **Scope and scale** Headliner. **When to go** Before 10:30 a.m., after 6:30 p.m., or use Fastpass. **Special comments**

Great effects, though a relatively tame ride; must be 40" tall to ride; those age 8 and younger must ride with an adult; switching-off option provided (see page 150). **Duration of ride** 3½ minutes. **Average wait in line per 100 people ahead of you** 3 minutes. **Assumes** 5 trains operating. **Loading speed** Moderate–fast.

Scary Lose Things Queasy Rough

DESCRIPTION AND COMMENTS A roller-coaster ride through and around a Disney "mountain." The idea is that you are on a runaway mine train during gold rush days. Along with the usual thrills of a roller-coaster ride (about a 5 on a "scary scale" of 10), the ride showcases some first-rate examples of Disney creativity: lifelike scenes depicting a mining town, falling rocks, and an earthquake, all humorously animated.

TOURING TIPS A superb Disney experience, but not too wild a roller coaster. The emphasis here is much more on the sights than on the thrill of the ride itself. Regardless, it's a not-to-be-missed attraction. Finally, give Big Thunder a try after dark. The lighting gives the attraction a whole new feel.

As an example of how differently guests experience Disney attractions, consider this letter that we received from a reader in Brookline, Massachusetts:

> Being in the senior citizens' category and having limited time, my friend and I confined our activities to those attractions rated as 4 or 5 stars for seniors.
>
> Because of your recommendation and because you listed it as "not to be missed," we waited for 1 hour to board the Big Thunder Mountain Railroad, which you rated a 5 on a scary scale of 10. After living through 3½ minutes of pure terror, I will rate that attraction a 15 on a scary scale of 10. We were so busy holding on and screaming and even praying for our safety that we did not see any falling rocks, a mining town, or an earthquake. In our opinion the Big Thunder Mountain Railroad should not be recommended for seniors or preschool children.

A woman from New England discovered that there's more to consider about Big Thunder than being scared:

> Big Thunder Mountain Railroad was rated 5 on the scary scale. I won't say it warranted a higher scare rating, but it was much higher on the lose-your-lunch meter. One more sharp turn and the kids in front of me would have needed a dip in Splash Mountain!

Frontierland Shootin' Exposition ★★

| APPEAL BY AGE | PRESCHOOL ★★★★ | GRADE SCHOOL ★★★★ | TEENS ★½ |
| YOUNG ADULTS ★★★★½ | | OVER 30 ★★½ | SENIORS ★★ |

Thumbs Up for the Whole Family

What it is Electronic shooting gallery. **Scope and scale** Diversion. **When to go** Whenever convenient. **Special comments** Costs extra; a nifty shooting gallery.

DESCRIPTION AND COMMENTS A very elaborate electronic shooting gallery that costs $1 to play. One of the few attractions in Disneyland Park not included in the admission pass.

TOURING TIPS Good fun for those who like to shoot, but definitely not a place to blow time if you are on a tight schedule. Try it on your second day if time allows.

The Golden Horseshoe ★★★★½

| APPEAL BY AGE | PRESCHOOL ★★★ | GRADE SCHOOL ★★★ | TEENS ★★★ |
| YOUNG ADULTS ★★★★ | OVER 30 ★★★★½ | | SENIORS ★★★★½ |

What it is Western dance-hall stage show. **Scope and scale** Minor attraction. **When to go** Catch a show and lunch at the same time. **Special comments** Delightfully zany show; food is available. **Duration of show** 30 minutes.

DESCRIPTION AND COMMENTS The Golden Horseshoe has always offered a decent show, hearty sandwiches, and a nice air-conditioned respite from the sun. A while back, however, either intentionally or accidentally, Disney signed up an act so good that it turned the humble venue into one of the best attractions in either park. The talent, the unfortunately named Billy Hill and the Hillbillies, consists of a quartet of master bluegrass fiddlers who also happen to be born comics. The show is double-over funny, zany, and totally engaging. And did we mention that the fiddling is phenomenal? At the end of the show, we noticed something that we've never seen at any Disney stage production—the audience refused to leave. Instead, they stood clapping and cheering like at a rock concert, trying to bring back the performers for an encore. They stayed at it so long that the fiddlers were forced to return and take a second bow (though they didn't perform another song). Still the audience lingered, departing only reluctantly after many minutes. We rate the Golden Horseshoe ★★★★½ and classify it as not to be missed.

TOURING TIPS The Golden Horseshoe has first-come, first-served seating. Performance times are listed in the daily *Times Guide*. Note that Billy Hill and the Hillbillies do not perform on Tuesday or Wednesday. We recommend arriving 30 minutes early if you want to find a table and grab some grub. Food service can be slow; look for the shortest of three service lines, usually on the far left. The best view is from the center balcony near the sound technician, but Walt liked the opera box seats best.

Mark Twain Riverboat ★★★

| APPEAL BY AGE | PRESCHOOL ★★½ | GRADE SCHOOL ★★★ | TEENS ★★★ |
| YOUNG ADULTS ★★ | OVER 30 ★★★½ | | SENIORS ★★★★ |

Thumbs Up for the Whole Family

What it is Scenic boat ride. **Scope and scale** Minor attraction. **When to go** 11 a.m.–5 p.m. **Special comments** Provides an excellent vantage point; suspends operation at dusk. **Duration of ride** About 14 minutes. **Average wait to board** 10 minutes. **Assumes** Normal operations. **Loading method** En masse.

DESCRIPTION AND COMMENTS Large-capacity paddle-wheel riverboat that navigates the waters around Tom Sawyer Island and Fort Wilderness. A beautiful craft, the riverboat provides a lofty perch from which to see Frontierland and New Orleans Square. The *Mark Twain,* Sailing Ship *Columbia,* and Davy Crockett's Explorer Canoes travel through the Rivers of America, which was refurbished in 2010. The show scenes were updated to include a home for Mike Fink (and one of his keelboats, a former Disneyland attraction) and 26 new audio-animatronic animals, and the audio spiel now includes a musical nod to the New Orleans–set *The Princess and the Frog.*

TOURING TIPS One of three boat rides that survey the same real estate. Because the Explorer Canoes are slower in loading and the *Columbia* operates seasonally, we think the riverboat makes more efficient use of touring time. If you are not in the mood for a boat ride, many of the same sights can be seen by hiking around Tom Sawyer Island.

Pirate's Lair on Tom Sawyer Island ★★★

APPEAL BY AGE PRESCHOOL ★★★★★ GRADE SCHOOL ★★★★★ TEENS ★★★★
YOUNG ADULTS ★★★★ OVER 30 ★★★½ SENIORS ★★★★

What it is Walk-through exhibit and rustic playground. Scope and scale Minor attraction. When to go Midmorning–late afternoon. Special comments The place for rambunctious kids; closes at dusk.

DESCRIPTION AND COMMENTS Pirate's Lair on Tom Sawyer Island manages to impart something of a sense of isolation from the rest of the park. It has hills to climb, a cave and a treehouse to explore, tipsy bridges to cross, paths to follow, and a "rock-climbing" play area. It's a delight for adults but a godsend for children who have been in tow all day.

As an aside, a mother of four from Duncan, South Carolina, found Tom Sawyer Island as much a refuge as an attraction, writing:

I do have one tip for parents. In the afternoon, when the crowds were at their peak, the weather was hottest, and the kids started lagging behind, our organization began to suffer. We then retreated over to Tom Sawyer Island, which proved to be a true haven. My husband and I found a secluded bench and regrouped. Meanwhile, the kids were able to run freely in the shade. Afterwards, we were ready to tackle the park again refreshed and with direction once more.

The island has sets from the *Pirates of the Caribbean* films, such as William Turner's blacksmith shop, and story artifacts such as Elizabeth Swann's love letters tucked into every nook and cranny. Kids exploring the caverns of Dead Man's Grotto will encounter spooky voices, ghostly apparitions, and buried treasure. Elsewhere, a sunken chest can be discovered by operating a hoist.

Evidently, you can't have a pirate's lair without a bunch of gore. A pop-up head and moving skeletal arm are just the beginning. There's also a "bone cage," and our favorite—a treasure chest containing Davy Jones's beating heart. If your child doesn't have a playmate, don't worry. There's usually a gang of itinerant pirates on hand to administer the "pirate oath" and, somewhat incongruously, lead sing-alongs.

TOURING TIPS Pirate's Lair on Tom Sawyer Island is not one of Disneyland Park's more celebrated attractions, but it's certainly one of the most well done. Attention to detail is excellent, and kids particularly revel in its adventuresome atmosphere. We think it's a must for families with children ages 5–15. If your party has only adults, visit the island on your second day, or stop by on your first day if you have seen the attractions you most wanted to see. We like the island from about noon until the island closes at dusk. Access is by raft from Frontierland, and you may have to stand in line to board both coming and going. Two or three rafts operate simultaneously, however, and the round-trip is usually pretty time efficient. Tom Sawyer Island takes about 30 minutes or so to see, but many children could spend a whole day there.

Raft to and from Tom Sawyer Island

What it is Transportation ride to Tom Sawyer Island. Scope and scale Minor attraction. Duration of ride A little more than 1 minute one way. Average wait in line per 100 people ahead of you 4½ minutes. Assumes 3 rafts operating. Loading speed Moderate.

Sailing Ship *Columbia* (open seasonally) ★★★½

APPEAL BY AGE	PRESCHOOL ★★★★	GRADE SCHOOL ★★★★	TEENS ★★★
YOUNG ADULTS ★		OVER 30 ★★★★	SENIORS ★★

What it is Scenic boat ride. Scope and scale Minor attraction. When to go 11 a.m.– 5 p.m. Special comments Pirates on extremely busy days; a stunning piece of workmanship. Duration of ride About 14 minutes. Average wait to board 10 minutes. Assumes Normal operations. Loading method En masse.

Thumbs Up for the Whole Family

DESCRIPTION AND COMMENTS The *Columbia* is a stunning replica of a three-masted 18th-century merchant ship. Both its above and below decks are open to visitors, with below decks outfitted to depict the life and work environment of the ship's crew in 1787. The *Columbia* operates only on busier days and runs the same route as the canoes and the riverboat. As with the other rivercraft, the *Columbia* suspends operations at dusk.

TOURING TIPS The *Columbia*, along with the *Mark Twain* Riverboat, provides a short-wait, high-carrying-capacity alternative for cruising the Rivers of America. We found the beautifully crafted *Columbia* by far the most aesthetically pleasing and historically interesting of any of the three choices of boat rides on the Rivers of America.

If you have time to be choosy, ride aboard the *Columbia*. After boarding, while waiting for the cruise to begin, tour below deck. Once the ride begins, come topside and stroll the deck, taking in the beauty and complexity of the rigging.

The *Columbia* does not usually require a long wait, which makes it a good bet during the crowded afternoon hours.

▌ FANTASYLAND

TRULY AN ENCHANTING PLACE, spread gracefully like a miniature alpine village beneath the towers of Sleeping Beauty Castle, Fantasyland is the heart of the park. Fantasyland is the backbone of the Magic Mornings early-entry program, with nine rides open. If your group consists of older kids and adults, ride Matterhorn Bobsleds first during the early-entry period, followed by Peter Pan's Flight. If you have younger children in your group, start with Peter Pan and then ride Dumbo.

Alice in Wonderland ★★★

| APPEAL BY AGE | PRESCHOOL ★★★★½ | GRADE SCHOOL ★★★★½ | TEENS ★★★½ |
| YOUNG ADULTS ★★★ | OVER 30 ★★★★ | | SENIORS ★★★★ |

What it is Track ride in the dark. **Scope and scale** Minor attraction. **When to go** Before 11 a.m. or after 5 p.m. **Special comments** Good characterization and story line; do not confuse with Mad Tea Party ride. **Duration of ride** Almost 4 minutes. **Average wait in line per 100 people ahead of you** 12 minutes. **Assumes** 16 cars operating. **Loading speed** Slow.

DESCRIPTION AND COMMENTS This attraction recalls the story of *Alice in Wonderland* with some nice surprises and colorful effects. Guests ride nifty caterpillar cars in this Disney spook-house adaptation. Though not a spring chicken, Alice is a third-generation Disney dark ride with more vibrant, evocative, and three-dimensional sets and characters than Pinocchio's Daring Journey or Mr. Toad's Wild Ride. This is also the only two-story Disney dark ride with an outdoor section, though recently added safety railings now somewhat spoil the view.

TOURING TIPS This is a very well-done ride in the best Disney tradition, with familiar characters, good effects, and a theme you can follow. Unfortunately, it loads very slowly.

Casey Jr. Circus Train ★★½

| APPEAL BY AGE | PRESCHOOL ★★★★½ | GRADE SCHOOL ★★★★ | TEENS ★★★ |
| YOUNG ADULTS ★★½ | OVER 30 ★★★ | | SENIORS ★★★ |

What it is Miniature-train ride. **Scope and scale** Minor attraction. **When to go** Before 11 a.m. or after 5 p.m. **Special comments** A quiet, scenic ride. **Duration of ride** A little more than 3 minutes. **Average wait in line per 100 people ahead of you** 12 minutes. **Assumes** 2 trains operating. **Loading speed** Slow.

DESCRIPTION AND COMMENTS A long-standing attraction and a pet project of Walt Disney, Casey Jr. circulates through a landscape of miniature towns, farms, and lakes. There are some stunning bonsai specimens visible from this ride, as well as some of the most manicured landscaping you are ever likely to see.

TOURING TIPS This ride covers the same sights as the Storybook Land Canal Boats but does it faster and with less of a wait. Accommodations for adults, however, are less than optimal on this ride, with some passengers having to squeeze into diminutive caged cars (after all, it is a circus train). If you do not have children in your party, you can enjoy the same sights more comfortably by riding the Storybook Land Canal Boats, which also benefits from live narration instead of Casey Jr.'s canned soundtrack.

A father of two toddlers from Menlo Park, California, explains that issues of redundancy were not uppermost in his children's minds.

Contrary to your advice, the Casey Jr. Train and Storybook Land Boats are totally different experiences—if you are 4 or younger. Hey, one is a boat and one is a train! Seems obvious to the mind of a 4-year-old! We did both, and the kids loved both, and we loved it because they loved it.

Disneyland Railroad

DESCRIPTION AND COMMENTS   The Disneyland Railroad stops in Fantasyland/Mickey's Toontown on its circuit around the park. The station is located to the left of It's a Small World, next to the Fantasyland Theatre. From this usually uncrowded boarding point, transportation is available to Tomorrowland, Main Street, and New Orleans Square.

Dumbo the Flying Elephant   ★★★

APPEAL BY AGE PRESCHOOL ★★★★	GRADE SCHOOL ★★★★★	TEENS ★★★
YOUNG ADULTS ★★	OVER 30 ★★½	SENIORS ★★

What it is Disney-fied midway ride. **Scope and scale** Minor attraction. **When to go** Before 10 a.m. or during late evening parades, fireworks, or *Fantasmic!* performances. **Special comments** An attractive children's ride. **Duration of ride** 1 minute and 40 seconds. **Average wait in line per 100 people ahead of you** 12 minutes. **Assumes** Normal staffing. **Loading speed** Slow.

DESCRIPTION AND COMMENTS   A nice, tame, happy children's ride based on the lovable Disney flying elephant. An upgraded rendition of a ride that can be found at state fairs and amusement parks across the country. Shortcomings notwithstanding, Dumbo is the favorite Disneyland Park attraction of most preschoolers. A lot of readers take us to task for lumping Dumbo in with state-fair midway rides. These comments from a reader in Armdale, Nova Scotia, are representative:

I think you have acquired a jaded attitude. I know [Dumbo] is not for everybody, but when we took our oldest child (then just 4), the sign at the end of the line said there would be a 90-minute wait. He knew and he didn't care, and he and I stood in the hot afternoon sun for 90 blissful minutes waiting for his 90-second flight. Anything that a 4-year-old would wait for that long and that patiently must be pretty special.

TOURING TIPS   This is a slow-loading ride that we recommend you bypass unless you are on a very relaxed touring schedule. If your kids are excited about Dumbo, try to get them on the ride before 10 a.m., during the parades or *Fantasmic!*, or just before the park closes. Also, consider this advice from an Arlington, Virginia, mom:

Grown-ups, beware! Dumbo is really a tight fit with one adult and two kids. My kids threw me out of their Dumbo and I had to sit in a Dumbo all by myself. Pretty embarrassing, and my husband got lots of pictures.

Fantasyland Theatre/Disney Princess Fantasy Faire

DESCRIPTION AND COMMENTS Originally installed as a teen nightspot called Videopolis, this venue has been converted into a sophisticated amphitheater where concerts and elaborate stage shows are performed according to the daily entertainment schedule. Better productions that have played the Fantasyland Theatre stage include *Beauty and the Beast Live, Snow White,* and *The Spirit of Pocahontas,* all musical stage adaptations of the respective Disney-animated features. In 2007, adding fuel to the fire of little girls' infatuation with Disney princesses, an elaborate, interactive meet and greet called the Princess Fantasy Faire was installed. Here, little ones can meet princesses, participate in a crafts project, join in a combination stage show and coronation, listen to a princess read a story, and, of course, shop for princess duds and other regalia. The usual Disneyland queue must be endured to meet and be photographed with the duty princess on the Disney Princess Royal Walk, but no lines are required for the other activities and events. The coronation ceremony is a stage show involving several princesses with help from the children. Performed several times daily, showtimes are listed in the *Times Guide.* Kids learn dance steps and courtly gestures before the ceremony and cap the coronation with a maypole dance. This last is clearly something that most kids have never seen and that typically leaves them dumbfounded. There are great photos to be had, however, as the kids circle in conflicting directions tying the maypole in knots. It too is billed as interactive, but children's participation in the less-than-10-minute event is minimal to nonexistent. The princesses don't stick around after the show for autographs and photos; for those, you'll need to stand in the Royal Walk queue, which regularly reaches a 45–60 minutes' wait at the peak of the day.

TOURING TIPS Little girls love the Princess Fantasy Faire, as do boys age 6 and under. The best way to take in the whole thing is to arrive about 10 minutes in advance of a coronation and then stay after the show for crafts, princess meet and greet, and storytelling. Incidentally, you won't believe how many of the kids come in costume. If you do everything, you'll spend about an hour, not counting shopping time.

It's a Small World ★★★½

What it is World brotherhood–themed indoor boat ride. Scope and scale Major attraction. When to go Anytime except after a parade. Special comments A pleasant change of pace. Duration of ride 14 minutes. Average wait in line per 100 people ahead of you 2½ minutes. Assumes Busy conditions with 56 boats operating. Loading speed Fast.

Thumbs Up for the Whole Family

DESCRIPTION AND COMMENTS A happy and upbeat attraction with a world-brotherhood theme and a catchy tune that will stick in your head for weeks. Small boats convey visitors on a tour around the world, with singing and dancing dolls showcasing the dress and culture of each nation. Almost everyone enjoys It's a Small World (well, there are those jaded folks who are put off by the dolls' homogeneous appearance, especially in light of the diversity theme), but it stands, along with the *Enchanted Tiki Room,* as an attraction that some could take or leave but that others consider one of the real masterpieces of Disneyland Park. In 2009 Disney inserted more than 20 new figures of Disney and Pixar characters into the classic attraction, over the vocal objections of some serious Disney fans. Tastefully crafted in the style of original artist Mary Blair, the additions don't detract from the ride, except in the tacky U.S.A. tribute tacked onto the end. In any event, a woman from Holbrook, New York, wrote with this devilish suggestion for improvement:

> Small World would be much better if each person got a few softballs on the way in!

A mom from Castleton, Vermont, added this:

> It's a Small World at Fantasyland was like a pit stop in the Twilight Zone. They were very slow unloading the boats, and we were stuck in a line of about six boats waiting to get out while the endless chanting of that song grated on my nerves. I told my husband I was going to swim for it just to escape one more chorus.

From November through New Year's, the attraction receives an annual holiday overlay inside the attraction as well as outside, featuring "Jingle Bells" and "Deck the Halls" instead of the usual earwig soundtrack. We particularly enjoy the light show and projection effects outside the attraction that happen every 15 minutes.

TOURING TIPS Totally renovated and upgraded in 2009 with a deeper flue to accommodate today's heavier guests, It's a Small World is a fast-loading ride that's usually a good bet during the busier times of the day. The boats are moved along by water pressure, which increases as boats are

added. Thus, the more boats in service when you ride (up to a maximum total of 60), the shorter the duration of the ride (and wait). Small World is taken off-line in mid-October and reopened in November with a special Christmas holiday theme. Two notes: While the loading can be very quick when there are many boats running, the unloading can be very slow. Second, the attraction has two loading zones, one which has wheelchair access and one without. Unless you need wheelchair access, we recommend using the loading zone on the far side of the entrance by choosing the right-hand side of the queue when it splits.

King Arthur Carrousel ★★★

APPEAL BY AGE PRESCHOOL ★★★★★ GRADE SCHOOL ★★★★ TEENS ★★★
YOUNG ADULTS ★★   OVER 30 ★★★   SENIORS ★★★★

What it is Merry-go-round. **Scope and scale** Minor attraction. **When to go** Before 11:30 a.m. or after 5 p.m. **Special comments** A showpiece carousel; adults enjoy the beauty and nostalgia of this ride. **Duration of ride** A little more than 2 minutes. **Average wait in line per 100 people ahead of you** 8 minutes. **Assumes** Normal staffing. **Loading speed** Slow.

DESCRIPTION AND COMMENTS A merry-go-round to be sure, but certainly one of the most elaborate and beautiful you will ever see, especially when lit at night. For the 50th anniversary in 2005, a special horse was added in tribute to Julie Andrews and her iconic role in *Mary Poppins*. It is a white horse with bells all over, hence her name, Jingles. She is the horse closest to the handicapped ramp.

TOURING TIPS Unless there are small children in your party, we suggest that you appreciate this ride from the sidelines. If your children want to ride, try to get them on before 11:30 a.m. or after 5 p.m. While nice to look at, the carousel loads and unloads very slowly.

Mad Tea Party ★★

APPEAL BY AGE   PRESCHOOL ★★★★★   GRADE SCHOOL ★★★½
TEENS ★★★★   YOUNG ADULTS ★★★★   OVER 30 ★★★★   SENIORS ★★★

What it is Midway-type spinning ride. **Scope and scale** Minor attraction. **When to go** Before 11 a.m. or after 5 p.m. **Special comments** You can make the teacups spin faster by turning the wheel in the center of the cup; fun but not worth the wait. **Duration of ride** 1½ minutes. **Average wait in line per 100 people ahead of you** 8 minutes. **Assumes** Normal staffing. **Loading speed** Slow.

DESCRIPTION AND COMMENTS Well done in the Disney style, but still just an amusement-park ride. *Alice in Wonderland*'s Mad Hatter provides the theme, and patrons whirl around feverishly in big teacups. A rendition of this ride, sans Disney characters, can be found at every local carnival and fair.

TOURING TIPS This ride, besides not being particularly special, loads notoriously slowly. Skip it on a busy schedule if the kids will let you. Ride in the morning of your second day if your schedule is more relaxed. A warning for parents who have not given this ride much thought: Teenagers like to lure an adult onto the teacups and then turn the wheel in the middle (which makes the cup spin faster) until the adults are plastered against the side of the cup and are on the verge of throwing up.

Matterhorn Bobsleds ★★★½

APPEAL BY AGE	PRESCHOOL ★★★★½†	GRADE SCHOOL ★★★★★
TEENS ★★★★½	YOUNG ADULTS ★★★★	OVER 30 ★★★★½ SENIORS ★★★★

† Some preschoolers loved Matterhorn Bobsleds; others were frightened.

What it is Roller coaster. **Scope and scale** Major attraction. **When to go** During the first 90 minutes the park is open or during the hour before it closes. **Special comments** Fun ride but not too scary; must be 35" tall to ride. **Duration of ride** 2½ minutes. **Average wait in line per 100 people ahead of you** 13 minutes. **Assumes** Both tracks operating with 10 sleds per track with 23-second dispatch intervals. **Loading speed** Moderate.

Scary   Lose Things   Queasy   Rough

DESCRIPTION AND COMMENTS The Matterhorn is the most distinctive landmark on the Disneyland scene, visible from almost anywhere in the park. Open since 1959, the Matterhorn maintains its popularity and long lines year in and year out. The Matterhorn Bobsleds is a roller-coaster ride with an alpine motif. On the scary scale, the ride ranks about 6 on a scale of 10. The special effects cannot compare to Space Mountain, but they do afford a few surprises. The Matterhorn was refurbished in 2011, replacing the original straddle seating with individual lap bars and upgrading some effects.

TOURING TIPS Lines for the Matterhorn form as soon as the gates open and persist throughout the day. Ride first thing in the morning or just before the park closes. If you are a roller-coaster person, ride Space Mountain and then hurry over and hop on the Matterhorn. If roller coasters are not the end-all for you, we recommend choosing one of the other coasters or saving one for a second day.

One of the things we like about the Matterhorn is that the entire queuing area is visible. This makes the lines look more oppressive than they actually are and also provides an opportunity to closely approximate the time of your wait. If the line extending toward Tomorrowland reaches a point across from the Kodak Photo Spot, your wait to ride the Matterhorn Bobsleds will be about 16 minutes. The line normally forms on the Tomorrowland side of the mountain, but during busy times, there is also a line along the Fantasyland side as well. Most people do not know about this, so if you have a party of two or more, have one person wait in line, and check out if there is a line on the other side. In our research, when the Fantasyland line is operating, it is a much shorter wait. When there is only one line along the Tomorrowland side, most people stay to the left when the queue splits, often leaving the right-hand loading station with a shorter line.

Mr. Toad's Wild Ride ★★½

APPEAL BY AGE	PRESCHOOL ★★★	GRADE SCHOOL ★★★★	TEENS ★★★
YOUNG ADULTS ★★★½	OVER 30 ★★★★		SENIORS ★★

What it is Track ride in the dark. **Scope and scale** Minor attraction. **When to go** Before 11 a.m. **Special comments** Past its prime. **Duration of ride** Almost 2 minutes. **Average wait in line per 100 people ahead of you** 9 minutes. **Assumes** 12 cars operating. **Loading speed** Slow.

DESCRIPTION AND COMMENTS Mr. Toad is a twisting, curving ride in the dark that passes two-dimensional sets and props. There are a couple of clever effects, but basically it's at the technological basement of the Disney attraction mix. Its sister attraction at Disney World was scrapped in 1999. Though Mr. Toad doesn't compare well with newer high-tech attractions, many Disneyland veterans appreciate it because it's one of a handful of attractions remaining from the park's beginning.

TOURING TIPS Not a great but certainly a popular attraction. Lines build early in the day and never let up. Catch Mr. Toad before 11 a.m.

Peter Pan's Flight ★★★★

APPEAL BY AGE	PRESCHOOL ★★★★★		GRADE SCHOOL ★★★★½
TEENS ★★★★★	YOUNG ADULTS ★★★★	OVER 30 ★★★★	SENIORS ★★★★½

What it is Indoor fantasy-adventure ride. **Scope and scale** Minor attraction. **When to go** Before 10 a.m. or after 6 p.m. **Special comments** Happy and mellow. **Duration of ride** Just over 2 minutes. **Average wait in line per 100 people ahead of you** 11 minutes. **Assumes** 13 ships operating. **Loading speed** Slow.

Thumbs Up for the Whole Family

DESCRIPTION AND COMMENTS Although it is not considered one of Disneyland Park's major attractions, Peter Pan's Flight is superbly designed and absolutely delightful, with a happy theme, a reunion with some unforgettable Disney characters, beautiful effects, and charming music. Tiny pirate ships suspended from an overhead track launch you from Wendy's window to fly over nighttime London and on to Never Land and an encounter with Captain Hook, Mr. Smee, and the ubiquitous crocodile.

TOURING TIPS Though not a major feature of Disneyland Park, we nevertheless classify it as the best attraction in Fantasyland. Try to ride before 10 a.m. or after 6 p.m., during the afternoon or evening parade(s), or during a performance of *Fantasmic!*

Pinocchio's Daring Journey ★★½

APPEAL BY AGE	PRESCHOOL ★★★	GRADE SCHOOL ★★★	TEENS ★★★
YOUNG ADULTS ★★★	OVER 30 ★★★½		SENIORS ★★★★

What it is Track ride in the dark. **Scope and scale** Minor attraction. **When to go** Before noon or after 3:30 p.m. **Special comments** A big letdown. **Duration of ride** Almost 3 minutes. **Average wait in line per 100 people ahead of you** 8 minutes. **Assumes** 15 cars operating. **Loading speed** Slow.

DESCRIPTION AND COMMENTS This is another twisting, curving track ride in the dark, this time tracing the adventures of Pinocchio as he tries to find his way home. The action is hard to follow, and it lacks continuity. Although the sets are three-dimensional and more visually compelling than, say, Mr. Toad, the story line is dull and fails to engage the guest. In the ride's defense, it features some deliciously trippy Pleasure Island imagery, a clever vanishing Blue Fairy effect, and almost always an empty queue.

TOURING TIPS   The word must be out about Pinocchio because the lines are seldom very long. Still, the longest waits occur 11:30 a.m.–4:30 p.m.

Sleeping Beauty Castle   ★ ★ ★

APPEAL BY AGE	PRESCHOOL ★ ★ ★	GRADE SCHOOL ★ ★ ★ ½	TEENS ★ ★
YOUNG ADULTS ★ ★ ½		OVER 30 ★ ★ ★ ½	SENIORS ★ ★ ½

What it is Walk-through exhibit. Scope and scale Minor attraction. When to go Anytime. Special comments Must be able to climb up and down two flights of stairs. Duration of exhibit Varies; about 10 minutes. Average wait Usually none.

DESCRIPTION AND COMMENTS   Disneyland Park's most famous icon, Sleeping Beauty Castle is at the heart of Disneyland and serves as a stage for shows and special events. For the non-claustrophobic, the Sleeping Beauty Castle walk-through exhibit is a miniature 3-D series, arranged along a narrow passage inside the castle, that tells the story of Sleeping Beauty. Originally opened on April 29, 1957, to "preview" the upcoming 1959 movie *Sleeping Beauty,* and then closed for most of a decade after 9/11, the attraction reopened in November 2008 with new dioramas reflecting the style of artist Eyvind Earle, who gave *Sleeping Beauty* its distinctive design. In this version there are animated scenes, interactive elements, and Pepper's Ghost projection effects (as also seen in the Haunted Mansion) that have re-energized this classic attraction.

TOURING TIPS   The entrance is on the Fantasyland side of the castle near the passageway to Plaza Gardens and Frontierland. The exhibit allows for one-way traffic only. It can get a bit crowded inside, but there should rarely be a line outside the attraction. For those guests unable to handle stairs, a small alcove is to the left of the bridge to Tomorrowland. Inside you will find a collection of the animations, as well as music, allowing you to experience the attraction's elements without walking. The viewing location runs on a loop, so you might have to watch it out of order.

Snow White's Scary Adventures   ★ ★ ★

APPEAL BY AGE	PRESCHOOL ★ ★ ★	GRADE SCHOOL ★ ★ ★ ★	TEENS ★ ★ ★
YOUNG ADULTS ★ ★ ★		OVER 30 ★ ★ ★ ½	SENIORS ★ ★ ★ ★

What it is Track ride in the dark. Scope and scale Minor attraction. When to go Before 11 a.m. or after 5 p.m. Special comments Quite intimidating for preschoolers; worth seeing if the wait is not long. Duration of ride Almost 2 minutes. Average wait in line per 100 people ahead of you 9 minutes. Assumes 10 cars operating. Loading speed Slow.

Dark   Scary

DESCRIPTION AND COMMENTS   Here, you ride in a mining car in the dark through a series of sets drawn from *Snow White and the Seven Dwarfs.* The attraction has a *Perils of Pauline* flavor and features Snow White as she narrowly escapes harm at the hands of the wicked witch. The action and effects are a cut above Mr. Toad's Wild Ride but not as good as Peter Pan's Flight. This ride is more condensed and less coherent compared to its now-closed Orlando cousin, but it does boast new high-tech projection effects enhancing the magic mirror and rainstorm scenes.

TOURING TIPS Enjoyable but not particularly compelling. Experience it if the lines are not too long or on a second-day visit. Ride before 11 a.m. or after 5 p.m. if possible. Also, don't take the "scary" part too seriously. The witch looks mean, but most kids take her in stride. Or maybe not. A mother from Knoxville, Tennessee, commented:

> The outside looks cute and fluffy, but inside, the evil witch just keeps coming at you. My 5-year-old, who rode Space Mountain three times [and took other scary rides] right in stride, was near panic when our car stopped unexpectedly twice during Snow White. [After Snow White] my 6-year-old niece spent a lot of time asking, "Will a witch jump out at you?" before other rides. So I suggest that you explain a little more what this ride is about. It's tough on preschoolers who are expecting forest animals and dwarfs.

In point of fact, we receive more mail from parents about this ride than about all other Disneyland Park attractions combined. The bottom line is that it really punches the buttons of the 6-and-under crowd, when other more traditionally scary rides don't. Many kids, once frightened by Snow White's Scary Adventures, balk at trying any other attractions that go into the dark, regardless how benign.

Storybook Land Canal Boats ★★★

APPEAL BY AGE	PRESCHOOL ★★★★	GRADE SCHOOL ★★★	TEENS ★★★
YOUNG ADULTS ★★		OVER 30 ★★★	SENIORS ★★★★

What it is Scenic boat ride. **Scope and scale** Minor attraction. **When to go** Before 10:30 a.m. or after 5:30 p.m. **Special comments** Pretty, tranquil, and serene. **Duration of ride** 9½ minutes. **Average wait in line per 100 people ahead of you** 16 minutes. **Assumes** 7 boats operating. **Loading speed** Slow.

Thumbs Up for the Whole Family

DESCRIPTION AND COMMENTS Guide-operated boats wind along canals situated beneath the same miniature landscapes visible from the Casey Jr. Circus Train. This ride, offering stellar examples of bonsai cultivation, selective pruning, and miniaturization, is a must for landscape-gardening enthusiasts. The landscapes include scenes from more recent Disney features, in addition to those from such classics as *The Wind in the Willows* and *The Three Little Pigs*.

TOURING TIPS The boats are much more comfortable than the train, the view of the miniatures is better, and the pace is more leisurely. On the downside, the lines are long, and if not long, definitely slow moving. The ride itself also takes a lot of time. Our recommendation is to ride Casey Jr. if you have children or are in a hurry. Take the boat if your party is all adults or your pace is more leisurely. Best of all, the boats' pilots deliver live narration that (depending on the driver) can be delightfully droll. If you ride the canal boats, try to get on before 10:30 a.m. If the queue isn't prohibitive, this ride is especially appealing after dusk, when the creative lighting adds a whole new dimension. Closed during parades.

MICKEY'S TOONTOWN

MICKEY'S TOONTOWN IS SITUATED across the Disneyland Railroad tracks from Fantasyland. Its entrance is a tunnel that opens into Fantasyland just to the left of It's a Small World. As its name suggests, Toontown is a fanciful representation of the wacky cartoon community where all of the Disney characters live. Mickey's Toontown was inspired by the Disney animated feature *Who Framed Roger Rabbit?*, in which humans were able to enter the world of cartoon characters.

Mickey's Toontown consists of a colorful collection of miniature buildings, all executed in exaggerated cartoon style with rounded edges and brilliant colors. Among the buildings are Mickey's and Minnie's houses, both open to inspection inside and out.

If you want to see characters, Mickey's Toontown is the place to go. In addition to Mickey, who receives guests all day (except during parades) in his dressing room, and Minnie, who entertains in her house, you are also likely to see Goofy and Pluto in front of Toontown Hall and bump into such august personages as Daisy, Roger Rabbit, and a host of others lurking around the streets. It would be a rare event to visit Toontown without bumping into a few characters. From time to time, horns sound and whistles blow atop the Toontown City Hall, followed by a fanfare rendition of the Mickey Mouse Club theme song. This indicates, as a mom from Texas explained to us, that "some characters are fixin' to come out." And there you have it.

Mickey's Toontown is rendered with masterful attention to artistic humor and detail. The colorful buildings each have a story to tell or a

---

DISNEY DISH WITH JIM HILL

FINE-TUNING TOONTOWN When the Imagineers were originally designing this part of the park, Mickey Land (as this proposed expansion area was then known) looked very different. The Hundred Acre Wood, featuring a meet and greet with Winnie the Pooh and pals, was supposed to be where Mickey's and Minnie's houses are now. And where Goofy's Playouse was eventually built, Imagineers initially dreamed of installing earlier incarnations of DCA's The Little Mermaid: Ariel's Undersea Adventure and *Muppet-Vision 3-D*. What's more, Roger Rabbit's Car Toon Spin would have literally burst through the roof of the Cab Company and then sent your car careening across the rooftops of Toontown before it then dropped back into the show building for the dark ride's gag-filled grand finale. But not everything the Imagineers propose actually makes it off the drawing board, which is how we wound up with today's version of Mickey's Toontown.

gag to visit upon an unsuspecting guest. There is an explosion at the Fireworks Factory every minute or so, always unannounced. Across the street, the sidewalk is littered with crates containing strange contents addressed to exotic destinations. If you pry open the top of one of the crates (easy to do), the crate will emit a noise consistent with its contents. A box of "train parts," for example, broadcasts the sound of a racing locomotive when you lift the top.

Everywhere in Mickey's Toontown are subtleties and absurdities to delight the imagination. Next to Goofy's Playhouse is a Goofy-shaped impact crater marking the spot where he missed his swimming pool while high diving. A sign in front of the local garage declares, "If we can't fix it, we won't."

While adults will enjoy the imaginative charm of Mickey's Toontown, it will quickly become apparent that there is not much for them to do there. Most of the attractions in Mickey's Toontown are for kids, specifically smaller children. Attractions open to adults include a dark ride drawn from *Who Framed Roger Rabbit?* (sort of a high-tech rendition of Mr. Toad's Wild Ride) and a diminutive roller coaster.

In many ways, Mickey's Toontown is a designer playground, a fanciful cousin to Tom Sawyer Island in Frontierland, where it's OK for the kids to run, climb, and let off steam. What distinguishes Mickey's Toontown is that the play areas are specially designed for smaller children; it's also much cleaner than Tom Sawyer Island (that is, no dirt—though this does not guarantee a dirt-free child upon leaving the area). Finally, in the noblest Disney tradition, you must wait in line for virtually everything.

Also, be forewarned that Mickey's Toontown is not very large, especially in comparison with neighboring Fantasyland. A tolerable crowd in most of the other lands will seem like Times Square on New Year's Eve in Mickey's Toontown. Couple this congestion with the unfortunate fact that none of the attractions in Mickey's Toontown are engineered to handle huge crowds, and you come face-to-face with possibly the most attractive traffic jam the Disney folks have ever created.

Mickey's Toontown opens 1 hour after the rest of the park. If you're touring with younger children, hit the Fantasyland attractions during the first hour the park is open, and then head for Mickey's Toontown.

Beating the crowds in Toontown is complicated by **Toontown Morning Madness,** an early-entry perk bundled with most tickets included in travel packages purchased through the Walt Disney Travel Company. On Monday, Wednesday, Friday, and Saturday, guests with the special tickets can enter Toontown 1 hour before the general public. Because Mickey's Toontown opens 1 hour later than the rest of the park, Toontown Morning Madness actually commences at

unofficial **TIP**
When Toontown Morning Madness begins at the same time as general park opening, it will take you 20 minutes or more to get through the turnstiles and walk or board the train to Toontown. To take advantage of the entire Morning Madness hour, therefore, you need to be among the first guests admitted to the park.

the same time that Disneyland Park opens. The festivities focus on character meet and greets—oddly, rides do not begin operating until the Morning Madness hour ends. If your tickets do not include Morning Madness admission, try to tour Toontown as soon as it opens on Tuesday, Thursday, or Sunday. Because Toontown Morning Madness days are subject to change, call Disneyland information in advance to verify them during your visit. Finally, be aware that all of Toontown, including the Roger Rabbit ride, will close early before every nighttime fireworks show. It seems that rockets are launched from a building behind the land, showering Mickey's city with fiery embers, which might prove inconvenient for anyone standing below.

Chip 'n Dale Treehouse ★★

APPEAL BY AGE	PRESCHOOL ★★★★	GRADE SCHOOL ★★	TEENS ★★
YOUNG ADULTS ★★★★		OVER 30 ★★	SENIORS ★

What it is Imaginative children's play area. **Scope and scale** Diversion. **When to go** Anytime. **Special comments** Good exercise for the small fry.

DESCRIPTION AND COMMENTS The play area consists of a treehouse with slides.

TOURING TIPS Located in the most remote corner of Mickey's Toontown and obscured by the crowd waiting to ride the roller coaster next door, the Treehouse is frequently overlooked. Of all the attractions in Mickey's Toontown, this is the easiest one to get the kids into without much of a wait. Most any child who can fit is allowed to rummage around in the Treehouse.

Disneyland Railroad

DESCRIPTION AND COMMENTS Mickey's Toontown and Fantasyland share a station on the Disneyland Railroad's route around the perimeter of the park. Usually the wait to board is short.

Gadget's Go Coaster ★★

APPEAL BY AGE	PRESCHOOL ★★★★½	GRADE SCHOOL ★★★★	TEENS ★★★
YOUNG ADULTS ★★★		OVER 30 ★★★	SENIORS ★★★

What it is Small roller coaster. **Scope and scale** Minor attraction. **When to go** Before 10:30 a.m., during the parades or *Fantasmic!* in the evening, or just before the park closes. **Special comments** Great for little ones but not worth the wait for adults; must be 35" to ride; expectant moms shouldn't ride. **Duration of ride** About 50 seconds. **Average wait in line per 100 people ahead of you** 10 minutes. **Assumes** Normal staffing. **Loading speed** Slow.

DESCRIPTION AND COMMENTS Gadget's Go Coaster is a very small roller coaster, the idea of which is that you are miniaturized and riding around in an acorn shell. The ride itself is pretty zippy, but it is over so quickly that you hardly know that you've been anywhere. In fact, of the 52 seconds the ride is in motion, 32 seconds are consumed in exiting the loading area, being ratcheted up the first hill, and braking into the off-loading area. The actual time you spend careening around the track is a whopping 20 seconds.

TOURING TIPS   Gadget's Go Coaster, a beginner roller coaster for young children, is the perfect attraction to gauge the pluckiness of your little ones before tossing them to the coyotes on Big Thunder Mountain Railroad. The coaster cars are not very comfortable for adults, and you can expect a fair amount of whiplash, but as noted, the ride takes less than a minute. The coaster is both slow-loading and visually attractive, so you can expect long waits except during the first 30 minutes that Mickey's Toontown is open.

Goofy's Playhouse   ★★½

APPEAL BY AGE	PRESCHOOL ★★★	GRADE SCHOOL ★★★	TEENS –
YOUNG ADULTS –	OVER 30 ★		SENIORS ★

What it is A whimsical children's play area. **Scope and scale** Diversion. **When to go** Anytime.

DESCRIPTION AND COMMENTS   Goofy's Playhouse is a small but nicely themed play area for the under-6 set. Usually not crowded, the playhouse is a pleasant place to let preschoolers ramble and parents relax while older sibs enjoy more adventurous attractions.

TOURING TIPS   There's not a lot of shade, so visits early or late in the day work best.

Mickey's House and Meet Mickey   ★★★

APPEAL BY AGE	PRESCHOOL ★★★★★	GRADE SCHOOL ★★★★	TEENS ★★★
YOUNG ADULTS ★★★	OVER 30 ★★★		SENIORS ★★★★

What it is Walk-through tour of Mickey's House and Movie Barn, ending with a personal visit with Mickey. **Scope and scale** Minor attraction and character-greeting opportunity. **When to go** Before 10:30 a.m. or after 5:30 p.m. **Special comments** Well done. **Duration of tour** 15–30 minutes (depending on the crowd). **Average wait in line per 100 people ahead of you** 20 minutes. **Assumes** Normal staffing. **Touring speed** Slow.

DESCRIPTION AND COMMENTS   Mickey's House is the starting point of a self-guided tour that winds through the famous mouse's house, into his backyard and past Pluto's doghouse, and then into Mickey's Movie Barn. This last stop harks back to the so-called "barn" studio where Walt Disney created a number of the earlier Mickey Mouse cartoons. Once in the Movie Barn, guests watch vintage Disney cartoons while awaiting admittance to Mickey's Dressing Room.

   In small groups of one or two families, guests are ultimately conducted into the dressing room where Mickey awaits to pose for photos and sign autographs. The visit is not lengthy (2–4 minutes), but there is adequate time for all of the children to hug, poke, and admire the star.

TOURING TIPS   The cynical observer will discern immediately that Mickey's House, backyard, Movie Barn, and so on are no more than a cleverly devised queuing area designed to deliver guests to Mickey's Dressing

Room for the Mouse Encounter. For those with some vestige of child in their personalities, however, the preamble serves to heighten anticipation while providing the opportunity to get to know the corporate symbol on a more personal level. Mickey's House is well conceived and contains a lot of Disney memorabilia. You will notice that children touch everything as they proceed through the house, hoping to find some artifact that is not welded or riveted into the set (an especially tenacious child during one of our visits was actually able to rip a couple of books from a bookcase).

Meeting Mickey and touring his house are best done during the first 2 hours the park is open or, alternatively, in the evening during *Fantasmic!* If meeting Mickey is at the top of your child's list, you might consider taking the Disneyland Railroad from Main Street to the Toontown/Fantasyland station as soon as you enter the park. Some children are so obsessed with seeing Mickey that they cannot enjoy anything else until they get Mickey in the rearview mirror.

Minnie's House ★★½

APPEAL BY AGE PRESCHOOL ★★★★★ GRADE SCHOOL ★★★★½ TEENS ★★★
YOUNG ADULTS ★★★   OVER 30 ★★★½   SENIORS ★★★½

What it is Walk-through exhibit. **Scope and scale** Minor attraction and character-greeting opportunity. **When to go** Before 11:30 a.m. or after 4:30 p.m. **Special comments** OK but not great. **Duration of tour** About 10 minutes. **Average wait in line per 100 people ahead of you** 12 minutes. **Touring speed** Slow.

DESCRIPTION AND COMMENTS Minnie's House consists of a self-guided tour through the various rooms and backyard of Mickey Mouse's main squeeze. Similar to Mickey's House, only predictably more feminine, Minnie's House likewise showcases some fun Disney memorabilia. Among the highlights of the short tour are the fanciful appliances in Minnie's kitchen. Like Mickey, Minnie is usually present to receive guests.

TOURING TIPS The main difference between Mickey's House and Minnie's House is that Minnie's House cannot accommodate as many guests. See Minnie early and before Mickey to avoid waiting outdoors in a long queue. Be advised that neither Mickey nor Minnie is available during parades.

Miss Daisy, Donald's Boat ★★

APPEAL BY AGE PRESCHOOL ★★★½ GRADE SCHOOL ★★★★ TEENS ★★★½
YOUNG ADULTS ★★★★★   OVER 30 ★★   SENIORS ★★

What it is Creative play area with a boat theme. **Scope and scale** Diversion. **When to go** Before 10:30 a.m. or after 4:30 p.m.

DESCRIPTION AND COMMENTS Another children's play area, this time with a tug-boat theme. Children can climb nets, ring bells, survey Toontown from the captain's bridge, and scoot down slides. The idea is that Donald Duck (who, as everyone knows, lives in Duckburg) is visiting Toontown.

TOURING TIPS Kids more or less wander on and off of the *Miss Daisy,* and usually there is not any sort of organized line or queuing area. Enjoy this play area at your leisure and stay as long as you like.

Roger Rabbit's Car Toon Spin (Fastpass) ★★★

What it is Track ride in the dark. **Scope and scale** Major attraction. **When to go** Before 10:30 a.m. or after 6:30 p.m. **Special comments** Ride with your kids, if you can stomach it. **Duration of ride** A little more than 3 minutes. **Average wait in line per 100 people ahead of you** 7 minutes. **Assumes** Full-capacity operation. **Loading speed** Moderate.

Dark   Rough   Queasy

DESCRIPTION AND COMMENTS A so-called dark ride where guests become part of a cartoon plot. The idea is that you are renting a taxicab for a tour of Toontown. As soon as your cab gets under way, however, weasels throw a slippery glop (known as "dip") on the road, sending the cab into a more or less uncontrollable spin. This spinning continues as the cab passes through a variety of sets populated by cartoon and audio-animatronic characters and punctuated by simulated explosions. As a child of the 1960s put it, "It was like combining Mr. Toad's Wild Ride with the Mad Tea Party while tripping on LSD." The ride features an elaborate indoor queue, and the best effects of any Disneyland cartoon dark ride, climaxing in a head-scratchingly effective "portable hole" gag that holds up under repeated viewing.

The main problem with the Car Toon Spin is that, because of the spinning, you are often pointed in the wrong direction to appreciate (or even see) many of the better visual effects. Furthermore, the story line is loose. The attraction lacks the continuity and humor of Splash Mountain or the suspense of The Haunted Mansion or Snow White's Scary Adventures.

The spinning, incidentally, can be controlled by the guests. If you don't want to spin, you don't have to. If you do elect to spin, you still will not be able to approach the eye-popping speed attainable on the teacups at the Mad Tea Party. Sluggish spinning aside, our advice for those who are at all susceptible to motion sickness is not to get near this ride if you are touring with anyone under 21 years of age.

A reader from Milford, Michigan, echoed our sentiments, lamenting:

> *The most disappointing ride to me was Roger Rabbit's Car Toon Spin. I stood 45 minutes for a fun-house ride, and the wheel was so difficult to operate that I spent most of my time trying to steer the bloody car and missed the point of the ride.*

TOURING TIPS The ride is popular for its novelty, and it is one of the few Mickey's Toontown attractions that parents (with strong stomachs) can enjoy with their children. Because the ride stays fairly thronged with people all day long, ride before 10:30 a.m., during parades or *Fantasmic!*, or in the hour before the park closes. The Car Toon Spin Fastpass machines are not connected to the park system, meaning that you can obtain a Fastpass at any time irrespective of whether you are holding another Fastpass. Because the attraction is in such an isolated part of the park, however, the inconvenience of returning to ride can be considerable. The best move is to obtain Fastpasses before 10:30 a.m., when the return time is an hour or less away, and then let your children enjoy the other Toontown attractions until it's time to ride.

TOMORROWLAND

LOCATED DIRECTLY TO THE RIGHT of the central hub is Tomorrowland. This themed area is a futuristic mix of rides and experiences that relates to technological development and what life will be like in the years to come.

Before its 2000 renovation, Tomorrowland's 40-year-old buildings more resembled 1970s motel architecture than anyone's vision of the future. Tomorrowland's current design is more enduring, reflecting a nostalgic vision of the future as imagined by dreamers and scientists in the 1920s and 1930s. Frozen in time, Tomorrowland conjures up visions of Buck Rogers (whom nobody under age 60 remembers), fanciful mechanical rockets, and metallic cities spread beneath towering obelisks. Disney refers to Tomorrowland as the "Future That Never Was." *Newsweek* has dubbed it "retro-future."

Astro Orbitor   ★★

APPEAL BY AGE	PRESCHOOL ★★★★	GRADE SCHOOL ★★★	TEENS ★★
YOUNG ADULTS ★½		OVER 30 ★★	SENIORS ★★½

What it is Very mild midway-type thrill ride. **Scope and scale** Minor attraction. **When to go** Before 10 a.m. or during the hour before the park closes. **Special comments** Not worth the wait. **Duration of ride** 1½ minutes. **Average wait in line per 100 people ahead of you** 13 minutes. **Assumes** Normal staffing. **Loading speed** Slow.

Queasy

DESCRIPTION AND COMMENTS The Astro Orbitor is a visually appealing midway-type ride involving small rockets that rotate on arms around a central axis. Be aware that the Astro Orbitor flies higher and faster than Dumbo and that it frightens some small children.

Thumbs Up for the Whole Family

TOURING TIPS Astro Orbitor is slow to load and expendable on any schedule. If you want to take a preschooler on this ride, place your child in the seat first and then sit down yourself.

Autopia (Fastpass)   ★★

APPEAL BY AGE	PRESCHOOL ★★★★★		GRADE SCHOOL ★★★★½
TEENS ★★	YOUNG ADULTS ★★	OVER 30 ★★½	SENIORS ★★½

What it is Drive-'em-yourself miniature cars. **Scope and scale** Minor attraction. **When to go** Before 10 a.m., after 5 p.m., or use Fastpass. **Special comments** Boring for adults; great for preschoolers; must be at least 32" tall to ride, and at least one guest in car must be 54". **Duration of ride** Approximately 4½ minutes.

Average wait in line per 100 people ahead of you 6 minutes. **Assumes** 35 cars operating on each track. **Loading speed** Slow.

DESCRIPTION AND COMMENTS An elaborate miniature freeway with gasoline-powered cars that will travel at speeds of up to 7 miles per hour. The attraction design, with its sleek cars, auto noises, highway signs, and even an "off-road" section, is quite alluring. In fact, however, the cars poke along on a track that leaves the driver with little to do. Pretty ho-hum for most adults and teenagers, but at least it's much more visually stimulating than the unthemed Magic Kingdom version.

TOURING TIPS This ride is appealing to the eye but definitely expendable on a schedule for adults. Preschoolers, however, love it. If your preschooler is too short to drive, place the child behind the wheel and allow him or her to steer (the car runs on a guide rail) while you work the foot pedal.

A mom from North Billerica, Massachusetts, writes:

I was truly amazed by the number of adults in the line. Please empha-size to your readers that these cars travel on a guided path and are not a whole lot of fun. The only reason I could think of for adults to be in line was an insane desire to go on absolutely every ride. The other feature about the cars is that they tend to pile up at the end, so it takes almost as long to get off as it did to get on. Parents riding with their preschoolers should keep the car going as slow as it can without stalling. This prolongs the preschooler's joy and decreases the time you will have to wait at the end.

Be aware that Fastpass is only offered on busier days and doesn't work very well at Autopia. It's typical for the wait in the Fastpass return line to exceed 20 minutes. If Autopia ranks high on your pop chart, you might be better off riding the first hour the park is open and using the standby line.

Buzz Lightyear Astro Blasters ★★★★

APPEAL BY AGE	PRESCHOOL ★★★★★	GRADE SCHOOL ★★★★★
TEENS ★★★★★	YOUNG ADULTS ★★★★★ OVER 30 ★★★★★	SENIORS ★★★★

What it is Space-travel interactive dark ride. **Scope and scale** Major attraction. **When to go** Before 10:30 a.m. or after 6 p.m. **Special comments** A real winner! **Duration of ride** About 4½ minutes. **Average wait in line per 100 people ahead of you** 3 minutes. **Loading speed** Fast.

DESCRIPTION AND COMMENTS This attraction is based on the space-commando character Buzz Lightyear from *Toy Story*. The marginal story line has you and Buzz Lightyear trying to save the universe from the evil Emperor Zurg. The indoor ride is interactive to the extent that you can spin your car and shoot simulated "laser cannons" at Zurg and his minions.

A similar attraction at the Magic Kingdom at Walt Disney World opened with little fanfare in 1998 but immediately became one of the most popular attractions in the park. The Disneyland version, situated across from Star Tours, is much the same except mobile guns allow more accurate aiming and one high-tech twist: Folks at home can play along with guests on the ride in real time via the Internet. Through Web-cam technology, guests on the attraction are virtually paired up with Internet partners.

Praise for Buzz Lightyear is almost universal. This comment from a Massachusetts couple is typical:

> Buzz Lightyear was the surprise hit of our trip! My husband and I enjoyed competing for the best score so much that we went on this ride several times during our stay. Definitely a must, especially when there's no wait.

TOURING TIPS Each car is equipped with two laser cannons and a scorekeeping display. Each scorekeeping display is independent, so you can compete with your riding partner. A joystick allows you to spin the car to line up the various targets. Each time you pull the trigger, you'll release a red laser beam that you can see hitting or missing the target. Most folks' first ride is occupied with learning how to use the equipment (fire off individual shots as opposed to keeping the trigger depressed) and figuring out how the targets work. The next ride (as with certain potato chips, one is not enough), you'll surprise yourself by how much better you do. *Unofficial* readers are unanimous in their praise of Buzz Lightyear. Some guests, in fact, spend several hours on the attraction, riding again and again. See Buzz Lightyear after riding Space Mountain and Star Tours first thing in the morning.

Captain EO ★★★★

APPEAL BY AGE	PRESCHOOL ★★★	GRADE SCHOOL ★★★★	TEENS ★★★★
YOUNG ADULTS ★★★		OVER 30 ★★★	SENIORS ★★★★

What it is 3-D film with special effects. **Scope and scale** Major attraction. **When to go** Before noon or after 4 p.m. **Special comments** Not to be missed. Adults should not be put off by the sci-fi theme or rock music. The loud, intense show with tactile effects frightens some young children. **Duration of show** Approximately 17 minutes. **Preshow** 8 minutes. **Probable waiting time** 15 minutes (at suggested times).

Loud

Scary

DESCRIPTION AND COMMENTS In response to pop music star Michael Jackson's death in 2009, Disney brought back Jackson's 3-D space-themed rock music video, *Captain EO*, for a limited engagement in its theme parks. *Captain EO* originally ran in Epcot 1986–1994. There's no telling how long it'll last on its second run in Disneyland, but we've heard that the King of Pop is posthumously pulling four times the audience that *Honey, I Shrunk the Audience* (his immediate predecessor) was drawing, so Michael may stick around for a while. The film has an exceptionally loud soundtrack and a propensity to frighten small children.

DESCRIPTION AND COMMENTS *Captain EO* is sort of the ultimate music video. Starring Jackson and directed by Francis Coppola, this 3-D space fantasy is more than a film; it's a happening. Action on the screen is augmented by in-theater lighting and hydraulic moving seats that enforce involuntary audience participation, though the original laser and fog effects have sadly not returned. There's not much of a story, but there's plenty of music and dancing performed by some of the most unlikely creatures ever to shake a tail feather. If nothing else, *Captain EO* reminds us that music videos once contained more than young urbanites dancing in clubs or five ill-dressed, unshaven guys whining onstage. Unfortunately, the 70-millimeter film looks fuzzy and faded compared to modern projection methods, and the aggressive bouncing with every bass beat grows bothersome.

TOURING TIPS Shows usually begin on the hour and half hour. The sound level is earsplitting, frightening some young children. Many adults report that the loud soundtrack is distracting, even uncomfortable. Avoid seats in the first several rows; if you sit too close to the screen, the 3-D images don't focus properly. If the bouncing floor bothers you, ask for a stationary seat in the last row.

Disneyland Monorail System ★★★

APPEAL BY AGE PRESCHOOL ★★★★★ GRADE SCHOOL ★★★★★ TEENS ★★★
YOUNG ADULTS ★★★★ OVER 30 ★★★½ SENIORS ★★★★½

What it is Scenic transportation. **Scope and scale** Major attraction. **When to go** During the hot, crowded period of the day (11:30 a.m.–5 p.m.). **Special comments** Nice, relaxing ride with some interesting views of the park; take the monorail to Downtown Disney for lunch. **Duration of ride** 12–15 minutes round-trip. **Average wait in line per 100 people ahead of you** 10 minutes. **Assumes** 3 monorails operating. **Loading speed** Moderate–fast.

Thumbs Up for the Whole Family

DESCRIPTION AND COMMENTS The monorail is a futuristic transportation ride that affords the only practical opportunity for escaping the park during the crowded lunch period and early afternoon. Boarding at the Tomorrowland monorail station, you can commute to the Disneyland Resort hotels and Downtown Disney complex, where it's possible to have a nice lunch without fighting the crowds. For those not interested in lunch, the monorail provides a tranquil trip with a nice view of Downtown Disney, Disney California Adventure theme park, Fantasyland, and Tomorrowland.

TOURING TIPS We recommend using the monorail to commute to Downtown Disney for a quiet, relaxing lunch away from the crowds and the heat. If you only want to experience the ride, go whenever you wish; the wait to board is usually 15–25 minutes except in the 2 hours before closing. Also note that you must disembark and then queue up to reboard at Downtown Disney.

Disneyland Railroad

DESCRIPTION AND COMMENTS The Disneyland Railroad makes a regular stop at the Tomorrowland Railroad Station. For additional details about the railroad, see pages 219–220.

TOURING TIPS This station becomes fairly crowded on busy days. If you are interested primarily in getting there, it may be quicker to walk.

Finding Nemo Submarine Voyage ★★★★

APPEAL BY AGE	PRESCHOOL ★★★★½	GRADE SCHOOL ★★★★½	TEENS ★★★
YOUNG ADULTS ★★½		OVER 30 ★★★	SENIORS ★★★

What it is Simulated submarine ride. **Scope and scale** Headliner. **When to go** First hour the park is open or the last 30 minutes before park closing. **Duration of ride** 11½ minutes. **Average wait in line per 100 people ahead of you** 7½ minutes. **Assumes** All 8 subs are operating. **Loading speed** Slow–moderate.

DESCRIPTION AND COMMENTS The Finding Nemo Submarine Voyage ride is based on the story line of the hit Disney/Pixar animated feature *Finding Nemo*. Here you board a submarine in a loading area situated below the Disneyland monorail station in Tomorrowland. After a quick lap of the open-air lagoon, the sub passes through a waterfall and inside to follow the general *Finding Nemo* story. Special effects center on a combination of traditional audio-animatronics and, once you're inside the dark interior of the building, what appear to be rear-projection screens, underwater, at a distance of 3–10 feet from the sub's windows. Encased in rock and shipwrecks, the screens are natural looking and allow the animated characters to appear three-dimensionally in the undersea world. Other elements include traveling through a minefield, a sea of jellyfish (very cool), and entering the mouth of a whale. The onboard sound system allows the story to "travel" from front to back of the sub, and the visual experience is different depending on what seat you're in.

The attraction is well done and rates at or close to four stars for all age groups. You don't have to be a Nemo fan to be impressed by the scale and effects. It's not fast-paced but, rather, leisurely in the way that Pirates of the Caribbean is.

TOURING TIPS Finding Nemo Submarine Voyage is a theatrical and technical success but in many ways an engineering failure. By lengthening the duration of the voyage, by failing to provide adequate loading facilities, and by being slowed down due to a technical dispatching constraint, the Imagineers have reduced the attraction's capacity to about 900 guests per hour, a shockingly small capacity for a headliner attraction. Further, owing to the low carrying capacity, the subs are not a good candidate for Fastpass (all Fastpasses would be gone before noon). The bottom line is that the Submarine Voyage is the most difficult attraction in the park to experience without a long wait in line, and by long we mean 1–2½ hours.

In collecting data for the touring plans in this guide, we discovered that none of the arrive-early, beat-the-crowds strategies work very well. Our researchers entered the park via both the monorail and the main entrance after lining up as much as 1 hour before park opening at the monorail station or turnstiles. We did this on both early-entry days and non-early-entry days. On average, we arrived at the Finding Nemo queue about 12–15 minutes after the park opened or the early-entry period commenced. By that time, the wait to ride was already 1 hour.

Because Finding Nemo is immensely popular, a huge percentage of the guests on hand at park opening head straight for the subs—only if you are literally among the first 70 people to enter the park and arrive at the subs will you be rewarded with a short wait. But here's the kicker: Adding the time it takes to reach the subs, wait to board, ride, and disembark, you will invest 35–70 minutes to ride Finding Nemo first thing in the morning, sacrificing in the process the most crowd-free touring period of the day for the other popular attractions.

We've determined that, taking the day as a whole, you make much better use of your time enjoying Space Mountain, Splash Mountain, Peter Pan's Flight, and other popular attractions during the first hour the park is open and saving the subs for later, when a parade, fireworks show, or *Fantasmic!* has siphoned a large number of guests from the line. By lining up for the subs 15 minutes before one of these events, we were able to whittle the wait from 1–2 hours down to 30–40 minutes. Even 30–40 minutes by *Unofficial Guide* standards is a very long wait, but with the engineering constraints and popularity of Finding Nemo, it's pretty much the best you can do without messing up the rest of your day. Incidentally, arriving 15 minutes before a parade or other presentation is not an arbitrary suggestion—during this time window, the Finding Nemo line (or lines at other popular attractions) will be its shortest. The last 30 minutes before park closing is another good time to get in line.

Claustrophobes may not be comfortable with the experience, even though the sub doesn't actually submerge (we saw one 30-ish woman who started hyperventilating before the sub left the dock). Children may be scared of the same thing, or of the encounter with sharks (they keep their distance). The sharks here are a bit less menacing than in the movie too.

The bright-yellow subs, revived from the previous attraction, have been reengineered with electric power to minimize noise and pollution. The subs fit 40 people. It's not easy to get 40 aboard, however, because the seats are narrow and a few guests take up two. Ideally, large guests should aim to be in one of the four seats at the front or back, but this may be difficult to negotiate. Wheelchair-bound guests or those who can't get down the spiral staircase into the sub can view the experience from a special topside viewing room (seats about six able-bodied persons plus two wheelchairs). With the exception of one small animated effect, the visual is identical (perhaps faster), but despite a large monitor the creatures appear smaller than when viewing them through a real porthole.

A reader from Sydney, Australia, disagrees with our Finding Nemo rating, writing:

> The ride that was the most overrated was Finding Nemo. Perhaps it would rate high for the under 8-year-olds, but for our group it was one of the worst rides. It was boring, had rushing water, moved slowly, and creaked with age. What made it worse was that it had a high rating and this raised expectations.

If there's a silver lining attached to the long queues for the Submarine Voyage, it's that it draws a lot of guests away from other Disneyland favorites such as Splash Mountain, Space Mountain, and Indiana Jones Adventure.

Innoventions ★★★

APPEAL BY AGE	PRESCHOOL ★★★½	GRADE SCHOOL ★½	TEENS ★★★½
YOUNG ADULTS ★★		OVER 30 ★★	SENIORS ★½

What it is Multifaceted attraction featuring static and hands-on exhibits relating to products and technologies of the near future. **Scope and scale** Major diversion. **When to go** On your second day or after you have seen all the major attractions. **Special comments** Most exhibits demand time and participation to be rewarding; not much gained here by a quick walk-through; very commercial, but well presented.

DESCRIPTION AND COMMENTS Modeled after a similar attraction at Epcot in Walt Disney World, Innoventions was part of the 1996–2000 Tomorrowland renovation. In 2008 Disney scrapped the trade-show-like collection of high-tech gizmos and games and borrowed a page from the park's ancient past. One of the most beloved and often remembered attractions of Disneyland's early years was the Monsanto House of the Future, a stand-alone building with a curved spaceship-style exterior and rooms outfitted with furniture and appliances forecast to be in everyone's home before the millennium. This time around, sans Monsanto, it's the Dream Home, located in the middle of the ground floor of Innoventions. Surrounding the Dream Home are rooms from equally futuristic "neighbors'" homes, complete with actors playing the neighbors. Between the neighbors and a member of the Dream Home family, you are guided on a tour of the home's wondrous rooms and the technology within them. A grand piano in the great room is networked to a music teacher across the country. In the dining room, touch screens in the dinner table allow the family to assemble a scrapbook. A 100-inch television dominates the family room. The kitchen, which will remind you of the bridge of the Starship *Enterprise*, is of course the mother lode: Among its many amazements is a computer that reads RFID (radio-frequency identification) "smart" labels on food packages and warns you if you're about to chug a glass of milk past its expiration date; the same computer will alert you if you don't have an ingredient on hand for a recipe you're making. A story line concerning the Dream Home family, the Eliases, sort of ties everything together. On the second floor you'll find an entertaining 15-minute show demonstrating Honda's ASIMO, an impressive humanoid robot capable of running autonomously, climbing stairs, and kicking soccer balls. Also upstairs are some Xbox video game consoles, Siemens' "Project Tomorrow" simulations (as also seen at Epcot's Spaceship Earth), and St. John's Hospital's interactive health-living play area.

A reader from Washington state likes the Dream Home but sees it as a Band-Aid:

Innoventions seems a little more coherent than it was, now that the model house has been installed, but I don't get the whole point. It still strikes me as filling up room until the Disney people figure out what "real attraction" they're going to put in there.

TOURING TIPS The Dream Home creates order and continuity at Innoventions, where previously there was an almost random assemblage of games, gadgets, and imponderables. It also provides structure, with the house tour regimenting the way you view the exhibit and probably extending the amount of time you would have spent there otherwise. Crowds are rarely an issue at this attraction. We recommend that you spend time at Innoventions on your second day. If you have only 1 day, visit sometime during the evening if you have the time and endurance. Be forewarned that when you return home, your wife will want to remodel the kitchen.

Jedi Training Academy ★★★½

APPEAL BY AGE	PRESCHOOL ★★★★★	GRADE SCHOOL ★★★★★	TEENS ★★
YOUNG ADULTS ★★★		OVER 30 ★★★★	SENIORS ★★★★

What it is Live entertainment where young audience members are trained to be Jedis. **Scope and scale** Major diversion. **When to go** See *Times Guide* for performance times. **Duration of show** 25 minutes.

DESCRIPTION AND COMMENTS Staged at the Tomorrowland Terrace Theater, the *Jedi Training Academy* recruits 30 young volunteers and trains them to fight with a lightsaber (an elegant, if plastic, weapon). The training consists of practicing a surprisingly long set of fencing-style moves while the audience gets to enjoy the minimal comprehension by some of the youngest Jedis. Just when the training ends, Darth Vader and Darth Maul arrive with a couple of Stormtroopers, and the young recruits meet them in "battle," with each Jedi getting his or her turn to take a whack at a Darth. All volunteers are awarded a *Jedi Training Academy* diploma. It's a great photo op for parents and a major hoot for everyone else. For a London, England, mother, Jedi boot camp was a highlight of the trip:

My 8-year-old son literally cried with joy after participating in the Jedi Experience in Tomorrowland. You advise sitting in the front two rows to be picked, but actually, they picked my son only after my husband launched him onto his shoulders to draw their attention. I noticed they especially picked other kids on their parents' shoulders.

TOURING TIPS There are two prime viewing locations: standing room on the show floor underneath the overhang, and seating at the Terrace counter-service restaurant. There are only 10–20 tables with decent views of the show, so make sure to stake them out early. Otherwise, there is plenty of standing room space around the sides of the stage.

To be chosen to participate, arrive 20–30 minutes early and seat your child in the first couple of rows surrounding the stage. Jedis look for energetic and excited children to recruit; wearing a *Star Wars* T-shirt helps, but don't bring your own lightsaber because those are supplied.

Space Mountain (Fastpass) ★★★★½

APPEAL BY AGE	PRESCHOOL ★★	GRADE SCHOOL ★★★★	TEENS ★★★★
YOUNG ADULTS ★★★★½		OVER 30 ★★★★	SENIORS ★★★

What it is Roller coaster in the dark. **Scope and scale** Super-headliner. **When to go** Right after the park opens or use Fastpass. **Special comments** Much improved; must be 40" tall to ride. **Duration of ride** 2 minutes and 45 seconds. **Average wait in line per 100 people ahead of you** 3½ minutes. **Loading speed** Moderate.

Dark　　Scary　　Lose Things　　Queasy　　Rough

DESCRIPTION AND COMMENTS Space Mountain is an indoor roller coaster with a theme of high-speed interstellar travel. Roller-coaster aficionados will tell you (correctly) that Space Mountain is a designer version of the Wild Mouse, a midway ride that's been around for at least 50 years. There are no long drops or swooping hills as there are on a traditional roller coaster—only quick, unexpected turns and small drops. Disney's contribution essentially was to add a space theme to the Wild Mouse and put it in the dark. And this does indeed make the Mouse seem wilder.

The most surprising thing about the new Space Mountain is its aesthetic beauty. No, we're not kidding. The vistas of the solar system and the stars, the distant galaxies, and passing comets are intoxicating and very realistic. Because you cannot see the ride's infrastructure, Space Mountain is no longer simply a roller coaster in a dimly lit building with some Buck Rogers planets and meteors projected on the ceiling. Because you can't see the track or anticipate where your vehicle will go, your eyes are free to feast on the rich visuals. Since 2009, Disney has transformed Space Mountain into Ghost Galaxy for Halloween, adding atmospheric audio and video projections of an angry space ghost (no, not that Space Ghost) chasing you through the cosmos. The interstellar specter is more goofy than genuinely scary, but it makes a fun novelty for the spooky season. Nighttime video projections, which make the iconic conical building look like it's crumbling to dust or crackling with electricity, are the most impressive element of the overlay.

TOURING TIPS Space Mountain is the park's most popular attraction. Experience it immediately after the park opens or use Fastpass.

Starcade

DESCRIPTION AND COMMENTS Starcade is nothing more or less than a large electronic-games arcade. Since the Sega jet-combat simulator was removed, the most interesting items in here are a Guitar Hero Arcade game and a few skill-crane claw machines. In other words, move along; there's nothing to see here.

TOURING TIPS Enjoy your time in the area with a pocket full of quarters.

Star Tours: The Adventures Continue
(Fastpass) ★★★★½

APPEAL BY AGE   PRESCHOOL ★★★½   GRADE SCHOOL ★★★★   TEENS ★★★★
YOUNG ADULTS ★★★★   OVER 30 ★★★★   SENIORS ★★★★

What it is Space-flight simulation ride. **Scope and scale** Major attraction. **When to go** Before 11 a.m. or use Fastpass. **Special comments** A blast; not to be missed; frightens many small children; expectant mothers are also advised against riding; must be 40" tall to ride. **Duration of ride** Approximately 7 minutes. **Average wait in line per 100 people ahead of you** 6 minutes. **Assumes** 4 simulators operating. **Loading speed** Moderate.

Scary   Queasy   Rough

DESCRIPTION AND COMMENTS When Disney's first modern flight simulator ride debuted in 1987, guests lined up for hours (us included) for their hyperspace voyage into a galaxy far, far away. But time and technology march on, and because George Lucas is never finished tinkering with the *Star Wars* universe, Star Tours received a top-to-bottom overhaul in 2011. The original StarSpeeder 3000 cabins (retro-christened as the model 1000) have been upgraded with cutting-edge digital 3-D screens (the sharpest and clearest that we've ever seen) and new in-cabin audio-animatronic figures of C-3PO, your golden droid pilot. During your inevitably turbulent travels, you'll bump, twist, and dive into a who's-who of *Star Wars* icons, with heroes Master Yoda and Admiral "It's A Trap!" Akbar on your side, and villains Darth Vader and Boba Fett on your back. Jedi junkies will want to know that the refreshed ride takes place between episodes III and IV, so you'll be visiting planets from both the classic trilogy—such as icy Hot and arid Tatooine—and the not-so-classic prequels, including Geonosis (home of the dreaded Death Star) and Naboo (home of the equally dreaded Jar Jar Binks).

The big twist is that the six possible cosmic destinations and five celebrity cameos are randomly combined into 54 different story variations, giving the attraction unprecedented re-ridability (though you may see all 11 potential ride elements in as few as three voyages). Fans of the former ride will be thrilled to find a wealth of references (along with hidden Disney characters and *Star Wars* inside jokes) inside the detailed queue, and those made uncomfortable by the old experience's jerkiness will be surprised at how smooth and well-synchronized the reprogrammed ride now is.

TOURING TIPS Disney has a galactic-size smash on its hands with the refreshed Star Tours, and lines should remain long well into early 2012. With only two-thirds the carrying capacity of Walt Disney World's version, Disneyland's Star Tours frequently sees multihour waits, so grab a Fastpass as early in the morning as possible. If you have young children (or anyone) who are apprehensive about this attraction, ask the attendant about switching off (see page 150).

LIVE ENTERTAINMENT
and SPECIAL EVENTS

LIVE ENTERTAINMENT IN THE FORM OF BANDS, Disney character appearances, parades, singing and dancing, and ceremonies further enliven and add color to Disneyland Park on a daily basis. For specific information about what's happening on the day you visit, check the daily entertainment schedule in the *Times Guide*. Be forewarned, however, that if you are on a tight schedule, it is impossible to both see the park's featured attractions and take in the numerous and varied live performances offered. In our 1-day touring plans, starting on page 276, we exclude the live performances in favor of seeing as much of the park as time permits. This is a tactical decision based on the fact that the parades and *Fantasmic!*, Disneyland Park's river spectacular, siphon crowds away from the more popular rides, shortening waiting lines.

The color and pageantry of live events around the park are an integral part of the Disneyland Park entertainment mix and a persuasive argument for second-day touring. Though live entertainment is varied, plentiful, and nearly continuous throughout the day, several productions are preeminent.

Fantasmic!

Loud   Scary

DESCRIPTION AND COMMENTS *Fantasmic!* is a mixed-media show presented one or more times each evening that the park is open late (10 p.m. or later). Staged at the end of Tom Sawyer Island opposite the Frontierland and New Orleans Square waterfronts, *Fantasmic!* is far and away the most extraordinary and ambitious outdoor spectacle ever attempted in any theme park. Starring Mickey Mouse in his role as the sorcerer's apprentice from *Fantasia*, the production uses lasers, images projected on a shroud of mist, fireworks, lighting effects, and music in combinations so stunning that you can scarcely believe what you have seen.

The plot is simple: good versus evil. The story gets lost in all the special effects at times, but no matter—it is the spectacle, not the story line, that is so overpowering. While *beautiful, stunning,* and *powerful* are words that immediately come to mind, they fail to convey the uniqueness of this presentation. In recent years, the production has been upgraded with brighter high-definition projectors and a 45-foot-tall full-bodied fire-breathing dragon (nicknamed Murphy) for the finale. It could be argued, with some validity, that *Fantasmic!* alone is worth the price of Disneyland Park admission. Needless to say, we rate *Fantasmic!* as not to be missed.

TOURING TIPS It is not easy to see *Fantasmic!* For the first show particularly, guests begin staking out prime viewing spots along the edge of the New Orleans Square and Frontierland waterfronts as much as 4 hours in advance. Similarly, good vantage points on raised walkways and terraces are also grabbed up early on. A mom from Lummi Island, Washington, dismantled her Disney stroller to make a nest:

> We used the snap-off cover on the rental stroller to sit on during Fantasmic! since the ground was really cold.

Along similar lines, a middle-aged New York man wrote, saying:

> Your excellent guidebook also served as a seat cushion while seated on the ground waiting for the show to begin. Make future editions thicker for greater comfort.

The best seats in the house are at the water's edge. For adults, it is really not necessary to have an unobstructed view of the staging area because most of the action is high above the crowd. Children standing in the closely packed crowd, however, are able to catch only bits and pieces of the presentation.

Probably the most painless strategy for seeing *Fantasmic!* is to attend the second show. Usually, the second performance follows the first performance by about 90 minutes. At the second *Fantasmic!* fewer people are in the park and viewing conditions are less crowded. If you let the crowd for the first show clear out and then take up your position, you should be able to find a good vantage point, as a Salt Lake City reader found:

> During the first showing, I perused the shops in New Orleans Square and then found a place to sit for awhile. When the show was almost over, I worked my way to Pirates and stationed myself in front of the entrance. When the show was over and the crowd started to disperse, I worked my way down to the riverfront and into prime seating where I was able to watch the fireworks and the second showing of Fantasmic!

Rain and wind conditions sometimes cause *Fantasmic!* to be canceled. Unfortunately, Disney officials usually do not make a final decision about

The Smith family from East Wimple stakes out their viewing spot for Fantasmic!

whether to proceed or cancel until just before showtime. We have seen guests wrapped in ponchos sit stoically in rain or drizzle for more than an hour with no assurance that their patience and sacrifice would be rewarded. Unless you can find a covered viewing spot, we do not recommend staking out vantage points on rainy or especially windy nights. On nights like these, pursue your own agenda until 10 minutes or so before showtime, and then head to the waterfront to see what happens.

You can view *Fantasmic!* from a special reserved viewing area located near the Tom Sawyer Island raft dock. To make reservations, call ☎ 714-781-4400. The price for the dock-viewing area runs $59 for adults and $49 for children ages 3–9. A dessert box is included, but be aware of this Petaluma,California, family's experience:

> *We did the reserved seating for* Fantasmic!, *and that was pretty much a waste of money. After picking up our tickets earlier in the day, we stood in line at the designated spot at 7:50 p.m. for the 8 p.m. opening of first-come, first-serve seating. Somehow every seat was taken by the time we got to the front of the line at 8:15 p.m., except for four seats in the very back. When the show began at 9 p.m., we had a terrible view of the show between the light pole and people's heads in front of us. Note that they serve hot coffee/chocolate and give a dessert box, but bring your own treats for the kids—the dessert box is full of fancy desserts that no child recognizes or wants to eat.*

Finally, make sure to hang on to children during *Fantasmic!* and to give them explicit instructions for regrouping in the event you are separated. Be especially vigilant when the crowd disperses after the show.

PARADES

DISNEY THEME PARKS ARE FAMOUS THE WORLD OVER for their parades. On days when the park closes early, there is an afternoon parade. On days when the park closes late (10 p.m.–midnight), there are always evening parades, and often an afternoon parade as well.

The parades are full-blown Disney productions with some combination of floats, huge inflated balloons of the characters, marching bands, old-time vehicles, dancers, and, of course, literally dozens of costumed Disney characters. Themes for the parades vary from time to time, and a special holiday parade is always produced for Christmas. Mickey's Soundsational Parade, Disneyland's latest daytime processional, premiered in 2011. It features a whimsical marching band theme with brand-new floats dedicated to *The Princess and the Frog*, *The Little Mermaid*, and a Keith Moon–channeling Drummer Mickey. The new parade is a big improvement over Disneyland's previous street party, and well worth watching from the stick-twirling drum-line kickoff to the Mary Poppins finale.

Parades always draw thousands of guests from the attraction lines. We recommend, therefore, watching from the departure point. With this strategy you can enjoy the parade, and then while the parade is continuing on its route, take advantage of the diminished lines at the

Disneyland Parade Route

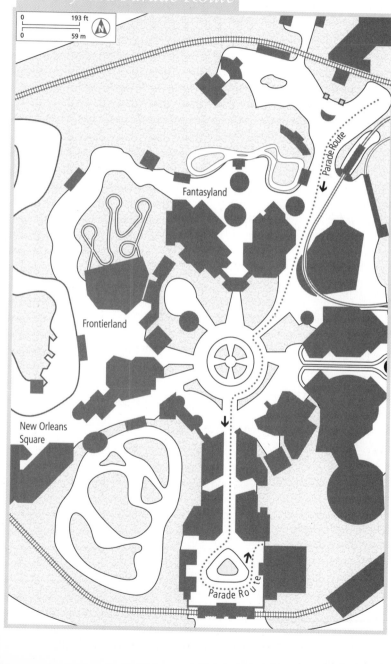

0   193 ft

0   59 m

Parade Route

Fantasyland

Frontierland

New Orleans
Square

Parade Route

attractions. Watching a parade that begins in Fantasyland from Small World Mall affords the greatest mobility in terms of accessing other areas of the park when the parade has passed.

Main Street is the most crowded area from which to watch a parade when it begins at Town Square. The opposite is true when the parade begins in Fantasyland. The upper platform of the Main Street train station affords the best viewing perspective along the route. The best time to get a position on the platform is when the parade begins in Fantasyland. When this happens, good spots on the platform are available right up to the time the parade begins. When you are at the end of the parade route, you can assume that it will take the parade 15–18 minutes to get to you. Some recent Disney parades have included show stops, meaning that the floats freeze in place for a few minutes while the cast dances in the streets. When this happens, show stop viewing spots will be marked on the park map. There are usually three locations (two on Main Street and one in Fantasyland), with the Small World Mall providing the best perspective.

Keep an eye on your children during parades and give them explicit instructions for regrouping in the event you get separated. Children constantly jockey for better viewing positions. A few wiggles this way and a few wiggles the other, and presto, they are lost in the crowd. Finally, be especially vigilant when the crowd starts dispersing after the parade. Thousands of people suddenly strike out in different directions, creating a perfect situation for losing a child or two.

LIVE ENTERTAINMENT THROUGHOUT THE PARK

PARADES AND *FANTASMIC!* MAKE UP only a part of the daily live-entertainment offerings at Disneyland Park. The following is an incomplete list of other performances and events that are scheduled with some regularity and that require no reservations.

DISNEY CHARACTER APPEARANCES Disney characters appear at random throughout the park but are routinely present in Mickey's Toontown, Fantasyland, and on Main Street. Rapunzel, still riding high on the popularity of 2010's *Tangled,* draws long line at her meet and greet tower in Fantasyland. An irregularly used greeting area that sometimes features Aladdin and Jasmine is located at Aladdin's Oasis in Adventureland (see the *Times Guide*). Disney princesses are on call daily at the Fantasyland Theatre (see page 239). Subsequent to the release of the *Tinker Bell* animated feature, pixies and fairies are all the rage (and have been in LA for years, but that's another story). A new character-greeting area, Pixie Hollow, situated on the path connecting the Matterhorn Bobsleds to the central hub, features Tink and a squad of her buddies.

DISNEY CHARACTER BREAKFASTS AND DINNERS Disney characters join guests for breakfast each morning until 11 a.m. at the **Plaza Inn** on Main Street and **Storytellers Café** at the Grand Californian Hotel. Disney

characters also join guests for breakfast and dinner at
at the Disneyland Hotel and **Disney's PCH Grill** at Para
Ariel's Grotto at Disney California Adventure serves
lunch with Ariel and friends.

DISNEY ROCK GROUPS High-energy Disney rock group
sonally in Tomorrowland according to the *Times Guide*

FANTASYLAND THEATRE The park's premier
venue for full-fledged musical productions starring the Disney characters. Also the home of the
Disney Princess Fantasy Faire (see page 239). See
the *Times Guide* for showtimes.

unofficial **TIP**
If you plan to leave the
park after the fireworks,
the second-floor platform
of the Main Street train
station affords one of the
best views you'll find.

**FIREWORKS REMEMBER . . . DREAMS COME
TRUE** Since it debuted in 2005, *Remember* has
been the go-to fireworks show in between sea-
sonal varieties and is a particular favorite among locals. The show runs
the full gamut of special effects: a rousing score, spectacular firework
effects, castle lighting, lasers, and an impressive flight from the fairy
Tinker Bell. Julie Andrews narrates this pyrotechnic tribute to classic
Disneyland attractions—featuring a pirate cannon assault on Sleeping
Beauty Castle and audio from Adventure Thru Inner Space—with
music from Walt Disney World's popular *Wishes* fireworks. We rate this
show as five stars and not to be missed.

During the summer season, *Remember* is replaced by *Magical*.
Tinker Bell is your host and kicks it off with a zany flight path that
makes you wonder what she's on besides pixie dust. *Magical* features
an array of Disney's most magical characters, including Peter Pan,
Mary Poppins, and the three good fairies from *Sleeping Beauty*.
Dumbo (in the form of a giant puppet) joins Tink in flight and steals
the show. Broadway singer Eden Espinosa belts out the theme song,
and the program also features sentimental classic Disney tunes such as
"Baby Mine" from *Dumbo* and "So This Is Love" from *Cinderella*.

Without a doubt, the central hub is the best vantage point for
watching fireworks. Unfortunately, every guest in the park won't fit in
the hub at the same time. The next-best positions are at any open
(that is, not canopied by trees) spots facing Sleeping Beauty Castle.
We've stood between the castle and the Matterhorn, for example, and
found the view just gorgeous. If those spots are taken, try any open
spot without something really big, such as a Disney mountain, in the
way. Concerning the latter, you'll be able to see the fireworks fine but
will miss Tinker Bell. Other interesting (and less crowded) viewing
angles can be found in Fantasyland and Tomorrowland.

GOLDEN HORSESHOE–LAUGHING STOCK CO. The Laughing Stock Company is a Frontierland comedy show that performs inside the Golden
Horseshoe Saloon on Billy Hill's days off (Tuesday and Wednesday)
and on weekends outside the building (sometimes on the second
floor!). Each show is different and includes a set of zany Wild

st–style characters. A particular favorite of ours is the "find a suitor," where three unsuspecting members of the crowd are selected to answer questions from the Mayor of Frontierland's less-than-handsome daughter (played by a man).

The showtimes are in the *Times Guide* as well as our Lines app, and we recommend showing up just 1 or 2 minutes before the show. They don't perform daily, but when they do perform, they can have up to eight shows throughout the late morning until late afternoon.

JEDI TRAINING ACADEMY An interactive show for young Padawans-in-training is staged several times daily at the Tomorrowland Terrace Theater (see page 259). See the *Times Guide* for showtimes.

THE MAGIC, THE MEMORIES, AND YOU! Tied to Disney Parks' 2011 marketing campaign, this nightly show uses cutting-edge projection mapping technology, along with a smattering of pyrotechnics, to display striking animated images onto the outside of It's A Small World. During the 10-minute show, the ride's white facade is transformed into a child's coloring book, a pirate's battlement, a blizzard of balloons and birthday candles, and a cartoon construction zone. There's some gimmickry involving that day's guests' PhotoPass pictures being mixed into the imagery, but the odds of you actually seeing yourself up there are practically nil, so just relax and enjoy the eye candy. Small World doesn't make as dramatic a canvas as Cinderella Castle (where the show is projected in the Magic Kingdom), but Disneyland's setting is more intimate and accessible. Rumor is that the show hasn't surveyed well with guests, so it may be gone by the time you visit.

PLAZA GARDENS This tented venue, located just beyond the central hub and to the left of the castle, hosts visiting high school and university bands, as well as swing dance bands.

RETREAT CEREMONY Daily at around dusk in Town Square, an honor guard lowers the flag.

STREET ENTERTAINMENT Various bands, singers, comics, and strolling musicians entertain in spontaneous (that is, unscheduled) street performances throughout the park. Musical styles include banjo, Dixieland, steel drum, marching, and fife and drum. You don't want to miss the Dapper Dans, a slapstick barbershop quartet that has been performing on Main Street, U.S.A. in Disneyland since 1959. While the cast changes on a regular basis, the Dans really liven up the street.

UNHERALDED TREASURES *at* DISNEYLAND PARK

UNHERALDED TREASURES ARE SPECIAL FEATURES found in all of the Disney theme parks that add texture, context, beauty, depth, and subtlety to your visit. Generally speaking, Unheralded Treasures are nice surprises that should be accorded a little time. They are the proverbial Disney roses you should stop to smell. Lani Teshima, *Unofficial Guide* friend and writer for **mouseplanet.com,** knows them all. Her list follows.

TREASURE Snow White's Grotto and Wishing Well
LOCATION The front right of Sleeping Beauty Castle
A SLOW STROLL AROUND THE SLEEPING BEAUTY CASTLE can be romantic, but sitting quietly to its right is Snow White's Grotto and Wishing Well. If you stop for a few moments, you can hear the voice of Snow White singing "I'm Wishing" in the area. The grotto includes a trickling waterfall framing statues of Snow White and the Seven Dwarfs, placed on three tiers in such a way as to make Snow White appear to be off in the distance in an optical illusion that masks the fact that her statue is the same height as those of the dwarfs. Next to the grotto is a wishing well, where you can toss a coin and make a wish. This area is a popular place for Disney to trot out its princesses for photos, so don't be surprised to see a group of people milling around.

TREASURE Disneyland Railroad | **LOCATION** Stations in Main Street, U.S.A.; New Orleans Square; Toontown/Fantasyland; and Tomorrowland
AFTER A LONG DAY, the Disneyland Railroad offers a nice way to get from one end of the park to another. But trains held a special place in Walt Disney's heart, and the railroad offers much more than just a ride back to the park gates. Pause and turn around before you enter Main Street Station for a beautiful view of the entire length of Main Street, U.S.A. Inside the station, you can enjoy looking at model trains and other little exhibits. If you get off at the New Orleans Square Station, stop and listen—that beeping sound you hear is Walt Disney's 1955 Disneyland park opening speech in land-line telegraphic code. And don't forget to ride from Tomorrowland back to Main Street so you can enjoy an unexpected treat: two large indoor dioramas inside the train tunnel, one depicting the Grand Canyon and another depicting a primeval world, complete with large-scale dinosaurs!

TREASURE Windows on Main Street | **LOCATION** Main Street, U.S.A.
EVER WONDER IF THE NAMES ON ALL THOSE WINDOWS on Main Street mean anything? Like guardian angels looking over everyone who walks through the park, these are the names of very special people who have had a profound influence on the park in some way. The names are also often associated with "professions" related to what they used to do when they worked for Disney. For example, the inscription for a window dedicated to the person who modeled Disneyland's waterways reads, "Decorative Fountains and Watercolor by Fred Joerger." Disneyland still occasionally bestows this window honor in official dedication ceremonies in the park.

TREASURE Frontierland Shootin' Exposition | **LOCATION** Frontierland
SMACK IN THE MIDDLE OF FRONTIERLAND is the shooting gallery where cowpokes can close an eye and squeeze the trigger to try to get their target to ping, ting, move, or light up. Don't discount the Frontierland Shootin' Exposition as just another arcade gimmick. Everything about this well-themed attraction is dusty and rustic—except the laser-powered guns, which are both safe and cause little

wear on the targets—and about the only things missing are blowing tumbleweeds and Clint Eastwood.

TREASURE Edible Plants | **LOCATION** Tomorrowland
DON'T BE SO SURE THAT ALL YOU CAN FIND in Disneyland is junk food. The Disney theme parks are known for their magnificent landscaping, but did you know that many of the plants in Tomorrowland are edible, emphasizing the practicality of a future where the garden plants do double duty as your vegetable garden? For example, the entryway to Tomorrowland is lined with orange trees, and the bushes along the walkways are planted with leafy vegetables such as lettuce, kale, and rhubarb, as well as herbs such as sage, chives, and basil.

TREASURE Carnation Plaza | **LOCATION** Central Hub
IF YOU STILL HAVE ENERGY LEFT AT THE END of a long Saturday at Disneyland, did you know you don't even have to leave the park to put on your dancin' shoes? Near Frontierland at the castle-end of Main Street is Carnation Plaza, where every Saturday (and also on Fridays in the summer), swingers can dance the night away. Even if you're too tired to dance, you might catch some guys in crazy zoot-suit getups or seasoned veterans twirling in their poodle skirts.

TREASURE Flag Retreat Ceremony | **LOCATION** Main Street Square
EVERY DAY IN THE AFTERNOON, THE DISNEYLAND BAND or Dapper Dans vocal group marches to the front of Main Street to perform a number of Americana tunes. Park security guards then lower the American flag as the band plays "The Star-Spangled Banner" in this very respectful ceremony. Though this 20-minute event (including the band's march down Main Street) has been happening for years, it has enjoyed a larger audience in recent years because of its patriotic feel.

TREASURE *Partners* Statue | **LOCATION** Central Hub
AT THE CASTLE-END OF MAIN STREET, in the center of the circular hub, is a bronze statue of Walt Disney holding the hand of Mickey Mouse. With his right hand, Walt points outward to the park as if to say, "Look at this wonderful place." The statue, simply called *Partners*, pays homage to the two original ambassadors of Disneyland. If you stand in front of the statue, you can get a nice shot of it with Sleeping Beauty Castle in the background. The spot is encircled by a stone bench, and it's a great place to meet should your family decide to split off to visit different lands. There's more bronze in the area too; smaller statues of other popular Disney figures such as Dumbo, Goofy, and Pluto form a ring around this little garden oasis in the middle of the park.

QUIET PLACES AT DISNEYLAND PARK

PEACE AND QUIET ARE ANYTHING BUT THE NORM at Disneyland. Yet sometimes when you're overwhelmed by it all, a place to decompress is worth a lot, as a reader from Culver City, California, points out:

> *I confess that I can't tolerate the hyperstimulation as well as my husband and kids. Sometimes when I'm on my ninth nerve, I'd give anything to*

put myself in time-out and just collapse for a while. Are there any nice
out-of-the-way places in the park where this is possible?

Actually, there are a few. There's a **pier** with a canopy and benches opposite the Matterhorn Bobsleds loading area. Created for a long-departed boat ride, the pier overlooks a quiet pool. There's still ambient noise, of course, but the pier is far enough removed from the action to afford both tranquillity and a lovely setting. The **Hungry Bear Restaurant** in Critter Country offers upper and lower covered outdoor decks overlooking the Rivers of America. In between major feeding periods, the decks are decidedly low-key. **Snow White's Grotto and Wishing Well,** described on page 269, is also very pleasant, though there is a modest but continuous flow of pedestrian traffic there. Finally, the alfresco dining area of **Troubadour Tavern,** adjacent to Fantasyland Theatre, is very relaxing between shows.

TRAFFIC PATTERNS *at* DISNEYLAND PARK

WHEN WE BEGAN OUR RESEARCH on Disneyland, we were very interested in traffic patterns throughout the park, specifically these issues:

I. WHAT ATTRACTIONS AND WHICH SECTIONS OF THE PARK DO VISITORS HEAD FOR WHEN THEY FIRST ARRIVE? When guests are admitted to the various lands, the flow of people to Tomorrowland (Space Mountain, Buzz Lightyear, and Finding Nemo Submarine Voyage) is heaviest. The next most crowded land is Fantasyland, though the crowds are distributed over a large number of attractions. Critter Country is likewise crowded with its small area and only two attractions (Splash Mountain and The Many Adventures of Winnie the Pooh). Adventureland, Frontierland, and New Orleans Square fill more slowly, with Mickey's Toontown not really coming alive until later in the morning. As the park fills, visitors appear to head for specific favored attractions that they wish to ride before the lines get

---

ATTRACTIONS HEAVILY ATTENDED IN EARLY MORNING

ADVENTURELAND
- Indiana Jones Adventure
- Jungle Cruise

CRITTER COUNTRY
- Splash Mountain

FANTASYLAND
- Alice in Wonderland
- Dumbo the Flying Elephant

FANTASYLAND (CONT'D)
- Matterhorn Bobsleds
- Peter Pan's Flight

TOMORROWLAND
- Buzz Lightyear Astro Blasters
- Finding Nemo Submarine Voyage
- Space Mountain
- Star Tours: The Adventures Continue

long. This, more than any other factor, determines traffic patterns in the mornings and accounts for the relatively equal distribution of visitors throughout Disneyland.

2. HOW LONG DOES IT TAKE FOR THE PARK TO REACH PEAK CAPACITY FOR A GIVEN DAY? HOW ARE THE VISITORS DISPERSED THROUGHOUT THE PARK? There is a surge of early birds who arrive before or around opening time but are quickly dispersed throughout the empty park. After the initial onslaught is absorbed, there is a bit of a lull that lasts until about an hour after opening. Following the lull, the park is inundated with arriving guests for about 2 hours, peaking 10–11 a.m. Guests continue to arrive in a steady but diminishing stream until around 2 p.m.

Sampled lines reached their longest length noon–3 p.m., indicating more arrivals than departures in the early afternoon. For general touring purposes, most attractions develop substantial lines 9:30–11 a.m. In the early morning, Tomorrowland, Critter Country, and Fantasyland fill up first. By late morning and into early afternoon, attendance is fairly equally distributed throughout all of the "lands." Mickey's Toontown, because it is comparatively small, stays mobbed from about 11:30 a.m. on. By midafternoon, however, we noted a concentration of visitors in Fantasyland, New Orleans Square, and Adventureland, and a slight decrease of visitors in Tomorrowland.

In the late afternoon and early evening, attendance continues to be more heavily distributed in Tomorrowland, Critter Country, and Fantasyland. Though Space Mountain, Buzz Lightyear, Splash Mountain, and especially Finding Nemo Submarine Voyage remain inundated throughout the day, most of the other attractions in Tomorrowland and Critter Country have reasonable lines. In New Orleans Square, The Haunted Mansion, Pirates of the Caribbean, and the multitudes returning from nearby Critter Country keep traffic brisk. Frontierland and Adventureland (except the Indiana Jones ride) become less congested as the afternoon and evening progress.

3. HOW DO MOST VISITORS GO ABOUT TOURING THE PARK? IS THERE A DIFFERENCE IN THE TOURING BEHAVIOR OF FIRST-TIME VISITORS AND REPEAT VISITORS? Many first-time visitors accompany friends or relatives who are familiar with Disneyland and who guide their tour. These tours sometimes do and sometimes do not proceed in an orderly (clockwise or counterclockwise) touring sequence. First-time visitors without personal touring guidance tend to be more orderly in their touring. Many first-time visitors, however, are drawn to Sleeping Beauty Castle on entering the park and thus commence their rotation from Fantasyland. Repeat visitors usually proceed directly to their favorite attractions or to whatever is new.

4. WHAT EFFECT DO SPECIAL EVENTS SUCH AS PARADES, FIREWORKS, AND FANTASMIC! HAVE ON TRAFFIC PATTERNS? Special events such as parades, fireworks, and *Fantasmic!* pull substantial numbers of visitors from the lines for rides. Unfortunately, however, the left hand taketh what the right hand giveth. A parade or *Fantasmic!* snarls traffic flow throughout Disneyland so much that guests find themselves captive wherever they are. Attraction lines in Tomorrowland, Mickey's Toontown, Adventureland, and Fantasyland (behind the castle) diminish dramatically, making Space Mountain, Finding Nemo Submarine Voyage, Buzz Lightyear, Star Tours, the Jungle Cruise, Indiana Jones Adventure, Peter Pan's Flight, and Snow White's Scary Adventures particularly good choices during the evening festivities. The remainder of the park (Critter Country, New Orleans Square, Frontierland, Main Street, and Small World Plaza in Fantasyland) is so congested with guests viewing the parade or *Fantasmic!* that it's almost impossible to move.

5. WHAT ARE THE TRAFFIC PATTERNS NEAR TO AND AT CLOSING TIME? On our sample days, which were recorded in and out of season, park departures outnumbered arrivals beginning in midafternoon, with a substantial number of guests leaving after the afternoon parade. Additional numbers of visitors departed during the late afternoon as the dinner hour approached. When the park closed early, there were steady departures during the 2 hours preceding closing, with a mass exodus of remaining visitors at closing time.

When the park closed late, departures were distributed throughout the evening hours, with waves of departures following the evening parade(s), fireworks, and *Fantasmic!* Though departures increased exponentially as closing time approached, a huge throng was still on hand when the park finally shut down. The balloon effect of this last throng at the end of the day generally overwhelmed the shops on Main Street, the parking lot, trams, and the hotel shuttles, and the exits onto adjoining Anaheim streets. In the hour before closing in the lands other than Main Street, touring conditions were normally uncrowded except at Indiana Jones in Adventureland and Splash Mountain in Critter Country.

DISNEYLAND PARK TOURING PLANS

THE DISNEYLAND PARK TOURING PLANS are step-by-step plans for seeing as much as possible with a minimum of time wasted standing in line. They are designed to assist you in avoiding crowds and bottlenecks on days of moderate to heavy attendance. On days of lighter attendance (see "Selecting the Time of Year for Your Visit," page 22), the plans will still save you time but will not be as critical to successful touring.

Choosing the Right Touring Plan

Six different touring plans are presented:

- 1-day Touring Plan for Adults

- Author's Select 1-day Touring Plan
- Dumbo-or-Die-in-a-Day Touring Plan for Adults with Small Children
- 2-day Touring Plan for Adults with Small Children
- 2-day Touring Plan A, for Daytime Touring or for When the Park Closes Early (before 8 p.m.)
- 2-day Touring Plan B, for Morning and Evening Touring or for When the Park Is Open Late (after 8 p.m.)

If you have 2 days to spend at Disneyland Park, the 2-day touring plans are by far the most relaxed and efficient. The 2-day Touring Plan A takes advantage of early-morning touring, when lines are short and the park has not yet filled with guests. This plan works well all year and is particularly recommended for days when Disneyland Park closes before 8 p.m. On the other hand, 2-day Touring Plan B combines the efficiencies of early-morning touring on the first day with the splendor of Disneyland Park at night on the second day. This plan is perfect for guests who wish to sample both the attractions and the special magic of Disneyland Park after dark, including *Fantasmic!*, parades, and fireworks. The 2-day Touring Plan for Adults with Small Children spreads the experience over 2 more-relaxed days and incorporates more attractions that both children and parents will enjoy.

For readers who have requested a 3-Day Park Hopper Touring Plan, we recommend using the 2-Day Disneyland Park Touring Plan of your choice and mixing it with the 1-Day Disney California Adventure Touring Plan as you see fit. Enter Disneyland Park first, and then when DCA opens, send a runner across the Esplanade with your entire group's tickets. Because the Fastpass systems of the two parks are disconnected, you can collect Fastpasses for *World of Color* and Soarin' Over California (or Radiator Springs Racers) simultaneously with any you've already claimed in Disneyland Park (such as Space or Splash mountains).

If you have only 1 day but wish to see as much as possible, use the 1-day Touring Plan for Adults. This plan will pack as much into a single day as is humanly possible, but it is pretty exhausting. If you prefer a more relaxed visit, try the Author's Select 1-day Touring Plan. This plan features the best Disneyland Park has to offer (in the author's opinion), eliminating some of the less impressive attractions.

If you have small children, you may want to use the Dumbo-or-Die-in-a-Day Touring Plan for Adults with Small Children. This plan includes most of the children's rides in Fantasyland and Toontown and omits roller-coaster rides and other attractions that small children cannot ride (because of Disney's age and height requirements), as well as rides and shows that are frightening for small children. Because this plan calls for adults to sacrifice many of the better Disney attractions, it is not recommended unless you are touring Disneyland Park primarily for the benefit of your children. In essence, you pretty much stand around, sweat, wipe noses, pay for stuff, and watch the children have fun. It's great.

An alternative to the Dumbo Plan would be to use the 1-day Touring Plan for Adults or the Author's Select 1-day Touring Plan, and take advantage of switching off, a technique whereby children accompany adults to the loading area of rides with age and height requirements but do not actually ride (see page 150). Switching off allows adults to enjoy the wilder rides while keeping the whole group together.

Park-opening Procedures

Your progress and success during your first hour of touring will be affected by the particular opening procedure the Disney people use that day.

A. All guests are held at the turnstiles until the park opens (which may or may not be at the official opening time). On admittance, all "lands" are open. If this is the case on the day you visit, blow right past Main Street and head for the first attraction on whatever touring plan you are following.

B. Guests are admitted to Main Street 30 minutes–1 hour before the remaining "lands" open. Access to the other lands is blocked by a rope barrier at the central-hub end of Main Street on these days. On admittance, move to the rope barrier and stake out a position as follows:

(1) If you are going to Indiana Jones or Splash Mountain first, take up a position in front of Plaza Pavilion at the central-hub end of Main Street on the left. Wait next to the rope barrier blocking the walkway to Adventureland. When the rest of the park opens, proceed quickly to Adventureland for Indiana Jones, or Critter Country by way of Adventureland and New Orleans Square for Splash Mountain.

(2) If you are going to Finding Nemo Submarine Voyage or Space Mountain first, wait on the right at the central-hub end of Main Street. When the rope drops at opening time, bear right and zip into Tomorrowland.

(3) If you are going to Fantasyland or Frontierland first, proceed to the end of Main Street and line up at the rope right of center.

Clip-out Touring Plans

For your convenience, we have prepared outline versions of all the touring plans presented in this guide. These pocket outlines present the same touring itineraries as the detailed touring plans but with vastly abbreviated directions. First, select the touring plan that is most appropriate for your party, and then familiarize yourself with the detailed version of the plan. Once you understand how the touring plan works, clip out the pocket-outline version of your selected plan from the back of this guide and carry it with you as a quick reference when you visit the theme park.

PRELIMINARY INSTRUCTIONS FOR ALL DISNEYLAND PARK TOURING PLANS

ON DAYS OF MODERATE to heavy attendance, follow the touring plans exactly, deviating only when you do not wish to experience a listed show or ride. For instance, the touring plan may direct you to go next to Big Thunder Mountain, a roller-coaster ride. If you do not like roller coasters, simply skip that step and proceed to the next activity.

1. Buy your admission in advance (see "Admission Options" on page 19).
2. Call ☎ 714-781-7290 the day before you go for the official opening time.
3. Become familiar with the park-opening procedures (described on the previous page) and read over the touring plan of your choice so that you will have a basic understanding of what you are likely to encounter as you enter the park.

DISNEYLAND PARK 1-DAY TOURING PLAN FOR ADULTS

FOR Adults without small children.

ASSUMES Willingness to experience all major rides (including roller coasters) and shows.

Be forewarned that this plan requires a lot of walking and some back-tracking; this is necessary to avoid long waits in line. A little extra walking coupled with some hustle in the morning will save you 2–3 hours of standing in line. Also be aware that you might not complete the tour. How far you get will depend on the size of your group, how quickly you move from ride to ride, how many times you pause for rest or food, how quickly the park fills, and what time the park closes.

ABOUT EARLY ENTRY If you are eligible for early entry, arrive at the turnstiles 45–60 minutes before the early-entry period begins on Tuesday, Thursday, Saturday, or Sunday (days subject to change) with admission in hand. Upon admission to the park, experience (1) Space Mountain, (2) Buzz Lightyear, (3) Matterhorn Bobsleds, and (4) Peter Pan's Flight, in that order. If you're not able to enjoy all of the above during the early-entry hour, see as many as you can. When the park opens to the general public, join the touring plan at Step 7 and proceed from there.

If you are not eligible for early entry, use the following plan on a non-early-entry day (currently Monday, Wednesday, or Friday). Do not attempt to use the plan on an early-entry day—Disneyland Park will be packed with early-entry guests before you even make it past the turnstiles. If you wish to tour on an early-entry day but are not eligible for early entry, visit DCA (which does not participate in the early program) and save Disneyland Park for a non-early-entry day.

Note: The success of the touring plan hinges on you entering the park when it first opens.

1. Arrive at the park, admission in hand, at least 40 minutes before opening.

Line up at Gate 13. Once you get through the turnstiles, entrust all your admission passes to one very speedy person.

2. Go to Space Mountain and obtain Fastpasses.

3. Ride the Matterhorn Bobsleds if they're on your priority list.

4. Proceed to Fantasyland via the entrance next to the Mad Tea Party. Experience Peter Pan's Flight.

5. Return to Tomorrowland via the central hub and ride Buzz Lightyear.

6. Ride Space Mountain using your Fastpasses.

7. While in Tomorrowland, obtain Fastpasses for Star Tours.

8. Turn left toward the central hub. Enter Frontierland and ride Big Thunder Mountain Railroad.

9. Keeping the waterfront on your right, head for Critter Country. Experience The Many Adventures of Winnie the Pooh.

10. While in Critter Country, obtain Fastpasses for Splash Mountain.

11. From Critter Country, head to Adventureland. Ride Indiana Jones Adventure.

12. Exit Indiana Jones to the right and take the Jungle Cruise. If you don't care about the Jungle Cruise, skip to Step 13.

13. Continue to New Orleans Square and experience Pirates of the Caribbean.

14. Also in New Orleans Square, tour The Haunted Mansion.

15. The best way to ride Finding Nemo Submarine Voyage without a wait in excess of an hour (see pages 256–258) is to ride during a parade, fireworks show, or *Fantasmic!* Using the *Times Guide,* determine when one or another of these events is scheduled and join the line for Nemo 15 minutes before the event begins. This is the time when the wait should be shortest, usually 35–50 minutes as opposed to 60–110 minutes.

16. In nearby Frontierland, ride either the Sailing Ship *Columbia* or the *Mark Twain* Riverboat.

17. Ride Splash Mountain using your Fastpasses.

18. Return to Adventureland and see the show at the *Enchanted Tiki Room.*

19. Nearby, explore Tarzan's Treehouse.

20. Cross the central hub and return to Tomorrowland. Ride Star Tours using the Fastpasses obtained earlier.

21. Also in Tomorrowland, see *Captain EO.*

22. Take the Disneyland Railroad from the Tomorrowland Station to the Fantasyland/Mickey's Toontown Station.

23. Exit the station to the left and pass under the railroad bridge to Mickey's Toontown. Though imaginative and colorful, Toontown is primarily for small children and expendable for most adults.

24. Pass back under the railroad bridge, bear left, and ride It's a Small World.

25. While in Fantasyland, sample any rides you missed earlier.

26. Check the *Times Guide* for parades, fireworks, and *Fantasmic!* Work these shows into the remainder of your day as time and energy allow.

27. Backtrack to pick up any attractions that you may have missed earlier.

28. Continue to tour, saving Main Street for last. If you have any oomph left, see *The Disneyland Story,* presenting *Great Moments with Mr. Lincoln* on your way out of the park.

AUTHOR'S SELECT DISNEYLAND PARK 1-DAY TOURING PLAN

FOR Adults touring without small children.

ASSUMES Willingness to experience all major rides (including roller coasters) and shows.

This touring plan is selective, including only attractions that, in the author's opinion, represent the best Disneyland Park has to offer.

Be forewarned that this plan requires a lot of walking and some backtracking; this is necessary to avoid long waits in line. A little extra walking coupled with some hustle in the morning will save you 2–3 hours of standing in line. Note that you might not complete this tour. How far you get will depend on the size of your group, how quickly you move from ride to ride, how many times you pause for rest or food, how quickly the park fills, and what time the park closes. With a little zip and some luck, it is possible to complete the touring plan even on a busy day when the park closes early.

ABOUT EARLY ENTRY If you are eligible for early entry, arrive at the turnstiles 45–60 minutes before the early-entry period begins on Tuesday, Thursday, Saturday, or Sunday (days subject to change) with admission in hand. Upon admission to the park, experience (1) Space Mountain, (2) Buzz Lightyear, (3) Matterhorn Bobsleds, and (4) Peter Pan's Flight, in that order. If you're not able to enjoy all of the above during the early-entry hour, see as many as you can. When the park opens to the general public, join the touring plan at Step 7 and proceed from there.

If you are not eligible for early entry, use the following plan on a non-early-entry day (currently Monday, Wednesday, or Friday). Do not attempt to use the plan on an early-entry day—Disneyland Park will be packed with early-entry guests before you even make it past the turnstiles. If you wish to tour on an early-entry day but are not eligible for early entry, visit DCA (which does not participate in the early program) and save Disneyland Park for a non-early-entry day.

Note: The success of the touring plan hinges on your entering the park when it first opens.

1. Arrive at the park, admission in hand, at least 40 minutes before opening. Line up at Gate 13. Once you get through the turnstiles, entrust all your admission passes to one very fast person.

2. Move quickly to Space Mountain and obtain Fastpasses.

3. Ride the Matterhorn Bobsleds if they're on your priority list.

4. Proceed to Fantasyland via the entrance next to the Mad Tea Party. Experience Peter Pan's Flight.

5. Return to Tomorrowland via the central hub and ride Buzz Lightyear.

6. Ride Space Mountain using your Fastpasses.

7. While in Tomorrowland, obtain Fastpasses for Star Tours.

8. Turn left toward the central hub. Enter Frontierland and ride Big Thunder Mountain Railroad.

9. Keeping the waterfront on your right, head for Critter Country and enjoy The Many Adventures of Winnie the Pooh.

10. While in Critter Country, obtain Fastpasses for Splash Mountain.

11. From Critter Country, head to Adventureland. Ride Indiana Jones Adventure.

12. Continue to New Orleans Square and experience Pirates of the Caribbean.

13. Also in New Orleans Square, tour The Haunted Mansion.

14. Feel free at this time to grab a bite to eat if you're hungry. Now's also a good time to look over the *Times Guide* handout for live entertainment offerings. Whatever else, don't miss the show at the Golden Horseshoe in Frontierland.

15. The best way to ride Finding Nemo Submarine Voyage without a wait in excess of an hour (see pages 256–258) is to ride during a parade, fireworks show, or *Fantasmic!* Using the *Times Guide,* determine when one or another of these events is scheduled and join the line for Nemo 15 minutes before the event begins. This is the time when the wait should be shortest, usually 35–50 minutes as opposed to 60–110 minutes.

16. In nearby Frontierland, ride either the Sailing Ship *Columbia* or the *Mark Twain* Riverboat.

17. Ride Splash Mountain using your Fastpasses.

18. Cross the central hub and return to Tomorrowland. Ride Star Tours using the Fastpasses obtained earlier.

19. Also in Tomorrowland, see *Captain EO.*

20. Take the Disneyland Railroad from the Tomorrowland Station to the Fantasyland/Mickey's Toontown Station.

21. Exit the station to the left and pass under the railroad bridge to Mickey's Toontown. Though imaginative and colorful, Toontown is primarily for small children and expendable for most adults.

22. Pass back under the railroad bridge, bear left, and ride It's A Small World.

23. Check the *Times Guide* for parades, fireworks, and *Fantasmic!* Work these shows into the remainder of your day as time and energy allow.

24. Backtrack to pick up any attractions that you may have missed earlier.

25. Continue to tour, saving Main Street for last. If you have any oomph left, see *The Disneyland Story,* presenting *Great Moments with Mr. Lincoln* on your way out of the park.

DUMBO-OR-DIE-IN-A-DAY TOURING PLAN
FOR ADULTS WITH SMALL CHILDREN

FOR Parents with children under age 7 who feel compelled to devote every waking moment to the pleasure and entertainment of their small children, and rich people who are paying someone else to take their children to the theme park.

ASSUMES Periodic stops for rest, restrooms, and refreshment.

The name of this touring plan notwithstanding, this itinerary is not a joke. Regardless of whether you are loving, guilty, masochistic, truly selfless, insane, or saintly, this touring plan will provide a small child with about as perfect a day as is possible at Disneyland Park.

This touring plan represents a concession to those adults who are determined, even if it kills them, to give their small children the ultimate Disneyland Park experience. The plan addresses the preferences, needs, and desires of small children to the virtual exclusion of those of adults or older siblings. If you left the kids with a sitter yesterday, or wouldn't let little Marvin eat barbecue for breakfast, this is the perfect plan for expiating your guilt. This is also a wonderful plan if you are paying a sitter, nanny, or chauffeur to take your children to Disneyland Park.

If this description has intimidated you somewhat or if you have concluded that your day at Disneyland Park is as important as your children's, use the 1-day Touring Plan for Adults, making use of the switching-off option (see page 150) at those attractions that impose height or age restrictions.

Because the children's attractions in Disneyland Park are the most poorly engineered in terms of handling large crowds, the following touring plan is the least efficient of the six plans we present. It does represent the best way to experience most of the child-oriented attractions in 1 day if that is what you hope to do. We do not make recommendations in this plan for meals. If you can, try to hustle along as quickly as is comfortable until about noon. After noon, it won't make much difference if you stop to eat or take it a little easier.

ABOUT EARLY ENTRY Do not attempt to use the plan on an early-entry day if you're not eligible for early entry—Disneyland Park will be packed with early-entry guests before you even make it past the turnstiles. If you wish to tour on an early-entry day but are not eligible for early entry, visit DCA (which does not participate in the early program) and save Disneyland Park for a non-early-entry day.

If you are eligible for early entry, experience (1) Alice in Wonderland, (2) Dumbo, and (3) Peter Pan's Flight, in that order, followed by the other Fantasyland attractions. At the end of the early-entry hour, pick up the touring plan at Step 7.

Note: The success of this touring plan hinges on you being among the first to enter the park when it opens.

1. Arrive 40 minutes before the official opening time with your admission

in hand. Line up in front of Gate 13.

2. When you're admitted to the park, head directly to Fantasyland via the castle and ride Dumbo the Flying Elephant.

3. After Dumbo, experience Peter Pan's Flight.

4. Also in Fantasyland, ride Storybook Land Canal Boats, or alternatively ride Casey Jr. Circus Train. Both attractions cover the same real estate.

5. In Fantasyland, ride the Mad Tea Party.

6. Near the Mad Tea Party and across from Matterhorn Mountain, experience Alice in Wonderland.

7. Next, head toward It's a Small World in the far corner of Fantasyland. Bypassing the ride for the moment, cross under the Disneyland Railroad tracks into Mickey's Toontown. In Mickey's Toontown, try Roger Rabbit's Car Toon Spin if your children are plucky. Do not use Fastpass unless the wait exceeds 30 minutes.

8. In Mickey's Toontown, ride Gadget's Go Coaster.

9. While in Mickey's Toontown, let off some steam in Goofy's Playhouse.

10. Tour Mickey's House and visit Mickey in his dressing room.

11. After seeing Mickey, turn right to enjoy Chip 'n Dale Treehouse.

12. Go to the far side of Mickey's House and tour Minnie's House.

13. Round out your visit to Mickey's Toontown with an inspection of Donald's Boat tied up next to Goofy's Playhouse.

14. Depart Toontown. Take the Disneyland Railroad from the Fantasyland/Toontown Station to New Orleans Square. Walk if you have a stroller that does not collapse.

15. Bear left on exiting the train station and follow the waterfront to Critter Country. Experience The Many Adventures of Winnie the Pooh.

16. Return to New Orleans Square and see Pirates of the Caribbean. If your children were frightened by Roger Rabbit's Car Toon Spin in Mickey's Toontown, skip ahead to Step 18.

17. Go left on leaving Pirates of the Caribbean to experience The Haunted Mansion. If your children were not frightened at Pirates of the Caribbean, they will do fine at The Haunted Mansion.

18. Go down to the waterfront and take a raft to Tom Sawyer Island. Allow the kids plenty of time to explore.

19. Catch the Disneyland Railroad at the New Orleans Square Station and return to the Fantasyland/Mickey's Toontown Station.

20. In Fantasyland, ride It's a Small World.

21. Visit the Disney Princess Fantasy Faire at the Fantasyland Theatre to the left of the Fantasyland Railroad Station.

22. Return to the heart of Fantasyland and ride the King Arthur Carrousel.

23. In Fantasyland, also ride Pinocchio's Daring Journey if the wait does not exceed 15 minutes. Otherwise, skip ahead to Step 24.

24. Exit Pinocchio to your left and head to Frontierland. In Frontierland,

ride the *Mark Twain* Riverboat or the Sailing Ship *Columbia,* whichever departs first.

25. Leave Frontierland and go to Adventureland. Explore Tarzan's Treehouse if the wait is less than 15 minutes. Otherwise, skip ahead to Step 26.

26. In Adventureland, see the *Enchanted Tiki Room* show.

27. Leave Adventureland, cross the central hub, and enter Tomorrowland via the path that runs along the right side (as you face it from the central hub) of the Matterhorn. In Tomorrowland, obtain Fastpasses for Autopia.

28. Check your *Times Guide* for parades and live performances. The Jedi Training Academy at the Tomorrowland Terrace is especially worthwhile.

29. In Tomorrowland, take the Disneyland monorail for a round-trip ride. Be aware that you must disembark and then reboard at the Downtown Disney Station to make a round-trip circuit.

30. While in Tomorrowland, ride Autopia using your Fastpasses.

31. Ride Buzz Lightyear Astro Blasters.

32. This concludes the touring plan. Use any time remaining to revisit favorite attractions, see attractions that were not included in the touring plan, or visit attractions you skipped because the lines were too long. Also, consult your daily entertainment schedule for parades, Fantasyland Theatre productions, or other live entertainment that might interest you. As you drag your battered and exhausted family out of the park at the end of the day, bear in mind that it was you who decided to cram all this stuff into 1 day. We just tried to help you get organized.

DISNEYLAND PARK 2-DAY TOURING PLAN FOR ADULTS WITH SMALL CHILDREN

FOR Parents with children under age 7 who wish to spread their Disneyland Park visit over 2 days.

ASSUMES Frequent stops for rest, restrooms, and refreshments.

This touring plan represents a compromise between the observed tastes of adults and the observed tastes of younger children. Included in this touring plan are many of the midway-type rides that your children may have the opportunity to experience (although in less exotic surroundings) at local fairs and amusement parks. These rides at Disneyland Park often require long waits in line, and they consume valuable touring time that could be better spent experiencing the many rides and shows found only at a Disney theme park and which best demonstrate the Disney genius. This touring plan is heavily weighted toward the tastes of younger children. If you want to balance it a bit, try working out a compromise with your kids to forgo some of the carnival-type rides (such as Mad Tea Party, Dumbo, King Arthur Carrousel, and Gadget's Go Coaster) or such rides as Autopia.

Another alternative is to use one of the other 2-day touring plans and take advantage of the switching-off option (see page 150). This technique allows small children to be admitted to rides such as Space

Mountain, Indiana Jones, Big Thunder Mountain Railroad, and Splash Mountain. The children wait in the loading area as their parents ride one at a time; the nonriding parent waits with the children.

TIMING The following 2-day touring plan takes advantage of early-morning touring. On each day you should complete the structured part of the plan by 3 p.m. or so. We highly recommend returning to your hotel by midafternoon for a nap and an early dinner. If the park is open in the evening, come back to the park by 7:30 or 8 p.m. for the evening parade, fireworks, and *Fantasmic!*

ABOUT EARLY ENTRY Do not attempt to use the touring plan on early-entry days if you are not eligible for early entry—Disneyland Park will be packed with early-entry guests before you even make it past the turnstiles. Do day 1 of the plan on a non-early-entry day. The next day will be an early-entry day, so visit DCA on that day (DCA does not participate in the early program). Come back to Disneyland Park on the following non-early-entry day and proceed with day 2.

If you are eligible for early entry, experience (1) Alice in Wonderland, (2) Dumbo, and (3) Peter Pan's Flight, in that order, followed by the other Fantasyland attractions. At the end of the early-entry hour, begin the touring plan, skipping any attractions called for in the touring plan that you experienced during early entry.

Note: Because the needs of small children are so varied, we have not built specific instructions for eating into the touring plan. Simply stop for refreshments or a meal when you feel the urge. For best results, however, try to keep moving in the morning. In the afternoon, you can eat, rest often, and adjust the pace to your liking.

DAY 1

1. Arrive 30–40 minutes before the official opening time with your admission in hand. Line up in front of Gate 13.

2. When you are admitted to the park, move quickly to the far end of Main Street. If there is no rope barrier, continue without stopping to Critter Country and Splash Mountain. Ride Splash Mountain, taking advantage of the switching-off option if your children are too young or too short to ride.

3. While in Critter Country, ride The Many Adventures of Winnie the Pooh.

4. Backtrack to New Orleans Square and experience The Haunted Mansion. If your children seem intimidated by the prospect of The Haunted Mansion, skip ahead to Step 6.

5. After The Haunted Mansion, turn right and try Pirates of the Caribbean.

6. Bear right into Adventureland. Ride the Jungle Cruise.

7. Exit the Jungle Cruise to the left. Ride Indiana Jones Adventure, also in Adventureland.

8. Exit to the left (back toward The Haunted Mansion) and go to the Frontierland/New Orleans Square Station. Take the Disneyland

Railroad one stop to the Fantasyland/Mickey's Toontown Station.

9. Cross under the Disneyland Railroad tracks into Mickey's Toontown. In Mickey's Toontown, try Roger Rabbit's Car Toon Spin if your children are plucky and have strong stomachs. Obtain Fastpasses if the wait exceeds 30 minutes.

10. In Mickey's Toontown, ride Gadget's Go Coaster.

11. While in Mickey's Toontown, let off some steam in Goofy's Playhouse.

12. Tour Mickey's House and visit Mickey in his dressing room.

13. After seeing Mickey, turn right to enjoy Chip 'n Dale Treehouse.

14. Go to the far side of Mickey's House and tour Minnie's House.

15. Round out your visit to Mickey's Toontown with an inspection of Donald's Boat tied up next to Goofy's Playhouse.

16. Depart Mickey's Toontown the same way you entered, bearing left after you pass under the railroad tracks. Proceed to It's a Small World and ride.

17. Visit the Disney Princess Fantasy Faire at the Fantasyland Theatre to the left of the Fantasyland Railroad Station.

18. Next, return to the Fantasyland/Toontown Station. Take the Disneyland Railroad all the way around the park (back to Toontown); then stay on for one more stop and disembark in Tomorrowland. If you have a stroller that cannot go on the train, make a complete circuit on the train without the stroller and then walk from Toontown to Tomorrowland.

19. In Tomorrowland, obtain Fastpasses for Autopia.

20. Also in Tomorrowland, enjoy a performance of *Captain EO* (see the Small-child Fright-potential Chart on pages 142–146).

21. After the performance, take the monorail for a round-trip. Be aware that you must disembark and then reboard at the Downtown Disney Station.

22. Return with your Fastpasses to ride Autopia.

23. This concludes the touring plan for day 1. Use any time remaining to revisit favorite attractions, see attractions that were not included in the touring plan, or visit attractions you skipped because the lines were too long. Also, consult your daily entertainment schedule for parades, Fantasyland Theatre productions, or other live entertainment that might interest you. If the park is open in the evening, consider going back to your hotel for a nap and dinner and returning after 7 p.m. for a parade and *Fantasmic!*

DAY 2

1. Arrive at the park, admission in hand, at least 40 minutes before opening. Line up at Gate 13.

2. If members of your party want to ride Space Mountain, proceed

directly to Space Mountain and obtain Fastpasses as soon as you're admitted to the park. The Fastpasses can be used until park closing, so don't worry about the return-time window on the Fastpass.

3. Continue through Tomorrowland to Fantasyland and the Matterhorn Bobsleds. Ride.

4. Head to Fantasyland via the central hub. Ride Dumbo the Flying Elephant if the wait is tolerable.

5. Backtracking toward the castle, ride Peter Pan's Flight.

6. Exiting Peter Pan to the right, ride Mr. Toad's Wild Ride.

7. Exit Mr. Toad to the right and bear right around the corner to Alice in Wonderland. Ride.

8. After Alice in Wonderland, try the Mad Tea Party next door.

9. Next, ride the Storybook Land Canal Boats, across the walk from the Mad Tea Party.

10. Bear right after the Canal Boats and return to the center of Fantasyland by the castle. Ride the King Arthur Carrousel.

11. Across from King Arthur Carrousel, experience Pinocchio's Daring Journey (we recommend skipping the nearby Snow White's Scary Adventures).

12. Exit Pinocchio to your left, leave Fantasyland, and go into Frontierland. If you want, ride Big Thunder Mountain Railroad, taking advantage of the switching-off option. Use Fastpass if the wait exceeds 30 minutes.

13. The best way to ride Finding Nemo Submarine Voyage without a wait in excess of an hour (see pages 256–258) is to ride during a parade, fireworks show, or *Fantasmic!* Using the *Times Guide,* determine when one or another of these events is scheduled and join the line for Nemo 15 minutes before the event begins. This is the time when the wait should be shortest, usually 35–50 minutes as opposed to 60–110 minutes.

14. Take a cruise on the *Mark Twain* Riverboat or the Sailing Ship *Columbia,* whichever departs first.

15. Keeping the waterfront on your right, proceed to the rafts for transportation to Tom Sawyer Island. Allow the children to explore the island.

16. Leave Frontierland and pass through New Orleans Square into Adventureland. Explore Tarzan's Treehouse.

17. See the *Enchanted Tiki Room* show, also in Adventureland.

18. Return to Tomorrowland and ride Buzz Lightyear.

19. Ride Space Mountain using your Fastpasses. Take advantage of switching off if you have children too young or too short to ride.

20. Also in Tomorrowland, ride Star Tours and catch a performance of the *Jedi Training Academy.*

21. This concludes the touring plan for day 2. Use any time remaining to revisit favorite attractions, see attractions that were not included in the touring plan, or visit attractions you skipped because the lines were too long. Also, consult your daily entertainment schedule for parades, Fantasyland Theatre productions, or other live entertainment

of interest. If the park is open in the evening, consider going back to your hotel for a nap and dinner and returning after 7 p.m. for a parade and *Fantasmic!*

DISNEYLAND PARK 2-DAY TOURING PLAN A, FOR DAYTIME TOURING OR FOR WHEN THE PARK CLOSES EARLY

FOR Parties wishing to spread their Disneyland Park visit over 2 days and parties preferring to tour in the morning.

ASSUMES Willingness to experience all major rides (including roller coasters) and shows.

TIMING The following 2-day touring plan takes advantage of early-morning touring and is the most efficient of all the touring plans for comprehensive touring with the least time lost waiting in line. On each day you should complete the structured part of the plan by 3 p.m. or so. If you are visiting Disneyland Park during a period of the year when the park is open late (after 8 p.m.), you might prefer our 2-day Touring Plan B, which offers morning touring on 1 day and late afternoon and evening touring on the other day. Another highly recommended option is to return to your hotel around mid-afternoon for a well-deserved nap and an early dinner, and to come back to the park by 7:30 or 8 p.m. for the evening parade, fireworks, and live entertainment.

ABOUT EARLY ENTRY Do not attempt to use the plan on early-entry days if you are not eligible for early entry—Disneyland Park will be packed with early-entry guests before you even make it past the turnstiles. Do day 1 of the plan on a non-early-entry day. The next day will be an early-entry day, so visit DCA on that day (DCA does not participate in the early program). Come back to Disneyland Park on the following non-early-entry day and proceed with day 2.

If you're eligible for early entry, experience (1) Space Mountain, (2) Buzz Lightyear, (3) Matterhorn Bobsleds, and (4) Peter Pan's Flight, in that order. If you're not able to enjoy all of the above during the early-entry hour, ride as many as you can. When the park opens to the general public, continue the sequence until you've experienced all four. At that point, begin the touring plan, skipping any attractions you've already seen.

DAY 1

1. Arrive at the park, admission in hand, at least 40 minutes before opening. Line up at Gate 13. If members of your party want to ride Space Mountain, entrust all your admission passes to one person who can fly like the wind.

2. Dispatch the person with the passes to Space Mountain to obtain Fastpasses.

3. Everyone else, hurry to the Matterhorn Bobsleds.

4. Proceed to Fantasyland via the entrance next to the Mad Tea Party. Experience Peter Pan's Flight.

5. Also in Fantasyland, ride the Storybook Land Canal Boats.

6. In Fantasyland, experience Mr. Toad's Wild Ride.

7. Still in Fantasyland, ride Snow White's Scary Adventures.

8. Next door to the left, ride Pinocchio's Daring Journey.

9. Return to Tomorrowland. Ride Space Mountain using your Fastpasses.

10. Also in Tomorrowland, ride Buzz Lightyear.

11. Proceed to Frontierland and ride Big Thunder Mountain Railroad. Get Fastpasses and return later to ride if the wait exceeds 25 minutes.

12. If you are hungry, try Rancho del Zocalo, across from the entrance to Big Thunder Mountain Railroad.

13. While in Frontierland, ride the *Mark Twain* Riverboat or the Sailing Ship *Columbia,* whichever departs first.

 Note: At this point, check your *Times Guide* daily entertainment schedule to see if there are any parades, fireworks, or live performances that interest you. Make note of the times and alter the touring plan accordingly. Because you've already seen all of the attractions for day 1 that cause bottlenecks and have big lines, an interruption of the touring plan here will not cause you any problems. Simply pick up where you left off before the parade or show.

14. The best way to ride Finding Nemo Submarine Voyage without a wait in excess of an hour (see pages 256–258) is to ride during a parade, fireworks show, or *Fantasmic!* Using the *Times Guide,* determine when one or another of these events is scheduled, and join the line for Nemo 15 minutes before the event begins. This is the time when the wait should be shortest, usually 35–50 minutes as opposed to 60–110 minutes.

15. While in Frontierland, take a raft to Tom Sawyer Island.

16. After you return to the mainland, proceed through New Orleans Square to Adventureland. Tour Tarzan's Treehouse.

17. Exit to your right and see the *Enchanted Tiki Room* show.

18. Return to Main Street via the central hub. See *The Disneyland Story,* presenting *Great Moments with Mr. Lincoln.*

19. This concludes day 1 of the touring plan. If you have any energy left, backtrack to pick up attractions you would like to ride again or may have missed or bypassed because the lines were too long. Check out any parades or live performances that interest you. Alternatively, return to your hotel and fall, exhausted, into bed.

DAY 2

1. Arrive 30–40 minutes before the official opening time with your admission in hand. Line up in front of Gate 13.

2. After passing through the turnstiles, continue to the end of Main Street,

U.S.A. If there is no rope barrier, move as fast as you can to Adventure-land and ride Indiana Jones Adventure.

3. Exit Indiana Jones to the left and pass through New Orleans Square to Critter Country. Ride Splash Mountain.

4. While in Critter Country, experience The Many Adventures of Winnie the Pooh.

5. After you ride Winnie the Pooh, leave Critter Country and return to Adventureland. Ride the Jungle Cruise.

6. Exit the Jungle Cruise to the left and go to New Orleans Square. Ride Pirates of the Caribbean.

7. While in New Orleans Square, experience The Haunted Mansion.

8. Take the Disneyland Railroad to the Fantasyland/Mickey's Toontown Station, one stop down the line.

9. After you get off the train, bear to your left and cross under the railroad tracks to Mickey's Toontown. In Mickey's Toontown, ride Roger Rabbit's Car Toon Spin. If the wait is prohibitive, obtain Fastpasses and ride later.

10. If you have children in your party, tour Mickey's House and visit Mickey in his dressing room.

11. Do the same at Minnie's House.

12. Leave Mickey's Toontown the same way you entered. Bear left after passing under the tracks and ride It's a Small World.

13. Passing between the lagoon and the Matterhorn, proceed to Tomorrow-land. The loading platform for the monorail is built over the docks for the lagoon. An escalator takes you up to the monorail loading area. If you are hungry, consider having lunch at Downtown Disney. Be aware that you must disembark and then reboard at the Downtown Disney Station to make a round-trip circuit.

14. Return to Tomorrowland on the monorail. In Tomorrowland, see *Captain EO*.

15. Also in Tomorrowland, ride Star Tours and catch a performance of the *Jedi Training Academy*.

16. This concludes the touring plan. Revisit your favorite attractions, or try any rides and shows you may have missed. Check your daily entertainment schedule for parades or live performances that interest you.

DISNEYLAND PARK 2-DAY TOURING PLAN B, FOR MORNING AND EVENING TOURING OR FOR WHEN THE PARK IS OPEN LATE

FOR Parties who want to enjoy Disneyland Park at different times of day, including evenings and early mornings.

ASSUMES Willingness to experience all major rides (including roller coasters) and shows.

TIMING This 2-day touring plan is for those visiting Disneyland Park on days when the park is open late (after 8 p.m.). The plan offers morning touring on the first day and late afternoon and evening touring on the other day. If the park closes early, or if you prefer to do all of your touring during the morning and early afternoon, use the 2-day Touring Plan A, for Daytime Touring or for When the Park Closes Early.

ABOUT EARLY ENTRY If you are not eligible for early entry, do not try to use day 1 of the plan on an early-entry day. Disneyland Park will be packed with early-entry guests before you even get past the turnstiles.

If you're eligible for early entry and want to use day 1 of the plan on an early-entry day, experience (1) Space Mountain, (2) Buzz Lightyear, (3) Matterhorn Bobsleds, and (4) Peter Pan's Flight, in that order. If you're not able to enjoy all of the above during the early-entry hour, ride as many as you can. When the park opens to the general public, continue the sequence until you've experienced all four. At that point, begin the touring plan, skipping any attractions you've already seen.

DAY 1

1. Arrive at the park, admission in hand, at least 30 minutes before opening. Line up at Gate 13.

2. If members of your party want to ride Space Mountain, proceed directly to Space Mountain and obtain Fastpasses as soon as you're admitted to the park. The Fastpasses can be used until park closing, so don't worry about the return-time window on the Fastpass.

3. Continue through Tomorrowland to Fantasyland and the Matterhorn Bobsleds. Ride.

4. Proceed to Fantasyland via the entrance next to the Mad Tea Party. Experience Peter Pan's Flight.

5. Return to Tomorrowland via the central hub and ride Buzz Lightyear.

6. Ride Space Mountain using your Fastpasses.

7. Exit Space Mountain and turn left toward the central hub. Enter Frontierland and ride Big Thunder Mountain Railroad.

8. Keeping the waterfront on your right, head for Critter Country and Splash Mountain. Obtain Fastpasses.

9. Also in Critter County, enjoy The Many Adventures of Winnie the Pooh.

10. From Critter Country, head to Adventureland. Ride Indiana Jones.

11. Continue to New Orleans Square and experience Pirates of the Caribbean.

12. Also in New Orleans Square, tour The Haunted Mansion.

13. Feel free at this time to grab a bite to eat if you're hungry. Now is also a good time to look over the *Times Guide* handout for

live-entertainment offerings. Whatever else, don't miss the show at the Golden Horseshoe in Frontierland.

14. The best way to ride Finding Nemo Submarine Voyage without a wait in excess of an hour (see pages 256–258) is to ride during a parade, fireworks show, or *Fantasmic!* Using the *Times Guide,* determine when one or another of these events is scheduled, and join the line for Nemo 15 minutes before the event begins. This is the time when the wait should be shortest, usually 35–50 minutes as opposed to 60–110 minutes.

15. In nearby Frontierland, ride either the Sailing Ship *Columbia* or the *Mark Twain* Riverboat.

16. Ride Splash Mountain using your Fastpasses.

17. Continue to tour, saving Main Street for last. If you're not completely pooped, see *The Disneyland Story,* presenting *Great Moments with Mr. Lincoln* on your way out of the park.

18. This concludes the touring plan for day 1.

DAY 2

1. Eat an early dinner and arrive at the park about 5:30 or 6 p.m.

2. Go to Adventureland and explore Tarzan's Treehouse.

3. Nearby, catch the show in the *Enchanted Tiki Room.*

4. Cross the central hub to Tomorrowland. Ride Star Tours if the wait isn't prohibitive.

5. Also in Tomorrowland, see *Captain EO.*

6. Take the Disneyland Railroad from the Tomorrowland Station to the Fantasyland/Mickey's Toontown Station.

7. Exit the station to the left and pass under the railroad bridge to Mickey's Toontown. Though imaginative and colorful, Toontown is primarily for small children and expendable for most adults. Ride Roger Rabbit's Car Toon Spin if the wait is tolerable.

8. Pass back under the railroad bridge and bear left to It's a Small World. Ride.

9. Check the *Times Guide* for parades, fireworks, and *Fantasmic!* Work these shows into the remainder of your day as time and energy allow.

10. This concludes day 2 of the touring plan. Backtrack to pick up any attractions you may have missed earlier.

PART SIX

DISNEY CALIFORNIA ADVENTURE

A MOST ANTICIPATED SEQUEL

DISNEY CALIFORNIA ADVENTURE held its grand opening on February 8, 2001. Now known as DCA among Disneyphiles, the park is a bouquet of contradictions conceived in Fantasyland, starved in utero by corporate Disney, and born into a hostile environment of Disneyland loyalists who believed they'd been handed a second-rate theme park. Its parts are stunningly beautiful yet come together awkwardly, failing to compose a handsome whole. And perhaps most lamentable of all, the California theme is impotent by virtue of being all-encompassing. But despite the long odds, just a decade after its inauspicious debut, DCA is emerging from a billion-dollar metamorphosis that may finally make it an honorable companion to its storied older sibling across the Esplanade.

The history of the park is another of those convoluted tales found only in Robert Ludlum novels and corporate Disney. Southern California Disney fans began clamoring for a second theme park shortly after Epcot opened at Walt Disney World in 1982. Although there was some element of support within the Walt Disney Company, the Disney loyal had to content themselves with rumors and half-promises for two decades while they watched new Disney parks go up in Tokyo, Paris, and Florida. For years, Disney teasingly floated the "Westcot" concept, a California version of Epcot that was always just about to break ground. Whether it was a matter of procrastination or simply pursuing better opportunities elsewhere, the Walt Disney Company sat on the sidelines while the sleepy community of Anaheim became a sprawling city and property values skyrocketed. By the time Disney emerged from its Westcot fantasy and began to get serious about a second California park, the price tag—not to mention the complexity of integrating such a development into a mature city—was mind-boggling.

Disney California Adventure

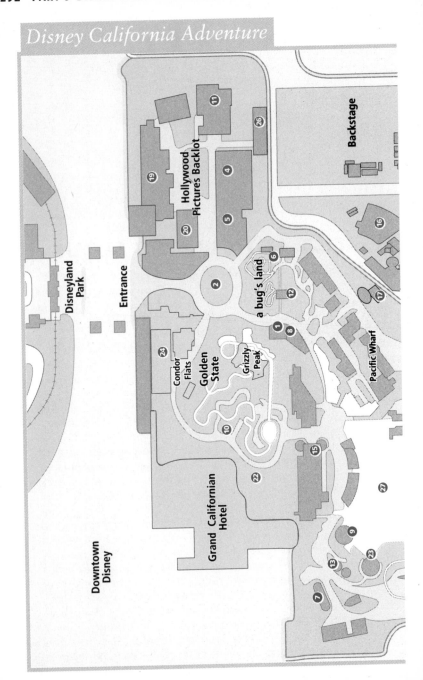

Disneyland Park

Entrance

Hollywood
Pictures Backlot

Backstage

a bug's land

Condor
Flats

**Golden
State**

Grizzly
Peak

Pacific Wharf

Downtown
Disney

**Grand Californian
Hotel**

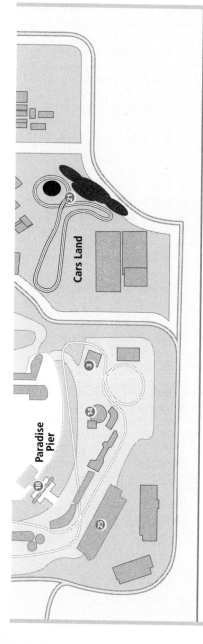

Paradise Pier

Cars Land

1. Blue Sky Cellar
2. Buena Vista Steet (central hub)
3. California Screamin'
4. Disney Animation
5. Disney Junior–
   Live on Stage!
6. Flik's Fun Fair
7. Goofy's Sky School
8. Golden Vine Winery
9. Golden Zephyr
10. Grizzly River Run

11. Hyperion Theater
12. *It's Tough to Be a Bug!*
13. Jumpin' Jellyfish
14. King Triton's Carousel
15. The Little Mermaid:
    Ariel's Undersea
    Adventure
16. Luigi's Flying Tires
17. Mater's Junkyard Jamboree
18. Mickey's Fun Wheel
19. Monsters, Inc. Mike &
    Sulley to the Rescue

20. *Muppet-Vision 3-D*
21. Radiator Springs Racers
22. Redwood Creek
    Challenge Trail
23. Silly Symphony
    Swings
24. Soarin' Over
    California
25. Toy Story Midway
    Mania!

26. The Twilight Zone
    Tower of Terror
27. *World of Color*

Westcot had been billed as a $2- to $3-billion, 100-plus-acre project, so that was what the Disney faithful were expecting when Disney California Adventure was announced. What they got was a park that cost $1.4 billion (slashed from an original budget of about $2.1 billion), built on 55 acres, including a sizable piece carved out for the Grand Californian Hotel. It's quite a small park by modern theme-park standards, but $1.4 billion, when lavished on 55 acres, ought to buy a pretty good park.

Then there's the park's theme. Although flexible, California Adventure comes off like a default setting, lacking in imagination, weak in concept, and without intrinsic appeal, especially when you stop to consider that two-thirds of Disneyland guests come from Southern California. As further grist for the mill, before the arrival of The Little Mermaid and Cars Land, there was precious little new technology at work in Disney's newest theme park. Of the headliner attractions, only two—Soarin' Over California, a simulator ride, and Toy Story Midway Mania!, a "virtual dark ride"—broke new ground. All the rest are recycled, albeit popular, attractions from the Animal Kingdom and Disney's Hollywood Studios. When you move to the smaller-statured second half of the attraction batting order, it gets worse. Most of these attractions are little more than off-the-shelf midway rides spruced up with a Disney story line and facade.

From a competitive perspective, Disney California Adventure was an underwhelming shot at Disney's three Southern California competitors. The Hollywood section of DCA takes a hopeful poke at Universal Studios Hollywood, while Paradise Pier offers midway rides à la Six Flags Magic Mountain. Finally, the whole California theme has for years been the eminent domain of Knott's Berry Farm. In short, there's not much originality in DCA, only Disney's now-redundant mantra that "whatever they can do, we can do better."

Finally, after more than 8 years of basically being in denial about Disney California Adventure, the Walt Disney Company seemed willing to admit that this theme park (which only pulls in about a third of Disneyland's attendance annually) needed some help. The Mouse has nearly completed a $1.1 billion effort, originally announced in 2007, to address DCA's problems. And that's only one portion of the $10 billion Disney has budgeted over 10 years for an extreme makeover of the entire Disneyland Resort.

Starting at the park entrance, the Imagineers have scoured every inch of DCA, injecting charm, character, and ride capacity wherever they could. A new entryway embraces the legacy of Disneyland's founder with a nostalgic re-creation of 1920s Los Angeles. That freshly poured-on theming flows all the way to Paradise Pier, where the tacky seaside amusements have been softened with new-old Victorian-era stylings. An original family-friendly dark ride based on a popular Piscean princess has been added, and the central lagoon now sports a Vegas-quality water show designed expressly to keep crowds in DCA after dark. The final element of DCA's transformation falls into place with 2012's opening of Cars Land, an entire area dedicated to the best-selling Pixar property. Cars Land has shaped up to be the biggest project to hit theme parks since Universal Orlando's Wizarding World of Harry Potter, and could be the final puzzle piece needed to rehabilitate DCA's poor reputation. While the park spent its first decade as a punch line, we predict DCA's popularity to steadily build in 2012 and beyond.

Mind you, the rest of Disneyland Resort is experiencing its own gussying up. Look for Downtown Disney to increase in size, adding at least five new shops, clubs, and restaurants to its lineup. Likewise, Disneyland Hotel is completing a face-lift as festive new furnishings and the most up-to-date amenities are folded into the 56-year-old resort. Disneyland Park is also rumored to see an expansion in 2013, after the major work on DCA is done. There's also at least one new hotel on the drawing boards, plus a Disney Vacation Club property. According to the rumor mill, there might even be a third theme park in the works, possibly to be built on the Disneyland employee parking lot.

Meanwhile, as the Disneyholics churn up cyberspace debating DCA's theme and worrying whether expensive additions and patched-on personality can compensate for a flawed foundation, the rest of us will have some fun enjoying the park that is.

ARRIVING *and* GETTING ORIENTED

THE ENTRANCE TO Disney California Adventure faces the entrance to Disneyland Park across a palm-shaded pedestrian plaza called the **Esplanade.** If you arrive by tram from one of the Disney parking lots, you'll disembark at the Esplanade. Facing east toward Harbor Boulevard, Disneyland Park will be on your left and DCA will be on your right. In the Esplanade are ticket booths, the group sales office, and resort information.

Seen from overhead, Disney California Adventure is roughly arrayed in a fan shape around the park's central visual icon, **Grizzly Peak.** At ground level, however, the park's layout is not so obvious. From the Esplanade, where huge block letters spelling CALIFORNIA originally stood, you now pass through a new Streamline Modern entrance facade, designed after Los Angeles's Pan Pacific Auditorium. If it looks familiar, that's because it can also be recognized as the entrance to Disney's Hollywood Studios park in Florida.

Once past the turnstiles, you'll find yourself on **Buena Vista Street** (scheduled for completion in 2012), a re-creation of 1920s Hollywood as Walt saw it when he first arrived. To your left and right you'll find Guest Services, as well as a variety of shops and eateries with back stories referring to Disney's early biography. To your right you'll find lockers, restrooms, an ATM, and phones. Among the shops is **Elias and**

NOT TO BE MISSED AT DISNEY CALIFORNIA ADVENTURE

GOLDEN STATE
- Grizzly River Run
- Soarin' Over California

HOLLYWOOD PICTURES BACKLOT
- Hyperion Theater
- *Muppet Vision 3-D*
- The Twilight Zone Tower of Terror

A BUG'S LAND
- *It's Tough to Be a Bug!*

PARADISE PIER
- California Screamin'
- Toy Story Midway Mania!
- *World of Color*

Company Department Store (named after Walt's father), offering the park's largest selection of Disney-trademark merchandise. Other retail outlets include **Julius Katz & Sons Appliances, Los Feliz Five and Dime,** and **Kingswell Camera Shop.** Stroller and wheelchair rentals are immediately to your left as you enter the park in **Oswald's Filling Station.** Winding past the new shops and facades, the Red Car Trolley transports guests from the park entrance to The Twilight Zone Tower of Terror and back again along freshly laid tracks.

The original hub area, called Sunshine Plaza, was dominated by a an arresting metal sculpture of the sun. In its place now stands a replica of the **Carthay Circle Theater,** which premiered *Snow White and the Seven Dwarfs* in 1937; in this incarnation, it encloses a restaurant. In addition to serving as a point of departure for the various themed areas, Carthay Circle is one of the best places in the park to encounter the Disney characters and is also a great photo op.

"Lands" at DCA are called "districts," and there are five of them. A left turn at the hub leads you to the **Hollywood Pictures Backlot** district of the park, celebrating California's history as the film capital of the world. The **Golden State** district of the park is to the right or straight. Golden State is a somewhat amorphous combination of separate themed areas that showcase California's architecture, agriculture, industry, history, and natural resources. Within the Golden State district, you'll find **Condor Flats** by taking the first right as you approach the hub. **Grizzly**

DISNEY DISH WITH JIM HILL

WHERE'S WALT-O? You'll find all sorts of sly Walt-related references hidden among the buildings along Buena Vista Street, a re-creation of 1920s Los Angeles. Most visitors know that Oswald's Filling Station is a tribute to the popular cartoon character Oswald the Lucky Rabbit, which Disney Brothers' Studio created prior to Mickey Mouse. But how many people will realize that the Julius Katz & Sons store was named after one of the studio's first cartoon characters (Julius the Cat from *Alice Comedies*)? And if you want to get all the references, be sure to study your early Disney history before heading out to this theme park.

Peak will likewise be to your right, though you must walk two-thirds of the way around the mountain to reach its attractions. **Pacific Wharf,** the remaining Golden State–themed area, is situated along a kidney-shaped lake and can be accessed by following the walkway emanating from the hub at 7 o'clock and winding around Grizzly Peak. A third district, **a bug's land,** is situated opposite the **Golden Vine Winery** and can be reached by taking the same route. The fourth district, **Paradise Pier,** recalls sea-side amusement parks of the first half of the 20th century. It is situated in the southwest corner of the park, around the large lake. Opening in 2012, **Cars Land** is the fifth district, claiming a former parking lot behind the Pacific Wharf and Hollywood Pictures Backlot, with its primary entrance across from the Golden Vine Winery.

SINGLES LINES

YOU CAN OFTEN SAVE TIME WAITING in line by taking advantage of singles lines, a separate line for people who are alone or don't mind riding alone or with a stranger. The objective of singles lines is to fill odd spaces left by groups who don't quite fill the entire ride vehicle. Because there aren't many singles and most groups aren't willing to split up, singles lines are usually much shorter than the regular line. Four attractions at DCA offer singles lines: California Screamin', Goofy's Sky School, Grizzly River Run, and Soarin' Over California.

PARK-OPENING PROCEDURES

GUESTS ARE USUALLY HELD AT THE TURNSTILES until official open-ing time. Disneyland Resort hotel guests get a 30-minute jump on the public through the Grand Californian's exclusive entrance. You'll be required to show a hotel key card (a same-day receipt from a hotel restau-rant or store works as well) before being allowed through. Fastpasses for *World of Color* are also distributed inside the hotel to resort guests 1 hour prior to park open (see page 320 for more information). On especially busy days, guests are admitted to Golden Gateway and Condor Flats 30 minutes before official opening time. During this early-entry period, only Soarin' Over California and Grizzly River Run will operate, and guests are prevented from crossing into the Paradise Pier area. Be aware that DCA usually opens at 10 a.m., 1 or 2 hours later than Disneyland Park.

HOLLYWOOD PICTURES BACKLOT

HOLLYWOOD PICTURES BACKLOT OFFERS attractions and shop-ping that are inspired by California's (and Disney's) contribution to tele-vision and cinema. Visually, the district is themed as a studio backlot with sets, including an urban street scene, soundstages, and a central street with shops and restaurants that depict Hollywood's golden age.

As with most of DCA, the Backlot has not been immune to refurbishment. While plans are still in flux, the current direction is for the Backlot to be recast as 1930s-era Hollywood Land (which may be its new name by the time you visit). The new red trolleys run from Buena Vista Street to here, and a host of further enhancements are on the drawing board.

Disney Animation ★★★½

APPEAL BY AGE	PRESCHOOL ★★★½	GRADE SCHOOL ★★★★★
TEENS ★★★★★	YOUNG ADULTS ★★★★	OVER 30 ★★★★ SENIORS ★★★★

What it is Behind-the-scenes look at Disney animation. **Scope and scale** Major attraction. **When to go** Anytime. **Special comments** Quite amusing, though not very educational. **Duration of experience** 35–55 minutes. **Probable waiting time** 5 minutes.

Thumbs Up for the Whole Family

DESCRIPTION AND COMMENTS The Disney Animation building houses a total of 10 shows, galleries, and interactive exhibits that collectively provide a sort of crash course in animation. Moving from room to room and exhibit to exhibit, you follow the Disney animation process from concept to finished film, with a peek at each of the steps along the way. Throughout, you are surrounded by animation, and sometimes it's even projected above your head and under your feet!

Because DCA's Animation building is not a working studio, the attraction does not showcase artists at work on real features, and the interactive exhibits are more whimsical than educational. Sorcerer's Workshop, for example, is an interactive exhibit where you can act and sing with various cartoon scenes through a touch-screen computer interface.

The Animation Academy, hosted by a Disney cartoonist, teaches you how to draw a Disney character; if you have any artistic inclination, you may consider it DCA's best-kept secret and find yourself taking the class repeatedly, as a Salt Lake City reader suggests:

> [Animation Academy] turned out to be one of my absolute favorite things. I did it four times in a row and would have gone more if I wasn't starving. I plan to devote quite a bit of time to it on my next trip. I don't think you give it enough credit in your book.

Both Sorcerer's Workshop and Animation Academy provide a good foundation on the animation process and will enhance your appreciation of the other exhibits. *Turtle Talk with Crush* is also located here (see page 301). Finally, for a WOW! moment, be sure to check out the amazing zoetrope (no, don't worry, it's not that thing that the urologist threatened you with).

TOURING TIPS On entering the Animation building, you'll step into a lobby where signs mark the entrances of the various exhibits. Look up in the lobby for a moment at the oversize projections of animations in process, including Pixar's latest hits. It takes 40–55 minutes to do all the interactive stuff and see everything. You probably won't experience much of a wait for the Disney Animation offerings except on weekends and holidays. Even then, the Animation building clears out considerably by late afternoon.

Disney Junior—Live on Stage! ★★★★

APPEAL BY AGE	PRESCHOOL ★★★★½	GRADE SCHOOL ★★★	TEENS ★★
YOUNG ADULTS ★★★	OVER 30 ★★★½		SENIORS ★★★★

What it is Live show for children. **Scope and scale** Minor attraction. **When to go** Per the daily entertainment schedule. **Special comments** Audience sits on the floor. A must for families with preschoolers. **Duration of show** 20 minutes. **Probable waiting time** 25 minutes.

DESCRIPTION AND COMMENTS   The show features characters from the Disney Channel's *Little Einsteins, Mickey Mouse Clubhouse, Jake and the Never Land Pirates,* and *Handy Manny,* plus other Disney Channel characters. Reengineered in 2011, *Disney Junior* uses elaborate puppets instead of live characters on stage. A simple plot serves as the platform for singing, dancing, some great puppetry, and a great deal of audience participation. The characters, who ooze love and goodness, rally throngs of tots and preschoolers to sing and dance along with them. All the jumping, squirming, and high-stepping is facilitated by having the audience sit on the floor so that kids can spontaneously erupt into motion when the mood strikes. Even for adults without children, it's a treat to watch the tykes rev up. If you have a younger child in your party, all the better: Just stand back and let the video roll.

For preschoolers, *Disney Junior* will be the highlight of their day, as a Thomasville, North Carolina, mom attests:

> [It] was fantastic! My 3-year-old loved it. The children danced, sang, and had a great time.

Disney Junior is the second iteration of the stage show since 2007. Both versions replaced live characters with puppets, a fact that has left some parents less than enthralled. These comments from a Virginia Beach, Virginia, couple are typical:

> We were disappointed with the newly updated [show]. This did not consist of live characters, and I think the level of excitement from the kids was lower because of this. I mean, the kids enjoyed it, but you would think they would be more excited when it's a show with some of their favorite characters.

TOURING TIPS   The show is headquartered in what was formerly the ABC Soap Opera Bistro restaurant to the right of the entrance to the Hollywood Pictures Backlot. It now has a new Art Deco marquee. Because the tykes just can't get enough, it has become a hot ticket. Show up at least 25 minutes before showtime. If you arrive to find a line that extends out of the main queuing area and onto the sidewalk, you might not get into the show. Count two palm trees to the left of the theater entrance; if the line extends to the left of the second palm, you probably won't make the cut. If the line hasn't extended past the second palm tree, go ahead and get in line—chances are about 90% that you'll be admitted to the next show. Once inside, pick a spot on the floor and take a breather until the performance begins.

Hyperion Theater ★★★★

| APPEAL BY AGE | PRESCHOOL ★★★★½ | GRADE SCHOOL ★★★★★ | TEENS ★★★★★ |
| YOUNG ADULTS ★★★★½ | | OVER 30 ★★★★½ | SENIORS ★★★★ |

What it is Venue for live shows. **Scope and scale** Major attraction. **When to go** After experiencing DCA's rides. **Special comments** Great venue; not to be missed. **Duration of show** 50 minutes. **Probable waiting time** 30 minutes.

Thumbs Up for the Whole Family

DESCRIPTION AND COMMENTS This 2,000-seat theater is DCA's premier venue for live productions, many of which are based on Disney-animated films and feature Disney characters. Shows exhibit Broadway quality in every sense, except duration of the presentation, and alone are arguably worth the price of theme-park admission. In 2011 the Hyperion was supposed to debut *Toy Story—The Musical,* an adaptation of the first Pixar film crafted for Disney's cruise ships. That plan hasn't happened yet, nor have rumors of an indoor lobby replacing the theater's current false front. For now, *Aladdin—A Musical Spectacular* is continuing its run as the most elaborate show staged at any stateside Disney theme park. A breezy stage version of the *Aladdin* story, it features familiar film tunes ("Friend Like Me" and "Prince Ali") plus one newly written ballad, along with jaw-dropping overhead flying carpet effects. If *Aladdin* is still running when you visit, we rate it not to be missed, thanks largely to the actors playing the Genie, who are given remarkably long leashes to ad lib up-to-the-minute pop-culture references that sail right over younger audience members' heads. In the evening the Hyperion is often used as a stage for separate-admission concerts and special events.

TOURING TIPS The lavish productions hosted by the Hyperion Theater are rightly very popular and commonly sell out on busier days. Presentations are described, and showtimes listed, in the park *Times Guide.* The theater is multilevel. Though all the seats provide a good line of sight, we recommend that you sit on the ground level relatively close to the entrance doors (if possible) to facilitate an easy exit after the performance. Finally, be forewarned that the sound volume for Hyperion Theater productions would give heavy-metal rock concerts a good run for the money.

Monsters, Inc. Mike & Sulley to the Rescue ★★★½

| APPEAL BY AGE | PRESCHOOL ★★★★★ | GRADE SCHOOL ★★★★ | TEENS ★★★★ |
| YOUNG ADULTS ★★★★ | | OVER 30 ★★★★ | SENIORS ★★★★ |

What it is Dark ride. **Scope and scale** Major attraction. **When to go** Before 11 a.m. **Special comments** Disney's best dark ride in years. **Duration of ride** 3¾ minutes. **Average wait in line per 100 people ahead of you** 4 minutes. **Loading speed** Moderate.

DESCRIPTION AND COMMENTS Based on characters and the story from the Disney/Pixar film *Monsters, Inc.,* the ride takes you through child-phobic Monstropolis as Mike and Sulley try to return baby Boo safely to her bedroom. If you haven't seen the film, the story line won't make much sense. In a nutshell, a human baby gets loose in a sort of parallel universe populated largely by amusing monsters. Good monsters Mike and Sulley try to return Boo to her home before the bad monsters get their hands on her.

The Disney Imagineers did a very good job on the Monsters, Inc. ride, re-creating the humor, characters, and setting of the film in great detail. The section of the attraction where you ride through the door warehouse with all of its lifts and conveyors is truly inspired. Special effects are first-rate, and lots of subtle and not-so-subtle jokes are worked into the whole experience. As in the Tower of Terror, you'll have to ride several times to catch them all. Before disembarking, be sure to banter with sluglike supervisor Roz, an animatronic "living character" that can see and interact with riders.

TOURING TIPS The attraction is very popular. It should be a Fastpass attraction but it isn't. Try to ride the first hour the park is open, during a parade, or during the last hour before closing. Because it's near several theater attractions, the ride is subject to experiencing a sudden deluge of guests when the theaters disgorge their audiences.

Monsters, Inc. is an iffy attraction for preschoolers: Some love it and some are frightened. Increase your odds for a positive experience by exposing your little ones to the movie before leaving home.

Muppet-Vision 3-D ★★★★½

APPEAL BY AGE PRESCHOOL ★★★½ GRADE SCHOOL ★★★★½ TEENS ★★★★
YOUNG ADULTS ★★★★   OVER 30 ★★★★   SENIORS ★★★★

What it is 3-D movie featuring the Muppets. Scope and scale Major attraction. When to go Before noon or after 4 p.m. Special comments Must see; 3-D effects and loud noises frighten many preschoolers. Duration of show 17 minutes. Probable waiting time 20 minutes.

Thumbs Up for the Whole Family

DESCRIPTION AND COMMENTS Muppet-Vision 3-D provides a total sensory experience, with wild 3-D action augmented by auditory, visual, and tactile special effects. If you're tired and hot, this show will make you feel brand-new.

TOURING TIPS Although extremely popular, this attraction handles crowds exceedingly well. Your wait should not last longer than 20 minutes except on days when the park is jam-packed. Special effects and loud noises may frighten some preschoolers.

Turtle Talk with Crush ★★★★

APPEAL BY AGE PRESCHOOL ★★★★★ GRADE SCHOOL ★★★★½ TEENS ★★★★
YOUNG ADULTS ★★★★   OVER 30 ★★★½   SENIORS ★★★★

What it is An interactive animated film. Scope and scale Minor attraction. When to go After you see the other attractions in the Animation building. Duration of show 17 minutes. Probable waiting time 10–20 minutes.

DESCRIPTION AND COMMENTS Turtle Talk with Crush is an interactive theater show starring the 153-year-old surfer-dude turtle from Finding Nemo. Although it starts like a typical Disney-theme-park movie, Turtle Talk quickly turns into a surprise interactive encounter as the on-screen

Crush begins to have actual conversations with guests in the audience. Real-time computer graphics are used to accurately move Crush's mouth when forming words.

A mom from Henderson, Colorado, has a crush on Crush:

Turtle Talk with Crush is a must-see. Our 4-year-old was picked out of the crowd by Crush, and we were just amazed by the technology that allowed one-on-one conversation. It was adorable and enjoyed by everyone from Grammy and Papa to the 4-year-old!

TOURING TIPS The animation is brilliant, and guests of all ages list *Crush* as their favorite Animation-building feature. By late afternoon, the building has usually cleared out. Save this for your last stop at the building.

The Twilight Zone Tower of Terror (Fastpass) ★★★★½

APPEAL BY AGE	PRESCHOOL ★★	GRADE SCHOOL ★★★★	TEENS ★★★★★
YOUNG ADULTS ★★★★★		OVER 30 ★★★★	SENIORS ★★★★

What it is Sci-fi-theme indoor thrill ride. **Scope and scale** Super-headliner. **When to go** The first hour the park is open or use Fastpass. **Special comments** Not to be missed; must be 40" tall to ride; switching-off option provided (page 150). **Duration of ride** About 4 minutes plus preshow. **Average wait in line per 100 people ahead of you** 4 minutes. **Assumes** All elevators operating. **Loading speed** Moderate.

Dark Scary Rough Lose Things Queasy

DESCRIPTION AND COMMENTS The Twilight Zone Tower of Terror is a unique species of Disney thrill ride, though it borrows elements of The Haunted Mansion at Disneyland Park. The story is that you're touring a once-famous Hollywood hotel gone to ruin. As at Star Tours, the queuing area integrates guests into the adventure as they pass through the hotel's once-opulent public rooms. From the lobby, guests are escorted into the hotel's library, where Rod Serling, speaking on an old black-and-white television, greets the guests and introduces the plot.

The Tower of Terror is a whopper at 13-plus stories tall. It breaks tradition in terms of visually isolating themed areas. The entire park is visible from the top, but you have to look quickly!

The ride vehicle, one of the hotel's service elevators, takes guests to see the haunted hostelry. The tour begins innocuously, but at about the fifth floor things get pretty weird. You have entered The Twilight Zone. Guests are subjected to a full range of special effects as they encounter unexpected horrors and optical illusions. The climax of the adventure occurs when the elevator reaches the 13th floor and the cable snaps.

DCA's Tower of Terror is very similar to the Walt Disney World version, but they are definitely not clones. In Florida, you start by slowly approaching the tower through mood-setting decayed gardens, while in DCA you simply step off the street and through the hotel's front door. From there, the adventure begins the same way—you pass through the hotel lobby and into the library for the preshow, after which you enter the boarding area. DCA's boiler room is much bigger with colorful (that is, less creepy) lighting, and it's decorated with additional insider nods to the original TV series.

Once you're on the elevator, however, the two attractions really part company. In the Disney World version, the elevator stops at a couple of floors to reveal some eerie visuals, but then actually moves out of the shaft onto one of the floors. The effects during this brief sojourn are remarkable, and more remarkable still is that you don't know that you've reentered the shaft until the elevator speeds skyward. In the DCA Tower of Terror, the elevator never leaves the shaft. The visuals and special effects are equally compelling, especially the unique ghostly mirror not found in Orlando, but there's never that feeling of disorientation that distinguishes the Florida attraction. The DCA Tower of Terror is more straightforward, and consequently a little less mysterious. Once the elevator dropping ensues, both versions are similar, but Florida features multiple randomized drop profiles, making each re-ride a surprise, while every stay in DCA's hotel is the same. Regardless of which version you try, unless you're already fanatically familiar with the superior original, you're unlikely to be disappointed.

The Tower has great potential for terrifying young children and rattling more mature visitors. If you have teenagers in your party, use them as experimental probes—if they report back that they really, really liked it, run as fast as you can in the opposite direction. Seriously, avoid assuming this attraction isn't for you. A senior from the United Kingdom tried The Tower of Terror and liked it very much, writing:

> I was thankful I read your review of The Tower of Terror, or I would certainly have avoided it. As you say, it is so full of magnificent detail that it is worth riding, even if you don't fancy the drops involved.

TOURING TIPS Because of its height, the tower is a veritable beacon, visible from outside the park and luring curious guests as soon as they enter. Because of the attraction's popularity with schoolkids, teens, and young adults, you can count on a footrace to get there when the park opens. The tower used to be mobbed most of the day, but newer attractions such as Toy Story Midway Mania! and The Little Mermaid have siphoned away some of the lines.

To access The Tower of Terror, bear left from the park entrance into the Hollywood Pictures Backlot. Continue straight to the Hyperion Theater and then turn right. To save time, when you enter the library waiting area, stand in the far back corner across from the door where you entered and at the opposite end of the room from the TV. When the doors to the loading area open, you'll be one of the first admitted.

A BUG'S LAND

THIS DISTRICT IS DISNEY'S RESPONSE to complaints that DCA lacked appeal for younger children. A bug's land incorporates the vestiges of Bountiful Valley Farm, which celebrated California's agri-business, into a bug's-eye world of giant objects, children's rides, and the *It's Tough to Be a Bug!* attraction.

Flik's Fun Fair ★★★½

APPEAL BY AGE	PRESCHOOL ★★★★½	GRADE SCHOOL ★★★★½	TEENS ★★
YOUNG ADULTS ★★★		OVER 30 ★★★	SENIORS ★★★½

What it is Children's rides and play areas. **Scope and scale** Minor attraction. **When to go** Before 11:30 a.m. for the rides; anytime for the play areas. **Special comments** Preschool heaven. **Duration of tour** About 50 minutes for a comprehensive visit.

DESCRIPTION AND COMMENTS   Flik's Fun Fair is a children's park as seen through the eyes of an insect. Children can wander among 20-foot-tall blades of grass, tunnel-size garden hoses, an enormous anthill, and the like. Princess Dot's Puddle Park is a kid's water-maze play area fashioned from giant-size garden sprinklers (we're not making this up). Kiddie rides include Flik's Flyers, with a balloon-ride theme; a drive-it-yourself car ride called Tuck and Roll's Drive 'Em Buggies; Heimlich's Chew Chew Train, a miniature-train ride; and a mini–Mad Tea Party ride titled Francis' Lady-bug Boogie, where you can spin your own "ladybug."

TOURING TIPS   Though they're colorful and magnetically alluring to the under-8 crowd, all of the rides are low capacity, slow loading, and ridiculously brief. Our advice is to ride them before 11 a.m. if you visit on a weekend or during the summer. The play areas can be enjoyed anytime, but then you're faced with the prospect of the kids caterwauling to get on the rides.

Following is the relevant data on the kiddie rides (note that waiting times are per 50 people ahead of you as opposed to the usual 100 people):

FLIK'S FLYERS *(suspended "baskets" swing around a central axis)*
   Ride time   Almost 1½ minutes
   Average wait in line per 50 people ahead of you   6 minutes

FRANCIS' LADYBUG BOOGIE *(adaptation of the Mad Tea Party)*
   Special comments   Unlike most teacup-style rides, turning the center wheel won't spin you faster. Instead, squeeze together on one side of the car and lean your weight into the turns.
   Ride time   1 minute
   Average wait in line per 50 people ahead of you   8 minutes

HEIMLICH'S CHEW CHEW TRAIN *(train ride)*
   Special comments   Adults as well as children can ride and should enjoy the surreal narration and scent effects.
   Ride time   Almost 2 minutes
   Average wait in line per 50 people ahead of you   5 minutes

TUCK AND ROLL'S DRIVE 'EM BUGGIES *(bumper cars)*
   Special comments   Adults as well as children can ride. Cars are much slower than on normal bumper-car rides.
   Ride time   Almost 2 minutes
   Average wait in line per 50 people ahead of you   12 minutes

It's Tough to Be a Bug! ★★★★

What it is 3-D movie. **Scope and scale** Major attraction. **When to go** After experiencing DCA's better rides. **Special comments** 3-D effects and loud noises frighten many preschoolers. **Duration of show** 8½ minutes. **Probable waiting time** 20 minutes.

Dark   Scary   Loud

DESCRIPTION AND COMMENTS *It's Tough to Be a Bug!* is an uproarious 3-D film about the difficulties of being a very small creature and features some of the characters from the Disney/Pixar film *a bug's life*. *It's Tough to Be a Bug!* is similar to *Captain EO* at Disneyland Park in that it combines a 3-D film with an arsenal of tactile and visual special effects. In our view, the special effects are a bit overdone and the film somewhat disjointed. Even so, we rate the *Bug* as not to be missed.

TOURING TIPS Because it's situated in one of the sleepier themed areas, *Bug* is not usually under attack from the hordes until late morning. This should make *It's Tough to Be a Bug!* the easiest of the park's top attractions to see.

Be advised that *It's Tough to Be a Bug!* is very intense and that the special effects will do a number on young children as well as anyone who is squeamish about insects. Check out the following comments from readers who saw *It's Tough to Be a Bug!* at Walt Disney World. First, from a mother of two from Mobile, Alabama:

> *It's Tough to Be a Bug! was too intense for any kid. Our boys are 5 and 7 [years old], and they were scared to death. They love bugs, and they hated this movie. All of the kids in the theater were screaming and crying. I felt like a terrible mother for taking them into this movie. It is billed as a bug movie for kids, but nothing about it is for kids.*

But a Williamsville, New York, woman had it even worse:

> *We almost lost the girls to any further Disney magic due to the 3-D movie* It's Tough to Be a Bug! *It was their first Disney experience, and almost their last. The story line was nebulous and difficult to follow—all they were aware of was the torture of sitting in a darkened theater being overrun with bugs. Total chaos, the likes of which I've never experienced, was breaking out around us. The 11-year-old refused to talk for 20 minutes after the fiasco, and the 3½-year-old wanted to go home—not back to the hotel, but home.*

Most readers, however, loved the movie, including this mom from Brentwood, Tennessee:

> *It's intense like* Honey, I Shrunk the Audience *but mostly funny. The bugs are cartoonlike instead of realistic and icky, so I can't understand what all the fuss is about. Disney has conditioned us to think of rodents as cute, so kids think nothing of walking up to a mouse the size of a portable toilet but go nuts over some cartoon bugs. Get a grip!*

PARADISE PIER

WRAPPED AROUND THE SOUTHERN SHORE of the kidney-shaped lake, Paradise Pier is Disney's version of a Victorian-era seaside amusement park from the 1920s. It covers about one-third of Disney California Adventure and contains about half of the attractions.

Paradise Pier was the focal point during the early phases of the refurbishment activity being completed at DCA. The biggest addition was Disney's *World of Color Nighttime Spectacular,* an evening show complete with more than a thousand water fountains shooting water hundreds of feet into the sky, synchronized to music and Disney film clips. A new *Little Mermaid*–themed dark ride, as well as the removal or retheming of several existing attractions and restaurants, rounded out the rehabilitation of an area that was once widely considered an eyesore.

Paradise Pier's original tacky mid-20th-century theme at DCA was ironic, and in a perverse way it brought the story of Walt Disney and Disneyland full circle. Walt, you see, created Disneyland Park as an alternative to parks such as this—parks with a carnival atmosphere, simple midway rides, carny games, and amply available wine, beer, and liquor. Amazingly, corporate Disney had made just such a place the centerpiece of Disneyland's sister park, slaughtering in effect one of the last of Walt's sacred cows. The refurb's clapboard buildings and retro carnival games gave the area much-needed charm, but not everything is perfect in Paradise; the now-removed Maliboomer tower was supposed to become a lush park, but it turned out to be a few benches on concrete and a patch of green behind barricades to gaze at longingly. The foregoing notwithstanding, Paradise Pier is spotlessly clean, exciting during the day, and eye-popping in the evening with all its colorful lights.

Note: Many of the attractions in Paradise Pier will close early for *World of Color* performances.

California Screamin' (Fastpass) ★★★★

APPEAL BY AGE	PRESCHOOL ★½	GRADE SCHOOL ★★	TEENS ★★★★★
YOUNG ADULTS ★★★★½		OVER 30 ★★★★★	SENIORS ★★★½

What it is Big, bad roller coaster. **Scope and scale** Super-headliner. **When to go** Ride first thing in the morning, or use Fastpass. **Special comments** Long and smooth; may induce motion sickness; must be 48" tall to ride; switching-off option provided (see page 150). **Duration of ride** 2½ minutes. **Loading speed** Moderate–fast.

Scary   Lose Things   Queasy

DESCRIPTION AND COMMENTS This apparently antiquated wooden monster is actually a modern steel coaster, and at 6,800 feet, it's the second longest in the United States. California Screamin' gets off to a 0-to-55-mph start by launching you up the first hill like a jet fighter plane off the deck of a carrier (albeit with different technology). From here you will experience tight turns followed by a second launch that sends you over the crest of a 110-foot hill with a 107-foot drop on the far side. Next, you bank and complete an elliptical loop. A diving turn followed by a series of camelbacks brings you back to the station. Speakers play a synchronized soundtrack complete with recorded canned screaming and a carnival barker cameo by actor Neil Patrick Harris.

We were impressed by the length of the course and the smoothness of the ride. From beginning to end, the ride is about 2½ minutes, with 2 minutes of actual ride time. En route the coaster slows enough on curves and on transition hills to let you take in the nice view. On the scary-o-meter, Screamin' is certainly worse than Space Mountain but doesn't really compare with some of the steel coasters at nearby Magic Mountain. What Screamin' loses in fright potential, however, it makes up for in variety. Along its course, Disney has placed every known curve, hill, dip, and loop in roller-coaster design.

A Carlsbad, California, woman found the roller coaster to be a smooth operator:

> California Screamin' was WONDERFUL, and I am a 57-year-old mom, not an adrenaline-crazed young adult! It was my first ever upside-down ride, but it was so smooth and quick [that] I only felt a gentle pressure pushing me into the seat. It was so fun [that] I went again! Don't miss this one, at any age!

TOURING TIPS California Screamin' is a serious coaster, a coaster that makes Space Mountain look like Dumbo. Secure any hats, cameras, eyeglasses, or anything else that might be ripped from your person during the ride. Stay away completely if you're prone to motion sickness.

Engineered to run several trains at once, California Screamin' does a better job than any roller coaster we've seen at handling crowds, at least when the attraction is running at full capacity. The coaster is sometimes shut down two or more times a day for technical problems. Early in the morning, however, it's usually easy to get two or three rides under your belt in about 15 minutes. Ride in the first hour the park is open or use Fastpass or the singles line.

Golden Zephyr ★★

APPEAL BY AGE	PRESCHOOL ★★★★	GRADE SCHOOL ★★½	TEENS ★★½
YOUNG ADULTS ★½	OVER 30 ★★½		SENIORS ★★

What it is Zephyrs spinning around a central tower. **Scope and scale** Minor attraction. **When to go** The first 90 minutes the park is open or just before closing. **Special comments** Totally redundant; can't operate on breezy days. **Duration of ride** About 2½ minutes. **Loading speed** Slow.

Queasy

DESCRIPTION AND COMMENTS First, a zephyr is a term often associated with blimps. On this attraction, the zephyrs look like open-cockpit rockets. In any event, each zephyr holds about a dozen guests and spins around a central axis with enough centrifugal force to lay the zephyr partially on its side. As it turns out, the Golden Zephyrs are very touchy, as zephyrs go: They can't fly in a wind exceeding about 5 miles per hour. Needless to say, the attraction is shut down much of the time.

TOURING TIPS A colorful, beautiful attraction, it is another slow-loading cycle ride. Go during the 90 minutes the park is open or prepare for a long wait.

Goofy's Sky School (Fastpass) ★★★

APPEAL BY AGE   Too new to rate

What it is Disney's version of a Wild (or Mad) Mouse ride. Scope and scale Major attraction. When to go During the first hour the park is open. Special comments Space Mountain with the lights on; may induce motion sickness; a rethem-ing of Mulholland Madness, the previous ride in this location; must be 42" tall to ride; switching-off option provided (see page 150). Duration of ride About 1½ minutes. Loading speed Slow–moderate.

Scary   Lose Things   Lose Things

DESCRIPTION AND COMMENTS Themed as Goofy teaching a bunch of new pilots how to fly, Goofy's Sky School is a designer Wild Mouse (sometimes also called a Mad Mouse). If you're not familiar with the genre, it's a small, convoluted roller coaster where the track dips and turns unexpectedly, presumably reminding its inventor of a mouse tearing through a maze. To define it more in Disney terms, the ride is simi-lar to Space Mountain, only outdoors and therefore in the light. Goofy's Sky School is an off-the-shelf midway ride in which Disney has invested next to nothing in spiffing up. In other words, fun but nothing special.

TOURING TIPS A fun ride but also a slow-loading one, and one that breaks down frequently. Ride during the first hour that the park is open or use Fastpass.

Jumpin' Jellyfish ★★

APPEAL BY AGE	PRESCHOOL ★★★★	GRADE SCHOOL ★★★½	TEENS ★★
YOUNG ADULTS ★½		OVER 30 ★★	SENIORS ★★

What it is Parachute ride. Scope and scale Minor attraction. When to go The first 90 minutes the park is open or just before closing. Special comments All sizzle, no meat; can't operate on breezy days; must be 40" tall to ride. Duration of ride About 45 seconds. Loading speed Slow.

DESCRIPTION AND COMMENTS On this ride, you're raised on a cable to the top of the tower and then released to gently parachute back to earth. Mostly a children's ride, Jumpin' Jellyfish is paradoxically off-limits to those who would most enjoy it because of its 40-inch minimum-height restriction. For adults, the attraction is a real snore. Oops, make that a real bore—the paltry 45-second duration of the ride is not long enough to fall asleep.

TOURING TIPS The Jellyfish, so called because of a floating jellyfish's resem-blance to an open parachute, is another slow-loading ride of very low capacity. Get on early in the morning or prepare for a long wait.

King Triton's Carousel ★★★

APPEAL BY AGE	PRESCHOOL ★★★★★	GRADE SCHOOL ★★★★★	TEENS ★★★½
YOUNG ADULTS ★★★		OVER 30 ★★★½	SENIORS ★★★★

What it is Merry-go-round. Scope and scale Minor attraction. When to go

Before noon. **Special comments** Beautimus. **Duration of ride** A little less than 2 minutes. **Loading speed** Slow.

DESCRIPTION AND COMMENTS On this elaborate and stunningly crafted carousel, dolphins, sea horses, seals, and the like replace the standard prancing horses.

TOURING TIPS Worth a look even if there are no children in your party. If you have kids who want to ride, try to get them on before noon.

The Little Mermaid: Ariel's Undersea Adventure ★★★½

APPEAL BY AGE   Too new to rate

What it is Track ride in the dark. **Scope and scale** Headliner. **When to go** First thing in the morning or after 4 p.m. **Duration of ride** 6¼ minutes. **Loading speed** Fast.

DESCRIPTION AND COMMENTS The Palace of Fine Arts dome (former home of the Whoopi Goldberg–hosted *Golden Dreams* film) has been incorporated into an impressive new lagoon-facing facade modeled on early 20th-century aquariums. The seafoam-trimmed building, which is topped by a statue of King Triton, conceals Disney's newest old-school attraction. Opened in 2011, the basics of The Little Mermaid: Ariel's Undersea Adventure are similar to Disneyland's Haunted Mansion: A continuously loading ride system transports you through a series of elaborately themed, darkened scenes with sophisticated special effects. In this case, the Little Mermaid attraction takes you to the bottom of the ocean in clam-shell cars, where the ride recaps Ariel's journey from her father's undersea kingdom to marrying Prince Eric. After Scuttle the seagull recaps the back story for you, your vehicle descends backward beneath the simulated sea surface with a spritz of cool air. Assuming that you haven't drowned, you'll then meet a cutting-edge animatronic Ariel (featuring "floating" hair and synchronized lips); party down "Under the Sea" with Sebastian the crab; and be menaced by a 12-foot-wide, 7½-foot-tall undulating figure of Ursula, the evil sea witch. The adventure is all set to newly orchestrated versions of Alan Menken and Howard Ashman's classic songs, and original animator Glen Keane and actress Jodi Benson both returned to lend their talents.

DISNEY DISH WITH JIM HILL

THAT FISH IS KNOTTS SUPPOSED TO BE HERE   Keep a sharp eye out as your clam-shell cruises through the "Under the Sea" sequence in DCA's The Little Mermaid: Ariel's Undersea Adventure. When you get to Ariel and her swirly hair, look behind you to your right. There—hidden in the grass—you'll find a beautifully sculpted version of the cartoon character that Don Knotts voiced in *The Incredible Mr. Limpet*, a live-action/animated feature that Warner Brothers released in 1964. When I asked the Imagineers why they thought it was OK to feature a Warner Brothers character inside a Disney theme park ride, their response was, "If you'll look closely at one of the crowd scenes in the animated feature, you'll notice that Mr. Limpet is in the 1989 version of *The Little Mermaid* as well.")

Unfortunately, though the ride is colorful and kinetic, it suffers from shortchanged storytelling and several sections that feel unfinished. While it's a welcome addition to DCA's short roster of kid-friendly indoor rides, anyone expecting a modern-day classic to compete with Haunted Mansion and Pirates of the Caribbean (as the reported $100-million budget might suggest) will come away sorely disappointed.

TOURING TIPS   As one of the park's newest attractions and one that's suitable for most small children, expect long lines for The Little Mermaid as soon as the park opens. (On a positive note, this should reduce some of the early-morning demand for Toy Story Midway Mania!) This attraction does not have Fastpass. However, the Omnimover ride system is capable of efficiently handling more than 2,000 guests per hour, keeping lines moving swiftly even on busy days. Try The Little Mermaid right after Toy Story Midway Mania! in the morning or in the 2 hours before park closing. Disneyland Resort hotel guests may be offered early entry to this attraction, 30 minutes before the general public. This can lead to a long line in the hours after opening, so check back later in the afternoon.

Mickey's Fun Wheel   ★★

APPEAL BY AGE   PRESCHOOL ★★★★   GRADE SCHOOL ★★★★½   TEENS ★★★★½
YOUNG ADULTS   ★★★   OVER 30   ★★★½   SENIORS   ★★

What it is Ferris wheel. **Scope and scale** Major attraction. **When to go** The first 90 minutes the park is open or just before closing. **Special comments** The world's largest chicken coop; may induce motion sickness. **Duration of ride** 2 minutes. **Loading speed** Slow.

DESCRIPTION AND COMMENTS   Higher than the Matterhorn attraction at Disneyland Park, this whopper of a Ferris wheel tops out at 150 feet. Absolutely spectacular in appearance, with an enormous Mickey in the middle of its wheel, the aptly named Mickey's Fun Wheel offers stunning views in all directions. Unfortunately, however, the view is severely compromised by the steel mesh that completely encloses the passenger compartment. In essence, Disney has created the world's largest revolving chicken coop. As concerns the ride itself, some of the passenger buckets move laterally from side to side across the Fun Wheel in addition to rotating around with the wheel. Because it feels like your bucket has become unattached from the main structure, this lateral movement can be a little disconcerting if you aren't expecting it. If the movement proves too disconcerting, motion sickness bags are thoughtfully provided in each swinging car.

TOURING TIPS   Ferris wheels are the most slow loading of all cycle rides. Thus, we were very curious to see how the loading and unloading of the Fun Wheel is engineered. The Fun Wheel has a platform that allows three compartments to be loaded at once. The lateral sliding buckets are loaded from the two outside platforms, while the stationary compartments are loaded from the middle platform. Loading the entire wheel takes about 6½ minutes, following which the Fun Wheel rotates for a 2-minute ride. And speaking of the ride, the Fun Wheel rotates so slowly that the wonderful rising and falling sensations of the garden-variety Ferris wheel are completely absent. For our money, the Fun Wheel is beautiful to behold but terribly boring to ride. If you decide to give it a whirl, ride the first hour the park is open or in the hour before the park closes.

Silly Symphony Swings ★★★

What it is Swings rotating around a central tower. **Scope and scale** Minor attraction. **When to go** The first 90 minutes the park is open or just before closing. **Special comments** Simple but fun; must be 48" tall to ride. **Duration of ride** Less than 1½ minutes. **Loading speed** Slow.

Lose Things   Queasy

DESCRIPTION AND COMMENTS Originally opened as the Orange Stinger, with guests seated in swings flying around a giant citrus fruit, the ride was redone in 2009 as part of the DCA refurbishment and expansion. The new theme pays tribute to the 1935 Mickey Mouse cartoon *The Band Concert,* the first color Mickey cartoon released to the public, but the net effect is still the same. Ride junkies said that the Orange Stinger had good "foot chop," which essentially means that your feet come very close to the ride's walls. In the scary department, it's a wilder ride than Dumbo, but foot chop notwithstanding, SSS is still just swings going in circles. Lamentably, the height requirement precludes from riding those who would most enjoy the attraction.

TOURING TIPS This is a fun and visually appealing ride, but it's also one that loads slowly and occasions long waits unless you ride during the first hour or so the park is open. Be aware that it's possible for the swing chairs to collide when the ride comes to a stop—the author once picked up a nice bruise when an empty swing smacked him during touchdown.

Toy Story Midway Mania! ★★★★½

What it is 3-D ride through indoor shooting gallery. **Scope and scale** Headliner. **When to go** First thing after the park opens. **Special comments** Not to be missed. **Duration of ride** About 6½ minutes. **Average wait in line per 100 people ahead of you** 4½ minutes. **Loading speed** Fast.

DESCRIPTION AND COMMENTS Toy Story Midway Mania! ushers in a whole new generation of Disney attractions: virtual dark rides. Since Disneyland opened in 1955, ride vehicles have moved past two- and three-dimensional sets often populated by audio-animatronic (AA) figures. Designed by the Imagineers and constructed by skilled craftsmen, these amazingly detailed sets and robotic figures literally defined the Disney creative genius in attractions such as Pirates of the Caribbean, The Haunted Mansion, and Peter Pan's Flight. Now for Toy Story Midway Mania!, the elaborate sets and endearing AA characters are gone. Imagine long corridors, totally empty, covered with reflective material. There's almost nothing there . . . until you put on your 3-D glasses. Instantly, the corridor is full and brimming with color, action, and activity, thanks to projected computer-graphic imagery (CGI).

Conceptually, this is an interactive shooting gallery much like Buzz Lightyear Astro Blasters (see page 253), but in Toy Story Midway Mania!, your ride vehicle passes through a totally virtual midway, with booths offering such games as ring tossing and ball throwing. You use a cannon on your ride vehicle to play as you move along from booth to booth. Unlike the laser guns in Buzz Lightyear, however, Toy Story Midway Mania's pull-string cannons take advantage of CGI technology to toss rings, shoot balls, and even throw eggs and pies. Each game booth is manned by a *Toy Story* character who is right beside you in 3-D glory cheering you on. In addition to 3-D imagery, you experience various smells, vehicle motion, wind, and water spray. The ride begins with a training round to familiarize you with your cannon and the nature of the games and then continues through a number of "real" games in which you compete against your riding mate. The technology has the ability to self-adjust the level of difficulty so that every rider is challenged, and there are plenty of easy targets for small children to reach. *Tip:* Let the pull-string retract all the way back into the cannon before pulling it again. If you don't, the cannon won't fire.

Finally, and also of note, a new generation of "living character" AA figures was introduced in the preshow queuing area of Toy Story Midway Mania! A 6-foot-tall Mr. Potato Head breaks new ground for an AA character by interacting with and talking to guests in real time.

TOURING TIPS Much of the queuing area for Toy Story Midway Mania! is across the pedestrian walkway from the attraction's entrance. The queuing is covered, which is good, but it's not air-conditioned, which is very bad, with temperatures escalating into the 90s and higher. Not roasting in this oven is a great incentive to experience Toy Story Midway Mania! in the early morning, before it gets crowded.

As you might expect, Toy Story Midway Mania! is addictive, and though it's great fun right off the bat, it takes a couple of rides before you really get the hang of the pull-string cannon and the way the targets are presented. To rack up a high score, you must identify and shoot at high-value targets: Low-value targets are larger and easier to hit, while high-value targets are small and often moving. Toward the end of the ride, the top score of the day and the top all-time score are posted.

Toy Story Midway Mania! is one of the park's most popular attractions and gets jammed about 20–30 minutes after the park opens. If you're a newbie and you'd like to ride several times in order to gain experience and get your skill level up, consider making the attraction your first stop after the park opens.

The challenge of seeing Toy Story Midway Mania! without a horrendous wait is a hot topic among *Unofficial Guide* readers. First, from an English mother of three:

> We got to the gates well before the park opened, and there was already a long queue. My 4-year-old loved it!

From a Brentwood, California, family of five:

Be sure to include Toy Story Midway Mania! at DCA as a MAJOR attraction that you should RUN to right when they drop the rope. We walked quickly and were able to walk right on, but by the time we got off, the wait time was 40 minutes.

A couple from Minneapolis with two teens had this to say:

At DCA we found it essential to do Toy Story Midway Mania! as soon as the park opened. We got to the gate about 30 minutes before the official opening. At about 15 minutes before official opening, the gates were opened and signs directed us to a line for this attraction. Cast members assembled us at Grizzly River Run and marched us to Toy Story Midway Mania! so that we were right there when the attraction opened at 10 a.m. We were able to ride twice in 40 minutes.

CARS LAND

OPENING IN 2012, CARS LAND is the crowning capstone on DCA's transformation, and the first major "land" in an American Disney theme park devoted solely to a single film franchise. Tucked in the park's southeast corner on 12 acres of repurposed parking lot, Cars Land's main entrance is across from the Golden Valley Winery, though there are secondary gateways near the Tower of Terror and in Pacific Wharf. The Cadillac Mountain Range—topped with 125-foot-high peaks patterned after a 1959 Caddy Pinnacle tail fin—cradles Ornament Valley, home to a screen-accurate re-creation of Radiator Springs. That's the sleepy single-stoplight town along Route 66 populated by Pixar's anthropomorphized automobiles. Along its main drag, in addition to the three rides detailed below, you find eateries themed to the film's minor characters such as Fillmore's Taste-in, serving smoothies and healthy snacks; Cozy Cone Motel, with chili, popcorn, and corn on the cob; and Flo's V8 Cafe, serving burgers and milk shakes. Souvenir shops include **Radiator Springs Curios, Ramone's House of Body Art,** and **Sarge's Supply Hut.** Toys of Lightning McQueen and his petrol-powered pals have been flying off store shelves since before the 2006 debut of *Cars*, and sales have only accelerated with the release of a sequel in 2011. Once Cars Land opens, expect the area to draw large crowds all day, and even significantly increase DCA's overall attendance.

Luigi's Flying Tires

APPEAL BY AGE   Not yet open at press time

What it is Floating bumper cars. **Scope and scale** Minor attraction. **When to go** The first 30 minutes the park is open. **Loading speed** Slow (estimate).

DESCRIPTION AND COMMENTS Unless you are over the age of 50, you're unlikely to remember Disneyland Park's Flying Saucers, a long-lost Tomorrowland attraction that only lasted 5 years in the early 1960s. But

Imagineers have long memories, and have retreaded the concept of hovercraft bumper cars as the basis for a tribute to the Radiator Springs resident Ferrari fanatic. Passing an Italian garden of tire-shaped topiaries, you'll queue inside the Casa Della Tires shop (where Guido the forklift is on duty) before boarding your own supersize tire. Using a system similar to an air hockey table, your tire will lift up on a thin cushion of air as you scoot among teetering towers of (you guessed it) more tires, trying to bump against other riders.

TOURING TIPS   Luigi's will be a slow-loading cycle ride under the best circumstances, and its forefather, Flying Saucers, was notoriously unreliable. Even if this new version isn't a maintenance nightmare, expect long lines all day. A small playground out front should help tire out younger ones (pun intended).

Mater's Junkyard Jamboree

APPEAL BY AGE   Not yet open at press time

What it is Midway-type whip ride. Scope and scale Minor attraction. When to go The first 30 minutes the park is open. Loading speed Slow (estimate).

DESCRIPTION AND COMMENTS   On the outskirts of town sits the junkyard home of Mater, the redneck tow truck voiced by Larry the Cable Guy. In his yard sit 22 baby tractors, each towing an open-air two-seater trailer. While an animated Mater emerges from an oversize jukebox and sings a square-dancing tune, the tractors travel in overlapping figure-8 patterns along interlocking turntables. The vehicles are transferred from one revolve to another, creating near-miss moments much like Francis' Ladybug Boogie. The difference is that Mater's trailers swing freely from side to side, creating a centripetal snapping sensation similar to vintage whip carnival rides.

TOURING TIPS   Mater is the breakout hit character of the *Cars* franchise, and his namesake ride is visually attractive but slow-loading. Expect long lines from shortly after park opening. Near the entrance are some interactive musical instruments, sure to delight kids and deafen adults.

Radiator Springs Racers (Fastpass)

APPEAL BY AGE   Not yet open at press time

What it is Automotive dark ride with high-speed thrills. **Scope and scale** Super-headliner. **When to go** The first 30 minutes the park is open or use Fastpass.**Special comments** Must be 40" tall to ride; switching-off option provided (see page 150). **Duration of ride** About 5½ minutes. **Loading speed** Moderate–fast (estimate).

DESCRIPTION AND COMMENTS   At the far end of Radiator Springs's main street, the old courthouse doubles as the entrance for the most ambitious attraction built at Disneyland Resort in more than a decade. Disney's Imagineers have wedded an enhanced version of the high-speed slot-car vehicles developed for Epcot's Test Track with immersive sets and elaborate animatronics. The ride, which covers nearly 6 of Cars Land's 12 acres, mixes slow indoor sections with thrilling open-air acceleration in a way that will appeal to every end of the demographic spectrum.

You begin your road trip by walking through Stanley's Oasis, the town's original 1909 settlement, and end up in a cave filled with fender-shaped rock formations. There you'll board a six-passenger convertible, each with a smiling face on its front grill. After the sheriff gives you a few safety tips, you're off on a tour of Ornament Valley, on your way to compete in today's big race. Along the way, you'll be sidetracked by a tractor-tipping expedition with Mater, which leads to a run-in with an angry harvester. Before reaching the starting line, you'll need some new tires or a fresh coat of paint. Then it's time to line up alongside another carload of guests as you await the countdown. The last third of the ride is a flat-out race over camelback hills, past geysers, and around banked curves, with a randomly chosen car crossing the finish line first. Exiting your vehicle in Tail Light Cavern, you'll emerge into the gift shop and (if the concept art is even halfway accurate) immediately get back in line for another ride.

TOURING TIPS   As the $200 million big megillah of DCA's makeover, Radiator Springs Racers is expected to be a massive draw from the minute it opens. Luckily, the ride is reportedly engineered to handle large crowds, and Fastpass and single rider lines are expected to be available.

GOLDEN STATE

THIS DISTRICT CELEBRATES California's cultural, musical, natural, and industrial diversity. The centerpiece of the district is Grizzly Peak—one of the subdistricts within Golden State and yet another of Disney's famed "mountains" (with Boulder Bear at its summit). Surrounding **Grizzly Peak** are **Golden Vine Winery, Condor Flats,** and **Pacific Wharf,** home to bread-baking and chocolate-making factory tours.

CONDOR FLATS

SITUATED JUST TO THE RIGHT of the central hub, Condor Flats pays homage to California aviation. The pedestrian walkway is marked like a runway, and all of the buildings look like airplane hangars. Condor Flats is the home of one of the park's super-headliner attractions, **Soarin' Over California.**

Soarin' Over California (Fastpass) ★★★★½

APPEAL BY AGE PRESCHOOL ★★★★½ GRADE SCHOOL ★★★★★ TEENS ★★★★★
YOUNG ADULTS ★★★★★   OVER 30 ★★★★★   SENIORS ★★★★★

What it is Flight-simulation ride. **Scope and scale** Super-headliner. **When to go** The first 30 minutes the park is open, or use Fastpass. **Special comments** The park's best ride for the whole family; must be 40" tall to ride; switching-off option provided (see page 150). **Duration of ride** 4½ minutes. **Loading speed** Moderate.

Thumbs Up for the Whole Family

DESCRIPTION AND COMMENTS Once you enter the main theater, you're secured in a seat not unlike the ones used on inverted roller coasters (in which the coaster is suspended from above). Once everyone is in place, you are suspended with your legs dangling. Thus hung out to dry, you embark on a hang glider tour of California with IMAX-quality images projected below you, and with the simulator moving your seat in sync with the movie. The immersive images are well chosen and slap-dab beautiful, though scene transitions are jarringly abrupt. Special effects include wind, sound, and even olfactory stimulation. The ride itself is thrilling but perfectly smooth, exciting, and relaxing simultaneously. We think Soarin' Over California is a must-see for guests of any age who meet the 40-inch minimum-height requirement. And yes, seniors we interviewed were crazy about it.

TOURING TIPS Aside from being a true technological innovation, Soarin' Over California also happens to be located near the entrance of the park, thus ensuring heavy traffic all day. Because of its popularity, on days of higher attendance, Disney will sometimes begin admitting guests into Soarin' 30 minutes before the rest of the park opens. This alone should be incentive enough to get to the park early. Regardless of park opening time, Soarin' should be your very first attraction in the morning, or, alternatively, use Fastpass or the singles line. If you are among the first through the turnstiles at park opening, sprint to Soarin' Over California as fast as your little feet can carry you. If you arrive later and elect to use Fastpass, obtain your Fastpass before noon. Later than noon you're likely to get a return period in the hour before the park closes, or worse, find that the day's supply of Fastpasses is gone. Interestingly, while this ride is virtually identical to Soarin' at Epcot, the line for DCA's version moves much more efficiently.

GOLDEN VINE WINERY

THIS DIMINUTIVE WINERY situated at the base of Grizzly Peak and across from a bug's land is the smallest of the Golden State–themed areas. It would be a stretch to call it an attraction, much less a themed area.

Golden Vine Winery and Blue Sky Cellar ★★½

APPEAL BY AGE   PRESCHOOL ★   GRADE SCHOOL ★   TEENS ★
YOUNG ADULTS ★★★   OVER 30 ★★★½   SENIORS ★★★★

What it is Infomercial and exhibit about California wines. **Scope and scale** Minor attraction—exhibit. **When to go** Anytime. **Special comments** Quite informative. **Duration of film** 7½ minutes. **Probable waiting time** 15 minutes for film.

DESCRIPTION AND COMMENTS This Mission-style complex, squeezed into the side of Grizzly Peak, offers a demonstration vineyard. The rest of the facility, predictably, is occupied by shops, a tasting room, and a restaurant. Also located at the winery is the Walt Disney Imagineering Blue Sky Cellar preview center, a fantastic stop for the huge Disney fans in your group. It showcases the massive construction effort underway at DCA, including concept art, models, an interactive game, and a short film. The exhibit has been updated roughly every 6 months with the newest progress, but there's no word yet of what will become of the exhibit once the current construction wraps up in 2012.

TOURING TIPS The Blue Sky Cellar is a great way to kill 15–30 minutes. Make time to see this when you have some downtime, perhaps after a meal, while on the way back to Paradise Pier, or before watching Disney's *Aladdin—A Musical Spectacular.* Save the winery for the end of the day.

GRIZZLY PEAK

GRIZZLY PEAK, a huge mountain shaped like the head of a bear, is home to **Grizzly River Run,** a white-water raft ride, and the **Redwood Creek Challenge Trail,** an outdoor playground for children that resembles an obstacle course.

Grizzly River Run (Fastpass) ★★★★½

APPEAL BY AGE PRESCHOOL ★★★ GRADE SCHOOL ★★★★ TEENS ★★★★★
YOUNG ADULTS ★★★★½ OVER 30 ★★★★ SENIORS ★★★★

What it is White-water raft ride. **Scope and scale** Super-headliner. **When to go** First hour the park is open, or use Fastpass. **Special comments** Not to be missed; you are guaranteed to get wet, and possibly soaked; must be 42" tall to ride. **Duration of ride** 5½ minutes. **Average wait in line per 100 people ahead of you** 5 minutes. **Loading speed** Moderate.

Scary   Wet   Lose Things   Rough

DESCRIPTION AND COMMENTS White-water raft rides have been a hot-weather favorite of theme-park patrons for almost 20 years. The ride consists of an unguided trip down a man-made river in a circular rubber raft, with a platform mounted on top seating six to eight people. The raft essentially floats free in the current and is washed downstream through rapids and waves. Because the river is fairly wide with numerous currents, eddies, and obstacles, there is no telling exactly where the raft will go. Thus, each trip is different and unpredictable. The rafts are circular and a little smaller than those used on most rides of the genre. Because the current can buffet the smaller rafts more effectively, the ride is wilder and wetter.

What distinguishes Grizzly River Run from other theme-park raft rides is Disney's trademark attention to visual detail. Where many raft

DISNEY DISH WITH JIM HILL

BEARING UP   For more than a decade, guests floating through Grizzly River Run have heard those bruins a-growlin'. But they haven't actually seen any bears. All that changes in 2014 when the Imagineers take advantage of the development work they did for the Big Grizzly Mountain roller coaster, which opened late 2011 at Hong Kong Disneyland as part of its new Grizzly Gulch area. The Imagineers are looking to "borrow" some of the gags and audio-animatronic figures initially created for Hong Kong's thrill ride, so the bears can begin appearing along the shoreline of DCA's white-water raft ride. Which means that you're finally going to see some grizzlies when you ride Grizzly River Run.

rides essentially plunge down a concrete ditch, Grizzly River Run winds around and through Grizzly Peak, the park's foremost visual icon, with the great rock bear at the summit. Featuring a 50-foot climb and two drops—including a 22-footer where the raft spins as it descends—the ride flows into dark caverns and along the mountain's precipitous side before looping over itself just before the final plunge. As part of DCA's makeover, the ride's original extreme sports elements have been eliminated in favor of period-appropriate props supporting the new mid-century national parks theme.

When Disney opened the Kali River Rapids raft ride at the Animal Kingdom theme park at Walt Disney World, it was roundly criticized (and rightly so) for being a weenie ride. Well, we're here to tell you that Disney learned its lesson. Grizzly River Run is a heart-thumper, one of the best of its genre anywhere. And at 5½ minutes from load to unload, it's also one of the longest. The visuals are outstanding, and the ride is about as good as it gets on a man-made river. While it's true that theme-park raft rides have been around a long time, Grizzly River Run has set a new standard, one we don't expect to be equaled for some time.

TOURING TIPS This attraction is hugely popular, especially on hot summer days. Ride the first hour the park is open, after 4:30 p.m., or use Fastpass or the singles line. Make no mistake—you will certainly get wet on this ride. Our recommendation is to wear shorts to the park and bring along a jumbo-size trash bag, as well as a smaller plastic bag. Before boarding the raft, take off your socks and punch a hole in your jumbo bag for your head. Though you can also cut holes for your arms, you will probably stay drier with your arms inside the bag. Use the smaller plastic bag to wrap around your shoes. If you are worried about mussing your hairdo, bring a third bag for your head.

A Shaker Heights, Ohio, family who adopted our garbage-bag attire, however, discovered that staying dry on a similar attraction at Walt Disney World is not without social consequences:

I must tell you that the Disney cast members and the other people in our raft looked at us like we had just beamed down from Mars. Plus, we didn't cut armholes in our trash bags because we thought we'd stay drier. Only problem was once we sat down, we couldn't fasten our seat belts. The Disney person was quite put out and asked sarcastically whether we needed wet suits and snorkels. After a lot of wiggling and adjusting and helping each other, we finally got belted in and off we went looking like sacks of fertilizer with little heads perched on top. It was very embarrassing, but I must admit that we stayed nice and dry.

If you forget your plastic bag, ponchos are available at the adjacent Rushin' River Outfitters. Note that since the summer of 2010, the Grizzly River Run Fastpass booths have been partially taken over by *World of Color* Fastpass distribution. Depending on the day, all or half of the Fastpass booths are taken up by *World of Color*. The booths then slowly return to becoming Grizzly River Run booths as the *World of Color* Fastpasses have been fully distributed. The effect of *World of Color* has generally made Grizzly River Run more popular of an attraction, as well as getting a Fastpass a generally harder position, especially earlier in the day.

Redwood Creek Challenge Trail and Wilderness Explorer Camp ★★★½

APPEAL BY AGE PRESCHOOL ★★★★★ GRADE SCHOOL ★★★★★ TEENS ★★
YOUNG ADULTS ★★ OVER 30 ★★½ SENIORS ★★★★

What it is Elaborate playground and obstacle course. **Scope and scale** Minor attraction. **When to go** Anytime. **Special comments** Very well done; must be 42" tall. Plan to spend about 20 minutes here.

DESCRIPTION AND COMMENTS An elaborate maze of rope bridges, log towers, and a cave, the Redwood Creek Challenge Trail is a scout-camp combination of elements from Tarzan's Treehouse and Tom Sawyer Island. Built into and around Grizzly Peak, the Challenge Trail has eye-popping appeal for young adventurers.

Russell and Dug from Pixar's *Up* appear here daily to lead kids in a short but sweet Wilderness Explorer ceremony. Grab a map near the entrance and complete the self-guided activities to earn your own merit badge sticker.

TOURING TIPS The largest of several children's play areas in the park, and the only one that is dry (for the most part) and relatively shady, the Challenge Trail is the perfect place to let your kids cut loose for a while. Though the Challenge Trail will be crowded, you should not have to wait to get in. Experience it after checking out the better rides and shows. Be aware, however, that the playground is quite large, and that you will not be able to keep your children in sight unless you tag along with them.

PARADES *and* LIVE ENTERTAINMENT

Disney's World of Color Nighttime Spectacular ★★★★½ (Fastpass)

DESCRIPTION AND COMMENTS The 1,200 high-pressure water nozzles installed under the surface of DCA's Paradise Bay are the infrastructure for Disney's $75-million attempt to keep guests in the park (and spending money) until closing time. If you've seen or heard about the spectacular fountain show at the Bellagio in Las Vegas, *World of Color* is similar but larger, with more special effects and themed to Disney movies. The show includes a new musical score and incorporates dozens of Disney films and characters in its 27-minute performance. The show's backdrop includes Mickey's Fun Wheel, which was fitted with special lighting effects for use in the show. Giant projection surfaces sculpted by sprayed water—even larger than those used in *Fantasmic!*—display custom-made animations, and flamethrowers spew almost enough heat to dry off guests standing in the splash zones. What's most remarkable about the show is how the flashing colored lights and pulsating fountains combine to look like low-level fireworks. The effects are astounding, the colors are vibrant and deep, and the music includes some of Disney's best songs without being overloaded by overly sentimental ballads. But while *World of Color* is aesthetically entrancing, dramatically speaking it's a bit of a dud. Disney spectacles have never needed especially strong story lines, but *World of Color* is so plotless that it makes *Fantasmic!* next door look like a Russian novel. The show is essentially a 30-minute montage of movie moments with awkwardly edited segues straining to tie them together. Despite the show's titular association with Uncle Walt's 1960s NBC TV show, and the retro theme of DCA's overall rebranding, there's precious little vintage Disney referenced in *World of Color*. Aside from a brief cameo by 1937's *The Old Mill,* almost all the featured films are drawn from the last quarter century, with lots of mist-screen time given to modern Pixar heroes such as Buzz Lightyear and Wall-E, and footage from the fourth Pirates of the Caribbean film. There's also a handful of obscurities mysteriously tossed in: Was there a fan club somewhere clamoring for more of *Fantasia 2000*'s flying whales? Ultimately, there's enough dazzling eye candy to overwhelm any underlying emotional emptiness in the narrative. Finally, *World of Color* has more false finales than the last *Lord of the Rings* film, so stay put until you're absolutely sure that the show is over.

TOURING TIPS Entertainment value aside, *World of Color* is an operational nightmare. The effects were expressly designed to be viewed from Paradise Park, the tiered area along the lagoon in front of The Little Mermaid attraction. Unfortunately, only about 4,500 people—barely a quarter of the park's average daily attendance—are permitted to stand there for each show. Getting a decent view for *World of Color* requires time,

planning, and/or money, and therefore can alr
trouble to see than it's worth, but we still consid
couple from San Jose writes:

> Although the [World of Color] Fastpass line w
> ing for the show was horrible, the show itself w

If you want anything approaching a decent vie
you'll need a special Fastpass, the securing of which can be a.
adventure in and of itself. Here are your options for obtaining Fast
passes, beginning with the easiest (and most expensive) method:

World of Color Fastpasses are distributed to guests staying at Disney's
Grand Californian, Paradise Pier, and Disneyland Hotel in the Grand
Californian (near the exclusive entrance to DCA) 1 hour prior to the
park opening. You'll have to show a hotel key card to prove that you are
a resort guest before receiving your Fastpasses.

World of Color meal packages are offered by Ariel's Grotto and the
Wine Country Trattoria. The fixed-price meals run $40 per adult ($21
for kids) and include appetizer, your choice of entrée, dessert, and nonalcoholic beverages. Priority Seating reservations are a must, especially
during busy seasons (see Part 4 for dining details). After your meal,
you'll receive special Fastpasses for each member of your party, permitting entry into a VIP Preferred Viewing area reserved for dining package
patrons. Note that you don't actually watch the show from the restaurant, so you'll want to eat early enough to make it to the viewing area.
Though expensive, this is the only way to be guaranteed a central viewing spot with minimal crowding.

A counter near Wine Country Trattoria sells boxed picnics for $16
per person, including a light dinner, bottled water or soda, and a *World
of Color* Fastpass. Picnics can also be preordered online at **disneyland.
com** and may sell out on busy days. Wine or beer is available for an extra
charge, and you get a reusable *World of Color* tote bag in which to carry
your meals. Though served cold, the picnics are remarkably tasty; we
can vouch for the European cured meat and aged cheese antipasto, and
the Asian miso-glazed salmon and soba noodles. Kids pay the adult price
and can choose from PB&J or fried chicken. Even if you don't want the
food, many locals consider it worthwhile for the "$16 Fastpass" alone.
Note that the picnic Fastpasses do not entitle you to sit in the VIP section reserved for the higher-priced dinner packages.

Free Fastpasses are distributed on a first-come, first-served basis
from the Grizzly River Run Fastpass machines. Make sure that you get
passes for your whole party at once, or you may end up in different sections or showings. These machines are disconnected from the rest of
the park's Fastpasses system, so your *World of Color* ticket won't inter-
fere with other attractions. On busy days a queue forms for *World of
Color* Fastpasses before the park opens, and they may all be claimed by
early afternoon. If seeing the first *World of Color* show of the night is a
priority for you, we suggest getting a Fastpass within the first 30 minutes the park is open.

.ce you have your Fastpass, you'll notice that you've been assigned
of three color-coded sections. Yellow is the most central viewing
ea, red is to the right side (near the Golden Zephyr), and blue includes
the left side and and bridge. A special section is available upon request
for disabled guests, and a prime area in the middle is reserved for VIPs
and dining package purchasers.

Your Fastpass also includes a return time window. You won't be
allowed into Paradise Park before the start time, but the best viewing
spots will all be claimed shortly after opening, so don't be surprised
to see people lining up an hour before the area opens. Once inside
the viewing area, try to move to the front of an elevated area. You're
best off at the front of an elevated tier farther back, rather than at
the rear of a lower section, as these readers from Langley, British
Columbia, discovered:

*World of Color was great, but even with Fastpass it was hard for me
to see (wearing flat shoes and being 5'5"). My husband, who is 6'4", also
found himself bobbing around trying to see. When we got there, we had
good line of sight, but as people stood up and put their kids on their
shoulders, it became difficult.*

If you stand close to the railing, pay attention to the SPLASH ZONE
signs; on a calm night, you'll be seriously spritzed, and if the wind blows
the wrong way, you'll get soaked.

If all else fails, it's theoretically possible to view the show from various points around the park, but employees with flashlights will vigor-
ously shoo you away from all the obvious vantage points. The best
ticketless viewing spot is next to the Golden Zephyr, to the right of the
red section. You can see many of the fountain and lighting effects from
the opposite side of Paradise Pier, near the bases of Mickey's Fun Wheel
and Silly Symphony Swings, but the mist projections are illegible from
that angle, so we can't recommend it for first-time viewers. On nights
when there are multiple performances, you have better odds finding a
good spot for the last show.

After the show, if you are headed to the hotels or Downtown Disney, you can bypass the crowd at the main entrance by exiting through
the Grand Californian.

AFTERNOON AND EVENING PARADES Because of construction, DCA has
not hosted any parades for the past couple years. As renovations wrap
up, the former **Pixar Play Parade** (which featured characters from *Cars*,
Finding Nemo, and *Toy Story*) may reappear, or a new afternoon parade
may be announced.

DISNEY CHANNEL ROCKS! We can't fault Disney for trying to cash in
on the success of their Disney Channel pop musical programs, but
we wish that they'd find a more entertaining way of exploiting
Cheetah Girls and *Camp Rock* than this plot-free pageant, performed several times daily on a platform that rises out of Paradise
Park. The young adults who sing and dance their way through this

15-minute concert of songs from the Disney Channel's original movies and series give it their all, but Disney has saddled them with laughably "hip" costumes, simplistic choreography, and annoying "boys vs. girls" attitudes. The best performance is given by the *World of Color* water fountains that punctuate the opening and closing songs. The show does offer an opportunity for the younger crowd to dance along, and if you're a tween Jonas Brothers junkie who enjoys being exhorted to "pump it up!" at earsplitting volume, you'll be in heaven. Everyone else is advised to avoid.

ELECTRONICA To promote the release of *Tron: Legacy,* the 2010 sequel to the 1980s cult classic that introduced audiences to computer-generated graphics, Disney decided to throw weekend rave parties with techno music in DCA's Hollywood district. The evening kicks off with a short stage show starring an albino David Bowie impersonator. Guest DJs (many with authentic club cred) spin on a spectacularly lit sci-fi setup outside the Monsters, Inc. ride, attracting a crowd of often un-Disney-like dancers. A nearby soundstage becomes Flynn's Arcade, filled with vintage quarter-munchers from your youth, and the Muppet-Vision theater screens 3-D clips from the new *Tron* film. On certain nights, Laserman performs an expertly choreographed dance with laser lights and mirrors. There's even a TRONcore tag that is sometimes tacked onto the end of *World of Color* performances. At press time, ElecTRONica has proved remarkably popular, sticking around DCA much longer than the movie did in theaters. If the Blu-Ray sells well enough to warrant a sequel, ElecTRONica could still be running on select weekends for years to come. If not, don't be shocked if it's END OF LINE for this show by the time you visit.

HYPERION THEATER A state-of-the-art theater that hosts the best of DCA's live shows as well as special concerts and events. Check the daily entertainment schedule in the handout park map to see what's playing and for showtimes.

HOLLYWOOD BACKLOT STAGE This open-air stage that features small productions and Disney characters is one of our favorite venues in the park. Recently, the **Disney Dance Crew** has used this stage for a *So You Think You Can Dance*–style showcase of contemporary choreography. The dance remixes of Disney tunes won't be to everyone's taste, but watching Mickey Mouse (with blinking eyes and moving mouth) busting hip-hop moves is worth pausing a moment. Check the *Times Guide* to see what's playing.

STREET ENTERTAINMENT Unlike at Disneyland Park, where street entertainers appear on a more or less impromptu basis, most of DCA's street acts operate according to a specific performance schedule listed on the park *Times Guide*. The Miner 49ers, a bluegrass band that plays near Grizzly River Run, and the Delta Daddy-O's, a Hollywood-era doo-wop quartet, are both well worth your time.

DISNEY CHARACTERS Character appearances are listed in the daily *Times Guide*. In addition, Flik and Atta can usually be found at a bug's land, Chip 'n Dale hang out around the Redwood Creek Challenge Trail, Cruella De Vil makes appearances in the Hollywood Pictures Backlot, and Ariel's Grotto restaurant at Paradise Pier offers character dining featuring Ariel and her princess friends. Duffy the Disney Bear (a marketing creation imported from Tokyo DisneySea) greets guests across from Ariel's Grotto.

UNHERALDED TREASURES *at* DCA

TREASURE: Cove Bar | **LOCATION:** On the bridge to Paradise Pier

ARIEL'S GROTTO IS A FIXED-PRICE character-meal restaurant on the span connecting Paradise Pier to the Golden State area. Instead of heading downstairs to the restaurant from the entrance, though, go around the walkway. There, you'll find the Cove Bar, where you can enjoy a full-service bar and a small selection of food. For some, the thought of a cocktail at the end of a long day might be enticement enough, but this is a good spot even for teetotalers—it's one of the best places to enjoy the view. It's a bit too sunny during the day, but as the sun sets and the evening lights come on, the Cove turns into a mellow hideaway where you can enjoy a beautiful view of Paradise Pier. In the background, you hear music, laughter, and the occasional sounds of a roller coaster. You look out and see the small waves lapping against the pier that houses a brightly lit carousel—enough to make you forget that you're sitting in the middle of a completely artificial environment.

TREASURE: Redwood Creek Challenge Trail | **LOCATION:** Opposite Grizzly Peak

MAYBE A VISIT TO A THEME PARK was your kid's idea, and you prefer going on a quiet walk in the woods or enjoying a hike in a national park. If you just want to take a break from the hectic rush of a trip to DCA, hop over to the Redwood Creek Challenge Trail. Looking at the park map, you probably assume that this is just a playground designed for little kids, but the area is actually a good representation of a wilderness park. OK, so you don't really need to bring your birdwatching book, but there are various nooks and crannies, as well as a few "ranger buildings," that are very well themed (down to the wildlife books on the shelves). You could easily spend a portion of your day just enjoying the decidedly rustic feel of Redwood Creek.

TRAFFIC PATTERNS *at* DISNEY CALIFORNIA ADVENTURE

ONE OF THE PROBLEMS Disney had at DCA early on was that there was no traffic to create patterns. Attendance figures were far less than projected, though guests on hand did stack up daily at Soarin' Over

California and Grizzly River Run. On the relatively few crowded days (mostly weekends), the park didn't handle crowds particularly well. If Disney's gate projections had panned out, the park would have been in gridlock much of the time.

If you happen to hit DCA on a day of high attendance, here's what to expect. A high percentage of the early-morning arrivals will beat feet directly to Toy Story Midway Mania! and/or Soarin' Over California and then continue to The Little Mermaid and (on warmer days) Grizzly River Run. (Another reason why guests head to Grizzly River Run is to get Fastpasses for *World of Color.*) Once Cars Land opens in 2012, it should draw the lion's share of early-morning crowds. Other than The Tower of Terror and Monsters, Inc., the Hollywood Pictures Backlot is deserted, as are Golden Vine Winery, Pacific Wharf, and a bug's land until midmorning. As the lines build at Tower, Soarin', and Grizzly, and as guests begin opting for Fastpasses at these attractions, the crowd begins working its way into Paradise Pier. The super-headliner attraction Toy Story Midway Mania! has doubled the drawing power of Paradise Pier, and this has only increased since The Little Mermaid ride came online. California Screamin' sees its share of traffic, as locals in the know arrive to beat the crowd at the coaster and at the slow-loading cycle rides at Paradise Pier. By late morning on a busy day, you'll find sizable lines at most of DCA's rides. By noon or earlier, the ride queues are substantial and the crowds redistribute to the park's shows. *Disney Junior, MuppetVision,* and the Hyperion Theater each draw good-size crowds. By 2 p.m., the whole park is fairly socked in with guests, and even minor attractions and displays such as the sourdough-bread- and chocolate-making demonstrations build lines. Park departures increase significantly after 3 p.m., with lots of Park Hopper and Annual Passport holders heading over to Disneyland Park. By the dinner hour, crowds at DCA have thinned appreciably. As closing time approaches, long lines are found only at premier attractions. Guests with *World of Color* Fastpasses will begin queuing in the Golden State and Paradise Pier walkways an hour or more before showtime. The largest wave of departing guests occur at the end of *World of Color.* Just before closing, crowd levels are thin except, of course, at Soarin' Over California, The Tower of Terror, and The Little Mermaid; Radiator Springs Racers should be similar when it opens.

CALIFORNIA ADVENTURE 1-DAY TOURING PLAN

Before You Go

1. Buy your admission in advance (see page 19).
2. Call ☎ 714-781-7290 the day before visiting for official opening time.

At the Park

This touring plan assumes a willingness to experience all rides and shows. If the plan calls for you to experience an attraction that does not interest you, simply skip it and proceed with the plan. Height and age requirements apply to many attractions. If you have kids who aren't eligible to ride, try switching off (see page 150). This touring plan includes most of the amusement park rides on Paradise Pier. If you're short on time or wish to allocate more of the day to DCA's theatrical attractions, forgo a few of the rides in a bug's land. Because DCA doesn't participate in the early-entry program, crowds are smaller at DCA on Tuesday, Thursday, Saturday, and Sunday when Disneyland Park has early entry.

1. Arrive at the entrance 40 minutes before official opening time.
2. As soon as the park opens, ride Radiator Springs Racers in Cars Land (opens 2012). Save the rest of Cars Land for later.
3. In Condor Flats, obtain Fastpasses for Soarin' Over California.
4. Obtain Fastpasses for *World Of Color.*
5. In Paradise Pier, ride Toy Story Midway Mania!
6. Ride the California Screamin' roller coaster.
7. Experience Mickey's Fun Wheel.
8. If your party includes small children, ride King Triton's Carrousel.
9. Experience Goofy's Sky School if you have small children. If the wait exceeds 30 minutes, try again after The Golden Zephyr in step 23.
10. Head to Golden State and ride Grizzly River Run.
11. Head to Hollywood Pictures Backlot and ride The Twilight Zone Tower of Terror. Obtain Fastpasses if the wait exceeds 30 minutes.
12. See Monsters, Inc. Mike and Sulley to the Rescue.
13. Ride Soarin' Over California in Condor Flats using your Fastpasses.
14. Eat lunch and work in the current show at the Hyperion Theater, *Disney Junior,* or *Muppet-Vision 3-D.* Check the schedule for showtimes.
15. See the Disney Animation exhibit, including *Turtle Talk with Crush* and the Animation Academy.
16. Ride The Tower of Terror if you have not already done so.
17. Go to a bug's land. See *It's Tough to Be a Bug!*
18. If your party includes small children, experience Heimlich's Chew Chew Train, Flik's Flyers, Francis' Ladybug Boogie, and the Tuck and Roll Drive 'Em Buggies (in that order) at Flik's Fun Fair in a bug's land.
19. Also if you have small children, see Luigi's Flying Tires in Cars Land.
20. Next, ride Mater's Junkyard Jamboree.
21. Take the bakery and chocolate factory tours if time permits.
22. Ride Little Mermaid: Ariel's Undersea Adventure.
23. If time permits, experience the Redwood Creek Challenge Trail.
24. Also if time permits, ride the Golden Zephyr in Paradise Pier.
25. Check your daily entertainment schedule for parades, and check your *World of Color* Fastpass for the performance time.

PART SEVEN

UNIVERSAL STUDIOS HOLLYWOOD

UNIVERSAL STUDIOS HOLLYWOOD WAS THE FIRST film and TV studio to turn part of its facility into a modern theme park. By integrating shows and rides with behind-the-scenes presentations on moviemaking, Universal Studios Hollywood created a new genre of theme park, stimulating a number of clone and competitor parks. First came the Disney-MGM Studios (now Disney's Hollywood Studios) at Walt Disney World, followed shortly by Universal Studios Florida, also near Orlando. Where Universal Studios Hollywood, however, evolved from an established film and TV venue, its cross-country imitators were launched primarily as theme parks, albeit with some production capability on the side. Disney is also challenging Universal in California with Disney California Adventure. While DCA does not have production facilities, one of its themed areas focuses on Hollywood and the movies.

Located just off US 101 north of Hollywood, Universal Studios operates on a scale and with a quality standard rivaled only by Disney, Sea-World, and Busch Gardens parks. Unique among American theme parks for its topography, Universal Studios Hollywood is tucked on top of, below, and around a tall hill. The studios comprise an open-access area and a controlled-access area. The latter contains the working sound-stages, back lot, wardrobe, scenery, prop shops, postproduction facility, and administration offices. Guests can visit the controlled-access area by taking the Studio Tour. The open-access area, which contains the park's rides, shows, restaurants, and services, is divided into two sections. The main entrance provides access to the upper section, the Upper Lot, on top of the hill. Six theater shows and one ride, as well as the loading area for the Studio Tour, are located in the Upper Lot. The Lower Lot, at the northeastern base of the hill, is accessible from the Upper Lot via escalators. There are two rides (three when Transformers opens in 2012) and a walk-through exhibit in the Lower Lot. All attractions, including rides, shows, and tours, are profiled in this chapter.

The park offers all standard services and amenities, including stroller and wheelchair rental, lockers, diaper-changing and nursing

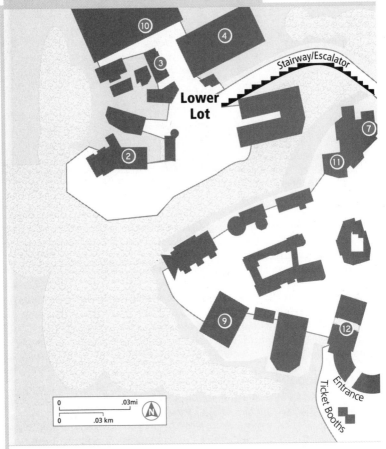

Universal Studios Hollywood

1. Adventures of Curious George
2. Jurassic Park—The Ride
3. The NBC Universal Experience
4. Revenge of the Mummy–The Ride
5. *Shrek 4-D*
6. The Simpsons Ride
7. Special Effects Stage
8. Studio Tour

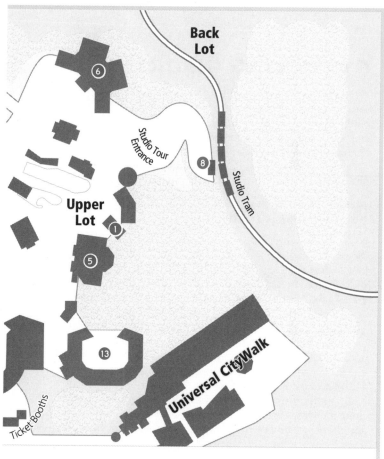

9. *Terminator 2: 3-D*
10. Transformers—The Ride
11. *Universal's Animal Actors*
12. Universal's House of Horrors

13. *WaterWorld*

facilities, car assistance, and foreign-language assistance. Most of the park is accessible to disabled guests, and TDDs are available for the hearing impaired. Almost all services are in the Upper Lot, just inside the main entrance.

GATHERING INFORMATION

THE MAIN UNIVERSAL STUDIOS information number is ☎ 818-622-3801. Calling this number, however, often results in up to 20 minutes of holding time or about 7 minutes on hold followed by a disconnect. If you have problems, try calling ☎ 818-622-3735 or 818-622-3750. While Universal Studios' website, **universalstudioshollywood.com,** is easy to navigate, obtaining information over the phone would try the patience of Buddha. To short-circuit the operating-hours litany, dial 3.

WHAT MAKES UNIVERSAL STUDIOS HOLLYWOOD DIFFERENT

WHAT MAKES UNIVERSAL STUDIOS HOLLYWOOD different is that the attractions, with a couple of exceptions, are designed to minimize long waits in line. The centerpiece of the Universal Studios experience is the Studio Tour. While on the tram, you experience an earthquake, are attacked by the killer shark from *Jaws,* and endure a simulated rain shower and a flash flood, among other things. In other parks, including Universal's sister park in Florida, each of these spectacles is presented as an individual attraction, and each has its own long queue. At Universal Studios Hollywood, by contrast, you suffer only one very manageable wait to board the tram and then experience all of these events as part of the tour.

In addition to the time saving and convenience provided by the tram tour, most of the live shows at Universal Studios Hollywood are performed in large theaters or stadiums. Instead of standing in line outside, guests are usually invited to enter the theater and wait in seated comfort for the production to begin.

TIMING *Your* VISIT

CROWDS ARE LARGEST IN THE SUMMER (Memorial Day to Labor Day) and during specific holiday periods during the rest of the year. Christmas Day to New Year's Day is extremely busy, as are Thanksgiving weekend, the week of Washington's birthday, spring break for schools and colleges, and the 2 weeks bracketing Easter. The least busy time is from after Thanksgiving weekend until the week before Christmas. The next slowest times are September through the weekend preceding Thanksgiving, January 4 through the first week of March, and the week following Easter to Memorial Day weekend.

SELECTING THE DAY OF THE WEEK FOR YOUR VISIT

WEEKENDS ARE MORE CROWDED than weekdays year-round. Saturday is the busiest day. Sunday, particularly Sunday morning, is the best bet if you have to go on a weekend, but it is still extremely busy. During the summer, Friday is very busy; Monday, Wednesday, and Thursday are usually less so; Tuesday is normally the slowest of all. During the off-season (September–May, holidays excepted), Tuesday is usually the least-crowded day, followed by Thursday.

HOW MUCH TIME TO ALLOCATE

ALTHOUGH THERE'S A LOT TO SEE and do at Universal Studios Hollywood, you can (unlike at Disneyland) complete a comprehensive tour in 1 day. If you follow our touring plan, which calls for being on hand at park opening, you should be able to check out everything by mid- to late afternoon, even on a crowded day.

Never mind that Universal Studios Hollywood claims to cover 400 acres; the area you will have to traverse on foot is considerably smaller. In fact, you will do much less walking and, miracle of miracles, much less standing in line at Universal Studios than at Disneyland.

UNIVERSAL STUDIOS HOLLYWOOD FOR YOUNG CHILDREN

WE DO NOT RECOMMEND UNIVERSAL STUDIOS HOLLYWOOD for preschoolers. Of 12 major attractions, all but 2 (*Universal's Animal Actors* and *Shrek 4-D*) have the potential for flipping out sensitive little ones. See the Small-child Fright-potential Chart on page 343.

COST

ONE-DAY TICKETS ARE AVAILABLE for about $77 for persons more than 48 inches tall and $69 for those less than 48 inches tall. A pass that allows you to skip to the front of the line at all attractions runs $149 for both adults and children. Annual passes cost $87 (with blackout dates) or $109 (without blackout dates) for all patrons over age 3 (add $30 for a pass with parking). Admission is free for those under age 3. By purchasing tickets online at **universalstudioshollywood.com,** you can buy 2 days' admission for the price of 1. Additionally, Universal almost always has some ticket special going online and at the park's ticket booths. You can print your tickets for $1 fee at the Universal website.

In addition to the website discounts, admission discounts are sometimes offered in area freebie publications available in hotels. Admission discounts are also periodically offered to AAA members. Vacation packages including lodging and park admission are available from Hilton and Sheraton hotels, both of which offer accommodations nearby.

In a groundbreaking initiative, Universal Studios Hollywood will issue you a rain check good for 30 days if it rains more than one-eighth of an inch by 2 p.m.

THE SHUTTLE

UNIVERSAL CITY is on the Red Line of **Los Angeles Metro Rail,** which makes it relatively easy to commute by light rail from downtown LA and many other places, though not from Anaheim. Across the street from the subway station and the bus stop, at Lankershim Boulevard and Universal Terrace Parkway, is a free shuttle bus that will conveniently take you to the main entrances of Universal Studios Hollywood and Universal CityWalk Hollywood. The bus runs 7 days a week, beginning at 7 a.m., with pickups about every 10–15 minutes; service continues until about 2 hours after the theme park closes. Refer to the posted times at each shuttle stop for information on the last departing shuttle. For rail and bus schedules and additional public-transportation information, call MTA at ☎ 800-COMMUTE or 213-626-4455, or visit **metro.net.**

ARRIVING *and* GETTING ORIENTED

MOST FOLKS ACCESS UNIVERSAL STUDIOS by taking US 101, also called the Hollywood Freeway, and following the signs to the park. If the freeway is gridlocked, you can also get to the Studios by taking Cahuenga Boulevard and then turning north toward Lankershim Boulevard. If you are coming from Burbank, take Barham Boulevard toward US 101, and then follow the signs.

Universal Studios has a big, multilevel parking garage at the top of the hill. Signs directing you to the garage are a bit confusing, so pay attention and stay to the far right when you come up the hill. Even after you have made it to the pay booth and shelled out $15 to park ($20 for premium parking, $17 if your RV is more than 15 feet long, and $10 after 3 p.m.), it is still not exactly clear where you go next. Drive slowly, follow other cars proceeding from the pay booths, and avoid turns onto ramps marked EXIT. You may become a bit disoriented, but ultimately you will blunder into the garage. Once parked, make a note of your parking level and the location of your space.

Walk toward the opposite end of the garage from where you entered and exit into Universal CityWalk, a shopping, dining, and entertainment complex (no admission required) situated between the parking structure and the main entrance of the park. As an aside, CityWalk is much like Downtown Disney at Disneyland. Some of Universal's better restaurants and more interesting shops are at CityWalk, and it's so close to the theme-park entrance that you can conveniently pop out of the park to grab a bite (don't forget to have your hand stamped for reentry).

Universal Studios' ticket booths and turnstiles are about 100 yards from the main parking garage. If you need cash, an ATM is outside and to the right of the main entrance. There is also an ATM inside the park next to the Cartooniversal store. Nearby is a guest-services window. As you enter the park, be sure to pick up a park map and a daily entertainment schedule.

THE UPPER LOT

THE UPPER LOT IS ESSENTIALLY a large, amorphous pedestrian plaza. In-park signage (which is inordinately confusing) references street names such as New York Street and Baker Street and place names such as Cape Cod and Moulin Rouge, but on foot these theme distinctions are largely lost and placement of buildings appears almost random. In other words, do not expect the sort of thematic integrity that you find at Disneyland.

Inside the main entrance, stroller and wheelchair rentals are on the right, as are rental lockers. Straight ahead is a TV Audience Ticket Booth, where you can obtain free tickets to join the audience for any TV shows that are taping during your visit (subject to availability).

Attractions in the Upper Lot are situated around the perimeter of the plaza. Near The Simpsons Ride (straight ahead) are the escalators and stairs that lead to the Lower Lot. The Upper Lot attractions are described in detail below.

THE LOWER LOT

THE LOWER LOT IS ACCESSIBLE ONLY via the escalators and stairs descending from the back left section of the Upper Lot. Configured roughly in the shape of the letter T, the Lower Lot is home to Jurassic Park and Revenge of the Mummy, both headliner attractions at Universal Studios Hollywood. In 2012 the new Transformers ride debuts down here, where Backdraft and the Special Effects Stages once stood. The Lower Lot attractions are described on page 339 following the Upper Lot attractions.

UNIVERSAL STUDIOS HOLLYWOOD ATTRACTIONS

UPPER-LOT ATTRACTIONS

Adventures of Curious George ★★★★

APPEAL BY AGE	PRESCHOOL ★★★★	GRADE SCHOOL ★★★★	TEENS ★★★★
YOUNG ADULTS ★★★½	OVER 30 ★★★½		SENIORS ★★★½

What it is Elaborate interactive playground. **Scope and scale** Major attraction. **When to go** Anytime. **Special comments** Almost overwhelming. Either set limits upfront or plan to stay all day.

DESCRIPTION AND COMMENTS The Adventures of Curious George has three interactive play areas. The first play area is a jungle-themed, two-story enclosure containing some 25,000 foam balls. Children

334 PART 7 UNIVERSAL STUDIOS HOLLYWOOD

(of all ages) can throw or (using air cannons) shoot the balls at each other. To add to the mayhem, an orangutan statue spits balls in all directions when irritated (and it's not hard to irritate him). The second area is also a two-story affair where the idea is to come as close as possible to drowning on dry land while fully clothed. There are geysers, water cannons, a rocket blasting water, and the periodic dumping of two 500-gallon water buckets (enough water to fill a 20-by-30-foot swimming pool). Some of the spewing, squirting, and dousing you can control yourself. Other soggy manifestations erupt periodically with little warning. Finally, a playground for children age 6 and under features slides, cargo nets, a climbing pole, and other assorted equipment.

TOURING TIPS The foam-ball extravaganza and the splash zone can be enjoyed by mischievous guests of any age. The balls neither hurt when they hit nor get you wet. As for the water playground, it's hard to participate without getting pretty soaked. Stay away on colder days, and bring a change of clothes on warmer ones. Be forewarned that even the toddler playground comes equipped with a set of little water jets.

The foam-ball palace and the drowning factory are both big places where you can lose sight of your kids in a hurry (or until they nail you with a foam ball or water cannon). Keeping an eye on your children at the toddler playground, by contrast, is easy.

Shrek 4-D ★★★★

APPEAL BY AGE PRESCHOOL ★★★★	GRADE SCHOOL ★★★★½	TEENS ★★★★½
YOUNG ADULTS ★★★★½	OVER 30 ★★★★½	SENIORS ★★★★

What it is 3-D theater show. Scope and scale Headliner. When to go The first hour the park is open or after 4 p.m. Duration of show About 20 minutes. Preshow 5-minute video. Probable waiting time About an hour.

DESCRIPTION AND COMMENTS Shrek 4-D is based on characters from the hit movie Shrek. A preshow presents the villain from the movie, Lord Farquaad, as he appears on various screens to describe his posthumous plan to reclaim his lost bride, Princess Fiona, who married Shrek. Lord Farquaad died in the movie, and it's his ghost making the plans, but never mind. Guests then move into the main theater, don their 3-D glasses, and recline in seats equipped with "tactile transducers" and "pneumatic air propulsion and water-spray nodules." As the 3-D film plays, guests are also subjected to smells relevant to the on-screen action (oh boy).

Technicalities aside, Shrek is a real winner. It's irreverent, frantic, laugh-out-loud funny, and iconoclastic. Concerning the latter, the film takes a good poke at Disney with Pinocchio, the Three Little Pigs, and Tinker Bell (among others) all sucked into the mayhem. The film quality and 3-D effects are great, and like the feature film, it's sweet without being sappy. Plus, in contrast to Disney's It's Tough to Be a Bug!, Shrek 4-D doesn't generally frighten children under 7 years of age.

TOURING TIPS Universal claims that they can move 2,400 guests an hour through Shrek 4-D. If true, that should keep things moving efficiently. Still, expect big crowds. Try to see Shrek before noon.

The Simpsons Ride ★★★★

APPEAL BY AGE	PRESCHOOL	GRADE SCHOOL ★★★★	TEENS ★★★★
YOUNG ADULTS ★★★★		OVER 30 ★★★★	SENIORS ★★★½

What it is Mega-simulator ride. **Scope and scale** Super-headliner. **When to go** First thing after park opening. **Special comments** Must be 40" tall to ride; not recommended for pregnant women or people prone to motion sickness. Switching-off option provided (see page 150). **Duration of ride** 4⅓ minutes, plus preshow. **Average wait time per 100 people ahead of you** 5 minutes. **Loading speed** Moderate.

Queasy

DESCRIPTION AND COMMENTS   In spring 2007 this ride, based on the Fox animated series that is now TV's longest-running sitcom, opened. Featuring the voices of Dan Castellaneta (Homer), Julie Kavner (Marge), Nancy Cartwright (Bart), Yeardley Smith (Lisa), and other cast members, the attraction takes a wild and humorous poke at thrill rides, dark rides, and live shows "that make up a fantasy amusement park dreamed up by the show's cantankerous Krusty the Clown."

Two preshows involve Simpsons characters speaking sequentially on different video screens around the line area. Their comments help define the characters for guests who are unfamiliar with the TV show. The attraction is a simulator ride similar to Star Tours at Disneyland Park, but with a larger IMAX-type screen more like that of Soarin' at DCA.

The story line has the conniving Sideshow Bob secretly arriving at Krustyland, the aforementioned amusement park, and plotting his revenge on Krusty and Bart, who, in a past *Simpsons* episode, revealed that Sideshow Bob had committed a crime for which he'd framed Krusty. Sideshow Bob gets even by making things go wrong with the attractions that the Simpsons (and you) are riding.

Like the show on which it's based, The Simpsons Ride definitely has an edge, and more than a few wild hairs. There will be jokes and visuals that you'll get but will fly over your children's heads—and most assuredly vice versa. A mom from Huntington, New York, had this to say:

The ride is lots of fun and suitable for all guests. I'm not a fan of wild motion [simulators], but I was fine on this ride. The field of vision makes it very engrossing, like Soarin'.

TOURING TIPS   You can expect large crowds all day. We recommend arriving at the park before opening and making the ride your first stop after passing through the turnstiles. Though not as rough and jerky as its predecessor, it's a long way from being tame. Several families we interviewed found the humor a little too adult for their younger children.

Special Effects Stage ★★★

APPEAL BY AGE	PRESCHOOL ★★½	GRADE SCHOOL ★★★	TEENS ★★★½
YOUNG ADULTS ★★★½		OVER 30 ★★★	SENIORS ★★★½

What it is A theater presentation on special effects. **Scope and scale** Major attraction. **When to go** Anytime. **Special comments** Predictable, but still interesting; may frighten young children. **Duration of show** 30 minutes. **Probable waiting time** 15 minutes.

DESCRIPTION AND COMMENTS Guests view a fast-paced presentation on special effects, with elements borrowed from both the old Special Effects Stages (formerly on the park's Lower Lot) and the *Horror Make-up* and *Disaster!* attractions found in Universal Studios Florida. Audience members participate in demonstrations of green screens, computer-generated imagery (CGI), and motion capture. For the finale, a volunteer is apparently attached to a flying rig (left over from the short-lived *Creature of the Black Lagoon* musical that once occupied this space) and sent sailing above the crowd. The educational content will already be familiar to anyone who has ever watched a DVD making-of documentary, and the thin through-line about a youthful digital-era director upstaging an aging analog artist may mildly offend viewers who still appreciate old-fashioned films that don't look like video games.

TOURING TIPS The best seats seem to be in the center of the theater, not directly up front. Or try the seats to the left of the stage.

Studio Tour including *King Kong 360/3-D* ★★★★★

APPEAL BY AGE   PRESCHOOL ★★★   GRADE SCHOOL ★★★★   TEENS ★★★★
YOUNG ADULTS ★★★★   OVER 30 ★★★★   SENIORS ★★★★

What it is Indoor-outdoor tram tour of soundstages and back lot. **Scope and scale** Headliner. **When to go** After experiencing the other rides. **Duration of tour** About 42 minutes. **Loading speed** Fast.

Loud

Scary

DESCRIPTION AND COMMENTS The Studio Tour is the centerpiece of Universal Studios Hollywood and is one of the longest attractions in American theme parks. The tour departs from the tram boarding facility to the *right* of The Simpsons Ride and down the escalator. (Note that there's also an escalator to the left of The Simpsons Ride, so don't get confused.)

The tour circulates through the various street scenes, lagoons, special-effects venues, and storage areas of Universal's back lot. The tram passes several soundstages where current films and TV shows such as *CSI* are in production and actually enters three soundstages where action inspired by *Earthquake, The Mummy,* and *King Kong* is presented. The Studio Tour was improved in 2006 with a robotic car chase from *The Fast and the Furious: Tokyo Drift* and the addition of sets and film-making demonstrations from *War of the Worlds.* Other famous sets visited include those from *Psycho, Jaws,* and *The Grinch Who Stole Christmas.* A simulated flash flood, long a highlight of the tour, was enhanced by increasing the volume of water used. A 2008 fire destroyed the New York Street section of the back lot, including the huge animatronic King Kong, the courthouse square from *Back to the Future,* and much of the contents of a video-archive storage vault. The back lot was restored more or less to its original appearance, but when King Kong returned in 2010, it was in a very different form. Instead of rebuilding the classic banana-breathing robotic monkey based on the 1976 version, the award-winning new *King Kong 360/3-D* is a virtual experience inspired by Peter Jackson's 2005 remake. Guests enter a darkened tunnel where tram-length curved projection screens transform into the jungles of Skull Island. A family of hungry V-Rexes decide to dine on your tour, and Kong himself swings to save you, with hydraulic lifts under the cars simulating the sensations of their tug-of-war. The experience is visceral and visually stunning, especially when seen from the middle of a row (sitting on the outside exposes the top of the screen, spoiling the illusion). At only about 90 seconds, *King Kong* is too short to be a satisfying standalone attraction, but it's a terrific addition to the overall tour.

As a great enhancement, all trams are equipped with high-definition monitors showing clips from actual movies that demonstrate how the various sets and soundstages were used in creating the films. In 2011 talk show host and former *Saturday Night Live* star Jimmy Fallon became the tour's pre-recorded host.

The great thing about the Studio Tour is that you see everything without leaving the tram—essentially experiencing four or five major attractions with only one wait.

TOURING TIPS Though the wait to board might appear long, do not be discouraged. Each tram carries several hundred people and departures are frequent, so the line moves quickly. We recommend taking the tram tour after experiencing the other rides plus the two theater-soundstage presentations on the Lower Lot.

Including your wait to board and the duration of the tour, you will easily invest an hour or more at this attraction. Remember to take a restroom break before queuing up. Though the ride as a whole is gentle, some segments may induce vertigo or motion sickness—especially The Curse of the Mummy's Tomb, inspired by *The Mummy* and adapted from the old avalanche-effect section of the tour. Finally, be aware that several of the scenes may frighten small children.

Terminator 2: 3-D ★★★★½

APPEAL BY AGE   PRESCHOOL ★★★   GRADE SCHOOL ★★★★★   TEENS ★★★★★
YOUNG ADULTS ★★★★★   OVER 30 ★★★★★   SENIORS ★★★★

What it is 3-D mixed-media presentation. **Scope and scale** Super-headliner. **When to go** First show of the day or after 4:30 p.m. **Special comments** Furiously paced high-tech experience; not to be missed; very intense for some preschoolers and grade-schoolers. **Duration of show** 20 minutes, including an 8-minute preshow. **Preshow** Short "promotional" video for Cyberdyne. **Probable waiting time** 20–40 minutes.

DESCRIPTION AND COMMENTS The Terminator "cop" from *Terminator 2* battles Arnold Schwarzenegger's T-100 cyborg character. For those who missed the *Terminator* flicks, here's the plot: A bad robot arrives from the future to kill a nice boy. Another bad robot (who has been reprogrammed to be good) appears at the same time to save the boy. The bad robot chases the boy and the rehabilitated robot while menacing the audience.

The attraction, like the films, is all action, and you really don't need to understand much. What's interesting is that it uses 3-D film and a theater full of sophisticated technology to integrate the real with the imaginary. Images seem to move in and out of the film, not only in the manner of traditional 3-D, but also in actuality. Remove your 3-D glasses momentarily and you'll see that the guy on the motorcycle is actually onstage.

We've watched this type of presentation evolve, pioneered by Disney's *Honey, I Shrunk the Audience* and *Muppet-Vision 3-D. Terminator 2: 3-D,* however, goes way beyond lasers, moving theater seats, blasts of hot air, and spraying mist. It creates a multidimensional space that blurs the boundary between entertainment and reality. Is it seamless? Not quite, but it's close. We consider *Terminator 2: 3-D* to be one of the best theme-park theater attractions in the country. The *Terminator* mythos has long since passed *Terminator 2: 3-D* by (with two more movies and a short-lived TV series), and the celluloid projection looks dated by digital *Avatar* standards. But the show still makes first-time viewers break into applause at the end.

TOURING TIPS Though not as popular as in years past, *Terminator 2: 3-D* still packs them in. On especially busy days the shows run almost back to back. The rest of the time, performances are scheduled according to the park schedule that's included with the park handout map. See *Terminator 2: 3-D* after experiencing the rides and *Shrek 4-D.* Families with young children should know that the violence characteristic of the *Terminator* movies is largely absent from the attraction. It has suspense and action but not much blood and guts.

Universal's Animal Actors   ★★★½

APPEAL BY AGE	PRESCHOOL ★★★★½	GRADE SCHOOL ★★★★	TEENS ★★★½
YOUNG ADULTS ★★★½		OVER 30 ★★★½	SENIORS ★★★½

What it is Trained-animals stadium performance. **Scope and scale** Major attraction. **When to go** After you have experienced all rides. **Special comments** Warm and delightful. **Duration of show** 20 minutes. **Probable waiting time** 15 minutes.

Thumbs Up for the Whole Family

DESCRIPTION AND COMMENTS *Universal's Animal Actors* features various critters, including some rescued from shelters, demonstrating behaviors that animals often perform in the making of motion pictures. The live presentation is punctuated by clips from films and TV shows. Of course, the animals often exhibit an independence that frustrates their trainers while delighting the audience.

TOURING TIPS Presented five or more times daily, the program's schedule is in the daily entertainment guide. Go when it's convenient for you; queue about 20 minutes before showtime.

Universal's House of Horrors   ★★★

APPEAL BY AGE	PRESCHOOL –	GRADE SCHOOL ★★★	TEENS ★★★½
YOUNG ADULTS ★★★½		OVER 30 ★★★	SENIORS ★★½

What it is A fun house–style walk-through of scenes based on classic Universal horror films, incorporating robotics, hydraulics, real people, smoke, and mirrors. **Scope and scale** Minor attraction. **When to go** Anytime. **Special comments** Not suitable for children age 10 and under. Switching-off option provided (see page 150). **Probable waiting time** 3–5 minutes.

Dark

Loud

Scary

DESCRIPTION AND COMMENTS This attraction is an extremely elaborate horror maze. It's quite similar to the walk-through haunted houses you see around Halloween. Basically, you walk in near darkness through the tight, winding corridors of Dracula's castle, occasionally coming upon a large set from the *Van Helsing* vampire-killing film (including a 50-foot bridge overlooking Frankenstein's monster while he enjoys a little electroshock therapy) or a more modern maniac such as Chucky or Leatherface. As you pick your way through the dark, there are lots of gruesome sights, disorienting devices such as mirrors, and worst of all, live people springing out of dark corners to startle you. If you don't like being startled but really want to see the attraction, follow some teenage girls through. The leaping, growling, menacing ghouls will expend lots of extra energy on the girls and be in a state of relative depletion when you pass through.

TOURING TIPS House of Horrors is located very near the main entrance to the park. It doesn't take long to tour (as the length of the experience depends on how badly you want out), and it can be gotten out of the way quickly. The only time things slow down is when a herd of guests clogs the entrance right after the adjacent *Terminator 2: 3-D* show lets out.

WaterWorld ★★★★

| APPEAL BY AGE | PRESCHOOL ★★★ | GRADE SCHOOL ★★★★ | TEENS ★★★★ |
| YOUNG ADULTS ★★★★ | | OVER 30 ★★★½ | SENIORS ★★★½ |

What it is Arena show featuring simulated stunt-scene filming. Scope and scale Major attraction. When to go After experiencing all of the rides and the tram tour. Duration of show 15 minutes. Probable waiting time 15 minutes.

Thumbs Up for the Whole Family

DESCRIPTION AND COMMENTS Drawn from the film *WaterWorld*, this outdoor theater presentation features stunts and special effects performed on and around a small man-made lagoon. The action involves various watercraft, and of course, a lot of explosions and falling from high places into the water. Fast-paced and well adapted to the theater, the production is in many ways more compelling than the film that inspired it.

TOURING TIPS Wait until you have experienced all of the rides and the tram tour before checking out *WaterWorld*. Because the show is located near the main entrance, most performances are sold out. Arrive at the theater about 30 minutes before the showtime listed in the daily entertainment schedule. Be careful where you sit; when this show says "splash zone," they mean it.

LOWER-LOT ATTRACTIONS

Jurassic Park—The Ride ★★★★

| APPEAL BY AGE | PRESCHOOL ★★★ | GRADE SCHOOL ★★★★½ | TEENS ★★★★½ |
| YOUNG ADULTS ★★★★ | | OVER 30 ★★★★ | SENIORS ★★★★ |

What it is Indoor-outdoor adventure ride based on the movie *Jurassic Park*. **Scope and scale** Super-headliner. **When to go** Before 10:30 a.m. **Special comments** Must be 46" tall to ride. Switching-off option provided (see page 150). **Duration of ride** 6 minutes. **Loading speed** Fast.

Scary

Lose Things

Queasy

Rough

DESCRIPTION AND COMMENTS Guests board boats for a water tour of Jurassic Park. Everything is tranquil as the tour begins; the boat floats among large herbivorous dinosaurs such as brontosaurus and stegosaurus. Then word is received that some of the carnivores have escaped their enclosure, and the tour boat is accidentally diverted into Jurassic Park's water-treatment facility. Here the boat and its riders are menaced by an assortment of hungry meat-eaters led by the ubiquitous *T. rex*. At the climactic moment, the boat and its passengers escape by dropping over a waterfall.

Jurassic Park is impressive in its scale, but the number of dinosaurs is a little disappointing. The big herbivores are given short shrift to set up the plot for the carnivore encounter, which leads to floating around in what looks like a brewery. When the carnivores make their appearance, however, they definitely get your attention. The final drop down a three-story flume to safety is a dandy, though not as impressive as its Orlando sibling.

TOURING TIPS You can get very wet on this ride, and extra jets enabled during hot weather practically ensure a soaking. Once the ride is under way, there's a little splashing but nothing major until the big drop at the end. When you hit the bottom, enough water will cascade into the boat to extinguish a three-alarm fire. Bring along an extra-large garbage bag and (cutting holes for your head and arms) wear it like a sack dress. If you forget to bring a garbage bag, you can purchase a poncho at the park for about $8.

Young kids must endure a double whammy. First, they are stalked by giant, salivating reptiles and then are catapulted over the falls. Wait until your kids are fairly stalwart before you spring Jurassic Park on them.

Jurassic Park stays jammed most of the day. Ride early in the morning after Revenge of the Mummy.

The NBC Universal Experience ★★★

APPEAL BY AGE	PRESCHOOL ★	GRADE SCHOOL ★★	TEENS ★★★
YOUNG ADULTS ★★★		OVER 30 ★★★	SENIORS ★★★

What it is Interactive walk-through exhibit. **Scope and scale** Diversion. **When to go** Anytime. **Duration of tour** 15–40 minutes. **Probable waiting time** None.

DESCRIPTION AND COMMENTS This exhibit features authentic props and costumes from many of Universal's most famous films—*Gladiator*, *To Kill a Mockingbird*, *Jurassic Park*, *E.T.*, *The Sting*, *Psycho*, and *Coraline*, just to name a few. Cinephiles will love it.

TOURING TIPS Never crowded—visit after you've experienced all of rides.

Revenge of the Mummy—The Ride ★★★½

APPEAL BY AGE	PRESCHOOL –	GRADE SCHOOL ★★★½	TEENS ★★★★½
YOUNG ADULTS ★★★★½		OVER 30 ★★★★	SENIORS ★★★½

What it is High-tech dark ride. **Scope and scale** Super-headliner. **When to go** The first hour the park is open or after 4 p.m. **Special comments** Must be 48" to ride. Switching-off option provided (see page 150). **Duration of ride** About 2 minutes. **Loading speed** Slow.

Dark

Scary

Lose Things

Queasy

Rough

DESCRIPTION AND COMMENTS It's kind of hard to wrap your mind around the actual attraction, but it pretty much lives up to the Universal press release, though the press release is generally incomprehensible. Here, quoting that press release, are some of the things you can look forward to: "authentic Egyptian catacombs; high-velocity show immersion system [we think this has something to do with very fast baptism]; magnet-propulsion launch wave system; and canopic jars containing grisly remains."

Of course the art of the press release is to create allure and excitement without actually spilling the beans. Actually, Revenge of the Mummy is an indoor dark ride based on the *Mummy* flicks, where guests fight off "deadly curses and vengeful creatures" while flying through Egyptian tombs and other spooky places on a high-tech roller coaster.

The queuing area serves to establish the story line: You're in a group touring a 1944 archeological dig of an Egyptian tomb when evil Imhotep decides to make another comeback. The theming includes authentic hieroglyphics and air-blasting "traps" as the queue makes its way to the loading area, where you board a somewhat clunky, jeep-looking vehicle. The ride begins as a slow, elaborate dark ride passing through various chambers, including one where golden treasures are offered in exchange for your soul. Suddenly the aforementioned "magnet-propulsion launch wave system" comes in. In more ordinary language, this means that you're shot at high speed straight forward into a minute of pitch-black hills and tight curves, dead-ending in an encounter with leg-tickling scarab beetles. We don't want to divulge too much, but the roller coaster part of the ride has no barrel rolls or any upside-down stuff.

After an all-too-brief backward section, the attraction anti-climaxes in a darkened dome, where the mummy moans and then blinds you with a strobe. Compared to Universal Studios Florida's ride of the same name, this abbreviated attraction severely disappoints with shorter drops, simpler animatronics, and no "Brain-Fire" pyrotechnics.

TOURING TIPS Revenge of the Mummy has a very low riders-per-hour capacity for the park's top draw. Your only prayer for a tolerable wait is to be on hand when the park opens and sprint immediately to the Mummy. If you can ride Space Mountain without getting sick, you should be fine on this.

Transformers

APPEAL BY AGE   NOT YET OPEN AT PRESS TIME

What it is Multisensory 3-D dark ride. **Scope and scale** Super-headliner. **When to go** The first 30 minutes the park is open or after 4 p.m. **Duration of ride** About 4 minutes. **Loading speed** Moderate–fast (estimate).

DESCRIPTION AND COMMENTS Hasbro's Transformers—those toy robots from the 1980s that you turned and twisted into tanks and planes—have been around long enough to go from commercial to kitsch to cool and back again. Thanks to director Michael Bay's recent movie trilogy, "Robots in Disguise" are again a blockbuster global franchise and in 2012, Transformers fans will finally have a theme-park attraction befitting their pop-culture idols. To do justice to the epic battle between good Autobots and evil Decepticons, Universal has harnessed the same ride system behind Island of Adventure's Amazing Adventures of Spider-Man ride. That's good news since Spidey, which broke ground by blending motion simulation and live effects with 3-D, is already acclaimed as one of the best attractions anywhere. Exact details are still under wraps at press time, but with high-definition video and towering animatronic figures rumored in the mix, we smell another groundbreaking hit.

TOURING TIPS Once Transformers opens (scheduled for 2012), it will draw heavy crowds to the attractions in the Lower Lot. The similar Spider-Man ride has a high hourly throughput, but if Transformers is as cutting-edge as Universal claims, it may suffer growing pains that kneecap its capacity. If it's running during your visit, ride immediately upon park opening or brace for a long wait.

LIVE ENTERTAINMENT *at* UNIVERSAL STUDIOS HOLLYWOOD

THE THEATER AND AMPHITHEATER ATTRACTIONS operate according to the entertainment schedule available with handout park maps. The number of daily performances of each show varies from as few as 3 a day during less busy times of year to as many as 10 a day during the summer and holiday periods. Blues Brothers impersonators offer a high-energy show in the Upper Lot near the front entrance. The instrumental track is prerecorded, but the show is a spirit lifter nonetheless. Look for the Doo Wop Singers belting out 1950s and 1960s harmonies near Mel's Diner.

DINING *at* UNIVERSAL STUDIOS HOLLYWOOD

THE COUNTER-SERVICE FOOD at Universal Studios runs the gamut from burgers and hot dogs to pizza, fried chicken, crêpes, and Mexican specialties. We rank most selections marginally better than fast food. Prices are comparable to those at Disneyland.

If you are looking for full-service dining, try **Wolfgang Puck's Cafe, Buca di Beppo, Wasabi,** or the **Hard Rock Cafe** in the Universal CityWalk

Universal Studios Hollywood Small-child Fright-potential Chart

Adventures of Curious George **Nature of the attraction encourages aggressive play. Getting soaked is a definite possibility at the Nickelodeon Splash section of the Zone.**

Jurassic Park—The Ride **Intense water-flume ride. Potentially terrifying for people of any age.**

Revenge of the Mummy—The Ride **Scares guests of all ages.**

Shrek 4-D **Special effects may frighten preschoolers.**

The Simpsons Ride **Motion simulator too intense for many children age 7 and younger tall enough to ride.**

Special Effects Stage **Some intense special effects. Shows how bloody fake wounds are created.**

Studio Tour **Certain parts of the tour are too frightening and too intense for many preschoolers.**

Terminator 2: 3-D **Extremely intense and potentially frightening for visitors of any age.**

Universal's Animal Actors **Not frightening in any way.**

Universal's House of Horrors **Frightens guests of all ages.**

WaterWorld **Fighting, gunplay, and explosions may frighten children age 4 and under.**

just outside the park entrance. Our favorite in the park is the **Hollywood Grill** burger joint across from *WaterWorld*. If you leave the park for lunch, be sure to have your hand stamped for reentry.

UNIVERSAL STUDIOS HOLLYWOOD 1-DAY TOURING PLAN

THIS PLAN IS FOR GROUPS OF ALL SIZES and ages and includes thrill rides that may induce motion sickness or get you wet. If the plan calls for you to experience an attraction that does not interest you, proceed to the next step. The plan calls for minimal backtracking.

Before You Go

1. Call ☎ 818-622-3801 the day before your visit for the official opening time. If you can't get through, call ☎ 818-622-3735 or 818-622-3750. On all numbers, press 4 for a live attendant.

2. If you have young children in your party, consult the Universal Studios Hollywood Small-child Fright-potential Chart on page 343.

At the Park

1. On the day of your visit, arrive at Universal Studios Hollywood 20 minutes before opening time. Park, buy your admission, and wait at the turnstiles. At the turnstile, ask an attendant whether any rides or shows are closed that day. Adjust the touring plan accordingly.

2. When the park opens, if Transformers is operating, take the escalators to the Lower Lot and ride it. Otherwise, head for the back-left section of the Upper Lot and experience The Simpsons Ride.

3. Take the escalators to the Lower Lot and make a hard right to Revenge of the Mummy.

4. Exiting the Mummy, experience Jurassic Park across the plaza.

5. Skip the other Lower Lot attractions for now. Return to the Upper Lot and take the Simpsons Ride if you missed it earlier.

6. Next see *Shrek 4-D*. Head toward the park entrance, bearing right before the turnstiles, to *Terminator 2: 3-D*. Note that *Terminator* sometimes runs back-to-back shows and at other times schedules shows at specific times as detailed in the daily entertainment schedule.

7. See the Special Effects Stage. Check the daily entertainment schedule for performance times.

8. Check your daily entertainment schedule for *WaterWorld* and *Universal's Animal Actors* showtimes. Plan the rest of your schedule around seeing these shows. Note that you should arrive at the theater 30 minutes before showtime for *WaterWorld* and 20 minutes before *Universal's Animal Actors*.

9. With your show schedule in mind, decide when you'd like to eat lunch and when you'd like to take the Studio Tour. Allocate an hour and 10 minutes for the tour (counting the 45-minute tour, coming and going, and waiting to load).

10. Return to the Lower Lot and check out The NBC Universal Experience. Return to the Upper Lot.

11. If you have time to kill between stage shows, check out Universal's House of Horrors and *The Blues Brothers* show. If you have children 12 years old and younger, try the Adventures of Curious George play area.

12. This concludes the touring plan. Spend the remainder of your day revisiting your favorite attractions or inspecting sets and street scenes you may have missed. Also, check your daily entertainment schedule for live performances that interest you.

APPENDIX

READERS' QUESTIONS
to the AUTHOR

QUESTION:

When you do your research, are you admitted to the park for free? Do the Disney people know you are there?

ANSWER:

We pay the regular admission, and usually the Disney people do not know we are on-site. Both in and out of Disneyland, we pay for our own meals and lodging.

QUESTION:

How often is the Unofficial Guide *revised?*

ANSWER:

We publish a new edition once a year but make corrections every time we go to press.

QUESTION:

I have an older edition of the Unofficial Guide. *How much of the information in it is still correct?*

ANSWER:

Veteran travel writers will acknowledge that 5%–8% of the information in a guidebook is out of date by the time it comes off the press! Disneyland is always changing. If you are using an old edition of the *Unofficial Guide,* the descriptions of attractions existing when the guide was published should still be generally accurate. Many other things, however—particularly the touring plans and the hotel and restaurant reviews—change with every edition. Finally, and obviously, older editions of the *Unofficial Guide* do not include new attractions or developments.

QUESTION:

Do you write each new edition from scratch?

ANSWER:

We do not. With a destination the size of Disneyland, it's hard enough keeping up with what is new. Moreover, we put great effort into communicating the most salient and useful information in the clearest possible language. If an attraction or hotel has not changed, we are very reluctant to tinker with its coverage for the sake of freshening up the writing.

QUESTION:

Do you stay at Disneyland hotels? If not, where do you stay?

ANSWER:

We do stay at Disneyland-area hotels from time to time, usually after a renovation or management change. Since we began writing about Disneyland in 1984, we have stayed in more than 40 different properties in various locations around Anaheim.

QUESTION:

How many people have you interviewed or surveyed for your age-group ratings on the attractions?

ANSWER:

Since the publication of the first edition of the *Unofficial Guide* in 1985, we have interviewed or surveyed more than 16,000 Disneyland patrons. Even with such a large sample, however, we continue to have difficulty with certain age groups. Specifically, we love to hear from seniors concerning their experiences with Splash Mountain, Big Thunder Mountain Railroad, Space Mountain, the Matterhorn Bobsleds, Star Tours, Indiana Jones, and Disney California Adventure attractions.

QUESTION:

How are your age-group ratings determined? I am 42 years old. During Star Tours, I was quite worried about hurting my back. If the senior-citizens rating is determined only by those brave enough to ride, it will skew the results.

ANSWER:

The reader makes a good point. Unfortunately, it's impossible to develop a rating unless the guest (of any age group) has actually experienced the attraction. So yes, all age-group ratings are derived exclusively from members of that age group who have experienced the attraction. Health problems, such as a bad back, however, can affect guests of any age, and Disney provides more-than-ample warnings on attractions that warrant such admonitions. But if you are in good health, our ratings will give you a sense of how much others your age enjoyed the attraction.

QUESTION:

I have heard that when there are two lines to an attraction, the left line is faster. Is this true?

ANSWER:

In general, no. We have tested this theory many times and usually have not gained an advantage of even 90 seconds by getting in one line versus another. The few rare exceptions are noted in the ride descriptions. What *does* occasionally occur, however, is after a second line has *just been opened*, guests ignore the new line and persist in standing in the established line. Generally, if you encounter a two-line waiting configuration with no barrier to entry for either and one of the lines is conspicuously less populated than the other, get in it.

AND FINALLY . . .

To end on a high note, consider this compliment from a Redding, California, reader:

Thanks to your book, this trip turned out much better than our last, so much in fact that I required only half as much Valium.

And so it goes . . .

INDEX

1-day Plan for Adults

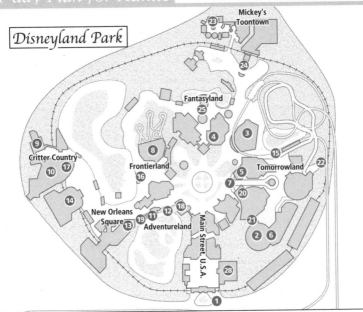

Disneyland Park

Mickey's Toontown

Fantasyland

Critter Country

Frontierland

Tomorrowland

New Orleans Square

Adventureland

Main Street, U.S.A.

1. Arrive at least 40 minutes before opening. Line up at Gate 13 and give all admission passes to one person.
2. Go to Space Mountain to obtain Fastpasses.
3. Ride the Matterhorn Bobsleds.
4. Go to Fantasyland and ride Peter Pan's Flight.
5. Return to Tomorrowland and ride Buzz Lightyear.
6. Ride Space Mountain using your Fastpasses.
7. Obtain Fastpasses for Star Tours.
8. Enter Frontierland and ride Big Thunder Mountain Railroad.
9. Go to Critter Country and ride The Many Adventures of Winnie the Pooh.
10. Obtain Fastpasses for Splash Mountain.
11. Go to Adventureland and ride Indiana Jones.
12. Take the Jungle Cruise.
13. Go to New Orleans Square and experience Pirates of the Caribbean.
14. Tour The Haunted Mansion.
15. The best way to ride Finding Nemo Submarine Voyage without a horrible wait is to ride during a parade, fireworks, or Fantasmic! Determine when one or another of these events

is scheduled, and join the line for Nemo 15 minutes before the event begins.
16. In Frontierland, ride either the Sailing Ship Columbia or the Mark Twain Riverboat.
17. Ride Splash Mountain using your Fastpasses.
18. Return to Adventureland and see the show at the Enchanted Tiki Room.
19. Explore Tarzan's Treehouse.
20. Return to Tomorrowland and ride Star Tours using your Fastpasses.
21. See Captain Eo.
22. Take Disneyland Railroad from the Tomorrowland Station to the Fantasyland Station.
23. Experience Mickey's Toontown if you have small kids.
24. Ride It's a Small World in Fantasyland.
25. Sample any rides in Fantasyland you missed earlier.
26. Check the Times Guide for parades, fireworks, and Fantasmic!
27. Visit any attractions you may have missed earlier.
28. See The Disneyland Story, presenting Great Moments with Mr. Lincoln.

Author's Select 1-day Plan

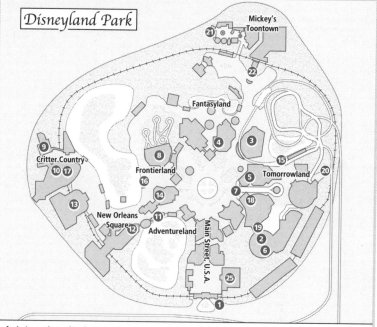

Disneyland Park

1. Arrive at the park at least 40 minutes before opening. Line up at Gate 13 and entrust all of your admission passes to one person.
2. Go to Space Mountain to obtain Fastpasses.
3. Ride the Matterhorn Bobsleds.
4. Go to Fantasyland and ride Peter Pan's Flight.
5. Return to Tomorrowland and ride Buzz Lightyear.
6. Ride Space Mountain using your Fastpasses.
7. Obtain Fastpasses for Star Tours.
8. Enter Frontierland and ride Big Thunder Mountain Railroad.
9. Head for Critter Country and ride The Many Adventures of Winnie the Pooh.
10. Obtain Fastpasses for Splash Mountain.
11. Head to Adventureland and ride Indiana Jones.
12. Continue to New Orleans Square and experience Pirates of the Caribbean.
13. Tour The Haunted Mansion.
14. Have lunch and see the show at the Golden Horseshoe Stage in Frontierland.

15. The best way to ride Finding Nemo Submarine Voyage without a horrible wait is to ride during a parade, fireworks, or *Fantasmic!* Determine when one or another of these events is scheduled, and join the line for Nemo 15 minutes before the event begins.
16. Ride either the Sailing Ship *Columbia* or the *Mark Twain* Riverboat.
17. Ride Splash Mountain using your Fastpasses.
18. Return to Tomorrowland and ride Star Tours using your Fastpasses.
19. See *Captain Eo.*
20. Take Disneyland Railroad from Tomorrowland Station to Fantasyland Station.
21. Experience Mickey's Toontown if you have small kids.
22. In Fantasyland, ride It's a Small World.
23. Check the *Times Guide* for parades, fireworks, and *Fantasmic!*
24. Visit any attractions you may have missed earlier.
25. See *The Disneyland Story,* presenting *Great Moments with Mr. Lincoln.*

Dumbo-or-Die-in-a-Day Plan

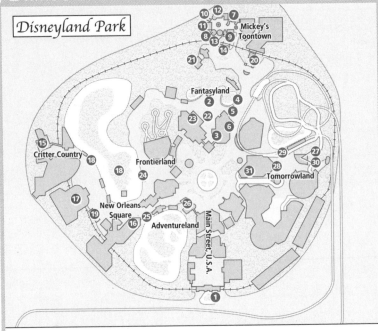

Disneyland Park

1. Arrive 40 minutes before the official opening time and line up in front of Gate 13.
2. Go to Fantasyland and ride Dumbo.
3. Ride Peter Pan's Flight.
4. Ride the Storybook Land Canal Boats or Casey Jr. Circus Train.
5. Ride the Mad Tea Party.
6. Ride Alice In Wonderland.
7. Go to Mickey's Toontown; try Roger Rabbit's Car Toon Spin.
8. Ride Gadget's Go Coaster.
9. Check out Goofy's Playhouse.
10. Tour Mickey's House and visit Mickey in his dressing room.
11. See Chip 'n Dale Treehouse.
12. Tour Minnie's House.
13. Check out Donald's Boat tied up next to Goofy's Playhouse.
14. Take Disneyland Railroad from Toontown Station to New Orleans Square.
15. Go to Critter Country and experience The Many Adventures of Winnie the Pooh.
16. Return to New Orleans Square and see Pirates of The Caribbean.
17. Experience The Haunted Mansion.
18. Take a raft to Tom Sawyer Island and explore.
19. Take Disneyland Railroad from New Orleans Square Station to Fantasyland.
20. In Fantasyland, ride It's a Small World.
21. Visit the Disney Princess Fantasy Faire at the Fantasyland Theatre.
22. Ride the King Arthur Carrousel.
23. Ride Pinocchio's Daring Journey.
24. Go to Frontierland and ride the *Mark Twain* Riverboat or the Sailing Ship *Columbia*.
25. Go to Adventureland and explore Tarzan's Treehouse.
26. See the *Enchanted Tiki Room* show.
27. Go to Tomorrowland and obtain Fastpasses for Autopia.
28. Check the *Times Guide* for parades and live performances. The *Jedi Training Academy* at the Tomorrowland Terrace is especially worthwhile.
29. Take the Disneyland monorail for a round-trip ride.
30. Ride Autopia using your Fastpasses.
31. Ride Buzz Lightyear.
32. Revisit favorite attractions or see others you missed. Check your daily entertainment schedule for parades, Fantasyland Theatre productions, or other live entertainment.

2-day Plan for Adults with Children: Day 1

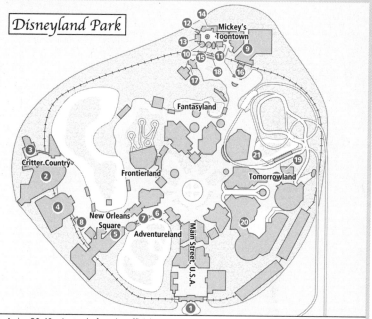

Disneyland Park

1. Arrive 30-40 minutes before the official opening time and line up in front of Gate 13.
2. Go to Critter Country and ride Splash Mountain.
3. Ride The Many Adventures of Winnie the Pooh.
4. Head to New Orleans Square and experience The Haunted Mansion.
5. Ride Pirates of the Caribbean.
6. Go to Adventureland and ride the Jungle Cruise.
7. Ride Indiana Jones.
8. Go from the Frontierland/New Orleans Square Station to the Fantasyland/Toontown Station on the Disneyland Railroad.
9. In Mickey's Toontown, try Roger Rabbit's Car Toon Spin.
10. Ride Gadget's Go Coaster.
11. Let off some steam in Goofy's Playhouse.
12. Tour Mickey's House and visit Mickey in his dressing room.
13. Enjoy Chip 'n Dale Treehouse.

14. Tour Minnie's House.
15. Check out Donald's Boat, tied up next to Goofy's Playhouse.
16. Go to Fantasyland and ride It's a Small World.
17. Visit the Disney Princess Fantasy Faire at the Fantasyland Theatre.
18. Take the Disneyland Railroad to Tomorrowland.
19. In Tomorrowland, obtain Fastpasses for Autopia.
20. Enjoy a performance of *Captain Eo*.
21. Take the monorail for a round-trip ride.
22. Return with your Fastpasses to ride Autopia.
23. Revisit favorites or see other attractions you missed. Check your daily entertainment schedule for parades, Fantasyland Theatre productions, or other live entertainment that might interest you. Return after 7 p.m. for a parade and *Fantasmic!*

2-day Plan for Adults with Children: Day 2

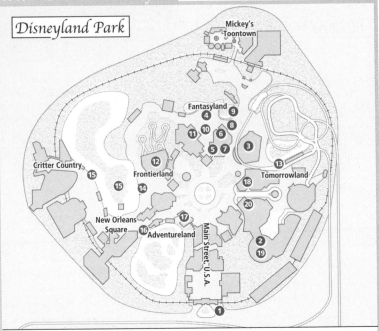

Disneyland Park

Mickey's Toontown

Fantasyland

Critter Country

Frontierland

Tomorrowland

New Orleans Square

Adventureland

Main Street, U.S.A.

1. Arrive at the park at least 40 minutes before opening and line up at Gate 13. Give all your admission passes to one person.
2. Go to Space Mountain to obtain Fastpasses.
3. Ride the Matterhorn Bobsleds.
4. Go to Fantasyland and ride Dumbo.
5. Ride Peter Pan's Flight.
6. Ride Mr. Toad's Wild Ride.
7. Ride Alice in Wonderland.
8. Visit the Mad Tea Party.
9. Ride the Storybook Land Canal Boats.
10. Ride the King Arthur Carrousel.
11. Experience Pinocchio's Daring Journey.
12. Go to Frontierland and ride Big Thunder Mountain.
13. The best way to ride Finding Nemo Submarine Voyage without a horrible wait is to ride during a parade, fireworks, or *Fantasmic!* Determine when one or another of these

events is scheduled, and join the line for Nemo 15 minutes before the event begins.
14. Cruise on the *Mark Twain* Riverboat or the Sailing Ship *Columbia*.
15. Explore Tom Sawyer Island.
16. Go to Adventureland and explore Tarzan's Treehouse.
17. See the *Enchanted Tiki Room* show.
18. Return to Tomorrowland and ride Buzz Lightyear.
19. Ride Space Mountain using your Fastpasses (your Fastpasses will still be valid).
20. Ride Star Tours and see *Jedi Training Academy*.
21. Revisit favorites or see attractions you missed. Check your daily entertainment schedule for parades, Fantasyland Theatre productions, or other live entertainment that might interest you. Return after 7 p.m. for a parade and *Fantasmic!*

2-day Plan A: Day 1

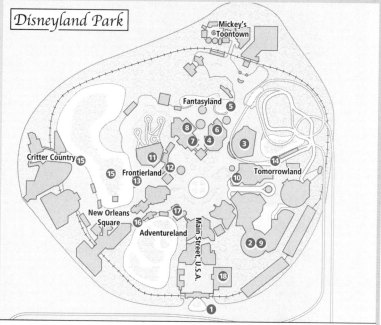

Disneyland Park

1. Arrive 40 minutes before opening and line up at Gate 13. Give all of your admission passes to one person.
2. Dispatch this person to Space Mountain to obtain Fastpasses.
3. Ride the Matterhorn Bobsleds.
4. Go to Fantasyland and ride Peter Pan's Flight.
5. Ride the Storybook Land Canal Boats.
6. Ride Mr. Toad's Wild Ride.
7. Ride Snow White's Scary Adventures.
8. Ride Pinocchio's Daring Journey.
9. Return to Tomorrowland. Ride Space Mountain using your Fastpasses.
10. Ride Buzz Lightyear.
11. Go to Frontierland and ride Big Thunder Mountain Railroad. If the wait exceeds 25 minutes, use Fastpass.
12. Try Rancho del Zocalo for lunch.
13. In Frontierland, ride the *Mark Twain* Riverboat or the Sailing Ship *Columbia.*
14. The best way to ride Finding Nemo Submarine Voyage without a horrible wait is to ride during a parade, fireworks, or *Fantasmic!* Determine when one or another of these events is scheduled, and join the line for Nemo 15 minutes before the event begins.
15. Take a raft to Tom Sawyer Island.
16. Go to Adventureland and tour Tarzan's Treehouse.
17. See the *Enchanted Tiki Room* show.
18. See *The Disneyland Story,* presenting *Great Moments with Mr. Lincoln.*
19. Revisit favorites or see attractions you missed earlier. Check out any parades or live performances that interest you.

2-day Plan A: Day 2

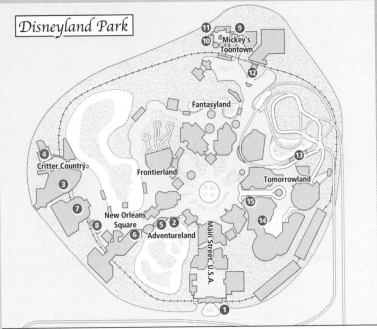

Disneyland Park

1. Arrive 30-40 minutes before the official opening time and line up in front of Gate 13.
2. Go to Adventureland and ride Indiana Jones.
3. Go to Critter Country and ride Splash Mountain.
4. Ride The Many Adventures of Winnie the Pooh.
5. Return to Adventureland and ride the Jungle Cruise.
6. Go to New Orleans Square and ride Pirates of the Caribbean.
7. Experience The Haunted Mansion.
8. Take the Disneyland Railroad to the Mickey's Toontown/Fantasyland Station.
9. Go to Mickey's Toontown and ride Roger Rabbit's Car Toon Spin.
10. Tour Mickey's House and visit Mickey in his dressing room.
11. Do the same at Minnie's House.
12. Go to Fantasyland and ride It's a Small World.
13. Go to Downtown Disney on the monorail for lunch. Have your hand stamped for reentry.
14. Return to Tomorrowland on the monorail and see *Captain Eo*.
15. Ride Star Tours and see *Jedi Training Academy*.
16. Revisit your favorites or see any attractions you missed. Check your daily entertainment schedule for parades or live performances that interest you.

2-day Plan B: Day 1

Disneyland Park

1. Arrive at the park at least 30 minutes before opening. Line up at Gate 13.
2. Obtain Fastpasses to Space Mountain.
3. Ride the Matterhorn Bobsleds.
4. Go to Fantasyland and ride Peter Pan's Flight.
5. Return to Tomorrowland and ride Buzz Lightyear.
6. Ride Space Mountain using your Fastpasses.
7. Go to Frontierland and ride Big Thunder Mountain Railroad.
8. Go to Critter Country and Splash Mountain. Obtain Fastpasses.
9. Ride The Many Adventures of Winnie the Pooh.
10. Go to Adventureland and ride Indiana Jones.
11. Continue to New Orleans Square and experience Pirates of the Caribbean.
12. Tour The Haunted Mansion.
13. Have lunch and see the show at the Golden Horseshoe Stage in Frontierland.
14. The best way to ride Finding Nemo Submarine Voyage without a horrible wait is to ride during a parade, fireworks, or *Fantasmic!* Determine when one or another of these events is scheduled and join the line for Nemo 15 minutes before the event begins.
15. Ride either the Sailing Ship *Columbia* or the *Mark Twain* Riverboat.
16. Ride Splash Mountain using your Fastpasses.
17. See *The Disneyland Story*, presenting *Great Moments with Mr. Lincoln*.

2-day Plan B: Day 2

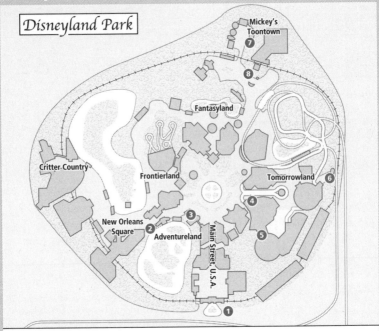

Disneyland Park

1. Eat an early dinner and arrive at the park about 5:30 or 6 p.m.
2. Go to Adventureland and explore Tarzan's Treehouse.
3. See the show in the *Enchanted Tiki Room*.
4. Go to Tomorrowland and ride Star Tours.
5. See *Captain Eo*.
6. Take the Disneyland Railroad from the Tomorrowland Station to the Fantasyland/ Mickey's Toontown Station.
7. In Mickey's Toontown, ride Roger Rabbit's Car Toon Spin.
8. Go to Fantasyland and ride It's a Small World.
9. Check the *Times Guide* for parades, fireworks, and *Fantasmic!*
10. Pick up any attractions you may have missed earlier.

1-day Plan

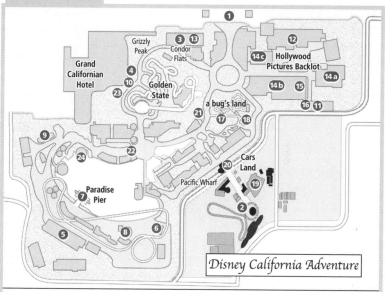

Disney California Adventure

1. Arrive at the entrance 40 minutes before official opening time.
2. Ride Radiator Springs Racers in Cars Land (opens 2012).
3. In Condor Flats, obtain Fastpasses for Soarin' Over California.
4. Obtain Fastpasses for *World Of Color*.
5. In Paradise Pier, ride Toy Story Midway Mania!
6. Ride the California Screamin' roller coaster.
7. Experience Mickey's Fun Wheel.
8. Ride King Triton's Carrousel.
9. Experience Goofy's Sky School.
10. Head to Golden State and ride Grizzly River Run.
11. Head to Hollywood Pictures Backlot and ride The Twilight Zone Tower of Terror. Obtain Fastpasses if the wait exceeds 30 minutes.
12. See Monsters, Inc. Mike and Sulley to the Rescue.
13. Ride Soarin' Over California in Condor Flats using your Fastpasses.
14. Eat lunch and work in the current show at a) the Hyperion Theater, b) *Disney Junior,* or c) *Muppet-Vision 3-D.* Check the schedule for showtimes.
15. See the Disney Animation exhibit, including *Turtle Talk with Crush* and the Animation Academy.
16. Ride The Tower of Terror if you have not already done so.
17. Go to a bug's land. See *It's Tough to Be a Bug!*
18. Experience Heimlich's Chew Chew Train, Flik's Flyers, Francis' Ladybug Boogie, and the Tuck and Roll Drive 'Em Buggies (in that order) at Flik's Fun Fair.
19. See Luigi's Flying Tires in Cars Land.
20. Ride Mater's Junkyard Jamboree.
21. Take the bakery and chocolate factory tours.
22. Ride Little Mermaid: Ariel's Undersea Adventure.
23. Experience the Redwood Creek Challenge Trail.
24. Ride the Golden Zephyr in Paradise Pier.
25. Check your daily entertainment schedule for parades, and check your *World of Color* Fastpass for the performance time.

Universal Studios 1-day Touring Plan

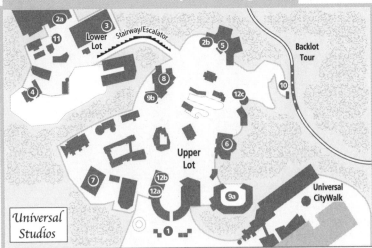

Lower Lot
Stairway/Escalator
Backlot Tour
Upper Lot
Universal CityWalk

Universal Studios

1. Arrive 20 minutes before opening time.
2. Ride a) Transformers if operating. Otherwise, b) try The Simpsons Ride.
3. Ride Revenge of the Mummy in the Lower Lot.
4. Check out Jurassic Park.
5. Take The Simpsons Ride if you missed it earlier.
6. See *Shrek 4-D.*
7. See *Terminator 2: 3-D.*
8. See the Special Effects Stage.
9. Check your daily entertainment schedule for a) *WaterWorld* and b) *Universal's Animal Actors* showtimes.
10. Eat lunch and take the Studio Tour. Allocate an hour and 10 minutes for the tour.
11. Return to the Lower Lot and check out The NBC Universal Experience. Return to the Upper Lot.
12. Check out a) Universal's House of Horrors and b) *The Blues Brothers* show or try the c) Curious George play area.
13. Revisit your favorites or see attractions you missed. Check your daily entertainment schedule for live performances that interest you.

2012 *Unofficial Guide* Reader Survey

If you would like to express your opinion in writing about Disneyland or this guidebook, complete the following survey and mail it to:

Unofficial Guide Reader Survey
P.O. Box 43673
Birmingham, AL 35243

Or fill out the survey online at **touringplans.com.**

Inclusive dates of your visit: _____

Your hometown: _____

Your e-mail address: _____

Members of your party:	Person 1	Person 2	Person 3	Person 4	Person 5
Gender:	M F	M F	M F	M F	M F
Age:	_____	_____	_____	_____	_____

How many times have you been to Disneyland? _____

CAR RENTALS Did you rent a car? _____
• If so, from what company? _____

Concerning your rental car, on a scale with 5 being best and 1 worst, how would you rate:
• Pickup-processing efficiency? _____

• Return-processing efficiency? _____
• Condition of the car? _____
• Cleanliness of the car? _____
• Airport-shuttle efficiency? _____

LODGING On your most recent trip, where did you stay? _____

_____

Have you stayed at any other hotels in the past 12 months? Yes ____ No ____

Please indicate the hotels you have stayed at in the past year, or write in others.

☐ Best Western ☐ Fairfield Inn ☐ Holiday Inn ☐ Omni ☐ Ritz-Carlton
☐ Days Inn ☐ Four Seasons ☐ Hyatt ☐ Quality ☐ Super 8
☐ Drury Inn ☐ Hampton Inn ☐ Marriott ☐ Radisson
☐ Embassy Suites ☐ Hilton ☐ Millenium ☐ Ramada Inn

Write in _____

Please tell us how important the following amenities were in your selection of a Disneyland-area resort/hotel. Select up to five amenities, and rank them in order of importance using 1 for the most important and 5 for the least. Feel free to add others in the margins or on another sheet of paper.

• cost_____
• bar _____
• distance to parks _____
• in-room dining/
  room service _____
• food court _____
• shuttle service to parks_____

• sit-down restaurant_____
• room size _____
• fine dining _____
• multiple bedroom suites ___
• spa/fitness center _____
• in-room kitchen _____
• pool _____

• shuttle to/from airport ____
• architecture/theme_____
• kids' activity center _____
• location inside
  Disneyland _____
• other _____
• other _____

On a scale with 5 being best and 1 being worst, please indicate how satisfied you were with your accommodations. Feel free to add other items you feel are important. *When rating food services, please rate only meals eaten at your resort.*

• ability to find your
  room, etc._____
• cleanliness of room _____

• size and layout of pool _____
• comfort of beds/pillows ____
• crowd level at the pool_____

• room size and layout_____
• cleanliness of pool area ____
• quietness of room _____

Continued on next page

LODGING *(continued)*

- check-in/out process _____
- overall layout of the resort_____
- shuttle to/from airport _____
- shuttle to/from parks_____
- staff accessibility, friendliness, and knowledge _____

- recreational amenities (marina, bikes, fitness center, etc.) _____
- overall food-court value_____
- overall food-court experience _____
- child care _____

- overall experience with full-service restaurant _____
  _____
- overall value of full-service restaurant_____

Please check the number that best describes how satisfied you were with your total resort experience during this trip.

1 Very dissatisfied   2 Somewhat dissatisfied   3 Neither satisfied nor dissatisfied
4 Somewhat satisfied 5 Very satisfied

Would you stay at this resort again? Yes ☐ No ☐

How likely are you to recommend this resort to a friend?
☐ Will definitely recommend   ☐ May recommend   ☐ Neutral
☐ Probably won't recommend   ☐ Definitely will not recommend

DINING **Concerning your dining experiences:**

How many restaurant meals (including fast food) did you average per day? _____

How much (approximately) did your party spend on meals per day? _____

Favorite restaurant outside Disneyland? _____

PARK TOURING On a scale with 5 being best and 1 being worst, please rate how the touring plans worked:

PARK	NAME OF PLAN	RATING
Disneyland Park		
DCA		
Universal Studios		

OTHER How did you hear about this guide?

What other guidebooks or websites did you use on this trip? On the 5-as-best, 1-as-worst scale, how would you rate them?

	NAME	RATING
Guidebooks		
Websites		

Using the same scale, how would you rate the *Unofficial Guide*? _____

Have you used other *Unofficial Guides*? Which ones? _____

Additional comments you would like to share with us about your Disneyland vacation or about the *Unofficial Guide:*

_____

_____

_____

_____

DISNEYLAND RESORT AND ANAHEIM RESTAURANT SURVEY

TELL US ABOUT YOUR DINING EXPERIENCES during your Disneyland visit. Listed below are the full-service restaurants at Disneyland Resort, followed by Anaheim-area restaurants profiled in this guide. Beside each restaurant are thumbs-up and thumbs-down symbols. If you enjoyed the restaurant enough that you would eat there again, circle the thumbs-up symbol; if not, circle the thumbs-down symbol. Mail the survey to:

Unofficial Guide Restaurant Survey
P.O. Box 43673
Birmingham, AL 35243

The survey is also available online at **touringplans.com**.

DISNEYLAND RESORT FULL-SERVICE RESTAURANTS (IN ALPHABETICAL ORDER)

Ariel's Grotto Disney California Adventure . . . . 👍 👎

Big Thunder Ranch Barbecue Disneyland Park . . . . 👍 👎

Blue Bayou Disneyland Park . . . . 👍 👎

La Brea Bakery Café Downtown Disney . . . . 👍 👎

Café Orléans Disneyland Park . . . . 👍 👎

Carnation Café Disneyland Park . . . . 👍 👎

Catal Restaurant & Uva Bar Downtown Disney . . . . 👍 👎

Disney's PCH Grill Paradise Pier Hotel . . . . 👍 👎

ESPN Zone Downtown Disney . . . . 👍 👎

The French Market Disneyland Park . . . . 👍 👎

Goofy's Kitchen Disneyland Hotel . . . . 👍 👎

House of Blues Downtown Disney . . . . 👍 👎

Napa Rose Grand Californian Hotel . . . . 👍 👎

Naples Ristorante e Pizzeria Downtown Disney . . . . 👍 👎

Napolini Downtown Disney . . . . 👍 👎

Pacific Wharf Café Disney California Adventure . . . . 👍 👎

Plaza Inn Disneyland Park . . . . 👍 👎

Rainforest Cafe Downtown Disney . . . . 👍 👎

Ralph Brennan's Jazz Kitchen Downtown Disney . . . . 👍 👎

Rancho del Zocalo Restaurante Disneyland Park . . . . 👍 👎

The River Belle Terrace Disneyland Park . . . . 👍 👎

Steakhouse 55 Disneyland Hotel . . . . 👍 👎

Storytellers Café Grand Californian Hotel . . . . 👍 👎

Tangaroa Terrace Disneyland Hotel . . . . 👍 👎

Tortilla Jo's Downtown Disney . . . . 👍 👎

Wine Country Trattoria Disney California Adventure . . . . 👍 👎

ANAHEIM-AREA FULL-SERVICE AND BUFFET RESTAURANTS
(IN ALPHABETICAL ORDER)

Anaheim White House Anaheim . . . . 👍 👎

Carolina's Italian Restaurant Garden Grove . . . . 👍 👎

La Casa Garcia Anaheim . . . . 👍 👎

The Catch Anaheim . . . . 👍 👎

Clancy's Clubhouse Anaheim . . . . 👍 👎

Gabbi's Mexican Kitchen Orange . . . . 👍 👎

Gandhi Palace Anaheim . . . . 👍 👎

Grand China Restaurant Anaheim . . . . 👍 👎

Harbor Seafood Buffet Garden Grove . . . . 👍 👎

In-N-Out Burger Anaheim . . . . 👍 👎

JW's Steakhouse Anaheim . . . . 👍 👎

Koisan Japanese Cuisine Orange . . . . 👍 👎

Luigi's D'Italia Anaheim . . . . 👍 👎

Mas' Chinese Islamic Restaurant Anaheim . . . . 👍 👎

McCormick & Schmick's Grille Anaheim . . . . 👍 👎

Morton's Anaheim . . . . 👍 👎

Mr. Stox Anaheim . . . . 👍 👎

Park Avenue Steaks & Chops Stanton . . . . 👍 👎

The Phoenix Club Anaheim . . . . 👍 👎

Prime Cut Café & Wine Bar Orange . . . . 👍 👎

Punjabi Tandoor Garden Grove . . . . 👍 👎

Los Sanchez Garden Grove . . . . 👍 👎

Souplantation Garden Grove . . . . 👍 👎

Tiffy's Family Restaurant Anaheim . . . . 👍 👎

Zankou Chicken Anaheim . . . . 👍 👎